The Ethos of Noh
Actors and Their Art

Harvard East Asian Monographs 232

The Ethos of Noh
Actors and Their Art

Eric C. Rath

Published by the Harvard University Asia Center
Distributed by Harvard University Press
Cambridge (Massachusetts) and London 2004

Printed in the United States of America

The Harvard University Asia Center publishes a monograph series and, in coordination with the Fairbank Center for East Asian Research, the Korea Institute, the Reischauer Institute of Japanese Studies, and other faculties and institutes, administers research projects designed to further scholarly understanding of China, Japan, Vietnam, Korea, and other Asian countries. The Center also sponsors projects addressing multidisciplinary and regional issues in Asia.

Library of Congress Cataloging-in-Publication Data

Rath, Eric C., 1967–
    The ethos of noh : actors and their art / Eric C. Rath.
        p. cm. – (Harvard East Asian monographs ; 232)
    Includes bibliographical references and index.
    ISBN 0-674-01397-2 (hardcover : alk. paper)
    1. Nōh–History. I. Title. II. Series.
    PN2924.5.N6R36 2004
    792'.0952–dc22

                                            2004001553

Index by the author

⊗   Printed on acid-free paper

Last figure below indicates year of this printing
14 13 12 11 10 09 08 07 06 05 04

To My Mother

Patricia M. Balsamo

Acknowledgments

This book's shortcomings exist despite the help I received from many kind and knowledgeable people.

The text first took shape as a doctoral dissertation at the University of Michigan; and I owe the greatest thanks to my advisor, Hitomi Tonomura, who guided the completion of that manuscript with her careful advice, support, and characteristic sense of humor. Jennifer Robertson's aid and enthusiasm for my research continues to motivate me, and the project would not have been completed without the help of Diane Hughes and Chun-shu Chang. The Department of History, the Center for Japanese Studies, and the Rackham Graduate School at the University of Michigan and the Japan-America Society of Chicago provided financial support. Haju Murray provided a mindful and peaceful environment for writing major parts of it.

Besides the University of Michigan, I studied Japanese language at Northwestern University, the University of Wisconsin, and the Inter-University Center for Japanese Language Studies in Yokohama. I appreciate the patient instruction of the teachers of these institutions, particularly the late Robert Danly, Tatematsu Kikuko, and Alexander Vovin. My deep thanks also extend to my undergraduate advisors at Skidmore College, William Brynteson, Tad Kuroda, Patricia-Ann Lee, Margaret Pearson, and Joel Smith, all of whom fostered my interest in Japanese history.

In Japan, I was fortunate to receive the assistance of Professor Wakita Haruko and later the guidance of Hosokawa Ryōichi. Professor Hosokawa allowed me to become the first male research student at Tachibana Women's University and gave freely of his time and knowledge of medieval history. A Japan Foundation Fellowship allowed me to study with both of them. Later, a fortuitous invitation from Professor Kasaya Kazuhiko to speak at the International Research Center for Japanese Studies in Kyoto allowed me to travel to Japan to obtain illustrations for this book. Professor Yamanaka Reiko of the Hōsei University Institute of Nōgaku Studies was extremely helpful in helping me obtain illustrations, as were the staff members of the Waseda University Theater Museum Library and the Mitsui Bunko Museum. I had a difficult time choosing among the excellent photographs of noh performers by the studios Ushimado Shashinkobō and Kin no Hoshi Watanabe Shashinjō. The publisher Hinoki Shoten allowed me to reprint a photo of Kongō Ukyō that appeared in the 1976 book edited by Miyake Noboru, *Nōgaku geiwa*. Takabayashi Kōji answered many of my questions about his father and allowed me to include Takabayashi Ginji's photograph. I also appreciate Takabayashi Shinji's assistance.

The first time I saw noh theater in Japan was during a summer session at Sophia University. My lack of understanding of what I saw motivated me to learn more about noh and resulted in this book. Noh shocked me because it was in such contrast to the Western theatrical forms I had gained some familiarity with by studying with Jeff Grygny, John Mills, Ray Nelson and others over the course of several summers.

My own study of noh dance, music, and movement helped me gain greater familiarity with its aesthetics and history. I was lucky to have an introduction to these through the "Kyoto Performance Institute" founded by Jonah Salz. I am fortunate that Jonah has continued to guide me in both scholarly and theatrical matters since then. My instructor for noh dance and music, Urata Yasuchika, has been extremely kind to me, as has his father, Urata Yasutoshi, and elder brother, Urata Yasuhiro. I credit Hisada Shun'ichirō with finally giving me some sense of rhythm, and both he and his daughter, Hisada Yasuko, are excellent instructors in the shoulder-drum (*kotsuzumi*). The late Kineya Emisuke kindly taught me a great deal about Japan in addition to the *nagauta shamisen* while I studied with him in Yokohama, and Kineya Shirosue guided me in the same instrument and manner in Kyoto. Professor Fujita Takanori helped clarify many points of noh history and performance for me, and I am indebted to him for introducing me to several resources essential to this project.

I was able to revise and add new material to this study thanks to a postdoctoral fellowship at the Reischauer Institute of Japanese Studies at Harvard University. During that time, I twisted Jay Rubin's arm to read an early draft of my chapter on masks; the same chapter benefited from the comments of Frank Hoff. Wayne Farris, who was also at Harvard at that time, kindly advised me.

Portions of several of this book's chapters have appeared earlier in print. I appreciate the permissions granted by these publications and the assistance of their editors: Rollo Koster, editor of *Medieval and Early Modern Rituals: Formalized Behavior in the East and West* published by Brill Press (2002), Samuel Leiter of *Asian Theatre Journal*, and Kate Wildman Nakai of *Monumenta Nipponica*. The discussion of the *shōmonji* in Chapter 2 formed a chapter in *Medieval and Early Modern Rituals*, the overview of the treatise *Hachijō kadensho* in Chapter 3 was published in *Monumenta Nipponica* in 1999, and the discussion of the Okina ritual that now makes up a portion of Chapter 7 appeared in *Asian Theatre Journal* in 2000.

I was able to complete this book thanks to the financial assistance of the University of Kansas Department of History, Center for East Asian Studies, and a General Research Fellowship awarded by the College of Liberal Arts and Sciences. I am grateful for the support of my colleagues at Kansas.

Personal support has proven to be the most crucial to this project's completion. I am thankful to my friends and family, especially my wife Kiyomi, her parents, Koshiba Hideo and Ruriko, my daughter Dana, and my stepfather Phil Balsamo. My mother, Patricia Balsamo, gave me my earliest example of how a scholar writes, and it is to her that this book is dedicated.

Sadly, there are several people who passed away while I was working on this project before I could offer them my full thanks. I often think of them, especially when I watch noh theater.

E.C.R.

Contents

Contents

Appendix

Reference Matter

Tables, Figures, and Color Figures

The Ethos of Noh
Actors and Their Art

Landmarks of Memory

A book about noh theater, Japan's classical masked drama, might be expected to begin with a definition. One of the first works to introduce noh to English readers was a 1916 book by Ernest Fenollosa and Ezra Pound, and it took the title of *Noh, or Accomplishment*. A display of a personal talent or "accomplishment" may be close to the original meaning of noh, since "noh" can be translated as "ability," and it is a dramatic form with beginnings in the demonstration of feats of wonder.[1] Yet, noh actors, almost from the art's inception, have resisted the notion that noh rests on natural talent alone. Correct performance, they have said, demands adherence to "traditions." At the same time, what constitutes noh's traditions and who can claim authority over them have been in dispute throughout noh's six-hundred-year history. This book traces how definitions of noh, both as an art and as an occupation, have changed historically. It contends that the definition of "noh" as an art is inseparable from its definition as an occupation. For these reasons, this book does not begin with a definition of noh; instead, it attempts to analyze the mechanisms and the agents who have determined what noh has meant both as an art and as a profession over the course of its history.

The Excommunication of Takabayashi Ginji

The case of Takabayashi Ginji (d. 1972) illustrates the extent to which noh's traditions as an art are bound up in its mores as a profession. Takabayashi was a professional noh actor until he made "impertinent" claims on noh's traditions and was disbarred from the profession. He belonged to the Kita school: an organization of professionals who perform the same roles and espouse the same artistic style (see the Appendix). Members of the Kita school follow a distinct mode of performance, which they trace to the early seventeenth century. However, individual members of the Kita can claim only varying degrees of authority over their school's traditions. The school's leader, the "family head" (*iemoto*), is the sole person in the Kita able to claim absolute authority over the school's traditions. His authority is based, first, on heredity, since he is the direct descendant of the school's founder, and, second, on his assumed mastery of the school's style, which he interprets in light of his supreme knowledge of the school's (his family's) traditions. The family head has the power to compel other performers in the school to obey his interpretations of traditions and even to disbar members who disobey him (see Table 8.1, p. 248). Takabayashi Ginji suffered this punishment when he offended the fourteenth family head of the Kita, Kita Roppeita (d. 1971). Takabayashi wrote about his experience and cast the blame for his exile not on his beloved teacher Roppeita but on the Roppeita's son, Minoru (d. 1986).

In May 1956 I received the maximum punishment of having my name removed from the school's register, and I was cast out by Minoru. In the noh world, I was dealt a death sentence. I was prevented from taking the stage and prohibited from interacting with other performers, and my life as a performing artist was dealt a death blow. My trial was the equivalent of a medieval inquisition. All the members of the school in Tokyo were in attendance, but as defendant I could not participate in the judgment, and so I could not say one word in my defense. Did my mere existence somehow harm the Kita school in some way? I was a defendant who did not know his crime. Yet, in a thundering voice I was declared to be "impertinent," and I was disbarred.[2]

Takabayashi's case reveals several points about noh and its traditions.[3] First, it highlights the inequalities in the power structure of noh. Although few performers suffer the "professional death sentence" that was Takabayashi's punishment, all of them are dependent on the head of their school for their livelihood. All performers must belong to a school, and their membership in a given school is determined by the type of part they perform and by family connections. Noh remains predominantly a hereditary profession, and performers join the same school as their parents, almost always the father, who typically trains them. Some performers also train directly under the

Fig. I.1 Takabayashi Ginji. Courtesy of Takabayashi Kōji.

supervision of the family head, and all need to seek the family head's endorsement at various times in their careers, as for example, when they attempt one of the more demanding works in the repertoire. This arrangement is not unique to noh. The control exercised by the family head is the norm in most traditional arts, including the tea ceremony, *nagauta shamisen*, Japanese dance (*Nihon buyō*), and flower arrangement. In most cases, the so-called family-head system (*iemoto seido*) functions smoothly and to the benefit of all the professionals involved. It provides mechanisms for training performers, setting standards, and ensuring the continuity of an art form. But in Takabayashi's view, the family head's monopoly over the school's artistic traditions was a recent phenomenon, one that he described as a disease. He claimed the "family-head sickness" had transformed the Kita school into a political party and turned the family head into a feudal lord or a mafia godfather. He concluded with deep regret that the artistic growth of the Kita school's performers and the development of noh as an art had suffered as a result of the family head's willfulness. Looking around him, Takabayashi found that the "family-head sickness" was plaguing not just noh but all of Japanese society.[4]

Besides the obvious power inequality that determines who has the authority to define tradition, Takabayashi's case reveals the instability of "tradition" itself. Takabayashi explained that his disbarment resulted from differences in interpretation in the traditions of the Kita school. He maintained that he was sole heir to a distinct, local variation of the Kita school's artistic style, namely, the style of the Horiike family, Kita school actors who had once served the imperial court in Kyoto. The account of his excommunication formed a prelude to his *Correct History of the Kita School* (*Hokuryū shōshi*), which he published privately in 1961. His book described the history of the Kita style as he defined it and made the point that the Kita school had once been more eclectic in its approach to traditions until Minoru and others had sought to standardize them. As Takabayashi demonstrated, traditions are neither natural nor necessarily agreed to by all involved: traditions are created and can be contested.

A final lesson from Takabayshi's case is the relationship among institutions, memory, and the formation of traditions. Although his perspective was radical in the context of the Kita school, all noh performers are cognizant of the long history of their art, and many have occasion to refer to the past to describe current aesthetics and the organization of their occupation. In Takabayashi's case, although he could document a distinct historical legacy, he lacked institutional backing to win wider adherence to his "memories" as accepted "traditions." Clearly, one person's memories of the past do not make a tradition, for that requires the support of an institution, because, as this book examines, memories as traditions are central to a group's self-understanding and exercise of power.

The aim of this book is to describe how memories of the past become traditions and the role of these traditions in the story of the institutional development of noh theater. Although the chronological scope of this book runs from noh's fourteenth-century beginnings to the twentieth century, its main intent is neither to provide a complete history of noh nor to explore its rich literary, musical, and dramatic features. Instead, it focuses on the development of the key traditions that constitute what is defined below as the "ethos of noh" and how this ethos fostered noh's professionalization: its growth from a loose occupation into a closed, regulated vocation. It further examines how certain performers, particularly the family head, can claim greater authority over noh's traditions than other actors.

Read chronologically, this book describes the maturation of noh as a profession and its ethos over six hundred years of history. It contends that the crystallization of noh's traditions facilitated occupational growth and eventually promoted noh's transformation into a profession by defining an ethos, an ideology that empowered certain groups of performers to the detriment of others. Read synchronically, the various traditions that are the components of noh's ethos, such as those surrounding masks and manuscripts, delineate the key traits that define it as an art. To grasp the meanings of noh as an art, it is necessary to have an understanding of its centuries-old traditions, for they have been the language by which noh performers and audiences have spoken about noh from the medieval age to the present.

This book must take such a long historical view to reflect the long institutional memory of noh. By taking a long view of noh's past, we can subject performers' claims about their traditions to historical analysis and can follow the evolution of these traditions across chronological divisions of Japanese history. Moreover, as I hope to show, the definition of noh as an art and as a profession is historically contingent and has been an ongoing and bitterly contested process; this becomes clearer if we follow the changes in noh's ethos over a long span of time.

Ethos, Myths, and Media

An ethos, as the term is used here, is the sum of a group's traditions, the memories that become important to the group. A study of noh's ethos not only reveals how performers view themselves and their art but also provides the story of the core ideals of an art that has been continuously enacted for over six hundred years, from the medieval to the modern period, a period of enormous changes in Japanese history. Noh as an occupation has also shared many characteristics with other institutions such as those encompassing the ruling samurai elite as well as other occupations and performing artists; therefore, the study of noh's ethos sheds light on the ways in which government and professions adapted their worldviews to fit the historical context, reshaping their institutional memory of the past—their traditions—to align themselves to current contingencies. The case of noh illustrates how one occupation borrowed from the ideology of rulers, the ideas of other artists, and the occupational tricks of tradespeople to transform a distinct and powerful core of traditions into an ethos, which became a focus for group identity and a vehicle for the construction of individual and group authority.

Tradition, as the historian Eric Hobsbawm has argued, is more than simply a function of memories of times past: traditions are invented to suit contemporary needs by creating a false continuity with the past in order to inculcate values and norms of behavior.[5] Yet Hobsbawm's notion of "invented tradition" is synonymous with the modern period, since the "traditional" is viewed as an opposite of the "modern"—although it could be argued that a similar process of inventing traditions has occurred throughout history. For clarity, this book refers to traditions, both modern and premodern, as "myths." These myths include tales of the supernatural and the deeds of heroes in accordance with the conventional meaning of the word, but "myth" also refers to assumptions taken for granted in daily life that are not rooted in historical fact. As the historian M. T. Clanchy noted, "Myth is not necessarily the 'purely fictitious narrative' of a dictionary definition . . . it can be a formulation of fundamental belief and experience handed down in a memorable way."[6] As "fundamental beliefs," myths are building blocks of an ethos that constitutes a group's mode of self-understanding.

The use of the term "myth" in this book follows the French literary critic Roland Barthes, who identified myths in objects, persons, or ideas—which he termed "signs"—that have been subsumed by the idea that they signify: as when soap stands for an obsession with cleanliness and purity. In Barthes's words, with these types of myths "the meaning leaves its contingency behind; it empties itself, it becomes impoverished, history evaporates, only the letter remains." For Barthes, the world of myth is timeless and enduring, and it is a disguise for the past. "Myth is constituted by the loss of the historical quality of things."[7] This loss of the past, according to Barthes, is not an accident. Instead, it is engineered to make assumptions look natural and disguise the exercise of power. Barthes's observation that myths engender a loss of history and that this loss supports hegemonic institutions serves as the entry point for the historical approach to noh's myths in this book. The purpose of investigating the history of the key myths that form noh's ethos is to understand, first, when and why certain myths appeared historically and, second, what function they played in noh's institutionalization.

This book asserts that media have played a fundamental role in the dissemination and crystallization of noh's myths. Printed texts, for instance, made wider knowledge of noh a possibility. Media, as Marshall McLuhan has forcibly argued, also effect changes in a message's content even as they amplify that message. For McLuhan, media are not only a technology that extends human senses but also a force whose use (re)formulates the conventions of communication and behavior. "When technology extends one of our senses, a new translation of culture occurs as swiftly as the new technology is interiorized," wrote McLuhan in *Gutenberg Galaxy*, his reflection of the impact of print on culture.[8] Although McLuhan's ideas have wide ramifications, for the purposes of this book, a definition of media as technologies of bodily extension can serve to broaden the term to include technologies important to noh actors, such as masks as well as manuscripts and printed texts. Moreover, his premise that a new medium influences discourse can serve as a method for charting pivotal changes in the evolution of noh's ethos, first, by drawing attention to actors' adoption of new media and, second, by highlighting the new myths these helped to engender. Thus, this book examines how noh's myths, expressed in terms of a contemporary medium, were displaced or reconfigured by newer technologies, which not only signified a new mode of expressing authority but also provoked a reformulation of prior myths, with results that reveal the implications of these new media for the whole of society.

This book follows a chronological telling of the adoption of new media and myths in the evolution of noh's ethos. Chapter 1 examines the importance of masks as a medium of group memory and identity for noh troupes of the fourteenth century. Chapter 2 focuses on the introduction of the technology of writing to noh in the fifteenth century and examines the impact of literacy and especially of secret, technical writings. Chapter 3 traces the popularization of these secret manuscripts in the sixteenth century. Genealogy replaced secret manuscripts as the fundamental medium of myth in the seventeenth century, and Chapter 4 describes this transition and the reasons behind it. Secret technical writings, however, gained new meanings in the print culture of the 1600s as published texts whose dissemination both benefited and challenged the attempts of performers to professionalize, as Chapter 5 relates. Chapter 6 probes the connection between control over the publishing industry and the family head's consolidation of the leadership of noh schools. Chapter 7 presents a discussion of ritual, which is the cornerstone of noh's ethos in the modern period.

The secondary aim of this book is to trace shifts in the myths of noh's ethos to delineate major turning points in the professionalization of noh. In *The Rise of Professionalism: A Sociological Analysis*, Magali S. Larson defines professionalization as a "process by which producers of special services sought to constitute and control a market for their expertise." Larson concluded that neither the state nor a particular elite group is responsible for creating professions. Occupations themselves gradually and sometimes unconsciously create the parameters for their profession in what she refers to as a "collective assertion of special social status."[9] Noh's formation of the myths that constitute its ethos facilitated its professionalization, which was neither idiosyncratic nor unique, as comparisons with other professions, arts, religious movements, and political institutions in Japan will illustrate. Therefore, as an example or case study, noh offers a springboard for considering larger issues of authority and social organization in Japanese history and allows us to understand the interplay of power, tradition, and artistic production.

Actors in Noh's History

Although it began in the 1300s and was practiced by a range of groups acting both full and part time, noh gradually became professionalized from the seventeenth century. By the end of that century, the four Yamato troupes (Kanze, Konparu, Hōshō, and Kongō) and the newer Kita troupe dominated it. Noh's professionalization and artistic development are usually attributed to the transition from the patronage of religious institutions in the fourteenth century to that of warriors by the seventeenth century; this has meant that the standard history of noh has focused on how the premodern military elite dominated noh's institutions and artistry.[10] Although this approach has illuminated the connections between noh and its military patrons, it unfortunately relegates performers to a secondary role in their history and their art. The present study turns the spotlight away from patrons to performers and their role in the formation of their ethos; it argues that actors played a more pivotal role than audiences in determining noh's central traditions on stage and off.

When actors are made the primary focus in the history of noh, the historical narrative often appears to have been written backward: that is, the modern noh theater composed of a few professional schools is seen to be the natural culmination of the development of the four Yamato troupes plus the Kita. Such an approach is itself a myth, for it ignores the numerous conflicts waged over noh's traditions through the centuries as well as the myriad of groups that once performed it. As this book explores, many other individuals and groups performed noh besides the four Yamato troupes. In the fourteenth through sixteenth centuries, noh was a much more inclusive practice and a full-time and part-time occupation and avocation by people of diverse social backgrounds. Historical records of the Muromachi period (1336–1573) describe noh groups composed of women, children, nobles, peasants, warriors, and social outcasts. Thus, long before noh was a closed, male-dominated and largely hereditary profession, it was an occupation that many could participate in and did. The distinction between amateur and professional in the noh world appeared only in the early modern period (1600–1868) at the time when the Yamato troupes were trying to secure their dominance. Yet rival groups persisted in performing, and it was not until the twentieth century that the modern noh schools achieved full domination. At this point, noh's institutional memory suffers amnesia in its willing forgetfulness of the contingencies of the past. This means that once-bitter rivals are presented as outside the main currents of noh; hence, they are usually excluded from standard histories or dealt with in a perfunctory fashion.[11] Nevertheless, as the present book describes, by their presence these rival actors played a central role in shaping the direction of noh through the centuries. Consequently, rather than assume the superiority of certain noh groups throughout history, I examine the various contests over noh's traditions, and analyze how certain performers succeeded in defining an ethos that transformed noh from a medieval entertainment enacted by a loosely defined occupation into a classic art performed by a closed profession dominated by a select elite.

CHAPTER I

Masks and Memory

Noh is Japan's masked theater. As theatrical props, the masks represent characters in a classical drama. As sculpture, they reveal superb
craftsmanship and refined artistic sensibilities, said to capture Japanese
ideals of beauty and horror. As artifacts, they point to the antiquity of
noh and testify to tradition. They are certainly the oldest sources for
its early history, surviving from a time before performers began to
write down their theories and plays. Yet, it is impossible to develop a
chronology of their invention and evolution because few of the earliest surviving masks can be dated conclusively. We cannot even know
which came first, the mask or the drama.

Scholars may debate the question of origins, but among actors the
consensus has long been that masks predate the creation of noh.[1] In
fact, the oldest family of actors claims to own the most ancient mask.
That family is the Konparu, and their mask is a hidden treasure, never
used in performance, and rarely photographed or displayed. A book
by the current family head of the Konparu, Nobutaka (b. 1920), claims
that the famous mask is over a thousand years old and that it was
carved by none other than the ancient statesman Prince Shōtoku
(d. 622) expressly for the founder of the Konparu line.[2] The legend of
the Shōtoku mask is itself ancient, found in the first noh treatise,
Zeami's (ca. 1363–ca. 1443) *Style and the Flower* (*Fūshikaden*), which is
approximately six hundred years old. However, this earliest written
account differs from the modern claim on a key point, namely, the
identity of the mask. According to Zeami, Shōtoku created a demon
mask, not the Okina mask—which represents an old man or wizened
deity—the one that the Konparu family now upholds as the "original."
The story of the Shōtoku mask is emblematic of how lore about

masks has changed historically in response to performers' understanding of their relationship to their art and livelihood.

This chapter focuses on the role of masks as a medium for constructing an ethos for noh in the late fourteenth century when it was beginning to take shape as a performing art and as an occupation. As we will see, noh actors adopted masks both for their theatrical value and for the lore surrounding them from earlier performing arts and traditions of object veneration. As a medium, masks not only assisted in the transmission of myths about noh but also shaped how that discourse was recalled and presented. Noh's earliest myths were inseparable from the masks used to convey them.

Noh Masks and Their Antecedents

Noh was not the first performing art in Japan to use masks. The origins of noh in earlier forms of theater are conjectural and a subject beyond the scope of this book. Noh did, however, draw from earlier masked dance arts such as *bugaku*, which flourished during the Heian period (794–1185).[3] *Bugaku* was performed to the accompaniment of the court music, *gagaku*. It arrived from the continent in the eighth century. Its predecessor was the dance form called *gigaku*, about which little is known since it quickly disappeared with *bugaku*'s arrival. About 250 *gigaku* masks, dating from the late sixth to early eighth century, survive in the treasure repositories of the Shōsōin and the Hōryūji temple in Nara.[4] These masks offer the best, and almost only, record for reconstructing *gigaku*. Scholars detect a strong continental influence in the surviving *gigaku* and *bugaku* masks and have concluded that most of these masks were either imported from China or Korea or made by craftsmen in Japan closely following continental models. *Gigaku* masks can be distinguished from their *bugaku* counterparts by their enormous size. Many *gigaku* masks would have covered the entire head of the performer. *Bugaku* masks are much smaller and cover only the face or sometimes, in the case of the largest masks, the sides of the face as well. Both *gigaku* and *bugaku* masks are carved from wood and painted; hair was sometimes added to *bugaku* masks. Apart from these wooden masks, *bugaku* also makes use of cloth masks (*zōmen*) with faces and designs painted in black.

Several noh masks appear to derive from *bugaku* models, but there is a puzzling gap of several centuries between *bugaku*'s heyday in the ninth century and the earliest noh masks. Demon masks and masks of the Okina variety (see Color Fig. 1), which in noh date from around the turn of the fourteenth century, are closest in appearance to earlier *bugaku* models. The masks representing women, men, and "old men" (*jō*), which date from the late fourteenth century, are the furthest removed stylistically from their *bugaku* predecessors.[5] Noh masks are closer to human form than *gigaku* and *bugaku* masks, as if noh masks were patterned after actual people as opposed to *gigaku* and *bugaku* masks, which are interpretations of lofty concepts or basic urges. To underline the connection between noh masks and the human world, modern performers and carvers prefer to use the word "face" (*omote*) in reference to noh masks and reserve the word "mask" (*kamen*) to refer to other types of masks. Carvers of *bugaku* masks occasionally signed their creations, and the names of *bugaku* mask carvers are known from as early as the twelfth and thirteenth century. But the earliest noh masks, as well as most other masks created in the medieval period, lack the carver's signature or other inscription that would allow for dating.[6] Some noh masks, including those recognized by the Japanese government as Important Art Objects and Important Cultural Properties, have been attributed to carvers from the late Kamakura period (1185–1333), but the masks and the traditions of attribution surrounding them date from centuries later.

The Features of Noh Masks

Masks are at the focal point of performances of noh because they are worn almost exclusively by the main actor (*shite*), whose story forms the crux of any play.[7] The features of a mask establish the character's gender, age, and social ranking; consequently, masks play an integral role in characterization. A change of masks reveals the transformation of a seemingly innocent figure into a deity or a demon. An actor's use of a mask can suggest psychological nuances to a role. By tilting the mask slightly upward, "brightening" it, the actor allows more light to strike the mask's features, making the mask appear to laugh or smile. Tilting the mask downward "clouds" it, causing the mask to appear to cry or brood. The ambivalence of the mask's features at such moments hint at a range of emotions left to the members of the audience to decipher. Actors consider masks not only to be more expressive than human faces because of their powers of suggestion but also, as the great performer Kanze Hisao (d. 1978) noted, to be a medium that allows an actor to transcend his own ego when he appears on stage.[8]

There are approximately 450 different noh masks, most of which are variations of sixty types. This great variety makes classification difficult and at times arbitrary. For example, the famous *hannya* mask, depicting a woman transformed into a snake-demon, might just as easily be included among demon masks as among woman's masks. The distinct masks of the horned demon in *Ikkaku sennin* and the drunken elf Shōjō are worn only in one or two plays and deviate from more representative masks. Scholars and performers categorize masks into five very general categories.[9]

1. Okina (and all masks used for the "three rites," *shikisanban*)
2. Demon
3. Old Men (*jō*)
4. Men
5. Women

In classical Japanese, the word *okina* was a generic term for old man, but the Okina mask is said to be the face of a god. At first glance, the mask looks like an old man's face with wrinkles and a broad smile. Wisps of a mustache lie under a flat nose, and a trailing white goatee indicates grandfatherly age. Yet, the smile of Okina is almost too broad to be human. The lines on the face are also more symmetrical than any mortal's wrinkles. Circular puffs of rabbit fur or hemp above the eyes cannot be taken as human eyebrows, since they are too spherical and fantastic. These features contribute to the mask's air of mystery.

Two other reasons argue for grouping the Okina mask along with the related masks of Sanbasō and Chichinojō in a separate category. First, these masks are used only for the "ritual" known as the *shikisanban* and are not employed in any play. Second, masks in the Okina category also differ from typical noh masks in having a detached lower jaw (*kiri ago*) that is tied to the upper jaw by knotted twine at either side of the lips. This unique feature, found also in the *bugaku* mask Saisōrō, distinguishes these masks; like the dance of Saisōrō, Okina is associated with arcane powers and the mysteries of old age.[10]

Demon masks are subdivided into two categories: those with an open mouth, as in the case of the "bulge" (*tobide*) and "black-beard" (*kurohige*) masks; and those with a closed mouth, for example, the different varieties of "frowning" (*beshimi*) masks. Masks of a "heavenly god" (*tenjin*), the Buddhist deity Fudō Myō'ō (see Color Fig. 5), and "lion-dog-mouth" (*shishiguchi*) fall into a third category of "miscellaneous" demon masks.

The term *jō* is sometimes translated as "old man." *Jō* masks blend both human and demonic features, and these masks are usually differentiated by their expressions. The more malevolent *jō* masks include the large and small versions of the "evil old man" (*ōakujō*, *koakujō*), the mask of the "frowning evil man" (*beshimi akujō*), and the "evil man with a swollen nose" (*hanakobu akujō*). The masks called the "laughing old man" (*waraijō*) and the "dancing old man" (*maijō*) reveal more benevolent features. The *sankōjō* and *ishiōjō* masks are traditionally attributed to the medieval carvers Sankōbō and Ishiōhyōe, although the veracity of this claim is uncertain.

Masks of men also encompass a range of emotions and ages. *Dōji* and *jidō* are masks of deities who have taken human form as young boys. *Imawaka* and *jūroku* represent adolescent males, and both are used for scenes in which a young warrior meets an early death. Actors wear the *heida* mask to depict a warrior cut down in his full maturity. The *ayakashi* mask is likewise used for roles of a slain warrior, but the mask shows greater malevolence and desire for revenge than the *heida*. The "starved man" (*yaseotoko*) and *kawazu* masks depict the onset of death. The masks of the blind men Semimaru and Yoroboshi are more specialized since they are used only in the two plays of the same names.

Masks of women come in even greater variety for roles ranging from girls to grandmothers to female spirits. The *ko'omote* mask for roles of beautiful young women is arguably the best-known noh mask (see Color Figs. 3 and 4), perhaps second only to the *hannya* mask. *Fukai* and *shakumi* depict women of advanced years but younger than the elderly faces of the "granny" (*uba*) and "old woman" (*rōjo*) masks used in plays about the faded beauty of the great Heian-era poetess Ono no Komachi. "Mud eyes" (*deigan*) and "long hair" (*masukami*) portray suffering and deranged women.

Mask as Medium of Myth

Stories of masks washing up from the sea, falling from the sky, and found enshrining deities were common in medieval noh and had their antecedents in earlier customs of relic worship, mask use, and the veneration of religious statuary. Such lore emphasized the latent power of masks as relics of immortal design or even as the embodiments of divine power. These earlier myths reveal the fascination and awe felt for masks in medieval Japan and show not only how masks served as a medium for conveying religious mysteries but also how noh actors successfully used masks to do just that.

Evidence of an object's divine origin and power can be deduced from its place of discovery. Uji shrine, in Uji city near Kyoto, enshrines a mask that is said to have fallen in a snowstorm.[11] Objects found drifting at sea are not only particularly mysterious but have the hallmark of sanctity. Fishermen in Misaki in modern Kanagawa prefecture told an anthropologist about finding a drifting noh mask in their nets and reported that the mask brought good luck and bountiful hauls of fish after it was properly enshrined.[12] Tales of objects including statues and masks originating from the sea can be found all over Japan. Many such found objects had been venerated as religious effigies (*shinzō*) long before the inception of noh. The eighth-century chronicle *Nihon shoki* (*Nihongi*) contains a story, which it dates to 553, of the first two Buddhist images created in Japan, which were carved from a luminous block of camphor wood found floating on the sea.[13] The origin story (*engi*) of Nishinomiya Ebisu shrine in Kobe describes how a fisherman repeatedly found a mysterious object in his nets; eventually he took it home and enshrined it. The deity Ebisu appeared to the fisherman in a dream and instructed him to build a worship hall, which later became the Nishinomiya shrine.[14] There are several examples of medieval folk masks discovered in the sea and then enshrined as deities; one mask continued to spit sea salt after being taken from the water.[15] Once the found object was enshrined and worshipped properly, it promised to be the source of magical blessings. A story about a statue of Kannon, the goddess of mercy, at Hasedera temple in the compilation *Tales of Times Now Past* (*Konjaku monogatari*; ca. 1107) further illustrates this point. A log that had drifted to shore in Ōmi province plagued villagers with floods and disease. The priest Tokudo, aided by Emperor Shōmu (r. 724–1), obtained it and had it carved into an eleven-faced statue of Kannon, which the famous ascetic Gyōgi installed at Hasedera in 733. *Miraculous Tales of the Hasedera Kannon* (*Hasedera Kannon genki*; ca. 1210) contains fifty-two stories that reveal the power of Kannon working through this statue.[16]

Cases of masks falling from the sky are even more illustrative of divine power, and these tales have a long history. *Kyōkunshō*, the oldest treatise on *bugaku*, by the thirteenth-century dancer Koma Chikazane, refers to several *bugaku* masks that fell from the heavens. And a mask dating from at least the Kamakura period at Hōryūji temple in Nara is similarly said to have dropped from the sky.[17]

Connections with the heavens and waters allowed some medieval masks to function as tools for rainmaking, just as Buddha relics were used in a similar manner from the ninth century.[18] One mask from Rengeji temple in Sabae city in Fukui prefecture causes rain when washed on a sunny day.[19] According to *Settsu meisho zue*, an early modern guide to Osaka, a dragon mask said to have been created by the famous ninth-century priest Kūkai, who pioneered the practice of using relics to pray for rain, was used for rainmaking ceremonies at Shitenōji temple.[20]

Masks need not have fallen from the sky or have been fished from the sea to be viewed as holy. Shrines throughout Japan use masks as the principal religious effigy; the shrine's deity is said to reside in the mask.[21] For example, masks dating from the Kamakura era are enshrined as effigies at the Upper and Lower Goryō shrines in Kyoto.[22] Shrine records dating from the fourteenth century from Nitta shrine in present-day Kawachi city in Kagoshima prefecture, describe a mask enshrined there as the incarnation (*keshin*) of the deity Hachiman.[23] *Munetaka gunki*, from the fifteenth century, records a priest's discovery of a mask that was miraculously dry floating on the surface of the sea. This mask of an old man was later enshrined at Munetaka shrine in Fukuoka prefecture, and it is still used there in performances of Okina every year on the first day of September.[24]

Masks viewed as religious effigies are referred to by the general term *shintai*, which designates any object in which a deity resides. Since masks—like statues, swords, rocks, and trees—might be viewed as sacred effigies, they came to be used in religious ceremonies. Demon masks were used for ceremonies of exorcism (*oni harai*). This rite, which includes the modern custom of *setsubun* (now celebrated at the beginning of February), dates back to the eight century; it was performed at court and religious institutions at the juncture of the seasons. In *setsubun*, a masked actor (or a member of a family) dresses as a demon and is driven away by an audience (or family) throwing beans. It is uncertain when masks were first used for exorcising demons, but demon masks (*tsuina*) from the Kamakura period used for this purpose survive at Hōryūji temple.[25]

Other masks at Hōryūji known as "parade masks" (*gyōdōmen*) were used in memorial services (*shōryōe*) in which a statue of the temple's founder, Prince Shōtoku, and Buddha relics were placed on biers and paraded from the Eastern Precinct (Tōin) to the Western Precinct (Saiin) and back. Masked dancers accompanied the procession and may have joined in the *bugaku* performance in the Eastern Precinct.[26] Masks were sometimes attached directly to processional biers (*mikoshi*) and religious floats (*hoko*), as in the case of the Gion festival of Kyoto, where masks adorn life-sized dolls riding the floats.[27]

Masks were also used in agricultural rites (*ta asobi*) in villages in premodern Japan. In these instances the masks are "hanging masks," *kakemen*, which are worn on the top of the head. One such mask, dated to 1509 and owned by Aburahi shrine in Shiga prefecture, was used in conjunction with a wooden doll with an enormous penis called *zuzuiko* in rites of fertility and agricultural blessing.[28] Many agricultural rites with masks, including Okina masks, persist throughout Japan today. The family head of the Kongō school, Kongō Iwao I (d. 1951), described his experiences performing Okina for a farming village, as had been his family's long-standing yearly custom. The villagers threw money during the performance, according to Iwao, and told him, "If Okina does not come, the rice will not grow."[29]

Mask Legends and Early Noh

Masks figured so prominently in early noh legends because they could serve both to recall and to convey a noh troupe's history in the absence of written texts. Even during the period when noh performers were becoming literate, around the turn of the fifteenth century, masks remained powerful icons. The historian M. T. Clanchy in *From Memory to Written Record*, who has analyzed the spread of literacy in medieval England, noted that even as written records were becoming more prevalent in society, objects continued to serve as reminders of events.[30] It is evident from the earliest artistic writings on noh that masks were the focal points of legends and origin stories and had the same function as cues to memory and evidence of custom for noh performers as the objects Clanchy describes for medieval England. More than any other object, masks symbolized the actors' occupation be cause their performances relied so heavily on them.[31] Sacred masks, those viewed as artifacts present at the creation of many noh troupes, were depicted as relics that fell from the sky or as masterpieces crafted by ancient carvers. Accordingly, as the earliest of these writings reveal, these masks embodied the history of the particular troupe and of the art itself.

The fourth chapter of Zeami's *Style and the Flower* provides a list of noh troupes active at the turn of the fifteenth century. Zeami cataloged noh troupes on the basis of their location and affiliation with a religious institution: four troupes in Yamato province who perform at Kasuga shrine, three troupes in Ōmi who perform at Hie shrine, two troupes in Ise, three that performed at the Hosshōji temple in Kyoto, and three more who performed in Settsu, modern Osaka.[32] The troupes from Yamato and Ōmi grew to be the most important and powerful in the capital region, and they are the ones whose early history is best known. Four of the five modern schools of *shite* actors (see Appendix), Konparu, Kanze, Kongō, and Hōshō, trace their lineages to the Enman'i (also known as the Emai), Yūzaki, Sakado (or Sakōdo), and Tobi troupes, respectively, from Yamato. The Ōmi troupes, which were later absorbed by the Yamato, had equally as long a history. Of the Ōmi, three "upper" troupes served at Hie shrine, the Yamashina, Shimosaka, and Hie, and three "lower" troupes, the Mimaji, Ōmori, and Sakaudo performed throughout Ōmi province and in nearby Kyoto.[33] The capital was in fact the proving ground where the Yamato and Ōmi troupes met, learned from one another, and competed for patrons. The Ōmi and Yamato troupes were well acquainted with their rivals' histories and approaches, as the secret writings of the Yamato troupes indicate.

Although masks, including those recognized today as noh masks, were employed in medieval Japan for the purpose of rainmaking, exorcisms, and other magic rites, noh performers borrowed most heavily from archetypal tales of the magical origin of masks when they crafted their own mask traditions.[34] The early lore of several of the Yamato and Ōmi troupes reveals a close connection with the founding of the troupe and the discovery of a mask. Place-names, such as Maskhill (Menzuka), were long associated with these troupes and mark the location where a founder discovered his first and most powerful mask. In Yūzaki, Kawanishi ward, Shiki district, Yamato province (modern Nara prefecture), a place long associated with the Kanze troupe—in fact, the origin of their former name—there is a mound associated with a legend of an Okina mask falling to earth. Near Yūzaki, at a place called Sixteen Masks (Jūrokusen), another Okina mask allegedly fell to earth at a site associated with the origins of the Konparu troupe.[35] Although absent from the earliest writings of the Konparu, *Oral Records of Sarugaku* (*Sarugaku kikigaki*) dated 1599, includes a tale of the Konparu troupe's "heavenly mask" (*ama no men*), which was said to have fallen from the sky into the hands of one of the troupe's founding ancestors.[36] Elsewhere, behind Kuwayama shrine in Kameoka, Kyoto, there is another hill called Fallen Mask Mountain (Menkudariyama) associated with the Yata troupe from Tanba. This shrine was an important patron of the Yata.[37]

Other stories of masks falling from heaven appear sporadically in the written lore of the Yamato and Ōmi troupes. The most detailed version is found in *Zeami's Talks on Sarugaku* (*Sarugaku dangi*) and describes the Yamashina (formerly Mimaji) troupe from Ōmi who performed at Hie shrine. The author, Zeami's son Kanze Motoyoshi, noted that the Yamashina enjoyed the exclusive right to perform Okina at New Year's at Hie shrine thanks to their possession of an Okina mask "dropped from heaven" in response to the prayers of the troupe's founder.[38]

At the *sarugaku* performances at the Hie shrine, which are now held from the first through the seventh day of the New Year, only the Yamashina troupe performs Okina. The Okina mask used on these occasions [is that dropped by the crow]. These *sarugaku* performances at the New Year came about because of the occasion when the head of the Yamashina troupe went with his wife to pray on the last day of the twelfth month, since their three-year-old child had suddenly died. They prayed to the deity that if the child lived, they and all their descendants would perform *sarugaku* on the first day of the New Year at the shrine. Indeed, the child revived, and the performances are a direct result of that prayer.[39]

The Yamashina troupe's performance is represented as a repayment to the divinity for saving the life of the troupe leader's son, whose death might have led to the end of the troupe. The mask myth of the Yamashina also justified the troupe's hereditary right to perform at the New Year's festivals. Their right was a god-given authority to be passed down, like the Okina mask itself, from generation to generation. This story may have been retold as part of the Okina performance at Hie shrine; versions of Okina performed as folk theater at local shrines throughout Japan today often begin with an explanation of the mask's origin, including certain instances in which masks are said to have fallen from the sky.[40] Medieval noh performers, such as those of the Yamashina troupe, conceivably may have added a similar story to their performances of this dance, since their authority and the efficacy of the performance hinged on their possession of the sacred mask. That may have been how Kanze Motoyoshi learned of the Yamashina troupe's mask. Motoyoshi's *Sarugaku dangi* includes several such legends, and the text purports to be a transcript of oral instructions dated 1430. In the colophon Motoyoshi indicated that he compiled it from teachings he had heard from his father, among others.[41]

Zeami completed the other important early source about noh masks, *Fūshikaden*, around 1420. Like Motoyoshi, Zeami stated that he based the text on his memories of oral teachings he had received from his deceased father, Kan'ami (d. 1384). Both authors signed these writings with the name Hada, which staked a claim to membership in a wider community of performers with a long historical legacy. The Konparu troupe claimed hereditary descent from the Hada line through Prince Shōtoku's minister Hada no Kōkatsu (seventh century), but as Zeami described in the opening of *Fūshikaden*, all members of the Yamato and Ōmi troupes were the artistic descendants of the Hada. This bond of commonality provided an incentive for Zeami and Motoyoshi to concern themselves with the lore of both the Yamato and Ōmi troupes, whom they viewed more as siblings than as rivals.

The most striking mask tale among the Yamato troupes is that of the Shōtoku mask possessed by the Konparu troupe, as recorded in *Fūshikaden*. In this story, the mask serves not only as evidence of the antiquity of the Konparu but also of the early history of noh. According to Zeami, noh originated when Prince Shōtoku commanded Hada no Kōkatsu to perform sixty-six entertainments and provided sixty-six masks, at least one of which the Konparu still treasured many generations later. Zeami wrote that the current leader, "Mitsutarō is the twenty-ninth-generation descendant in the Konparu family of Hada no Ujiyasu. . . . The same troupe possesses a demon mask created by Prince Shōtoku . . . along with a painting of the Kasuga deity and relics of the Buddha; all three of these are maintained by this family."[42] Like the painting and Buddha relics, the Konparu troupe's mask provided evidence of the family's legacy from Prince Shōtoku. Although the other relics were powerful and notable in their own right, the mask had arguably more significance for the Konparu, given its direct connection with their occupation. Above all, the mask proved the authenticity of the Konparu's artistic heritage. In *Sarugaku dangi*, Motoyoshi's discussion of the origins of noh troupes began with the Konparu, whom he referred to by their older name, Takeda, and he, too, called attention to their ownership of this ancient mask. He not only reiterated the antiquity of the mask but went so far as to call it the "original mask" (*konpon no men*); the implication is that this mask was the model for all subsequent masks, just as the Konparu family's ancestor Hada no Kōkatsu's entertainments were said by Zeami and others to form the basis for noh.[43] Although only the leadership of the Konparu troupe was able to lay full claim to noh's traditions, other noh performers associated with the Konparu, or those like Zeami who saw themselves as the artistic heirs of Kōkatsu, could bask in the honor of their distant connection with Prince Shōtoku through the Hada.

Prince Shōtoku, the early patron of Buddhism and the person traditionally credited with promoting Chinese-style bureaucracy in Japan, certainly qualifies as what Walter J. Ong in *Orality and Literacy* defines as a "heavy character." Ong identified the tendency in oral traditions to recall events through what he termed "heavy characters," "persons whose deeds are monumental, memorable and commonly public."[44] In addition to being honored for his accomplishments during his lifetime, in the medieval period Shōtoku was worshipped as an incarnation of the Bodhisattva Kannon.

Heavy characters, such as Shōtoku, not only help personify information, aiding its recollection, but also empower the individuals who claim a connection with them. This association between a narrator and a heavy character was verified through the invocation of relics, especially masks, which functioned as medium that signified and sanctified authenticity by recalling origins. Sacred masks, in other words, were the equivalent of the imperial regalia for performers. The emperor's authority to rule was incomplete without his possession of the three treasures of the Japanese imperial regalia: the Yata mirror, Mimata jewels, and Kusanagi sword, which, according to the eighth-century imperial chronicles *Kojiki* and *Nihongi*, the divine ancestor of the imperial line, the sun goddess Amaterasu, had bestowed on her heirs when she commanded them to go forth and rule.[45]

Comparable to the Konparu's link to Prince Shōtoku, the Kanze claimed special affinity with Sugawara no Michizane (d. 903), which they verified through their own collection of relics. Michizane, a famous statesman of the early Heian period, received posthumous deification as the god of learning and calligraphy called Tenjin. *Sarugaku dangi* included a story of how Zeami received a sample of Michizane's calligraphy from a monk of Tōnomine temple near Nara. The monk had received instructions in a dream to present the writing to Zeami. The tale attests to Zeami's personal authority and suggests a magical connection to Michizane and to Tōnomine, which was an important patron of the Yamato troupes in Zeami's day. Another passage in *Sarugaku dangi* describes a strange event concerning a Tenjin mask owned by the Kanze troupe. "The Tenjin mask takes its name from the play *Tenjin* in which it is used. When a person asked to borrow this mask, a mysterious spirit appeared in his dream, and he returned that mask. The mask was held in reverence at home and not used until there was another dream, and now the mask is used."[46]

Religious relics held significance throughout medieval society, but records from the fifteenth century confirm that noh performers viewed masks as especially symbolic of their livelihood. *Sarugaku dangi* indicates that the Kanze troupe was famous for its "great frowning demon mask" (*ōbeshimi*) attributed to the mask-maker Shakuzuru and dubbed the "Yamato *beshimi*" by other noh troupes. So significant were masks to the Yamato troupes that they even physically attacked performers of other traditions who tried to wear them on stage. In 1466, the actor Koinu (d. 1472?) from Yanagihara village in Kyoto faced punishment for wearing a mask at a public performance in the capital. As described in the next chapter, Koinu and his fellow villagers were *shōmonji*, members of an outcast group who were competitors of the Yamato troupes. According to *Inryōken nichiroku*, the journal of the secretary of Shōkokuji temple, the leader of the Kanze troupe, On'ami (d. 1467), used his connections with the Ashikaga bakufu to demand the punishment of Koinu. A similar dispute between noh actors and "field music" (*dengaku*) performers erupted in 1458 when a *dengaku* actor wore a noh mask. *Inryōken nichiroku* described another conflict between *dengaku* and noh performers in 1465 and cited an earlier precedent that prohibited *dengaku* performers from wearing noh masks. Based on these references, the scholar Nose Asaji contended that noh performers had a monopoly on wearing noh masks by the late 1450s.[47]

At turning points in their careers, noh performers turned to masks as a medium of expression significant to their occupation. According to some accounts, when Zeami's son Motomasa left the capital after falling out of favor with shogun Ashikaga Yoshinori (d. 1441), he embarked on a pilgrimage to the Amagawa Benzaiten shrine in Yoshino, where he donated a mask as an offering to the shrine. Motomasa may have prayed to the deity of the performing arts, Benzaiten, who was enshrined there as a last hope for a return to fame in the capital; or, he may have left the mask as a symbol of the end of his career.[48] Masks were also offered as dowry in marriage in the same way that Buddha relics (*shari*) had been occasionally exchanged among members of the imperial court in the Heian period.[49] The Hōshō school owns two masks that a son of the leader of the Kongō noh troupe brought with him when he was adopted by the fourth leader of the Hōshō in the sixteenth century. Another mask in the Hōshō collection bears the inscription Motokiyo on the reverse side and purports to be the gift from Zeami Motokiyo to the Hōshō, as mentioned in *Sarugaku dangi* (see below).[50]

In summary, from the earliest period of noh's history, masks served as a powerful medium of tradition within noh, as did similar artifacts in the larger cultural setting. The lore about masks resembled stories frequently told about relics and statues and gained saliency through this foundation in popular belief. Although the existence of relics such as ancient masks may have been widely known, performers asserted that they alone were the guardians of this legacy of masks that belonged to their troupe. This allowed them privileged control of the medium of masks. A few performers, chiefly the leaders of the troupes, were able to make special claims to legitimacy based on their assumed hereditary connections with "heavy" characters invoked in the masks legends. Masks thus simultaneously reinforced notions of group solidarity and lineage, although it is unclear whether, like the family head of today, troupe leaders in this early period could claim sole rights over their troupe's masks.[51] More important perhaps than the question of the ownership of masks was the right to interpret the lore about them and thereby control them as a form of media. This was to change dramatically in the early fifteenth century with the advent of writing.

How Writing Changed Mask Legends (and Noh)

The two-hundred-year period beginning in the fifteenth century when noh mask legends were first recorded up through the Edo period witnessed changes in the use of masks as noh gradually professionalized. These changes in discourse and in social organization were symbiotic, and they were catalyzed by the introduction of writing to noh. Writing had existed in Japan from as early as the fourth century,[52] but the first indications of the use of writing by noh performers for professional purposes date to the early 1400s.

Writing did not replace oral practices. Indeed, oral and bodily transmissions remain central to the teaching of acting styles and music in noh today. The introduction of writing, instead, inaugurated a dialectic between orality and literacy: thereafter the two were viewed in relation to each other. Secret manuscripts, for instance, constantly referred to the "existence of oral instructions" (*kuden ari*), and the texts to noh plays (*nōhon*) contained knowledge that was primarily learned and transmitted orally. Writing, therefore, defined the oral, and literacy itself was often an oral practice, since reading was done aloud or declaimed in the case of musical and poetic passages.[53]

The relationship between orality and literacy changed both the medium and contents of noh discourse. The following section examines changes in mask myths as a way to introduce the implications of writing for noh discourse and its effects on group organization, which are the subject of more detailed study in subsequent chapters. The method pursued here is to examine myths about masks chronologically, from the earliest ones recorded in the fifteenth century, which show a heavy debt to orality, to later ones of the late sixteenth and early seventeenth centuries, which demonstrate the effects of writing and literacy. Besides showing how the medium of writing reconfigured actors' discourse on masks, this approach suggests the gradual standardization of noh discourse that abetted noh's professionalization.

Masks and Oral Legends

As noted above, the earliest information about noh masks appears in writings purporting to be transcriptions of oral instructions and lore. The most detailed of these texts, *Sarugaku dangi*, is representative of a genre of writings called "transcriptions" (*kikigaki*) of oral teachings. *Kikigaki* are characterized by an effort to replicate a dialogue between a "speaker," who is the author, and the reader, who is cast in the role of "listener." This genre was typical of writings on the performing arts from the fifteenth to seventeenth centuries and was viewed as highly authoritative because it was thought to approximate an accurate transcript of specialized knowledge, which was otherwise conveyed only through secret, oral instructions.[54] *Sarugaku dangi* is subtitled *The Transcription of Hada no Motoyoshi* (*Hada no Motoyoshi kikigaki*) and claims to be a record of what Motoyoshi learned from other actors, chiefly his father, Zeami, who also helped edit the text. The dedication of *Sarugaku dangi*, which appears after the discussion of masks, reiterates that the sources included oral teachings truthfully recorded.[55] As transcriptions of oral teachings, *kikigaki* avoid extended analysis. Although proclaiming themselves an accurate reproduction of oral discourse, *kikigaki* nonetheless recontextualize information into a written format sometimes represented as a dialogue but organized by topics and themes, comparable to a list. When Motoyoshi recorded information about masks, he listed the data in the category headed by the phrase "concerning masks" (*omote no koto*).

Concerning masks. Okina masks are made by Nikkō and Miroku. Miroku made the Okina mask for our troupe. This mask was discovered at Iga when our troupe was first assembled at Obata in Iga. In Ōmi there was Shakuzuru, a *sarugaku* performer; he was talented in demon masks. Recently, there was a carver named Echi, who was from Zazen'in [in Enryakuji]. He was skilled in women's masks. In Echizen there was Ishiōhyōe, followed by Tatsuemon, followed by Yasha, followed by Bunzō, followed by Koushi, followed by Tokuwaka. Anyone can wear masks by Ishiōhyōe and Tatsuemon; after the time of Yasha, [success] depends on the person wearing the mask. The chief-attendant (*gon no kami*) of the Konparu troupe wears a mask created by Bunzō. Our troupe has a *toshi-yoritaru jō* mask by Tatsuemon. The "laughing old man" (*waraijō*) mask made famous in the play *Koi no omoni*, was made by Yasha. Koushi's [mask of *waraijō*] is worn in the second half of *Oimatsu*.

This example is typical of the way that *Sarugaku dangi* simply strings together small episodic details, in this case about masks, without any overall thesis. Some details probably came from independent stories about masks once transmitted orally. For instance, the Kanze troupe's origin is told in terms of the discovery of an Okina mask. Likewise,

Yasha's *waraijō* mask is mentioned because it recalls a successful presentation of the play *The Burden of Love* (*Koi no omoni*). The written list, as Walter Ong has noted, marks a significant departure from oral patterns of memory. Something as basic as a "shopping list" has no equivalent in oral methods of structuring memory, which rely on mnemonic devices to recall knowledge through association.[56] As a list of facts about masks, *Sarugaku dangi* ordered knowledge once told in the context of anecdote, legend, genealogy, and personal opinion into a new format that homogenized oral practices of memory into written information. Reflecting the transition from orality to writing, there is a detectable tension in this section that illustrates the problem of simply recording oral knowledge: the discussion jumps from Okina masks to masks by the carver Shakuzuru to masks by other makers, juxtaposing one bit of information against the next simply because all of them relate to masks.

Sarugaku dangi continues in the same vein with a discussion of masks by Echi, a carver from a subtemple in Enryakuji.

The mask carver Echi created masks that he gave to the *sarugaku* troupes of Ōmi. He presented a mask to the great Yamato *sarugaku* performer Zeami, using Iwao as an intermediary. These masks of a woman and of a "thin old man," *kaohosokijō*, are now in the Hōshō troupe. This mask was painted and sometimes used for the play *Genzanmi* [*Yorimasa*]. The mask carver Chigusa has recently created good men's masks. Tatsuemon makes masks of young men. The *tobide* mask used by the Deai troupe and the *tenjin*, *ōbeshimi*, and *kobeshimi* masks used by our troupe are all by Shakuzuru. This *ōbeshimi* mask is called the *Yamato beshimi* by other *sarugaku* troupes. . . . Masks should be worn with attention to their harmonizing with the level of dignity and atmosphere (*kurai*) of the play.[57]

Sarugaku dangi's section on masks is a rather disorganized list that weaves together brief legends with observations and other bits of information. The rambling nature of this section is reminiscent of a dialogue in which the speaker gradually recalls information by virtue of association. One mask story leads to another, and these are transcribed in succession; there is a semblance of speech that lacks the coherence of a developing argument. The fact that subsequent writings about masks did not recapitulate much of the lore contained in *Sarugaku dangi*, except the names of the mask carvers, indicates, first, that the surrounding details which had once served an essential mnemonic function in oral discourse became superfluous when recorded in writ-

ing, and, second, that mask lore itself had shifted away from the concrete and anecdotal grounded in reference to specific masks toward
the abstract and referential, as the following discussion of mask carvers illustrates.

Mask Legends and Writings

Sarugaku dangi was little if at all known among noh performers, since
it saw little dissemination from Zeami's time to the twentieth century,
but due to the publication of other writings, the names of the mask
carvers mentioned in the text became common knowledge in the noh
world by the early seventeenth century.[58] *Sarugaku dangi* names
eleven carvers; some of them are noted only by name, but most were
encapsulated in small vignettes. Noh writers of the latter half of the
sixteenth century ignored these contextualizing episodes and reformulated information about the carvers into a simple concept of the "ten
masters" (*jissaku*). One of the first uses of the term *jissaku* appears in
the writings of a noted performer affiliated with Kyoto's Honganji
temple, Shimotsuma Shōshin (d. 1616). Shōshin trained under the
leader of the Konparu troupe, Gyūren (d. 1583) and ranked among the
greatest actors of his age. He was also a mask carver and studied under
the direction of the Echizen branch of the Deme house of mask carvers. He is credited with helping Deme Hidemitsu, the second leader of
this house, create the woman's mask *Manpi*. In a section from *Transcriptions by Shōshin* (*Shōshin kikigaki*; ca. 1592), entitled the "Names of
the Skilled Mask Carvers" ("Men uchi jōsaku no na"), Shimotsuma
listed twelve great carvers by name: Nikkō and Miroku (whom he
grouped together with the notation that they made Okina masks),
Shakuzuru, Echi, Ishiōhyōe, Tatsuemon, Yasha, Bunzō, Koushi, Tokuwaka, Sankō, and Himi.[59] He offered the same list of mask carvers
in a different text titled *Sōdensho* (ca. 1596), adding that the members
of the group were also called the "ten masters." Surprisingly, although
there is no evidence to suggest that Shōshin had access to *Sarugaku
dangi*, the first ten names on both of Shōshin's lists correspond to the
names of the mask carvers mentioned in *Sarugaku dangi* and were
listed in the same order. The last two names, Sankō and Himi, derived
from the lore of the Deme family of mask carvers, who claimed them
as their ancestors. Shōshin asserted that he copied his information
about masks for *Shōshin kikigaki* from a text by the seventh leader of

the Kanze troupe, Sōsetsu (d. 1583). According to tradition, Sōsetsu's brother, Jūrō (*fl.* 1550), rediscovered Zeami's secret writings, including *Sarugaku dangi*. The current head of the Kanze family owns three versions of *Sarugaku dangi* said to have been copied by Sōsetsu. Therefore, Shōshin's list of mask carvers was probably based indirectly on *Sarugaku dangi* from a list that Sōsetsu had copied from it.

Why was just a list of names without anecdotal information important? A century after *Sarugaku dangi* was written, the names of mask carvers had become the chief way of determining the authenticity of noh masks and describing their styles. Whereas *Sarugaku dangi* mentioned the discovery of an Okina mask carved by Miroku as a means of recalling the founding of the Kanze troupe in Iga, subsequent noh discourse was more concerned with the general fact that Miroku was an important carver of Okina masks. Noh performers of the early modern era, as subsequent chapters examine, developed means other than masks to document their authority, although they never forgot the importance of masks to their trade.

By the era of Shōshin and Sōsetsu, noh mask carving had become a hereditary profession, and carvers no longer focused their energies on creating new masks but simply copied older models, relying on a standardized set of about sixty masks. The aesthetic favored old-looking masks, as a comment from the late sixteenth-century noh treatise, *Hachijō kadensho*, illustrates: "Masks that are too new tend to glisten and give a bad impression. More important, while new masks are unattractive, masks that are too old and worn-looking are even more unseemly. The right amount of aging is most essential."[60] Consequently, mask carvers took to replicating the signs of use on older masks and darkened new masks with compounds made from soot to age them. The biography of the warlord Toyotomi Hideyoshi, *Taikōki*, described how the mask carver Sumi no Bō (n.d.) copied several masks for Hideyoshi. The warlord could not distinguish the original (*hon*) from the copy (*utsushi*).[61] Sumi no Bō earned the title "the best in the world" (*tenga ichi*) for this accomplishment.

Sumi's success in producing exact replicas of older masks exemplified the need among carvers to differentiate originals from copies, and this problem appears to be the derivation of the term *jissaku*. For mask carvers, the creation of a recognized set of "original" ancient masks used for models was the first step in the process of standardizing mask production. By the early Edo period, the Deme family, which rose to dominate the mask-making profession, set the sizes for masks, using the dimensions of a young woman, *ko'omote*, as a standard measurement for all other masks.[62] The Deme preferred three noh masks as models for *ko'omote* masks, which were attributed to Tatsuemon and which Toyotomi Hideyoshi had dubbed Flower (*hana*), Snow (*yuki*), and Moon (*tsuki*)[63] (see Color Figs. 3 and 4 for the Flower mask). The best models, such as these, came to be classified as *jissaku*. The term *jissaku* can be translated "ten masters" since it was used in reference to a group of around ten ancient mask carvers. Yet, as the preceding example illustrates, the term also referred to the masks themselves rather than the carvers. In 1721, Kita Sadayoshi (d. 1750), leader of the Kita troupe, noted that the term *jissaku* might also be written as "true (*jitsu*) masterpieces" not "ten (*jū*) masters."[64] The collection of noh anecdotes *Rinchū kenmonshū* (1758) used the word *saku* in a similar way when its author characterized the forty-eight ancient masks of the Kongō troupe as masterpieces, "*saku no men.*"[65] The ninth leader of the Hōshō troupe, Tomoharu (d. 1728) also followed this definition and credited mask-makers with coining the term *jissaku*:

There were ten mask-makers a long time ago and they were termed the *jissaku*, and it is said that this custom was devised by mask-makers. In reference to masks by these makers, of the oldest ones, there are, for example, ones by Shakuzuru as well as Himi and Koushi. [Masks] that were made well were called masterpieces (*saku*) for convenience. The periodization may have been applied later, and this is unclear.[66]

Hōshō Tomoharu suggested that the practice of designating certain old masks as "masterpieces" (*saku*) predated the invention of the category of ten masters. By this account, well-made masks were called "masterpieces" (*saku*); the implication is that not all the masks ascribed to the ancient masters deserved to be designated masterpieces and deemed worthy of copying. Tomoharu's explanation draws attention to the utility of designations such as *saku* and *jissaku* as a way for the carvers who coined these terms to categorize masks and single out certain masks as good models for copies. This definition also explains why there were often more than ten names in lists of the *jissaku*.

The names of the carvers included among the ten masters also connoted certain styles of masks, and this further aided carvers in determining good models for copying. Some information about style was mentioned in *Sarugaku dangi*, but in later texts, individual carvers were portrayed as masters of specific types of masks. Thus, when Shimotsuma Shōshin used the term *jissaku* in *Sōdensho* to refer to the best mask carvers (*men'uchi jōsaku*), he added the types of masks these carvers created:[67]

> Nikkō, Miroku—Okina masks
> Shakuzuru—demons
> Echi
> Tatsuemon—women, men, *jō*
> Yasha
> Bunzō—women
> Koushi—*jō*
> Tokuwaka—"vengeful ghosts" (*ayakashi*)
> Sankō—"frowning demons" (*beshimi*), *jō*
> Himi—spirits

Sarugaku dangi distinguished Nikkō and Miroku as the carvers of Okina masks and described Shakuzuru as a master of demon masks, but it did not provide comparable information about the mask-makers found on Shōshin's list.

The subsequent publication of Shōshin's *Sōdensho* in the seventeenth century helped to popularize the term *jissaku*, although contemporary noh authorities sometimes disagreed as to who should be included among the top ten mask carvers. A treatise dated 1659 by the leader of the Ōkura school of kyōgen, Tora'akira (d. 1662), offered a slightly different version of the *jissaku* but nonetheless specified the types of masks attributed to them.[68]

> Nikkō—Okina related masks
> Miroku—Sanbasō
> Yasha—old woman
> Bunzō—male
> Kōji [Koushi]—*jō*
> Shakuzuru—demon
> Tatsuemon—woman
> Echi—woman
> Hibi (Himi)—"starved woman" (*yaseonna*)
> Tokuwaka—*ayakashi*

Tora'akira's claim that Miroku carved Sanbasō masks added prestige
to kyōgen, since this type of mask is used only by kyōgen actors. Despite a few differences, on the whole Tora'akira's list reproduced Shōshin's earlier texts. Tora'akira and Shōshin agreed on the types of
masks attributed to five of the ten masters; although Sankō is absent
from Tora'akira's list of *jissaku*, both nonetheless recognized him as a
master of *jō* masks.

Shōshin's and Tora'akira's writings on masks reveal the acceptance
of a standard classification scheme for masks by the seventeenth century. Such a schema was organized and ordered for its usefulness for
categorizing and judging mask quality rather than being a conglom-
eration of oral legends as in *Sarugaku dangi*. Whereas *Sarugaku dangi*
remained in manuscript form and barely disseminated, publication of
Shōshin's writings in the mid-seventeenth century helped to disseminate his concept of *jissaku*. By the late eighteenth century, mask makers were further categorized as "divine masters" (*shinsaku*), "six masters" (*rokusaku*), "old masters" (*kosaku*), and "masters of the middle
period" (*chūsaku*). Actors were also increasingly anxious about the historicity of their most ancient masks, and several leaders of the profession tried to offer guidelines for discerning real masks from copies (for
more on this subject, see Chapter 6).

When viewed chronologically, mask myths grew more abstract and
standardized over time, as they developed from a record of spoken wisdom to written references. The anthropologist Jack Goody explains
that the transition from orality to literacy induces changes in representation, which move toward greater abstraction: "In written codes there
is a tendency to present a single 'abstract' formula which overlays, and
to some extent replaces, the more contextualized norms of oral societies."[69] Nevertheless, this tendency cannot be attributed to the shift
from orality to literacy alone. Literacy and writing are technologies, as
Brian Street contends; their effects are not universal but are embedded
within specific ideological systems and dependent on particular social
contexts.[70] Other factors, such as the establishment of mask carving as a
profession and its focus on replicating old masks worked as an incentive for the creation of schemes to categorize mask types.

Masks remained powerful symbols of noh troupes even after the
adoption of writing and print, but as both of these new forms of media became more deeply ingrained, mask lore was increasingly an effect of the mediation of written texts. Thus, the spread of the technol-

ogy of writing among noh performers did not replace masks as a technology of memory; instead, writing subsumed memory, transposing memories about masks into a new context in which the manuscript and later the printed text became authoritative references. Changes in myths about masks also reveal the gradual codification of noh's aesthetics. Standardization, as Magali Larson has described it, is the depersonalization of knowledge. As information becomes more objectified, it transcends the bounds of the group that produced it. At the same time, "objective" standards provide legitimacy for a given occupational group when outsiders perceive that the group is functioning according to those measurable principles.[71] Standardization may be a prerequisite for a group's professionalization, but it is also a process of knowledge stratification within an occupational group as certain members of the group confirm their control through their right to create and impose standards. As the next chapter explores, the technology of writing in noh focused on creating secret manuscripts and therefore constituted a move to privatize knowledge, which strengthened the linkage between the production of myths and the maintenance of hierarchy within the noh troupe.

CHAPTER 2

Secret Manuscripts

If secrecy is maintained, the flower will exist, but when secrecy is not maintained, the flower cannot exist.

—Zeami, *Fūshikaden*

Was the founder of noh theater, Zeami Motokiyo, a beggar? This question has ramifications for our understanding of Zeami, early noh, and medieval society. The aristocrat Go'oshikōji Kintada (d. 1383), writing specifically of Zeami in 1378, commented in his diary, *Gogumaiki*: "*Sarugaku* is the occupation of beggars (*kotsujiki*)."[1] Kintada was registering his disgust that Shogun Ashikaga Yoshimitsu (d. 1408) had shown affection for the lowly Zeami and had even shared the same seat with him while watching the Gion festival. Some of Kintada's class doubtlessly shared his opinion, but other members of the Muromachi elite did not. Besides the shogun, the noted poet and high-ranking noble Nijō Yoshimoto (d. 1388) tutored Zeami in poetry and literature. Thanks to these supporters, Zeami gained an entrée to the highest circles of power, benefited financially, rose in prestige, and achieved firsthand knowledge of elite culture to enrich his art. Thus, in terms of literacy and achievements and in the eyes of his noble patrons, Zeami was not a beggar.

Nevertheless, recent scholarship has revived the view that Zeami's status was comparable to that of a beggar. The scholars who take this position do not seek to dismiss Zeami's achievements but hope instead to place them in context by reconsidering Zeami and his art from the standpoint of his perceived social inferiority. From this perspective, Zeami is depicted as striving not only to improve noh but also to raise his own position in society. As one scholar phrased it,

"Zeami was confronted with a formidable task: the transformation of a popular / religious / magic / pragmatic / temple-oriented art form known as *sarugaku* into an elitist / entertaining / representational / military-oriented artistic practice that had to please the patrons of noh."[2] According to this view, Zeami was at the lower end of the social infrastructure (economics, class, power) while marginal to its superstructure (art, religion, and politics) defined by the dominant classes of the military, aristocratic, and clerical elites. Proponents of this view further argued that only after the military appropriated noh as its own "ritual" theater did its performers cease being perceived as "objects of defilement."[3]

Although such considerations of Zeami's social standing have promoted historical contextualization of his plays and shed new interpretive light on some of his writings, structurally there is no difference between the modern scholarly focus on Zeami's perceived marginality and the medieval view of him as a beggar. Both representations of Zeami assert that (mis)perceived social status looms large in artistic production and identity, and both allow these perceptions to overshadow and determine production and identity. The effect is to reduce Zeami to a lowly person in need of a patron to lift him and his art from the social and aesthetic depths.

In recent decades, anthropology has grown sensitive to the issue of the representation of the subject as a voiceless "object" of study in the worst sense of the term. The conclusions of anthropologists who challenge structuralist modes of representation can be instructive in our assessments of views of Zeami as a beggar. Paul Rabinow writes: "We should be attentive to our historical practice of projecting our cultural practices onto the other; at best, the task is to show how and when and through what cultural and institutional means other people started claiming epistemology for their own."[4] A shift in emphasis away from *what* Zeami represented to *how* he represented allows us room to consider his personal role in defining himself and his art. Rather than take Zeami's marginal or low status as a given and then read his work and efforts through that lens, this approach scrutinizes Zeami's activity of representation itself (such as his myth-making), the medium he employed for representation (his secret manuscripts), and the implications of these for noh. This enables us to scrutinize how the adoption of a new medium and of myth changed noh without having to restrict ourselves to assumptions about the effects of Zeami's status, class, or "marginality" on their functions. Indeed, to do so would be to ignore the ways in which writing and literacy permeated and changed practices at all levels and sectors of society, even for the illiterate.

Zeami's secret treatises (*hidensho*) are the best key to his epistemology for three reasons. First, noh treatises by virtue of their content, intended audience, and purpose offer more determined views of how Zeami represented noh. Whereas plays are consciously fictional modes of representation dealing with specific topics and characters for dramatic presentation to an audience, treatises, especially the secret ones Zeami wrote, were intended to record authentic rules about noh practice for a very limited audience. Second, although variables such as changes in audience affected the reception and understanding of these theoretical writings, for example, when once-secret manuscripts became public, these factors are easier to address for the medieval period than those influencing the reception of his plays, which were performed publicly and were therefore contingent on the mediation of elements not limited to performers, staging, and audience. As Zeami explained, "The success of a noh depends on the time and place of its performance."[5] Finally, treatises addressed artistic practices such as plays, but plays did not present a comparable discourse on treatises, nor did they delimit general theories of representation.

This difference in representation between plays and treatises can further be contrasted by employing the definitions of hot and cool media coined by Marshall McLuhan. Drama is a "cool" medium dependent on audience reception to determine meaning. In contrast, theoretical treatises were "hot" in Zeami's age because the author had greater control over their interpretation by determining both content and reception through select transmission to readers. As McLuhan wrote, "A hot medium is one that extends one single sense in 'high definition.' High definition is the state of being well filled with data. . . . Hot media do not leave so much to be filled in or completed by the audience. Hot media are, therefore, low in participation, and cool media are high in participation or completion by the audience."[6] As a hot, high-definition medium, Zeami's treatises described the cool, less determined field of noh performance.

Later performers adopted the habit of writing treatises, and, as an epistemological practice and as a form of media, treatise writing changed noh's institutions and artistry. Specifically, treatise writing came to define art, ritual, and status and thereby established the parameters for noh's development as an occupation and as an art. This process was ideological, for it claimed parameters of authentic practice that consciously excluded techniques deemed aberrant as well as rival performance groups, which it presented as marginal. Writing defined legitimate performance customs and designated authorized practitioners. It attempted to bring order to a fluid environment of performance practices and, in the process, changed the way noh performers understood themselves, their place in society, and their art.

"Marginal Groups" and "Noh Troupes"

Zeami's epistemology drew distinctions between art and ritual, sacred and profane, center and periphery, and he brought these constructs to bear in his discussion of what constituted authentic performance. In his treatises these distinctions appear natural, reasoned, and supported with examples. However, the constructed nature of his representations becomes evident when placed against the backdrop of medieval society, in which the boundaries between art and ritual, authenticity and illegitimacy, and sanctity and blasphemy are less than apparent, a matter of perspective, value laden, and therefore ideological when imposed. The following overview of the groups performing noh in Muromachi-period Kyoto sheds light on Zeami's ideology in representing it.

Zeami's Kanze troupe of actors were only one group among many performing noh in Kyoto in the late fourteenth and early fifteenth centuries. The Kanze were one of four Yamato troupes affiliated with the religious institutions of Kasuga shrine, Kōfukuji temple, and Tōnomine temple in and around the old capital of Nara. In their relationship with these religious institutions, the Yamato troupes formed what the historian Wakita Haruko has termed noncommercial service guilds, characterized by the exchange of labor in return for benefits from a patron, such as tax-free land rights or exemption from tolls.[7] For the Yamato troupes, this meant performing in annual noh coinciding with the festival cycles of Nara's religious institutions in return for payment, protection, and patronage. Based closer to Kyoto were six troupes from Ōmi province, three of which were patronized by the powerful religious establishment of Enryakuji based on Mount Hiei, which loomed large in the capital's geo-

graphical and political landscape. Groups from neighboring Tanba
province, the Umewaka and Yata, also performed in religious institutions in the capital, and, as Zeami noted in *Fūshikaden*, troupes performing in more distant areas such as Ise province were also known
in Kyoto.[8]

One group of noh performers who resided in Kyoto whom Zeami
did not include in *Fūshikaden* were the *shōmonji*. *Shōmonji*, though esteemed as healers and ritual specialists, were an outcast group in the
medieval period and derived their livelihood by conducting ceremonies
and engaging in performing arts, including noh.[9] Zeami's omission of
them from his list of legitimate troupes is revealing of his ideology because *shōmonji* shared many characteristics with regional noh groups
such as the Kanze. Both Noh troupes and *shōmonji* appear in the historical record in the latter part of the fourteenth century. Like the Yamato noh troupes, *shōmonji* were often in the employ of religious institutions, sometimes even the same ones. *Shōmonji* were also an
important force for noh in Kyoto, where they lived in several villages.
And, as noh performers, they became major rivals of the Kanze troupe.
But rather than view *shōmonji* as brother performing artists and show
respect for their familiarity with supernatural forces, Zeami excluded
them and denied their legitimacy as performers. In response to the challenge of the *shōmonji*, Zeami and the Kanze troupe sought to prevent
shōmonji from performing noh, and their tactics succeeded. Scholars
view the Kanze and the Konparu troupes as responsible for driving
shōmonji from noh. This conflict with the *shōmonji* can be viewed as a
watershed in the growth of what Magali Larson terms the "evaluative"
and "normative" dimensions of noh as a profession.[10] Along the evaluative dimension, the Kanze troupe asserted its rights to perform noh by
denigrating *shōmonji*. In terms of the normative dimension, Zeami and
his peers rationalized their troupe's legitimacy by deploying representations of the theatrical and ritual parameters of performance that contested the *shōmonji*'s performances, which relied upon a more ambiguous interplay between ritual and entertainment. Who, then, were the
shōmonji?

Recent scholarship has highlighted the paradoxical view in the medieval imagination of the performing artist as an outsider, sometimes
called a "beggar-god."[11] As mentioned earlier, performing artists were
seen as comparable to beggars and were sometimes referred to by this
term. Typically from the lower strata of society, performers followed

an itinerant livelihood that depended on the charity of audiences. Yet, since some performing artists allegedly possessed the ability to summon and dispel magical forces of the universe—either by theatrical magic or directly through mystic rites—they became revered much like the powers they supposedly invoked. Although some have been inclined to apply the title of "beggar-god" to Zeami and his Kanze troupe,[12] the portrait of the performing artist as the beggar-god who functioned on the periphery of society and enjoyed close contact with the spiritual world better suits the *shōmonji*. Besides noh, *shōmonji* performed other theatrical arts and religious rites such as healings and exorcisms, and many of their performance specialties functioned simultaneously as entertainments and as thaumaturgy. The uncertainty of the boundaries between ritual and theater in their performance enhanced the mysterious power of *shōmonji* in society.

The two different sets of Chinese characters used to write the word *shōmonji* in the medieval period reflect the *shōmonji*'s ambiguous place in medieval society. The characters 唱門師 translate as "chanters at the gate"; 声聞師 as "those who hear the Buddha's word." The first set describes their itinerant livelihood as they traveled from house to house performing for alms. The second implied that a person who heard the teachings of the Buddha had some understanding of the Buddhist Law.[13] The Muromachi-period dictionary *Ainōshō* (1446) sought to differentiate between these two methods of writing *shōmonji* by classifying the first as itinerant performers and the second as novice priests.

Shōmonji stand at the gates of homes and beat gold bells (*konku*). The term does not refer to *shōmon* priests (*shōmonbō*, 声聞僧), and it should [therefore] be written as "chanter at the gate" (唱門師). Although there are many explanations about the priestly *shōmon*, according to one, they are novices who hear the explanation of the Buddhist Law, realize an understanding, and desire nirvana. References to those *shōmonji* who beat on gold bells should be written as "chanters at the gate." They appear at the gates of homes, intone the verses of the Buddha's vow, recite the Amida Sutra, and beat gold bells.[14]

The attempt here to disaggregate two groups—novice priests (*shōmonbō*) and itinerant performers (*shōmonji*)—reveals the difficulty contemporary observers had in distinguishing these two underprivileged groups, both of whom were affiliated with religious institutions and engaged in Buddhist liturgies. Yet, as *Ainōshō* notes, the itinerant livelihood of *shōmonji* marked them as distinct from novice monks. Unlike novice monks who entered into the institutional hierarchy of a religious order, *shōmonji* formed their own semi-autonomous groups and villages. In Nara, *shōmonji* were organized into guilds (*za*) under the supervision of the abbot of Daijōin, a subtemple of Kōfukuji temple. The fact that the same religious institution was a patron of the Yamato noh troupes, which were also organized into guilds suggests a close connection between *shōmonji* and Yamato noh. The first historical records of *shōmonji* in Kyoto date from the late fourteenth century. In Kyoto, *shōmonji* villages fell under the jurisdiction of Tōji temple and the Office of the Capital Police Force (Kebiishichō); scholars have not identified guilds among Kyoto's *shōmonji*.[15]

Although *shōmonji* were affiliated with religious institutions, another theory about the derivation of the name points to their connection with outcast groups. In Wakita Haruko's opinion, the term *shōmonji* originated as a corruption of *sanjō-hōshi*, literally, "a priest from a *sanjō*," an area associated with discriminated groups.[16] On the basis of occupational differences, Wakita differentiated the *shōmonji* from other groups such as the "defiled ones" (*eta*) and the "riverbank people" (*kawaramono*) who butchered animals, executed criminals, and engaged in other jobs considered spiritually impure. *Shōmonji* were also distinct from the so-called non-people (*hinin*), who lived in areas such as the vicinity of the Kiyomizu temple in Kyoto and assisted in funeral rites there. *Shōmonji* lived apart not only from these groups but also from the rest of society. In the fourteenth through sixteenth centuries, most of the *shōmonji* in Kyoto lived in the northern section of the city, in the villages of Yanagihara, Ōkurochō, Kitabatake, and Sakurachō.[17]

In summary, scholarly research as well as clues provided by the Chinese characters used to refer to the *shōmonji* ritualists suggests that in contrast to other discriminated groups, *shōmonji* could borrow from Buddhism to give their activities a moral resonance and legitimacy. The less flattering "chanter at the gate" reveals that the *shōmonji* earned a living performing peripatetic religious ceremonies.

Shōmonji *and Other Discriminated Groups*

Working at liminal areas such as household gateways through which both good and malevolent forces transgressed may have brought the *shōmonji* in contact with spiritual pollution. Yet, unlike *eta*, *hinin*, and *kawaramono, shōmonji* were not passive victims of spiritual contamination. Instead, they were the managers of sacred space, able to dispel defilement. The diary of the courtier Yamashina Tokitsugu (d. 1579), *Tokitsugu kyōki*, reveals that *shōmonji* were summoned to the homes of the nobility to perform a variety of rituals. In 1552, Yasutomi called them to conduct a purification rite when he had the kitchen hearth repainted. In 1576, he summoned *shōmonji* to perform a divination after someone had fallen ill.[18] According to the scholar Yamamoto Naotomo, the chief profession of *shōmonji* was as Daoist diviners (*onmyōji*); Murayama Shūichi agrees that the two occupations were practically synonymous in the medieval period. Accordingly, Yamamoto credited the *shōmonji* with popularizing Daoism and theories of the interaction of coequal forces of yin-yang (*onmyōdō*) in the medieval period.[19] On two occasions, Jinson (d. 1508), the abbot of Daijōin temple, the institution that patronized *shōmonji* in Nara, listed the activities of *shōmonji* in his diary *Daijōin jisha zōjiki*.[20] In 1463, Jinson described seven arts of *shōmonji*: noh (*sarugaku*), traveling priestesses (*aruki miko*), traveling female entertainers (*aruki shirabyōshi*), bell and bowl beating (*kane tataki* and *hachi tataki*) to accompany the chanting of sutras and as a means of collecting alms, something called "itinerant swaggering" (*aruki ōgyō*), and monkey training (*sarukai*). Some fourteen years later, in addition to *onmyōji* and bell beating (*konku*), he noted that *shōmonji* cast astrological calendars and performed the dance art of *kusemai*. During the Buddhist festivals of *obon* (in the seventh month) and *higan* (in the spring and fall), *shōmonji* chanted sutras to honor the deceased. Jinson also mentioned that they read from *Bishamon Sutra* (*Bishamonkyō*), which may have been used to provide protection, since Bishamon was one of the four guardian kings of Buddhism and the god of fortune. Scholars have also credited *shōmonji* with achievements in other performing arts such as originating the musical ensembles (*hayashi*) and the famous heron dance at Kyoto's yearly Gion festival and developing the performing art of *kowakamai* in the sixteenth century.[21]

Underlying *shōmonji* activities was a close interplay between acts of faith and entertainment. The two were closely connected in medieval performing arts. The reading of sutras formed part of the repertoire of an occupational performing art enacted by female entertainers called *asobime* during the Heian period. According to one reading of the twelfth-century collection of songs *Ryōjin hishō* that supports his claim, these "sutras" were as much entertainment as instruction because of the "humorous" manner in which they were read (*kiku ni okashikishi kyōyomi*).[22] It is unknown whether *shōmonji* recitations of the *Bishamon Sutra* and of sutras for *higan* (*higankyō*) may have been of this variety, but the implication of this poem in *Ryōjin hishō* is that sutras could be read for amusement.

In the fifteenth century *shōmonji* were most famous for noh. All the *shōmonji* villages in Kyoto formed noh troupes, and the names of the most famous *shōmonji* actors of the fifteenth century such as Inuwaka (d. 1430?) and Koinu were recorded in the diaries of the court, military, and ecclesiastical elite, who were their occasional patrons.[23] Koinu, for instance, won the praise and support of Prince Fushimi no Miya Sadafusa (d. 1456), whose diary *Kanmon gyoki* recorded Koinu's many visits to the prince's residence. After a performance of pine-music (*matsubayashi*—defined below) and five noh on the twelfth day of the first month in the fifth year of Eikyō (1433), Sadafusa commented that Koinu's performance was "extremely marvelous." He rewarded Koinu with a sword, a work of embroidery, food, drinks, and other gifts.[24] In addition to performing noh for the prince at the New Years, Koinu also sang while playing a small drum (*yatsubachi*) suspended at his waist.[25] The *shōmonji*'s ability to perform a variety of rituals and entertainments proved a lucrative combination since they gained greater rewards when they followed *senzumanzai* and *matsubayashi* with entertainments like noh.[26]

Matsubayashi and *senzumanzai* deserve special attention for the light the shed on *shōmonji* and their activities. Except for a few rural areas, pine-music has largely disappeared as a performing art.[27] Performances took place in the first weeks of the New Year and encompassed a range of different activities enacted by groups large and small. The first reference to *shōmonji* performing pine-music dates to 1416.[28] By adding their specialty entertainments, including noh, to their performances of pine-music, they turned them into a lucrative source of revenue.

The central image of pine-music performances was the pine tree, which had special significance for the New Year's holiday. The Japanese practice of decorating homes with pine boughs—analogous to the custom of the Christmas wreath in the West—dates from at least the twelfth century.[29] The practice took the name of "the pine of the Day of the Rat" (*ne no hi no matsu*), the first such day of the New Year when pine branches were placed at the threshold. In modern Japan the same practice of decorating homes with pine boughs is called "gate pines" (*kadomatsu*), and the decorations are left in place for the first seven days of the New Year's holiday, a time period referred to as "between the pines" (*matsu no uchi*).

For medieval Japanese the pine tree was more than just an attractive seasonal decoration: the pine held important spiritual power as a talisman that could purify a dwelling. Decking the gateway of homes with pine boughs was believed to prevent calamity and ensure prosperity. The sixteenth-century noh treatise *Hachijō kadensho* described this custom and its meaning.

The custom is for pine boughs to be placed as a mark of celebration by the entrance of everyone's home. Pine trees endure for a thousand years. . . . Among all the trees, the pine is famous for being auspicious. Consequently, at the New Year everyone enshrines a pine at their doorway like a sacred Shinto rope to serve as a barrier against evil. The pine welcomes the arrival of the benevolent deities of the New Year and serves as a talisman at the start of the year so that the residents of the house may be as long-lived as the pine.[30]

Besides serving as an auspicious symbol of the New Year's holiday, the pine magically concentrated benevolent energies within the threshold of a building and protected the boundary between the outer world and the sanctity of the home. In the hands of a performing artist, the pine branch served as a device to capture benevolent spirits and exorcise evil.

There is some debate whether the term *hayashi* in the word *matsubayashi* refers to a musical ensemble or ritual exorcisms. The controversy underlines the deep interplay in medieval performing arts between entertainment and thaumaturgy. The term *hayashi* in *matsubayashi* was usually written either with the Chinese character 奏 meaning "to play an instrument" or with two characters 囃子 meaning "musical ensemble."[31] Today, the two-character word *hayashi* is used to refer to an ensemble of musicians, such as those accompanying a noh play. Medieval *matsubayashi* performers employed similar instruments as noh musicians, and the word *hayashi*, therefore, might refer to the musicians. The Muromachi-era *Takanami Festival Drawings* in the collection of the Tokyo National Museum depict a parade of pine-music musicians playing shoulder-drums, hip-drums, stick-drums, and bells and carrying pine branches.[32] However, additional scholarly rumination on the term *hayashi* suggests that the word may instead derive from magical rites that permeated pine-music performances. The noted scholar of literature and folklore Orikuchi Shinobu (1887–1953) traced the derivation of *matsubayashi* to the word *hayasu*, "to exorcise a demon." According to Orikuchi, exorcists banished malevolent spirits with tree branches. *Hayashi* referred to the exorcism itself and to the branch, also termed a "spirit-expeller" (*tamahayashi*). Orikuchi noted that the pine branches decorating medieval dwellings at New Year's performed a similar function of driving away evil.[33] More recently, Morita Yoshinori (1994) argued that the word *hayashi* derived from a different archaic verb meaning to "burn out of gratitude."[34] Pine-music performers sometimes danced around bonfires of bamboo and pine called *sagichō*, which consisted of three large stalks of bamboo tied together and placed upright. Fans, poetry written at the New Year, and decorations including the pine branches that had adorned residences on New Year's day were placed on the *sagichō* and set ablaze to exorcise evil and celebrate the New Year. Abbot Mansai recorded in his diary, *Mansai Jugō nikki*, for the years 1411, 1413, and 1416 that pine-music performers, whom he called "pine-priests" (*matsuhōshi*), carried *sagichō* to his residence.[35] Morita, however, drew a distinction between the word *hayasu* meaning "to burn out of gratitude" and the custom of *sagichō*, which, he contended, was not an integral part of the pine-music performance itself. Pine-music performances occurred throughout the second half of first month of the year, but *sagichō* were set ablaze only on the fifteenth day of that month.

Two kyōgen plays in the modern repertoire of the Izumi school further explicate the meanings of *hayashi* as both a magical rite and a musical ensemble. The plays also illustrate the two main varieties of medieval pine-music: *furyū* (also *fūryū*) pine-music and *manzai* pine-music. The play *Matsuyani* (Pine resin), known also as *Matsu no sei* (The spirit of the pine), relates the story of a rehearsal for a *furyū* pine-music performance that ends with an unexpected turn of events.[36] Neighbors assemble at the home of the Master to practice for the yearly pine-music performance. The Master comments that "nothing is as auspicious as pine resin," and he suggests that they chant the words "pine resin," *matsuyani*.[37] The group begins to chant and play instruments until the Spirit of Pine-Resin (Matsuyani) unexpectedly appears. The Master and his servant try to capture the spirit but quickly abandon the idea. The spirit decides to dance, and he sings about the virtues of pine resin. Performances of *Matsuyani* feature a full instrumental accompaniment (*hayashi*) for the songs and dances of flute, shoulder-drum, hip-drum, and stick-drum, rare for kyōgen but comparable to noh and to the instruments depicted in the *Takanami Festival Drawings* of medieval pine-music.

In the medieval era, *furyū* pine-music, the type performed in *Matsuyani*, referred to group dancing or costumed parades accompanied by music. *Furyū* were not performed as an occupation but were acted intermittently by ad hoc groups as celebrations during, for example, the New Year's holiday or the Gion festival or as a means of averting calamity.[38] Fifteenth-century diaries record that villagers, farmers, low-ranking court retainers, townswomen of Kyoto, and the retainers of daimyo created impromptu *furyū* groups to perform pine-music. Although pine-music has largely disappeared, other examples of *furyū* survive as a folk art (*minzoku geinō*). According to Benito Ortolani, *furyū* retains its mystical aura: "The *furyū* tradition as it is still practiced in the guise of *minzoku geinō* is characterized by performances whose purpose is to avert pestilence. . . . The wild dancing and the bright costume colors are used to attract the harmful spirits of disease, and the gaudily decorated poles, umbrellas and hats are believed to become the place where the spirits are collected and drawn out of the village."[39] In the kyōgen play *Matsuyani*, the performers accidentally summoned a benevolent deity. The surprise twist to the play is typical of the humor of kyōgen and was meant to testify to the magical power of pine-music, albeit in kyōgen's satirical way.

Although *furyū* performers did not pursue pine-music as a means of livelihood, they typically received payment for their performances. If the practices noted in Prince Sadafusa's diary are representative, Muromachi-era nobles bestowed food and gifts on those who presented pine-music at their residences. Sadafusa recorded almost yearly performances of pine-music by the villagers under his stewardship (*jige*).[40] In the fourth year of Eikyō (1432), for example, he gave a pine-music band a sword, clothing, a letter or writing sample, and food and drink. This was typical of the types of remuneration that performers could expect from him.[41] Although the amount of payment was not enough to maintain a full-time company of performers, the prestige and value of the prince's gifts must have offered enough incentive to bands of performers to call upon him. Sadafusa wrote that he had to turn away many groups who asked to perform pine-music at his home.[42]

The kyōgen play *Matsubayashi* offers a view of another version of pine-music and features a character who may have been patterned on a

shōmonji. At the beginning of the play, the protagonist Manzai Tarō
enters the home of two brothers on New Year's Day to perform songs
and dances, as is his yearly custom. This year, however, Tarō offers
only abbreviated versions of his customary offerings because he has not
been paid. Realizing their error, the brothers make amends by paying
him a bonus. To show his gratitude, Tarō performs longer songs and
dances. In contrast to the rambunctious *furyū* pine-music, which required a large group of people, another medieval performing art enacted by *shōmonji* called *senzumanzai* provides a much closer model for
Manzai Tarō's program of pine-music. Manzai Tarō's name, which can
be translated as "Ten-thousand years Tarō," evokes the word *senzumanzai* (literally, "one-thousand autumns and ten-thousand years)."

Like Tarō of the play, *senzumanzai* performers operated in small
groups of two to three presenting songs and dances. The art dates from
at least the 1200s. A mid-thirteenth-century dictionary *Myōgoki* described *senzumanzai* performers as "begging priests from outcast areas"
(*sanjo no kojiki hōshi*) dressed as Daoist wizards (*sennin*) carrying pine
branches to bless dwellings at the beginning of the New Year.[43] A depiction of medieval *senzumanzai* performers in the painting *A Poetry
Contest of Thirty-two Artisans* (*Sanjūni ban shokunin uta'awase*) shows a
masked performer holding a fan and dancing to the accompaniment of
another performer playing a shoulder-drum.[44] Performers may have recited short poems or verses, and a few scripts of *senzumanzai* survive
from the early modern period.[45] To judge from diary records, the busi-
est time of the year for *senzumanzai* players was the same as that for
pine-music performances, particularly the Day of the Rat when homes
were adorned with pine branches. However, *senzumanzai* occurred
throughout the calendar year, because it was also a thaumaturgical rite.
It could, for example, be performed during the making of *sake* to bless
the production process or when trees were felled.[46]

Shōmonji fully embodied the role of "begging priests" when they
conducted *senzumanzai* or pine-music. In Muromachi-era Kyoto, the
same *shōmonji* villages supported both *senzumanzai* and *matsubayashi*
groups. *Senzumanzai* performers from the *shōmonji* villages of Kitabatake and Daikoku appeared annually at the imperial court on the
fifth day of the New Year in the fifteenth and sixteenth centuries according to the court record *Oyudono no ue no nikki*.[47] The *shōmonji* villages of Yanagihara and Sakurachō also gave their names to both pine-
music and *senzumanzai* groups.

Although targets of discrimination, *shōmonji* were mystical performers bearing magical pine branches to dispel evil, who coupled powerful rituals with dances and songs and performed both in the same settings. Although their solicitations of payment may have reminded some observers of the begging poor, for those who employed their services, the *shōmonji*'s mediation of supernatural forces through rites and dances warranted respect.

The dual proficiency of the *shōmonji* in the performing arts and mystical rituals was their chief asset in earning a living. On the one hand, *shōmonji* could draw on their knowledge of the performing arts to make their arcane rituals more appealing to potential customers. After presenting either *senzumanzai* or pine-music, *shōmonji* typically enacted other entertainments such as noh and the song and dance art of *kusemai*.[48] On the other hand, *shōmonji* could take full advantage of the hazy distinction between ritual and entertainment in the medieval period to give their performing arts an air of mystery.

Unfortunately, no records created by *shōmonji* survive that would provide their own perspectives about their livelihood and place in society. That absence (or perhaps disappearance) of a subjective voice has meant that *shōmonji* are objectified in writings by others. Their situation contrasts with that of noh performers belonging to regional troupes, chiefly the Kanze and Konparu of the Yamato troupes, who began writing down their plays and composing artistic treatises in the same period. The medium of writing gave the Yamato troupes a technological advantage over their *shōmonji* rivals, for it allowed them to seize the initiative in defining themselves and their performance practices. Not surprisingly, their empowerment came at the expense of *shōmonji*, as the discursive boundaries of noh as art and occupation were drawn to exclude them.

Writing in the Formation of Noh's Ethos

The adoption of writing was the most important innovation in the history of noh theater, and Zeami deserves recognition as the innovator behind that introduction. Zeami was probably the first member of his family to become fully literate. His father, Kan'ami, left no writings behind: no plays, treatises, or any other sort of text by Kan'ami exists. The oldest known written text of a noh play dates to 1414; this play, *The Plum of Naniwa* (*Naniwa no ume*, now shortened to *Naniwa*), is in

Zeami's hand. *Sarugaku dangi* attributes the "creation" but not the writing of three plays to Kan'ami: *Sotoba Komachi, Jinen Koji,* and *Kayoi Komachi.* The scholarly consensus is that the wording of these plays cannot be attributed to Kan'ami alone and that they were changed when written down by Zeami. Even if Kan'ami could read and write, he did not have comparable training in literature and poetry that his son pursued under the tutelage of the leading linked verse (*renga*) poet Nijō Yoshimoto and others.

Of course, literacy is not a prerequisite for knowledge of literate culture. The Heian-period women performers called *asobime* composed in the conventions of courtly poetry, and a few poems attributed to them were included in the imperial anthologies *Gosenshū* (commissioned 951) and *Senzaishū* (ca. 1188), even though there is no firm evidence that most *asobime* could read or write.[49] Many performers in Kan'ami's day were illiterate, notably the blind biwa players (*biwa hōshi*), who despite their handicap popularized epics such as the *Tale of the Heike*. Noh performers still rely heavily on rote memorization and oral transmission to learn the texts of plays and the mechanics of performance: the major difference between them and Kan'ami is that modern performers can use written texts as well.

Surprisingly, Zeami, whose literary talents are evident from his plays and theoretical writings, did not describe his writing as a radical departure from earlier practices. In fact, he was more interested in demonstrating the continuities in his approach to noh with that of his father, as if he were not yet comfortable with the practice himself. In the introduction to his first treatise, *Style and the Flower* (*Fūshikaden*), he explained that the text consisted of what he had learned from others as a youth.[50] In *Mirror Held to the Flower* (*Kakyō*), he attributed the information in *Fūshikaden* to his father, in contrast to the contents of *Kakyō*, which were his own thoughts.[51] Yet Zeami did articulate the importance of writing, not simply composition, in his notes on composing noh plays in *Fūshikaden*. Writing plays, he asserted, was central to the art of noh, and he emphasized the need to record them: "Writing the texts to noh plays (*nō no hon*) is the life of the Way."[52]

More important for this study than his writing of numerous plays was Zeami's creation of secret noh treatises. The twenty-one treatises attributed to Zeami provide an invaluable resource for understanding his approach to noh and its early history. Most of these writings remained hidden and scarcely known until they were rediscovered and published in the first decades of the twentieth century. Performers and scholars have subsequently found so much inspiration that it seems almost impossible to talk about noh without mentioning Zeami's ideas. Consequently, previous discussion of these writings, including Thomas Hare's *Zeami's Style: The Noh Plays of Zeami Motokiyo* (1986) and Sagara Tōru's *Zeami's Universe* (*Zeami no uchū*) (1990), have rightly focused on the interplay between Zeami's theories and his plays. However, these treatises also affected the structure of Zeami's troupe, the ways in which it presented its art to the outside world, and how audiences perceived them. Rather than focus on Zeami's aesthetic principles, which other authors have examined, the following section examines the social implications of Zeami's introduction of secret manuscripts and the impact of literacy on Zeami's noh troupe before discussing their effect on performance practices.

Zeami's Writing Practice

By taking the revolutionary step of committing his thoughts on noh to "secret" writings, that is, to privately transmitted writings, Zeami raised noh theater to the level of mystery and presumed expertise associated with other legitimate artistic endeavors, religious sects, and occupations that upheld the importance of secret manuscripts. Indeed, as described below, secret texts—writings transmitted only to select disciples—were essential for these trades and schools of thought not only as records of information but also as sources of legitimacy in the view of outsiders. The earlier performing arts of *bugaku* and *gagaku* had used secret writings, and some have argued that these works inspired Zeami.[53] Zeami likely would have gained knowledge of the extensive use of secret poetic treatises through contacts in the poetry schools at the court of the Ashikaga bakufu or during his studies with Nijō Yoshimoto, the author of *Secrets of Renga Composition* (*Renga hishō*). In Zeami's era, the aristocratic Nijō and Reizei families dominated the fields of poetry and literary criticism thanks to their possession of secret commentaries on celebrated works of poetry and literature, including *Kokinwakashū* and *Ise monogatari*. According to Susan Klein, familiarity with secret textual commentaries on poetry (*kochū*), many of which were held by the Nijō family, is evident in the play *Oshio* by Zeami's contemporary Konparu Zenchiku.[54] Similar writings probably influenced Zeami's practice of creating secret manuscripts.

Buddhist monastics in Japan were probably the first to commit oral secrets (*kuden*) to written form in what were termed "documents" (*kiroku*) and "written notes" (*kirikami*). Priests of the Tendai school and of Sōtō Zen Buddhism made use of these notes to record secret instructions from teachers. The practice began as an aide-mémoire, but the writings quickly acquired literal and symbolic value as reference works and as "proof" of the reception of oral teachings. Tendai priests made copies of oral secrets in *kiroku*, and other monastics compiled these notes into manuscripts. A class of specialists in these documents developed by the fourteenth century and were charged with organizing and interpreting these writings.[55] In this way, writing and the collation of manuscripts impinged on the reception and understanding of oral learning in the Tendai monastic community. Zen monks also compiled collections of answers to kōan, the spiritual conundrums used in Zen training that require insight gained through meditation to resolve. Masters transmitted kōan verbally to students to test their level of Zen realization. During and after kōan study, monks wrote down kōan and added their answers when they solved them. Masters might also ask students to write out their own or find suitable verses to "cap the kōan," to further illuminate their understanding. When a monk accumulated a complete set of kōan, called a *monsan*, it served as verification of succession in that lineage.[56] Possession of a *monsan* and of written notes authenticated mastery of Zen teachings before the advent of licenses in the early modern era assumed that function. Poets from the Kamakura era on employed *kirikami* as a means of transmitting secret information from master to student. As William Bodiford has noted, "In medieval Japan, *kirikami* were used at all levels of society for teaching almost any endeavor centered on private master-disciple lineages, such as theatrical performance, poetry composition, martial arts, secret religious practices, and especially Buddhism."[57] *Kirikami* and similar texts are thus the historical antecedents for the secret treatises of Zeami.

Besides serving as a medium that demonstrated mastery of orally transmitted knowledge, writings took over the earlier role of objects like relics as repositories of tradition and symbols of authority. Just as early noh troupes had venerated masks as symbols of legitimacy, Zen masters granted objects such as robes, bowls, and paintings to their disciples as indications of the transmission of the teachings, and—more important—official recognition of a student's religious attainments.

These practices date to seventh-century China when Shenhui (d. 758) used his possession of the robe of the sixth Chan (Zen) patriarch, Huineng (d. 713), to attest his reception of mind-to-mind transmission from Huineng. Later emperors of the Tang dynasty (618–907), as Bernard Faure recounts, appropriated this robe and incorporated it into the dynastic regalia to add luster to their own authority.[58] In medieval Japanese Zen, the regalia of transmission included robes, alms bowls, staffs, bamboo scepters, fly-whisks (*hossu*), paintings of Zen masters, and Buddhist scriptures. These objects continued to have value, but beginning in the thirteenth century they gradually lost ground to writings as the primary symbols of lineage and succession. After the era of Dōgen (d. 1253), in place of relics, Zen masters presented their successors with certificates of succession (*shisho*), which contained the names of the patriarchs and the master and the disciple written in a circle, and blood-lineage documents (*kechimyaku*), which detailed the procedures for the transmission of the Buddhist precepts.[59] The exchange of objects and manuscripts was not meant to replace the important extra-textual, mind-to-mind transmission in Zen; rather, it mediated how that the transmission from master to disciple was verified.

Like Zen enlightenment, the authority gained from being known to possess secret manuscripts was a public recognition of a self-referential truth. As long as the secret text (or enlightenment experience) was generally accepted as legitimate, ownership, provided it could be authenticated, conferred a similar degree of legitimacy. For Zen, enlightenment was recognized by the transmission of regalia and documents. In the case of secret manuscripts, the very secrecy of an unique treasury of knowledge served to authenticate the text. This gave an incentive to the text's owners to acknowledge the existence and importance of secret writings while simultaneously hiding the texts' contents. This was a difficult but by no means impossible task in an era when every pursuit from cooking to the martial arts to religious practices based its legitimacy on secret texts few ever saw.

This use of secrecy is akin to what Jean Baudrillard has called a "strategy of appearances." Secrecy, Baudrillard has written, "is the opposite of communication, and yet it can be shared. The secret maintains its power only at the price of remaining unspoken."[60] For Baudrillard, secrets are conspiratorial, but in medieval Japan the reverse was true. Secrecy defined orthodoxy, production, and interpretation. Secrecy is a play of appearances that permeates discourse, to borrow Baudrillard's phrasing. Secrets haunt discourse, but they are never made visible to the uninitiated.

Zeami grasped two key points in the game of secrecy: first, that the contents of the secrets sometimes mattered less than the secrecy itself, and second, that the existence of secret knowledge must be widely known. Evoking his metaphor of the flower for the actor's success on stage, he described in *Fūshikaden* how the audience would view an actor differently if they believed the actor had secret knowledge.

It is said that 'when there are secrets, the Flower exists; but without secrets, the Flower does not exist.' Understanding this distinction is the most crucial aspect of the Flower. Indeed, concerning all things and in any aspect of artistic endeavor, each family maintains its secrets, since those secrets are what make its art effective. However, when these so-called secret things are revealed openly, they often appear to be nothing special.[61]

According to Zeami's reasoning, if families in other artistic endeavors possessed secret writings, then so should his noh troupe. That is not to say that actors should tell their competitors their secrets, or even acknowledge their existence in reference to specific matters. Zeami wrote, "It is insufficient simply to hide the contents of secrets from people: a person who knows secrets must not even tell others of his knowledge. If an actor reveals himself to others, his enemies will be put on guard, take caution, and become circumspect themselves."[62] In the competitive marketplace, it served no purpose to brag about the specifics of one's secret knowledge since rivals could turn the same tactics against you and audiences would no longer gasp in awe.

Secret manuscripts amount to the creation of what Magali Larson has termed a "fictitious commodity."[63] Larson used the term to refer to any professional product that is knowledge based and consequently distinct from goods created by artisans. Zeami rationalized the necessity of the "fictitious commodity" of secrets by acknowledging that the information contained in secret manuscripts need not be relevant to performance practices for its owners to be esteemed. To quote Zeami again, "When these so-called secret things are revealed openly, they often appear to be nothing special." In other words, beyond the written information in the text, the secret treatise itself carried symbolic value as a signifier of expertise.

The Implications of Literacy for Noh

Zeami's introduction of secret manuscripts transformed the way in which knowledge of noh was viewed in relationship to its production. Before Zeami, performers could only convey the guidelines of their occupation through oral transmission. Everything, from the texts of plays to acting styles to techniques of musical performance was conveyed orally. Zeami's introduction of the practice of writing secret manuscripts brought a new medium to noh that reshaped oral practices by initiating a dialectic between orality and literacy in which authenticity was at stake in a game of secrecy and disclosure, silence and writing. Thus, instead of supplanting orality, Zeami added another dimension to it by juxtaposing oral teachings and written secrets. Thus, Zeami presented his first noh treatise, *Fūshikaden*, as a record of oral teachings he had heard from his father. He concluded Chapter Five of *Fūshikaden* with the words:

What I have written in all the various sections in this treatise does not come from my own strength or my own talents as an artist. From the time I was a small child, I received guidance from my late father, and so for more than twenty years, I have followed his teachings on the basis of what I have heard and seen, and so I have written all this not for any personal benefit but for the sake of our art and our house.[64]

In contrast, Zeami related that *Kakyō* represented his own discoveries about noh, "which he had continued to record" but referred nonetheless to what he had heard from his father.[65]

Zeami's act of committing his teachings to secret manuscripts did not undermine the value of oral teachings. Instead it upheld orality as a model and presented writing as an attempt to safeguard oral traditions for posterity. In the treatises *Fūshikaden* and *Finding Gems, Gaining the Flower* (*Shūgyoka tokka*, 1428), Zeami attempted to recreate a dialogue that recapitulated oral discourse by framing the text as a recording of an exchange (*mondō*) between an authoritative speaker and an inquisitive listener. As noted earlier, this format of writing, called "transcriptions" (*kikigaki*), was viewed in the medieval period as among the most authoritative of secret writings for its perceived achievement of capturing expertise conveyed only by speech. Such references to oral teachings in secret manuscripts not only revealed their existence but signified their importance. For Zeami, oral teachings were sometimes more sacred than their written counterparts. In *Flower of Returning* (*Kyakuraika*), he wrote that the "dance of Okina was the basis for noh dance," but he left the details to "an additional oral teaching . . . the most profound of all secrets."[66] After Zeami, oral teachings in noh were always made in reference to a written equivalent, and oral and written secrets reinforced one another. Secret writings, for instance, refer frequently to the "existence of oral teachings" (*kuden ari*), and the transmission of a series of oral teachings was often capped off by the transmission of a text and later by a license. Secrets, however, were not a substitute for a lifetime of hard practice, as Zeami noted at the conclusion of *Kakyō*.[67]

Zeami's introduction of written treatises provided a standard for gauging oral learning and consequently had an impact on the performance practices and social organization of his Kanze troupe. He transformed the troupe into a "textual community" to borrow the term Brian Stock used in *The Implications of Literacy*.[68] Stock analyzed the social ramifications of the spread of literacy during the eleventh and twelfth centuries in Europe, detecting the emergence of "textual communities," groups structured around similar interpretations of manuscripts. Textual communities relied on writings to guide members' behavior and to provide a sense of solidarity. For Stock, membership in a textual community depends only on the existence of a few people with mastery of a text who can convey that information to others. Membership does not rely on literacy but on contact with someone literate in the manuscripts acclaimed by a group. Stock emphasized the flow of information among members of literate communities as a means of fixing bonds of social cohesion and demonstrated that the introduction of literacy did not replace oral practices but instead restructured orality as even the discourse of non-literates came to be influenced by manuscripts. Stock's approach provides a way to theorize about the impact of Zeami's writings on his troupe. That is to say, although not every member of Zeami's troupe had access to all his manuscripts—or were even literate—the troupe became acquainted in varying degrees with Zeami's use of the medium of written texts and consequently realized that orality was neither the sole body of knowledge available nor the only means to express knowledge.

It is impossible to gauge the level of literacy within Zeami's troupe, but a few references are suggestive. Zeami's colleague, the kyōgen actor Gorō Yasutsugu (n.d.), admitted to being illiterate to the point of "not being able to write in the phonetic *katakana* syllabary."[69] Yet Gorō asked someone else to write a letter to Zeami in 1428 to convey his gratitude for what he had learned from the noh actor. In another example, Zeami addressed the treatise *Learning the Way* (*Shūdōsho*) to all the members of his troupe. *Learning the Way* is characterized by concrete directions about the preparations for performance and the duties of the troupe's different members. Zeami's decision to address this treatise to his troupe indicates his estimate of the ability of treatises to affect practices, and his unprecedented decision to allow troupe members access to it may have been provoked by a sense of desperation in the wake of a series of personal and professional setbacks.

At the time that he completed *Learning the Way* in 1430, the internal cohesion and clear lines of authority described in the text diverged from reality. The Kanze troupe was fractured into two opposing factions. One centered around Zeami and his son Motomasa. Zeami's estranged nephew On'ami headed the other troupe. Both troupes used the Kanze name and contested the right to the troupe's legacy. On'ami enjoyed the backing of Shogun Ashikaga Yoshinori, and the shogun sought to improve On'ami's standing at the expense of Zeami's. In the same year that Zeami completed *Learning the Way*, he lost the prestigious and lucrative position of "head of entertainment" (*gakutō*) at Daigoji temple, which he had held for six years. The previous year, Yoshinori had prohibited Zeami's group from performing for the retired emperor at the Sentō imperial palace in order to open the door there for Kanze On'ami. A far greater personal setback beset Zeami in 1430 when his son Motoyoshi decided to enter the priesthood and quit performing. Zeami's other son and heir, Motomasa, set off for Yamato province around the same time to escape the chilly reception he faced in the capital. The story of Zeami's subsequent exile to Sado Island in 1434 at the behest of Shogun Yoshinori is well known, although the circumstances are not. According to one theory, after the death of Motomasa in 1432, Zeami's refusal to recognize On'ami as the undisputed leader of the Kanze and to show On'ami his secret manuscripts provoked the shogun's retaliation.

Zeami's *Learning the Way* could not overcome his problems with the shogun, prevent the fracturing of the Kanze troupe, and counteract the rise to power of On'ami, but the text provides evidence that the members of the Kanze troupe knew about Zeami's practice of writing theoretical works since they were his intended audience. The noh scholar Nakamura Yasuo believes that Zeami's *Learning the Way* was an antecedent of the family-head system, since the text was meant to strengthen the authority of the lead performer (*shite*) over the troupe and unite its members.[70] In this case, the treatise failed to restore Zeami's control of his troupe, and the gambit was unsuccessful. However, the impact of Zeami's treatises extends beyond the contents of one text. Although his efforts to hold his troupe together failed, Zeami's practice of creating secret manuscripts had a far-reaching impact on noh by generating an inequality of expertise within the troupe that ensured those who could read and had access to secret writings a privileged place.

One particular effect of Zeami's treatise writing was to hasten the shift from seniority to heredity as the basis for authority in the Kanze troupe. Walter Ong has described how writing leads to a downgrading of age as a signifier of prestige as wise elders lose out to writings and writers as the chief keepers of tradition.[71] A similar process occurred in noh around this period. In the era of Zeami's father, an elder (*osa*) led the troupe. But by Zeami's time, elders no longer commanded undisputed authority over traditions by virtue of their advanced age and memory of old customs. Instead, the troupe leader (*tayū*) gained authority by virtue of his literacy, creation of plays, and access to writings that served as the enduring record of the troupe's activities and collective memory. The post of elder disappeared soon after Zeami's time, while that of troupe leader became hereditary. In *Sarugaku dangi*, Zeami's son Motoyoshi narrated the ascendancy of the troupe leader in terms of the elder's loss of the right to perform the sacred Okina dance (see below), which defined the troupe's core performance tradition. After Kan'ami danced Okina in place of the elder at a noted performance in 1374, the troupe leader and his descendants gained that prerogative. Even if other factors besides the leader's higher level of literacy may have contributed to his displacement of the elder, as described later in this chapter, the representation of this transition in writing heralded the importance of literacy to the way noh performers conceived of their artistic heritage, for it was troupe leaders, not the elders, who controlled this new medium.

With the elevation of the troupe leader as chief actor over the elder, other ranks and divisions within the Kanze troupe determined by seniority were effected. *Sarugaku dangi* described six grades of actors under the leadership of the elder in the "upper troupe" (*kamiza*). There was also a "middle group" (*nakaza*) led by an actor with the title "eldest" (*ichirō*), and perhaps also a "lower troupe" composed of boys.[72] In the case of the Konparu troupe, Zenchiku's writings delineate an adult troupe (*oza*) and a troupe for performers under the age of fourteen.[73] These age rankings and divisions disappeared from subsequent writings on noh by the end of the medieval period as the Kanze troupe adopted methods of organization that depended more on heredity and job specialty than age, as Chapter 4 describes.

The extant colophons in a few of Zeami's treatises that list the intended readers provide specifics on how Zeami sought to empower certain performers, chiefly his heirs who would take the position of *tayū*, with specialized knowledge. For instance, he dedicated a treatise on the composition of noh plays, *The Three Elements in Composing a Noh Play* (*Sandō*), to his son Motoyoshi and the writings *The Six Principles* (*Rikugi*) and *Finding Gems, Gaining the Flower* to Konparu Zenchiku. He concluded *Fūshikaden* with the words:

This separate secret teaching concerning the art of the noh is crucial to our family and should be passed down to only one person in each generation. . . . I have previously passed along these teachings to my younger brother Shirō, and I have given them as well to Mototsugu [Motomasa?], who is also a gifted player. They should only be passed on as an important secret.[74]

In this case, Zeami not only designated the readers of the text in his lifetime but also attempted to prohibit access to only one person per generation, presumably the subsequent leaders (*tayū*) of the troupe, his son and his descendants.

By restricting access to his secret writings, Zeami reinforced primogeniture within his noh troupe, which lent prestige to himself and the designated readers of his manuscripts. The most profound secrets were the inheritance of what Zeami called "one student per generation" (*ichidai hitori*), and that person was supposed to be the chosen successor of the leader of the troupe.[75] None of Zeami's extant writings bear the name of his son and chief heir, Motomasa, except for *Flower of Returning*, in which he lamented Motomasa's untimely death in 1432. However, the same text provides evidence that Motomasa received all of Zeami's secret treatises.

All the secrets of our art—from the legacy I received from my late father through what I had learned in old age—were transmitted to my son Motomasa, and I had only to await the Great Matter at the end of my life. Just at that time Motomasa unexpectedly departed from the world, and our school's line was broken: our house was already in ruin.[76]

After Motomasa's death, Zeami lost all hope for his family and his art, and On'ami became the undisputed heir to the Kanze name. Zeami explained in *Flower of Returning* that Konparu Zenchiku represented a potential successor to his artistic tradition. In that regard, he cited the fact that Motomasa had allowed Zenchiku to view a few of Zeami's treatises. Zeami himself presented Zenchiku with copies of treatises and the scripts of thirty-five plays.[77] Nevertheless, Zeami expressed his regret in *Flower of Returning* that Zenchiku lacked maturity as a performer.[78] As symbolized by his transmission of all his secret manuscripts, Zeami had invested the whole of his authority and knowledge in Motomasa. Ill fate robbed Zeami of his son and ruined his dreams.

In summary, secret treatises had both literal and symbolic value in Zeami's era, and as a medium they must be considered from both angles. Their literal value lay, for example, in their details about performance, playwriting, and training. The symbolic value of secret manuscripts was independent of the literal contents because most people did not have access to them. Symbolic value derived from close control of the circulation of manuscripts and the interplay of manuscripts and orality in the field of occupational expertise. Thus, although the audience for the literal information contained in Zeami's treatises was very select, the symbolic meanings of these manuscripts had a much wider impact within and beyond his noh troupe. Zeami socialized his troupe to the use of secret writings by making a few of his treatises such as *Learning the Way* available to all members, which fostered notions of primogeniture within the troupe and garnered popular respect for the troupe as a whole.[79] The effect of the symbolic power of Zeami's secret writing altered how performers and audiences interpreted noh, as examples of noh's changed relationship to theater and ritual indicates.

The Wind in the Pines Has Ended: The Kanze Troupe's Move Against Shōmonji

The growing boundaries around noh as an occupation and as an art in the early fifteenth century were defined by writing and strengthened in the competitive marketplace for performance. In Zeami's day, the main rivals of the Kanze troupe in Kyoto included the Hie from Ōmi province and the Yata and Umewaka from Tanba province. Perhaps out of

feelings of common identity or of grudging respect for their counterparts' popularity and powerful supporters, the Kanze did not directly
contest the prerogatives of the groups from Tanba and Ōmi until the
sixteenth century. Instead, Zeami and other early writers emphasized
the historical continuities among these regional groups and considered
all of them legitimate. In contrast, *shōmonji* performances of noh constituted a direct threat to Zeami's conceptualization of authority. *Shōmonji* did not specialize in noh or any single occupation but were instead proficient across a range of performing skills that blurred the
boundaries between magic and entertainment. This ambiguity and proficiency proved a lucrative combination that won *shōmonji* acclaim and
the occasional patronage of members of the military and courtly establishment. The Kanze troupe's disputes with the *shōmonji* over the right
to wear noh masks, hold benefit (*kanjin*) noh, and perform for the shogun reveal how the Kanze, beginning in words and culminating in vio-
lence, sought to lay claim to noh by ostracizing the *shōmonji*.

The Kanze troupe's first successful foray against *shōmonji* occurred
when they co-opted performances of pine-music for the shogun. As described above, *shōmonji* in large and small groups performed pine-
music during the New Year's holiday. Sometime during the first decades of the fifteenth century, *shōmonji* began enacting this rite for the
shogun. Unfortunately we do not know when; the first reference to
these performances, recorded in Abbot Mansai's diary, is dated 1431 and
mentions only that the Kanze had replaced the *shōmonji* as the shogun's
pine-music performers.[80] This move formed part of the Kanze troupe's
efforts to challenge the authority of the *shōmonji* and their influence
with the shogun. Prior to this reference, there are no known examples
of Yamato noh actors presenting pine-music.[81] This suggests that the
Kanze acted to strengthen their own position with the bakufu and to
challenge the *shōmonji*'s legitimacy as performing artists.

Sarugaku dangi suggests that the Kanze assumed responsibility for
performing pine-music at the bakufu in 1430, and that Zeami had been
consulted about this.

There were no longer any proper groups to continue performing pine-
music. The Gion festival might serve as a model, but in the first month of
the second year of Eikyō [1430], at a performance of pine-music at the shogun's mansion, it was learned that there were no longer any groups that
could continue this practice. Zeami was asked something about this matter,
and he replied that the words of celebration of the first solo part of a chant

should be sung: such as "The wind in the pines has ended, and all the clouds too have gone; Inari mountain, Inari Mountain, a gorgeous robe of blossoms adorns the imperial reign and blesses the spring. . . ." Zeami stated that performances today are generally too long.[82]

According to this account, by 1430 no suitable groups existed to perform pine-music for the shogun; this implies that these groups had disbanded or otherwise become unable to perform. This might be an indirect reference to the *shōmonji* Inuwaka, who had enacted pine-music for the emperor and Prince Sadafusa for over a decade. Inuwaka probably died that year, because the last reference to him in Sadafusa's diary dates from the fourth month of 1430.[83] Yet, besides Inuwaka, there were other actors and groups among the *shōmonji* who might have performed pine-music in 1430 had not the Kanze suggested themselves as replacements. Inuwaka hailed from Yanagihara village, and although records in Prince Sadafusa's diary are missing for the first three months of the year 1430, the following year he recorded pine-music performances at his residence by *shōmonji* from Yanagihara and Kitabatake villages.[84] The same diary indicates that two days later in 1431, the *shōmonji* performer Koinu, Inuwaka's successor, performed pine-music at Kōdaiji temple in Kyoto.[85] This is arguably the first time Sadafusa witnessed Koinu perform, but it is not Koinu's first appearance in the historical record: the diary of the courtier Made no Kōji Tosafusa (d. 1457), *Kennaiki*, records that Koinu performed at the palace of the retired emperor on the fourth day of the New Year in 1428.[86] In short, *Sarugaku dangi*'s claim that there were no longer any performers of pine-music was not accurate, because it ignored the fact that *shōmonji* groups who had previously performed pine-music and had enacted similar entertainments for the Gion festival were still alive and active.

According to *Sarugaku dangi*, as the new de facto expert on pine-music, Zeami proposed changes in the guidelines for the event. Zeami's suggestion of a verse to be chanted glorified the shogun's "imperial rule." Zeami's words "The wind in the pines has ended" exposes the scented garland that adorns the ruler. "Imperial reign" (*miyo*) refers to the emperor and, by extension, to the emperor's highest military officer, the shogun. On the one hand, Zeami's new verse for pine-music can be interpreted as an overt attempt to ingratiate his troupe with the capricious shogun, Yoshinori. On the other hand, Zeami's redefinition of pine-music softly asserted the prerogative of noh actors to judge the qualities of all performances for the bakufu.

Zeami never discussed *shōmonji* directly in his treatises, but an anecdote in *Fūshikaden* suggests that he did not approve of the modes of
dance associated with *shōmonji* pine-music. According to Zeami, during the life of the historical Buddha a group of heretics (*daiba*) bearing
tree branches and paper talismans (*shide*) sought to disrupt the Buddha's dedication of a new monastery. The Buddha's disciple Shāripu-
tra devised sixty-six entertainments set to flute and drum music to dis-
tract the rambunctious dancers and allow the Buddha to carry on his
work. These sixty-six entertainments were the forerunners of noh.[87]
Even if Zeami was not thinking about *shōmonji* when he recorded this
tale, his account represented noh as the sole authentic performing art
ideally suited for ceremonies. Performances by dancers waving
branches might give the appearance of magic, but for Zeami these
dances were powerless, heretical, offensive—not at all the stately
ceremonies befitting powerful people.

Another reason to suspect that the short reference to pine-music in
Sarugaku dangi contains elisions is that Zeami's influence with Ashikaga Yoshinori was at a nadir by 1430, and Zeami was no longer performing for him by that date. Yoshinori had favored Zeami's nephew
On'ami for many years before he assumed the office of shogun in
1428. A letter dated the fourth day of the eight month of 1428 in which
the kyōgen actor Gorō Yasutsugu apologized to Zeami for performing for Yoshinori indicates that Zeami's connections with the shogun
were strained.[88] In 1429, Mansai's note in his diary that "both Kanze
troupes" had performed for the shogun reveals that the split between
Zeami and On'ami had divided the Kanze troupe into two competing
factions.[89] Later that year, Yoshinori denied Zeami and his son Motomasa permission to perform for Retired Emperor GoKomatsu (d. 1433)
and granted On'ami the privilege instead. In 1430, the same year in
which *Sarugaku dangi* described Zeami's involvement with pine-music
for the shogun, at Yoshinori's whim Zeami lost the lucrative post of
musical director at the Kiyotaki shrine in favor of On'ami.[90] In short,
it is hard to believe that in 1430 the shogun would have consulted
Zeami.

Even if Zeami provided advice about pine-music, On'ami's faction
of the Kanze troupe were the ones who benefited. On'ami's group took
over the post of pine-music performers for the shogun in either 1430 or
1431, and the earlier date seems more likely. After the conflict over the
performance for the retired emperor in 1429, Zeami's group stopped

appearing before the shogun. In addition to the shogun, by 1430 On'ami had won other patrons who furthered his career at the bakufu. One of these was the powerful provincial military general (*shugo*), Akamatsu Mitsusuke (d. 1441), who had initiated the practice of bringing his retainers to perform their version of pine-music before the shogun. Mitsusuke may have been ordered to do so, or it may have been his own attempt to improve relations with Yoshinori. According to the first reference to these performances, which appears in Mansai's diary, Mitsusuke brought his retainers to perform pine-music at the shogunal residence in 1429 on the thirteenth day of the New Year.[91] Rival *shugo* such as the Hatakeyama, Isshiki, and Hosokawa followed suit and led their own retainers to perform *furyū* pine-music and noh before the shogun.[92] Mitsusuke became a patron of the Kanze around this period, and by 1432 Mitsusuke enlisted the shogun's favorite actor, Kanze On'ami, to aid him in the now annual custom of pine-music. That year, the Kanze troupe performed following a *furyū* performance by Mitsusuke's retainers.[93] Mansai's diary reveals that Mitsusuke was in attendance at the first Kanze pine-music for the shogun in 1430, which suggests that he may have helped facilitate the Kanze troupe's co-optation of the event. It seems likely that On'ami, too, had a hand in replacing *shōmonji* at the shogun's pine-music performances, and it was On'ami who emerged the victor of these machinations through Akamatsu Mitsusuke's assistance. On'ami was able to consolidate his claim to the Kanze troupe with the mysterious death of Zeami's son Motomasa in 1432 and Zeami's exile two years later. Ironically, On'ami was probably on stage when Shogun Yoshinori lost his life to Akamatsu Mitsusuke in 1441 at a noh performance by the Kanze. Having failed in his revolt, Mitsusuke took his own life later that year.

Kanze On'ami and the
Further Disparagement of Shōmonji

The kyōgen play *Gourd Beaters* (*Hachitataki*) is revealing of the attitudes of the Kanze troupe toward *shōmonji* in On'ami's day. The first recorded performance of the play, by Usagi Dayū (n.d.) on the fifth day of the fourth month of 1464 at a large benefit show at Tadasugawara in Kyoto, was organized by Kanze On'ami. The Kanze troupe's performance emulated an earlier one on the same spot in 1433, but it was on an unprecedented scale and was the crowning moment of

On'ami's long career. Many of the diaries of the period mentioned the event. *Tadasugawara kanjin sarugaku nikki* by the bakufu steward (*shitsuji*) Ise Sadayori (d. 1529) is devoted entirely to it and constitutes one of the earliest and most detailed descriptions of a benefit noh stage.[94] These sources reveal that the shogun, deputy shogun, powerful warlords, and prominent members of the nobility were in attendance. This entertainment gave the Kanze an opportunity to put on its best face, as well as to deride its *shōmonji* rivals during a time when the Kanze were attempting to prevent *shōmonji* from performing similar benefit performances. *Hachitataki* cast the *shōmonji* in poor light, and its performance on the first day of the benefit performance before the Muromachi ruling elite, not to mention townspeople who paid to attend, derided the efficacy and virtues of *shōmonji* performing arts in the public eye.

Unfortunately, the exact script of *Hachitataki* performed in 1464 does not survive. The oldest extant version of the play is found in *Tenshō kyōgenbon* of 1578.[95] This version, titled *Pot-Priests* (*Hachibō*), features *hachitataki*, whose specialty was beating on gourds to the accompaniment of chants. This itinerant performing art was one of seven *shōmonji* specialties, as Jinson noted in his diary in 1463 (see above).[96] In the play, two *hachitataki* priests make a pilgrimage to Kiyomizu temple, where they pray to rise above their present lowly status to become samurai. Kiyomizu temple was renowned for the powerful wish-granting statue of the Bodhisattva Kannon enshrined there. However, in the play, instead of Kannon, the Gourd God Fukube appears in the dreams of the two petitioners. The god presents one with an umbrella and the other with a begging bag (*ebukuro*). A third *hachitataki*, in an action reminiscent of *shōmonji* divination, interprets this dream, telling the two *hachitakaki* to forget about becoming samurai and to remain in their present occupation. The two priests rejoice in this revelation. Their joy proves their folly and draws attention to their inability to rise in status by ridiculing the idea. Even the deity who came to their aid, the comical Gourd God, refuses to supplicate his followers and chooses instead to reward them with items useful to their itinerant lifestyle and symbolic of their outcast status.[97] The play draws attention to the social stigma attached to the *shōmonji* and portrays them as blissfully ignorant.

Judging from the program of the 1464 performance, mocking disadvantaged groups was one of the themes of the kyōgen performed.

The play *Monkey Trainer* (*Saruhiki*), also performed on the first day, featured another occupation associated with *shōmonji*.[98] Two other plays spotlighted physical deformities that provoked discrimination: *Beard Fortress* (*Higeyagura*), a play about a man with an unusually long beard performed on the second day,[99] and *Tea Caddy Blind-Man* (*Chakin zatō*), a lost play enacted on the third day.

The Kanze's triumph over the *shōmonji* is exemplified by their persecution of the actor Koinu. Like his predecessor Inuwaka, Koinu was from the *shōmonji* village of Yanagihara, near Ninth Avenue in the capital. Although he was the most famous *shōmonji* of the era, enjoying the patronage of nobles including Prince Fushimi no Miya Sadafusa and Retired Emperor GoKomatsu, he left no surviving records of his own, and his career has to be pieced together from terse mentions in diaries, the best of these being Sadafusa's diary *Kanmon gyōki*.

Sadafusa's diary and others mention Koinu's performances at the residences of elite warriors and at the Sentō palace of the retired emperor beginning in 1431 and continuing to the end of the Bunshō era (1466).[100] Koinu was a regular performer of New Year's pine-music at these residences and usually added performances of around seven noh, if his performances for Sadafusa in the 1430s can be taken as standard. The prince praised Koinu's talent, but he also wrote that not everyone was satisfied with Koinu. On the fourth day of the first month of 1437, Koinu was apparently summoned to perform for the shogun, but Yoshinori abruptly changed his mind and had Koinu beaten away by guards. Four days later, Koinu was back in the shogun's favor and received his endorsement to perform.[101] The shogun's endorsement may not have been necessary to perform at the homes of commoners, but it helped to open doors at the more lucrative residences of the nobility. Sadafusa's diary indicates that *shōmonji* denied the shogun's approval were often turned away. Sadafusa himself turned away the Chōa group from his door in 1436 for their failure to obtain the shogun's endorsement.[102] Koinu, unfortunately, suffered the same loss of approval sometime between the years 1439 and 1442. The same years are missing from Sadafusa's diary, and it is uncertain—except for a comment in 1443 that Koinu had lost the shogun's approval and had been unable able to perform pine-music in recent years—when the shogun had acted against him or whether the shogun in question was Ashikaga Yoshinori or Ashikaga Yoshikatsu (d. 1443). In any case, by 1443 Koinu was again performing pine-music at both the court and

Sadafusa's residence, and Sadafusa expressed relief that Koinu would no longer suffer from this shogunal ban and immediately informed the court that the ban had been lifted.[103] But this does not mean that Koinu was welcome to perform for the shogun.

Koinu continued performing noh after the New Year's pine-music, but he was prevented from appealing to a larger audience by holding a public, benefit noh in the capital. Since admission was charged, benefit noh were extremely lucrative for performers, even though the proceeds were supposed to go toward a civil or religious project. *Dengaku*, noh, and *kusemai* actors alike enacted benefit performances in the capital in the fourteenth and fifteenth centuries. In 1423, *shōmonji* from Ōmi, Kawachi, and other provinces came to Kyoto for a benefit performance of *kusemai*.[104] Given their popularity as noh performers, it seems logical that *shōmonji* would also seek to hold benefit noh performances. Yet, when Koinu attempted this, he was twice thwarted by the Kanze. In the second month of 1450, Koinu was in the middle of enacting a benefit noh for Rokudō Chinkōji temple in Higashiyama when Deputy Shogun (*kanrei*) Hatakeyama Mochikuni (d. 1455) and guards from the shogunal board of retainers (*samurai dokoro*) drove him off the stage. The author of the diary *Yasutomiki*, Nakahara Yasutomi (d. 1457), who recorded this incident surmised that the Kanze and Konparu troupes were behind the move, noting that only they were allowed to perform benefit noh in the capital.[105] Yet, besides these two troupes, other groups did perform benefit noh in Kyoto in this period, including troupes from Tanba and Settsu provinces as well as groups of women noh performers (*onna sarugaku*) from Shikoku and Echizen. The scholar Nose Asaji has nonetheless affirmed that the Kanze and Konparu gained a virtual monopoly on benefit shows; he argues that the noh troupes from Settsu and Echizen relied on precedent to allow them to perform, and the women performers had received special dispensation from the shogun.[106] Even if the Kanze and Konparu troupes did not have a complete monopoly on benefit noh, that did not mean that they would tolerate the *shōmonji* on stage. Unlike the groups from the provinces, the Kyoto resident Koinu was a more immediate threat, especially since he had the obvious popularity and logistical support to mount a benefit performance.

Koinu survived the death of his great patron, Sadafusa, in 1456 and continued performing noh at the mansions of the nobility and warrior elite at New Year's and other occasions through the 1460s. In this period, Koinu's group caught the attention of Retired Emperor Go-Hanazono, thanks in part to his fondness for Koinu's grandson as indicated in the diary *Inryōken nichiroku*. In the second month of the first year of Bunsei (1466), Koinu was granted the unprecedented honor of performing for the retired emperor at the Sentō detached palace *after* the Kanze troupe. The author of *Inryōken nichiroku*, Kikei Shinsui (d. 1469), noted that Koinu's group was no rival for the Kanze, but that they had been summoned to perform due to GoHanazono's affections. This situation, coupled with the fact that the same grandson was receiving a stipend from GoHanazono, made them a target of derision, according to the same source.[107] Albeit brief, Shinsui's commentary is a telling record of the stigma attached to the *shōmonji*, their competition with the Kanze troupe over patronage, and the fact that their success was credited to a boy's sexual attractiveness instead of their skill as performers.

Two months after the incident at the Sentō palace, the Kanze troupe had revenge on Koinu when he attempted another benefit performance in neighboring Ōmi province. Koinu's crime this time was wearing a noh mask, and he was arrested in the capital on the fourth day of the fourth month.[108] This incident occurred on the eve of the Ōnin War (1466–77), and Koiniu's fate has been lost in the ensuing chaos of civil war that laid waste to large parts of Kyoto and damaged the authority of the bakufu. Koinu was probably imprisoned during this conflict and died in the early 1470s.[109]

The Shōmonji *After Koinu*

Koinu's demise marked the end of noh performances by *shōmonji*, although they continued to perform other arts into the sixteenth century, such as their traditional standbys, pine-music and *senzumanzai*, *kusemai*, and *kowakamai*, none of which was dominated by rigidly defined occupations like noh. The same *shōmonji* villages maintained their traditional ties with the court in the fifteenth and sixteenth centuries, as can be seen in the *Oyudono no ue no nikki*. In 1482 on the fourth day of the first month, a group from Daikoku Village enacted *senzumanzai*, and on the sixth day another group from Kitabatake Village performed. In 1572 on the fourth day of the New Year, the Daikoku group performed *senzumanzai*, as did a group from Kitabatake the next day.[110] *Shōmonji* were performing pine-music at the imperial court around *sagichō* on the eighteenth day of the first month into the mid-sixteenth century.[111]

Shōmonji also continued to be persecuted. When adherents of the Lotus sect ravaged Kyoto in 1533, they burned *shōmonji* villages east of the imperial palace twice in the fourth month. In defense, *shōmonji* formed their own armed bands (*ikki*) against the sect.[112] However, the biggest blow to *shōmonji* occurred in 1593 when the warlord Toyotomi Hideyoshi (d. 1598) rounded up all the *shōmonji* in Kyoto, Nara, and Osaka and exiled them to Owari province. The particulars of this move warrant further study but can be interpreted as part of Hideyoshi's effort to control the peasantry. Hideyoshi prohibited peasants from leaving the lands they farmed in 1586 and 1591. He also took steps to disarm them in a sword hunt in 1588 and to clarify their landholdings through countrywide cadastral surveys in the period 1582–98. Hideyoshi demanded ruthlessness in carrying out these provisions and ordered the deaths of peasants who opposed these measures. As he commanded one daimyo: "If they complain, kill all the peasants in the village. Even if the entire area or province is turned into a wasteland, it would not matter."[113] The itinerant, non-agricultural livelihood of the *shōmonji* was antithetical to Hideyoshi's policies of binding the peasantry to the land, and their presence was a potential source of defilement to the capital area, which he planned to remake, as symbolized by his construction of a huge, earthen rampart to surround Kyoto.

A few *shōmonji* remained in Kyoto after 1593, and they appear in the court records as *senzumanzai* performers as late as 1806.[114] However, by the Tokugawa period, *senzumanzai*, now simply called *manzai*, had become a more popularly enacted entertainment at New Year's and was no longer associated with *shōmonji*.[115] Similarly, pine-music was most commonly associated with performances by noh actors of a few sung portions of noh at the New Year in a recital also called "first songs," *utaizome*, as described in the following chapter. *Shōmonji* themselves disappeared as a recognizable social group in the Edo period. Some may have been pulled into other discriminated groups, which became increasingly scrutinized and restricted. Or they may have faded into the mass of common folk by virtue of their ability to adapt to any number of occupations.

Writing Okina and Defining Ritual

At the same time that they co-opted the ceremonial art of pine-music from *shōmonji*, noh actors of the Kanze and Konparu troupes also delimited their own technology of ritual in the dance of Okina, one of the "three rites," *shikisanban*. The dance of Okina lacks a plot, recognizable characters, and the dramatic elements found in a noh play.[116] Noh performers had enacted Okina at religious institutions since at least the early fourteenth century, and the dance itself may be older. In short, the performance elements and historical features of Okina set it apart from noh plays even in Zeami's day, and Zeami and his peers worked to accentuate these differences. In other words, rather than conflate all of noh with magic or ritual as the *shōmonji* did with their performing arts, actors of the Kanze and Konparu troupes, chiefly Zeami and Zenchiku, isolated ritual in the Okina dance, thereby distinguishing a frame of reference related to but apart from the artistic language used to describe the performance of plays. They created a technology of ritual that could be deployed at the artists' discretion as part of ceremonies at religious institutions or in discourse as a frame of reference to discuss the origins of noh. This distinction is evident in Zeami's treatises in which Okina plays an important sym-bolic role as a relic of noh's heritage, but remains extraneous to the discussion of performance practices, play writing, and aesthetics. Only four of Zeami's twenty-one treatises mention Okina, and only one of these works discusses it at length. Instead of being a dramatic work like any other noh play, Okina, as Zeami described it, had divine ori-gins. Its mystery and the apparent absence of transparent meaning suggested deeper, esoteric truths that were privileged knowledge. At its occasional performance, Okina served as a public display of a hid-den mystery, a counterpart to the actors' veneration of ancient masks described in the previous chapter. However, unlike the medium of masks, which made an origin story concrete, Okina's magic lay in its lack of clear meaning. In that sense, Okina was equivalent to secret treatises in Zeami's day. Both Okina and secret manuscripts contained hidden, private knowledge, whose power came more from what was hinted about them than from what was divulged. In that respect, Okina and manuscripts served as analogous myths for constructing authenticity and testifying to the efficacy of a performance tradition.

Three texts present the early perspectives of noh performers on Okina—Zeami's *Fūshikaden*, *Sarugaku dangi* by his son Motoyoshi, and *Writings to Clarify Okina* (*Meishukushū*) by Konparu Zenchiku.[117] The first has proved the most influential. Not only did *Fūshikaden* shape Motoyoshi's and Zenchiku's views of Okina, it also inspired sixteenth- and seventeenth-century interpretations.[118] Conversely, the writings by Motoyoshi and Zenchiku contain concrete details about Okina, but they were among the least known of theoretical writings about noh in the medieval and early modern periods. In contrast to *Fūshikaden*, which was published, albeit in bastardized form, in the early modern era, only eleven manuscript copies of *Sarugaku dangi* are known.[119] There are two surviving versions of Zenchiku's *Meishukushū*—the original and a copy dating from the mid-Edo period, both of which lay undiscovered in a storehouse until the 1960s.[120] Motoyoshi dedicated *Sarugaku dangi* to his father, who also expanded and edited the work. *Meishukushū* may have been intended for Zenchiku's eldest son, although the manuscript lacks a colophon.[121] Since Zeami's writings formed the basis for both Zenchiku's and Motoyoshi's discussions, they are the appropriate place to begin.

When Zeami observed in *Flower of Returning* that Okina was the source for his art, he asserted that noh was a distinct art with a sacred history.[122] In Zeami's three-part periodization of the history of noh, Okina occupied a midway point, somewhere between the misty era of noh's origins and his own era. This history, described below, mentioned but did not dwell on the annual occasions at which his troupe performed Okina, such as the Wakamiya festival at Kasuga shrine and the torch-lit noh of Kōfukuji temple in Nara. Thus, Zeami constructed his history of noh apart from the religious institutions that were his troupe's patrons. His history of noh was mythic in the sense that it depicted noh as an independent art set in motion by gods and buddhas, continued by great masters, and sustained by the actors of his era. Zeami might cite the role of famous men of state and religion in the development of Okina and noh, but he never subordinated the teleology of noh to any other historical phenomenon. Zeami made Okina an autonomous sign of noh's authenticity and a living relic of noh's origins. By foregrounding Okina as the essence of noh's history, Zeami empowered noh performers to define their traditions as they saw fit.

In *Sarugaku dangi*, Motoyoshi followed his father's view that Okina was the essence of noh: "When it comes to defining the basis for the dance in *sarugaku*, as far as our own traditions are concerned the dance in Okina should undoubtedly be cited. The basis of the chant is surely the *kagura* song in Okina, as well."[123] Konparu Zenchiku similarly followed Zeami in asserting that Okina was the foundation of noh, and he reiterated that noh developed from it. He began the last volume of notes to *Six Circles, One Dewdrop* by paraphrasing Zeami's view of the historical development of noh from *Okina*: "The way of *sarugaku* and *kagura* began in the age of the gods. Although the sixty-six entertainments later came into being, they are all governed by Okina (*shikisanba*)."[124]

In this sketch of noh's history, Zenchiku referred to three distinct historical moments, a beginning in the age of the gods, an era when sixty-six entertainments developed, and a culmination in the current age. Zeami devised this three-part periodization of noh in the prefatory remarks to *Fūshikaden*. For the first period, Zeami suggested two possible beginnings for noh: "It is said that the stories of the origins of *sarugaku* and *ennen* are traceable both to the land of the Buddha and to the age of the gods in Japan. But with the shifts of time and the passing of the ages, the power to learn about these traditions is out of our reach."[125] Here, Zeami hypothesized either that noh, like Buddhism came from India by way of China, or that it began in Japan as the creation of the native Shinto deities. In Chapter 4 of *Fūshikaden*, he elaborated on both possibilities. For the first, he traced noh's connection to India to the lifetime of the historical Buddha. The connection with Buddhism might also explain Zeami's decision to mention *ennen* noh, which was a performing art enacted primarily at Buddhist temples.[126] In the same chapter, Zeami located the native origins of noh in the familiar story of the Sun Goddess, Amaterasu, concealing herself in a heavenly rock cave and the efforts of the other deities to coax her out.

The beginnings of *sarugaku* in the age of the gods, it is said, occurred when Amaterasu, the Sun Goddess, concealed herself in the heavenly rock cave, and the whole earth fell under endless darkness. All the myriad deities gathered at the heavenly Kagu Mountain, in order to find a way to calm her. They played sacred music to accompany their comic dances. In the midst of this Ama no Uzume came forward, and, holding a sprig of *sakaki* wood and a *shide*, she raised her voice and, in front of a fire that had been lighted, she pounded out the rhythm of her dance with her feet and became possessed by divine inspiration as she sang and danced.[127]

When the Sun Goddess opened the rock door to see the source of the commotion, the assembled deities prevented her from returning to her retreat. The passage illustrates how Zeami borrowed freely from the great tales contained in the earliest mythologies—*Records of Ancient Matters* (*Kojiki*) and *Chronicles of Japan* (*Nihongi*). By taking these stories as the stuff for his history, Zeami interjected noh into the great narratives of the past and found a crucial reason for the inception of noh.

Uzume's "possession," described in the text as "descent of the deity" (*kamigakari* or *kangakari*), has given many scholars the impression that the passage demonstrates the shamanistic origins of Japanese theater and noh. Benito Ortolani has commented:

The function of divine possession (*kamigakari*) is extremely important . . . and fundamental for further developments of the Japanese performing arts. Its meaning is never clearly defined in Japanese tradition, and varies with the times. In antiquity it was probably understood simply as the dance of the gods; that is, the performers became the *kami* [deity]. Later, with the development of stronger shamanistic activity and consciousness, *kamigakari* referred to the act of divine presence in the medium; that is, the *kami* would make the shaman, or the object in the hand of the shaman, their temporary abode, and dance and speak through the shaman. This happened in ceremonies or entertainments (*asobi*) which the *kami*, through conjuration, were invited to preside over or take part in.[128]

In Ortolani's account, the meaning of the term *kamigakari* changed historically, from the "dance of the gods" to a "shamanistic practice." As I argue in the final chapter, at least in the case of noh, the notion of shamanistic possession as the inspiration for the performing arts dates from the twentieth century, much after the period of Zeami.[129] Modern scholars who read Zeami's stories as fragments of the "truth" about noh's origin should appreciate Zeami's creativity in devising myths that have retained some salience by continuing to fuel conjecture. In citing the story of Uzume, Zeami linked noh to a larger historical narrative. He no more meant noh to be understood as a form of frenzied possession than he wanted it to be seen as a women's performing art, which would have been an anathema to him.

By juxtaposing the two myths of noh's origin, Zeami denied primacy to either. He simultaneously associated noh with Buddhism and continental culture, on the one hand, and with Shinto and native origin myths, on the other. In his account, noh dates to the beginnings of time and recorded history, which he declared were ultimately unknowable. In both stories, Zeami described prototypes of noh and elaborated that noh did not remain in these archaic forms. Instead, noh, as Zeami defined it, was gradually refined in successive stages. Gods and buddhas served as the prime movers in this process, as they did for most worthwhile human activities, but noh continued to develop at the hands of mortals.

Zeami may have found the prototypes of noh in the actions of gods and the Buddha's disciples, but he attributed the origins of noh to one of Japan's greatest political leaders and his top advisor. "The origin of the nō, which we all enjoy today, goes back to the reign of the Empress Suiko, when Prince Shōtoku Taishi commanded Hata [Hada] no Kōkatsu (some say for the sake of peace in the country, some say to entertain the people) to create sixty-six public entertainments, which were named *sarugaku*. . . . Later, the descendants of Kōkatsu inherited this art and served at the Kasuga and Hie shrines."[130] The statesman Prince Shōtoku was beyond reproach in Zeami's era, and many worshipped him as an incarnation of the Bodhisattva Kannon. Credited with writing the *Seventeen Article Constitution* of 604, which laid down the earliest stipulations for ethical government, Shōtoku also promoted Buddhism, continental culture, and Confucianism and was the benefactor of several important religious institutions.

According to Zeami, Shōtoku's minister Hada no Kōkatsu (fl. 600) deserved the main credit for devising the forerunners of noh. The Hada clan are mentioned in *Nihon shoki* as descended from Hada no Kōkatsu, a local governor (*miyatsuko*) who received an image of the Buddha from Shōtoku, which he enshrined in a temple.[131] Zeami embellished the story of Kōkatsu's life much further. Chapter 4 of *Fūshikaden* has an elaborate legend about Kōkatsu's mysterious arrival: he was found as an infant floating in a vessel on the Hatsuse (Hase) River in Yamato province. The high official who discovered Kōkatsu reported the boy's radiant features to Emperor Kimmei (d. 571). The emperor discerned through a dream that the child was none other than the reincarnation of the first emperor of China, Qin Shi Huangdi (259–210 B.C.). The infant later received the surname Qin, read "Hada" in Japanese, and the name Kōkatsu, meaning "captured from the river." Kōkatsu's life ended as it began, in mystery. After conveying his teachings on the performing arts to his descendants, Kōkatsu departed from Naniwa (modern Osaka) in a boat for the province of Harima (modern Okayama prefecture). Apparently Kōkatsu morphed into a monster while on board. When the boat landed, the monster tormented the locals of Harima until they began to worship it, naming it the god Taikō daimyōjin, "The Great Raging God," who was said to be the incarnation of Bishamon (Sanskrit Vaisravana), one of the four guardian kings of Buddhism.[132]

The Kōkatsu myth was probably a time-honored story in the Konparu family, and Zeami cited relics and masks belonging to them as evidence for the truth of this myth, as described in the preceding chapter. He further claimed that Shōtoku had authored a treatise on noh: *Record of Sarugaku and Ennen* (*Sarugaku ennen no ki*).[133] According to Zeami, the work discussed the origin of *sarugaku* in the age of the gods and the time of the Buddha and then praised the power of *sarugaku* to spread the Buddhist Law, drive out evil, and ensure long life and happiness. Zeami did not admit to reading the work but hinted at its existence in a manner comparable to his descriptions of the hidden relics belonging to the Konparu—too sacred and ancient to be seen, even by Zeami.

After identifying relics that could testify to the historicity of the second stage of noh's development, Zeami then turned to the task of locating his own troupe in this history. He claimed he was a descendant of Hada no Kōkatsu both by blood and by occupation, and he signed the colophon at the end of Chapter 3 of *Fūshikaden* as Hada no Motokiyo.[134] He also affirmed that the members of his troupe followed the legacy of Kōkatsu, noting in the preface to *Fūshikaden*: "The descendants of Kōkatsu inherited this art and served at the Kasuga and Hie shrines."[135] He then traced the lineage of the four troupes that performed at the Kasuga shrine (the Konparu, Kanze, Kongō, and Hōshō) to a descendant of Hada no Kōkatsu, Hada no Ujiyasu (fl. 960). The noh troupes from Ōmi province who performed at the Hie shrine were in turn the offspring of the husband of Ujiyasu's sister, the gifted Ki no Gon no Kami (n.d.).

In Zeami's account, Hada no Ujiyasu and Ki no Gon no Kami refined the sixty-six entertainments into the three dances of the *shikisanban* and created the prototype for the Okina dance of his age. In the reign of Emperor Murakami (946–67), Ujiyasu and Ki no Gon no Kami concluded that performing all sixty-six entertainments in one day was too difficult; therefore, they edited the entertainments down to three pieces: Inatsumi no Okina, Yonasumi no Okina, and Chichinojō.[136] Zeami added a provisional definition of these three dances: they stood for the "symbolic representations of the three bodies of the Buddha"—The Essence Body, the Fruition Body, and the Transformation Body.[137] It is difficult to know exactly what Zeami meant by this interpretation, because he did not develop his ideas. The three bodies of the Buddha may indicate that the dances stood for different expressions of the absolute or of enlightenment. Yet Zeami did not reconcile this interpretation with the changes in the dances' performance in his own day; specifically that Chichinojō was seldom performed, and the three dances in the *shikisanban* were the Senzai, Okina, and Sanbasō, and not Inatsumi no Okina, Yonasumi no Okina, and Chichinojō. Nor did he grapple with the text of the *shikisanban* to reconcile it with his interpretation. The oldest script to the Chichinojō (see Chapter 7) indicates that the dancer portrayed the father of the historical Buddha, not one of the Buddha's bodies. How Zeami handled this disparity is unknown. His escape was a reference to "oral secrets that should be recorded elsewhere"—an odd statement since *Fūshikaden* was itself a secret treatise and Zeami's earliest.[138] There are no other known writings about Okina by Zeami.

In short, it appears Zeami had little to say about the substance of Okina and preferred allusion to definition. Okina's "meaning" may have been a mystery even to him. His son Motoyoshi recorded in *Sarugaku dangi* that the text of Okina was obtuse and a temptation for the actor to change. "The competition piece called *Torōkyō* is from long ago. Its text has been handed down just like the lyrics for Okina; consequently, it is not something that can be casually rewritten."[139] This passage suggests that even though performers did not fully understand Okina and might amend it, the leaders of the Kanze troupe nonetheless considered the age and sanctity of the dance and argued against alteration. The same case could apparently not be made for *Torōkyō*, for it was subsequently dropped from the repertoire.

Zeami's refusal to supply details about Okina may have been intended to preserve its mystery. If Zeami had designated Okina's nature, then he would have restricted Okina to a single religious or secular entity, hampering the potential of Okina to speak for the entire

legacy of noh in different circumstances. Even his provisional definition of the *shikisanban* as the three bodies of the Buddha recognized
the different ways that absolute Buddha-nature was manifest in the
relative world. Since all beings possess Buddha-nature, Zeami's definition could hardly be a less constraining one—it encompassed all spiritual phenomena and the creatures of the physical world. The very
lack of specificity allowed for any explanation of the meaning of the
dance, whether it was the Buddhist Law, the Way of the Gods, or the
history of the world. Thus Zeami made Okina carry the entire weight
of noh's history and spirituality: Okina became an open referent for
claims about the mysteries and profundity of the art, as Konparu Zenchiku would do in *Meishukushū*.

Zenchiku and Motoyoshi on Okina

Zenchiku, too, worked to expand Okina's mystery, but he took the
exact opposite approach. Where Zeami had hinted at a Buddhist interpretation but shied away from specifics, Zenchiku took Okina as
the symbol for divinity and listed name after name of the deities that
the dance represented. In describing the symbolism of the Okina
mask, Zenchiku equated it with both the historical Buddha and the
Shinto Lord of the Mountain, Sannō.

The [*Okina*] mask has seven holes for the eyes, ears, nose, and mouth.
Namely they are [metaphorically] the seven stars [that comprise the
North-pointing Constellation]. If we refer to these symbols as the seven
shrines of the Lord of the Mountain, we would be speaking of reverence
also for the Lord of the Mountain as the avatar of the Buddha. This also
applies to his epithet: The King of Physicians, Fully Enlightened, Teacher
of Healing as Lord of the Buddhas. Consequently, since the Lord of the
Mountain is the resident deity at Miwa, Mount Mimuro [on which his
home shrine is located] is accordingly worshipped as a form of the Ancient One in Triune Form.[140]

Zenchiku's definition placed no limits on the nature of Okina's divinity; by the time he concluded *Meishukushū*, he had equated Okina
with almost every known buddha, bodhisattva, and Shinto deity: the
Buddhas Dainichi Nyorai, Amida, Shakyamuni, the Bodhisattvas
Kannon and Jizō, and the Shinto deities of Kasuga, Sumiyoshi, Miwa,
and Sannō. Zenchiku further postulated that Okina represented the
Heian-era statesman and poet Sugawara no Michizane, worshipped

posthumously as the god (*tenjin*) of learning. The performing arts could not be omitted, and Zenchiku invoked Okina as the protective deity (*shukugami*) of all performers. Such an exhaustive list was made possible by Zenchiku's equation of Okina with the "source of divinity" (*kongen kami*). He compared Okina with the amniotic fluids of a womb that serves as the point of genesis for all that is sacred.[141]

If Okina stood for all of divinity, how then should an actor perform the role? Kanze Motoyoshi provided a long list of rules for performing Okina that reveals his interest in the outward look of the dance rather than a deep concern for the work's mystical core. He explicated the appropriate costumes to be used. He clarified that the mask-bearer should be young and handsome and that the kyōgen actor performing Sanbasō must dance with great seriousness and not provoke laughter. He recommended that musicians carry their instruments onto the stage with them and not leave them unattended on the stage when nobles were in the audience. And, he warned, the chorus must sing in unison. Violations of these rules did not necessarily risk divine punishment. Mistakes simply reflected poor taste or what Motoyoshi called "the horrid manner of the countryside."[142] The Okina dance could even be changed if the artistic outcome warranted it. For instance, in *Sarugaku dangi*, Motoyoshi described how Zeami made a surprise change in Okina during a competition performance and won praise for his clever innovation.[143] That is not to say that the actor should neglect the dance's sanctity. The most important element for Motoyoshi was that the actor preserve the appearance of sacredness, and he derided actors who behaved haughtily when they performed it:

On occasions when Okina is performed by request as a sacred offering, there are those who perform it in a perfunctory manner and receive a hundred *mon* from each of those present. If the crowd of contributors is too small, the actor makes a sour face. What can be done with performers of this description? One who possesses such attitudes cannot finish well. It can be said that in the life to come, he will surely fall into hell.[144]

Motoyoshi left it ambiguous whether a performer's bad attitude destined him for hell or whether the gods would damn the actor for arrogance.

Zenchiku spoke more concretely in *Meishukushū* about the proper attitude for portraying Okina. "With his costumes, the actor should

feel that he is putting on Okina's robe of forbearance and compassion.
. . . He should never, never treat these matters lightly."[145] Elsewhere
Zenchiku made the point that performers might receive divine favor
for their part in depicting the ways of the gods:

Our way follows Shinto and Buddhist ritual, not personal preference.
Still, it is true that [sarugaku] also serves as a vehicle [for the beauty] of
flowers and birds, the wind and the moon, an amusement for all under
heaven to enjoy. But even if a family of this sacred profession lacks fame,
by performing kagura and preserving the Way, it will be blessed with
divine protection. Evil conduct which does not accord with the Way in-
curs sin.[146]

Zenchiku's comment recalls Motoyoshi's criticisms of actors who performed Okina in a perfunctory manner if they were not paid well
enough. Invoking terms such as Shinto and Buddhist ritual (shinji, hōe)
and sacred profession (shinshiki) and characterizing his occupation as a
Way (michi) to religious understanding, Zenchiku confirmed the legitimacy of sarugaku performers even when their product was not entertaining.[147] He could then take comfort in the sanctity of his work,
even though audiences might not always appreciate it.

Zenchiku invited several commentators to add their thoughts to
his Rokurin ichiro, and their views provide an indication of how edu-
cated audience members interpreted noh and Okina. Abbot Shigyoku
(d. 1463) of the Kaidain-in subtemple of Tōdaiji justified noh and other
performing arts along lines similar to those found in the writings of
Zeami and Zenchiku; namely, that deities had once performed dances
and music. Shigyoku contended that songs provided expedient explanations of the Buddhist Law and dances reflected the spontaneity and
bliss of the enlightened state. Not everyone agreed with such a lofty
interpretation of noh. The Zen monk Nankō Sōgen (d. 1463), who
added the final commentary on Six Circles, tersely derided Shigyoku's
and Zenchiku's presumptuousness about religious interpretations of
noh. Nankō offered a Zen kōan that implied that performances were
better without references to any deep spiritual system.[148] At no point
did Zeami, Zenchiku, or Zenchiku's commentators describe the performance as the actor's own apotheosis, as modern performers do.[149]
Taking the role of Okina allowed the actor to represent but not become beings older and powers greater than himself. Still, as the monk
Nankō indicated, not everyone might agree with that interpretation.

Kan'ami and Developments in Okina

Even as Okina represented noh's origins, it also stood for the memory of more recent events critical to the development of noh. In *Sarugaku dangi*, Motoyoshi evoked Zeami's discourse on the sanctity of Okina to represent the redefined hierarchical structure of the Kanze troupe and glorify the troupe's founder, Kan'ami. Specifically, Motoyoshi dated Kan'ami's rise to dominance to the time when he was first allowed to perform Okina. After Chichinojō had been dropped from the *shikisanban*, the actor in the role of Okina enacted the centerpiece of the performance and was the only noh actor privileged to wear a mask in the performance (since a kyōgen performer took the role of Sanbasō). Because only one actor could take the part of Okina, that role had traditionally gone to the eldest performer in the group. Motoyoshi's description of Kan'ami's dance of Okina at Imagumano shrine in 1374 represented the performance not simply as his grandfather's first performance of Okina but as a fundamental shift in the history of noh.

In old days, the role of Okina was performed, according to the proper order, by the eldest actor in the troupe. At a performance of *sarugaku* at Imagumano, however, [in 1374] the Shogun Yoshimitsu was to see the art for the first time. When the subject came up as to who should dance, only the leader of the troupe, Kan'ami Kiyotsugu, seemed the appropriate choice. . . . This is how the practice began, and it has become a fundamental principle for the Yamato *sarugaku* troupe(s).[150]

When Zeami's father danced Okina, he established a precedent that the lead actor of the group, the *tayū*, should take the role.[151] In Motoyoshi's terms, the troupe's acquiescence in Kan'ami's performance acknowledged his fame and the importance of the lead actor in the troupe's hierarchy. Motoyoshi did not even bother recording the names of the actors who had once danced Okina or even of other possible candidates for the role.

Motoyoshi's glorification of his grandfather followed the pattern set by Zeami. From the time of his earliest treatise, Zeami credited his father with recreating noh. According to Zeami, Kan'ami introduced new dance forms and melodies and blended the art of imitation, or role-playing (*monomane*), for which the Kanze troupe was famous, with the refined grace (*yūgen*) that characterized the performances of *dengaku* and Ōmi noh.[152] Since Okina represented the roots of noh and signified its history, Motoyoshi's retelling of Kan'ami's first dance of Okina represented it as a new direction for his troupe and of the art as a whole. Kan'ami's right to perform Okina became in Motoyoshi's words, "a fundamental principle for the [four] Yamato *sarugaku* troupes," not just for the Kanze.[153]

Structurally, Motoyoshi's story of Kan'ami is the same as the tales Zeami told of Shōtoku and Hada no Kōkatsu. All these tales reduced the slow development of noh into short episodes involving well-known "heavy characters" and the performers' ancestral figures. These episodes also use Okina as a medium to represent legitimacy in terms of both religious and artistic authority. Motoyoshi included Ashikaga Yoshimitsu (d. 1408), whose power as shogun threatened to eclipse the imperial line, as principal witness to his father's dance of Okina—further testimony to the epoch-making nature of the event. The performance introduced Yoshimitsu to the Kanze troupe, and he became their greatest patron. Motoyoshi's decision to record only his grandfather's dance of Okina as the sole memory of an event he did not see firsthand serves as an indication of the symbolic importance of Okina to his troupe. Motoyoshi spotlighted his grandfather but remained silent about his father's contribution and that of other troupe members. In particular, Motoyoshi neglected to mention that his father's physical beauty captivated the young shogun and that the two subsequently had a sexual relationship.[154]

Scholars generally accept Motoyoshi's word that Kan'ami changed the history of noh when he danced Okina at Imagumano. As Thomas Hare commented, "This performance is often cited as a turning point in Japanese dramatic history; it not only marks the beginning of shogunal patronage for Kan'ami's troupe, but also signals a change in the orientation of *sarugaku*: with this performance, its ostensibly religious purpose was clearly subordinated to that of entertainment."[155] Motoyoshi's description of the Imagumano performance might argue for his farsightedness in grasping the significance of noh's development, but Kan'ami's noh troupe was only one of many groups performing noh in that age, and it is questionable that one performance could have such a profound impact on the history of a performing art. Motoyoshi instead reduced a much more complicated, slower, and contested process into a memorable moment that could be retold and, indeed, performed countless times.

Okina—The Eternal Mystery

Three generations after Zeami, Konparu Zenpō (1454–?), the grandson of Zenchiku, replied to a student's question about the meaning of Okina. Zenpō said that the words to Okina were themselves incomprehensible but were Buddhist in origin. Zenpō's student recorded in his notes, *Zenpō zōdan*, that the father of the historical Buddha created Okina and that like Buddhism, the dance had been transmitted through China to Japan, where it had become a Shinto rite.[156]

Zenpō's brevity was part of his direct style and his preference for concrete advice with examples drawn from daily life. Where his ancestors may have waxed philosophical, Zenpō drew comparisons to the Bizen and Ise ceramics used in the tea ceremony and referred to techniques used in swordplay (*kendō*) and kickball (*kemari*) to teach the correct posture necessary to produce the proper style of singing. His comments on Okina may reflect a reluctance to speak about the dance out of deference to its sacredness. Yet his comment that the lyrics of Okina were incomprehensible reflects an important continuity with Zeami's thinking. The importance of Okina did not depend on rational understanding. Okina was a great and impenetrable mystery that stretched back to the beginning of time and to the edges of the world. Okina was so mysterious that it did not lend itself well to direct comparisons with noh plays, except in the case where the mystery of a play was the topic.

In summary, Okina represented more than just a play in Zeami's, Zenchiku's, and Motoyoshi's writings. Okina was evidence of the history and the multivalent meanings of the whole of their art and suggested that such meanings were boundless. Zeami resisted the urge to circumscribe Okina's divinity. Zenchiku, who made the attempt, concluded that Okina represented all that was divine and the matrix that linked everything sacred. Zeami and Zenchiku in their depictions of Okina provided a way for noh performers to deploy philosophical and religious language about their work without having to defer to a particular saint or sect or to cite particular plays. Okina was the core of noh, a medium that expressed the multiplicity of the divine independently of any single religious system or institution. It transcended the artistic language and fictional stories used to create and perform plays. Thus, unlike the arts of *shōmonji*, which blended theater and ritual, Okina represented an isolated technology of ritual that allowed a distinction to be made between theater and religiosity while acknowledging the historical links between the two. This enabled Zeami and other performers to concentrate on exploring noh's dramaturgical possibilities in the writing of plays and in theorizing about them while enshrining noh's historical and spiritual roots.

The depiction of Okina in fifteenth-century noh discourse was structurally analogous to the introduction of secret manuscripts. Both secret writings and Okina contained the potential, contingent on the desires of the performers, to effect the reception of performances without necessarily informing artistic production. Both media were controlled by the leaders of noh troupes and could be selectively deployed as circumstances warranted. Their ultimate power was as symbols, or what are called "myths" in this book. As myths, they suggested a dimension of expertise for noh that confirmed their literate bearers' authority as the only ones who knew the truth of all mysteries. Thus, Okina and secret writings reshaped the discursive boundaries of noh, affecting power relations in this occupation by empowering interpreters with expertise while facilitating the disenfranchisement of those who could not claim to possess such intimate knowledge.

CHAPTER 3

The Power of Secret Manuscripts

By the mid-sixteenth century, a century after Zeami's death, noh treatises were no longer the sole preserve of the leaders of noh troupes, and performers often recorded their knowledge in secret writings intended for their descendants and principal students. Flute players and drummers, for instance, had their own secret writings. Performers collected writings, commented on them, and often compiled them into new works. Although there are several examples of this phenomenon, the Tenshō period (1573–91) *Treatise on the Transmission of the Flower in Eight Chapters* (*Hachijō kadensho*), is the most significant.

The incorporation of a wide range of source manuscripts into *Hachijō kadensho* reveals the state of noh in the mid- to late-sixteenth century. The work's comprehensive nature lent *Hachijō kadensho* authority and made it the most widely read treatise on noh until the twentieth century when Zeami's writings were rediscovered and published. *Hachijō kadensho* was frequently copied by hand, and a moveable-type printed (*kokatsuji*) version appeared as early as the 1590s and was followed, beginning in the early seventeenth century, by woodblock-print editions. One reason for the work's popularity was the concrete information it provided. In contrast to the philosophical writings of Zeami and Zenchiku, *Hachijō kadensho* gave detailed descriptions of performance practices in specific plays and provided advice on such topics as musical instruments, staging, and costumes. The level of detail indicates the trend toward standardization of performance by the late sixteenth century.

Another significant departure from Zeami's writings was *Hachijō kadensho*'s polemical nature. Although Zeami criticized performers on occasion, *Hachijō kadensho* reveals a much more competitive climate in the field of noh, which mirrored the political fragmentation and social upheaval of the late fifteenth and sixteenth centuries. Historians refer to this period as the Age of Warring States, an appropriate designation for late medieval Japan, which saw a fractured political order and warfare between regional warlords (daimyō). The Warring States period began with the Ōnin War, when two warrior factions battled in Kyoto, home to a shogun and imperial court powerless to stop the fighting. Several turning points mark the end of this period. In 1568, Oda Nobunaga (d. 1582) marched into Kyoto supposedly to restore the last Ashikaga shogun, whom he then banished in 1573. Subsequently, Toyotomi Hideyoshi, who continued Nobunaga's quest for political reunification, brought the period of civil war to a close. In this tumultuous period, once-friendly competitors in the noh world, particularly the Yamato and Hie troupes, became fierce rivals. As traditional bastions of both monetary and cultural capital crumbled, both noh troupes and warriors turned to means of constructing authority less dependent on the backing of time-honored institutions and more reliant on force. The warriors turned to the new technology of firearms introduced to Japan by the Portuguese in the 1530s. Military power enabled daimyō to claim public authority (*kōgi*) over their lands independent of external religious and governmental institutions. Noh performers, as *Hachijō kadensho* reveals, adapted secret manuscripts and changed them from a means of preserving family trade secrets into a medium for self-promotion through selective dissemination. Performers used secret artistic writings to lay claim to noh's traditions and secure a monopoly of legitimacy.

This chapter begins by reviewing the evidence for the spread of literacy in the sixteenth century among noh actors and then examines the world of sixteenth-century noh through the lens of *Hachijō kadensho*. It concludes by exploring the contribution of such writings to the standardization of noh performance practices.

The Spread of Literacy Among Noh Performers

The widespread use of secret manuscripts among sixteenth-century performers can be measured in the exponential growth in the number of treatises. This development suggests higher rates of literacy, although specific figures are impossible to determine. Only several dozen noh treatises can be dated to the fifteenth century, and nearly

all can be attributed to either Zeami or Zenchiku. It has been esti-
mated that as many as 200 extant treatises were composed a century
later, with several hundred more exemplars being copies with different titles or slight variations.

Moreover, the diversity in subject matter reveals that literacy and
the practice of secret manuscripts had spread among the members of
noh troupes. Treatises were no longer, as they had been in Zeami's
day, the preserve of the leaders of troupes. Musicians, for example,
had begun authoring their own secret treatises. The earliest examples
are by hip-drummers and appeared around the last decade of the fifteenth century. Manuscripts for other instruments soon followed.
Several treatises, including *Kinkan rakubaisho* and *Issōryū mugaidai fue
hidensho*, have been attributed to the flute player Hiyoshi Saemon
(fl. 1504–55) and his successors. The versatile drummer and playwright
Miyamasu Yazaemon (d. 1556) authored several texts on music, among
them *Collection of Oral Secrets for the Shoulder-Drum* (*Kotsuzumi
kudenshū*) and *Fuenukigaki*. *Zenpō zōdan*, a collection of notes by one
of Konparu Zenpō's amateur disciples, reveals that the practice of
writing about noh had grown to encompass students and patrons.

In comparison to the more focused writings of Zeami and Zenchiku, sixteenth-century noh treatises have been criticized for their
eclecticism and pastiche-like characteristics, but these same features attest to performers' increased reliance on manuscripts. Rather than
compose completely new texts devoted to theorizing about noh, sixteenth-century writers worked from both oral and written traditions
explaining the minutiae of performance.

A further indication of the increased use of texts among performers
is the rise in the numbers of scripts of noh plays from the fifteenth
through sixteenth centuries. The earliest texts of noh plays (*nōhon*)
date from the fifteenth century. Nine such texts in Zeami's hand have
survived, and approximately twenty more texts attributed to Konparu
Zenpō remain. A century after Zeami, even amateur students of noh
had amassed collections of hundreds of scripts. For instance, in 1556
the aristocrat Yamashina Tokitsugu recorded in his diary, *Tokitsugu
kyōki*, that an associate owned 300 *utaibon*, texts to noh plays with
musical notation.[1] Tokitsugu soon gathered enough texts to rival that
amount. Although there are no statistics on the increase in the number of noh texts from the fifteenth to the sixteenth centuries, these examples imply an exponential increase since even people at the periph-

ery of the noh world could assemble libraries of hundreds of hand-copied texts. Performers surely had many times more.

Forgeries of secret noh texts provide further evidence of the symbolic power of secret manuscripts and of their widespread acceptance and use by performers as commodities. If nothing else, the proliferation of forgeries attests to a growth of expertise in handling writings and a rise in their presumed value, as the historian Brian Stock has concluded about twelfth-century Europe, a period in which the gradual spread of literacy and respect for written proof was accompanied by an increase in forgery.[2] Although there is no statistical information to indicate if forgery was more prevalent in Japan than in medieval Europe, to judge from the severe punishments for forgery in Japan, which included banishment and execution, it evidently posed a threat to a society that placed pre-eminent value on documents to attest to legitimacy and authenticity.[3] Given the importance of documents in securing authority in Japan, the temptation to forge manuscripts from wills to artistic manuscripts was surely great. Samurai from the Kamakura period on utilized forged genealogies, landholding documents, and wills to obtain court ranks and win lawsuits. As the historian Hitomi Tonomura described, merchants from the Honai region of Ōmi province supported their trading privileges by citing a counterfeit imperial decree (*inzen*). For the merchants, the imperial decree proved irrefutable evidence in legal disputes, with the sumptuous outer wrapping of the document betokening as much as the contents in making the case for their rights.[4]

To have their productions accepted as authentic, would-be forgers needed to create documents according to established techniques, which meant they had to be fully versed in the conventions of writing. As the historian M. T. Clanchy has noted: "Forgers recreated the past in an acceptable literate form. They are best understood not as occasional deviants on the peripheries of legal practice, but as experts entrenched at the center of literary and intellectual culture."[5] Clanchy studied forgeries of written records such as deeds used as legal evidence in twelfth-century England, and his detection of orthodox practice and belief in the act of forgery is applicable to medieval Japan, where the prevalence of forgery similarly reveals the acceptance of the techniques of literacy and acknowledgment of the power of texts.

In the case of noh, the false ascription of the treatise *Hachijō kadensho* to four patriarchs of the four Yamato troupes not only disguised a hodgepodge of documents as a discrete and important text but also promoted the traditions of the four Yamato troupes. A leader of the Kanze troupe may have offered this work to a powerful warrior patron such as Tokugawa Ieyasu (d. 1616), as he did other writings. Judging by the polemic of the tome, particularly its glorification of the Yamato and denigration of the Hie, *Hachijō kadensho* reflected the heated rivalries among noh troupes and the aim of Yamato performers to use writings to present themselves as the legitimate interpreters of noh.

Hachijō kadensho

The original title of *Hachijō kadensho* was *Kadensho, Treatise on the Transmission of the Flower*.[6] The word "flower" (*hana, ka*), a metaphor for the actor's talent, is synonymous today with Zeami's theories about noh. It appears constantly in his writings, from his initial *Style and the Flower* (*Fūshikaden*) to his final major work, *The Flower of Returning* (*Kyakuraika*). By the sixteenth century, the word *kadensho* was a generic term found in the titles of several different noh treatises as well as in writings about other arts, especially flower arrangement (*rikka*). *Hachijō kadensho* employs the term in a similar manner as a synonym for authoritative knowledge about noh. The choice of the title is explained several times in the text; the citation in the first volume is the most illustrative: "The most important matter to be conveyed in teaching and learning noh is called the 'transmission of the flower'; therefore this work is called a 'writing to convey the flower' (*kadensho*) to express this meaning."[7] At times, *Hachijō kadensho* borrows the imagery of flower arrangement to describe the lead actor as the centerpiece of a flower display, or it uses "flower" as a metaphor for the slowly budding bloom produced by noh musicians restraining their playing on the first day of several days of performance. In general, however, in contrast to Zeami, it does not assign deep philosophical meaning to the term "flower."

As indicated by the modern title, *Hachijō kadensho* consists of eight chapters. These eight chapters range the gamut of information about noh—staging, costumes, dance, technical discussions of drum and flute playing, and even kyōgen. Chapter 1 describes the origin and meaning of noh and the ceremonial dance Okina. Chapter 2 focuses on pitch (*chōshi*) and flute playing. Chapter 3 examines noh chant (*utai*). Chapter 4 describes musical instrumentation for noh, particularly noh drums. Chapters 5 and 6 offer general information on noh performance. Chapter 7 returns to the subject of musical instruments, and Chapter 8 examines noh pedagogy and training. Each chapter contains short notes on discreet technicalities of performance. The discussions of performance are almost always grounded either in the context of a specific play or in terms of a performance venue. Complex points are expressed through a metaphysical language and artistic terminology that reveals the breadth of specialized terminology late medieval noh performers brought to bear on their art; for example, cosmological theories derived from Buddhism, Shinto, five-element theory, and the interplay between yin and yang (*onmyōdō*) as well as aesthetic theories of "introduction-break-climax" (*jo-ha-kyū*), which originated in *gagaku* music, and "formal-intermediate-casual" (*shin-gyō-sō*), used in calligraphy, flower arrangement, and the tea ceremony. There is, however, little sustained discussion of theory. Instead, *Hachijō kadensho* drew on these concepts to give concrete advice on selecting noh plays appropriate to a certain seasons, adjusting performances to the demands of specific audiences, and compensating for the effects of weather.[8]

Fond of esoterica, *Hachijō kadensho* nonetheless makes the case for applying abstract theories to specific performances. *Hachijō kadensho* demonstrates that late medieval noh performers were as willing to adapt ideas from the art of flower arrangement as they were to explore Buddhism and five-element theory or the theories of past actors such as Zeami. Yet the inclusion of these theories depended ultimately on their applicability to current performance practice.

Sources for Hachijō kadensho

Hachijō kadensho incorporated two of Zeami's writings, *Fūshikaden* and *Ongyoku kowadashi kuden* (Treatise on musical and vocal production), referring to them by name in two instances.[9] Unlike the majority of Zeami's theoretical writings, which remained the hidden property of only a few noh performers until the twentieth century, *Fūshikaden* and *Ongyoku kowadashi kuden* were disseminated to some extent in the medieval and early modern periods.[10] Yet *Hachijō kadensho* did not identify these texts as being by Zeami; nor did it indicate that they were by the same author.[11] Neither text is given in its entirety, and information from both appears in different sections of *Hachijō kadensho*.[12] *Hachijō kadensho* designated these two works by name but otherwise did not single them out.

With the exception of two texts by Zeami, the majority of contents of *Hachijō kadensho* derived from a variety of noh writings from the early sixteenth century that were incorporated in the text without citation. According to the scholar Nakamura Itaru, these include texts associated with the drummer and playwright Miyamasu Yazaemon, the lineage of the famous flute player Hiyoshi Saemon, and the playwright and fifty-ninth leader of the Konparu troupe, Konparu Zenpō, as well as several anonymous texts on music based on Zenpō's writings. Table 3.1 lists the best-known of these manuscripts and their location in *Hachijō kadensho*.[13]

As a pastiche of earlier noh writings, the *Hachijō kadensho* exemplified sixteenth-century noh treatises. Many of the anonymous texts found in the *Hachijō kadensho* were themselves second- or third-generation reworkings of earlier texts, such as Zenpō's theoretical treatises on music. The eclectic nature of the sources incorporated in *Hachijō kadensho* provides some clues about its authorship.

Table 3.1

Sources for *Hachijō kadensho*

Author	Title	*Hachijō kadensho* vol. no.
Zeami Motokiyo	*Fūshikaden*	6, 8
	Ongyoku kowadashi kuden	3, 8
Konparu Zenpō	*Go'on no shidai*	3
Miyamasu Yazaemon	*Kotsuzumi kudenshū*	2, 4, 7, 8
	Fuenukigaki	2, 4, 7, 8
Lineage of Hiyoshi Saemon	*Kinkan rakubaisho*	1
	Issōryū mugaidai fue hidensho	2, 4
Anonymous	*Eishō jūhachinen Motoyasu densho*	3
	Ongyoku no koto	3
	Ihon go'on no shidai	3

SOURCE: Nakamura Itaru, *Muromachi nōgaku ronko*, pp. 487–526.

Apocryphal Authors and Possible Compilers

In the Edo period. the anonymous *Hachijō kadensho* came to be attributed to Zeami, but the manuscript's original compiler(s) contended that it was a group effort by four authors, one from each of the four Yamato troupes: Kanze On'ami, Konparu Zenchiku, Hōshō Ren'ami (d. 1467?), and Kongō Sōsetsu (d. 1576) are collectively named as the authors in the fourth, fifth, and sixth chapters. All the attributions are similar; the one at the conclusion of Chapter 6 reads:

Lamenting that important teachings and secret matters had been abandoned as of no use, [His Highness] commanded Kanze On'ami, Konparu Zenchiku, Hōshō Ren'ami, and Kongō Sōsetsu, these four men, to gather from teachings on the various arts, past and present, to create a mirror for these arts for eternity. [What they compiled] was . . . recorded and given the name *Kadensho*.[14]

The putative sponsor of this project is not identified, and there is no explanation how the four masters divided their work or who contributed what. The individual authors are collapsed into a group.

Despite such claims, it is highly doubtful that any of these Yamato masters contributed directly or indirectly to *Hachijō kadensho*. Chronologically it would have been impossible for the four to have worked together, since Kongō Sōsetsu was born some thirty years after the other three had died. Moreover, the contents of *Hachijō kadensho* show little direct influence from these performers. Although Konparu Zenchiku is well known today as an author of noh plays and theoretical treatises, current scholarly consensus finds few of his theories in *Hachijō kadensho*. There is even less evidence for contributions by the other three. Kanze On'ami was well remembered in the medieval and early modern period as the third leader of the Kanze troupe and as a famous actor who won the patronage of the Muromachi shogunate and held spectacular benefit noh in Kyoto such as the grand performance at Tadasugawara in 1464. He was once believed to have written such treatises as *Jikkanshō*, but all these works have since been declared forgeries, and, in any case, there is no connection between them and *Hachijō kadensho*.[15] On'ami is believed to be the author of a collection of poems, but if he wrote anything else, it has not survived. Hōshō Ren'ami may have been a relative of Zeami, but his life is clouded in mystery.[16] Kongō Sōsetsu is the posthumous Buddhist name (hōmyō) of Kongō Ujimasa, nicknamed "The Nose" (hana), the most prominent of early Kongō leaders and one of the most colorful characters in the troupe's history. According to one story, Hana Kongō made a mask (see Color Fig. 5) out of the head of a statue of Fudō Myōō stolen from a temple in Nara; when he tried to remove it, his nose came off.[17] Other sources praise Hana Kongō's skill as an actor but attribute the loss of his nose to syphilis.[18] He may have been alive during the time when Hachijō kadensho was compiled, but scholars cannot detect his hand in the work.

Although the claim that these four actors authored Hachijō kadensho is dubious, the assertion that it was a joint compilation by figures personifying the authentic traditions of the Yamato troupes lent the text comprehensiveness and authority. These claims of authorship served as a hegemonic strategy to ascribe meaning to the text as a whole. As Michel Foucault has noted, the author is the name invoked to implant coherence and provide a link to reality for a text.[19] "A name," Foucault wrote, "can group together a number of texts and thus differentiate them from others."[20]

Similar claims appear to have been a useful means to garner authority for a text and its owner. Two examples from outside noh reveal how different groups used this method in the sixteenth century. Yoshida Kanetomo (d. 1511) resorted to false attributions to lend authenticity to his religious teachings on Shinto.[21] Kanetomo created the doctrine of "one and only Shinto" (yūitsu shintō) by combining Shinto and esoteric Buddhism. Yet instead of claiming the authorship of his texts, Kanetomo passed off his writings as the works of his ancestors and of four early Buddhist masters—Saichō, Kūkai, Ennin, and Enchin—and portrayed his own theories as revelations of his family's ancient teachings.[22] These texts supported Kanetomo's assertion of the supremacy of the Yoshida shrine over all official Shinto worship. In the seventeenth century, the Tokugawa bakufu granted Kanetomo's descendants the hereditary right to issue writs for all Shinto shrines. These writs governed rituals and the status of priests and even dictated the proper types of ceremonial clothing.[23] In the performing arts, Sendenshō played a pivotal role in the transformation of the art of flower arrangement. The founder of the Ikenobō school of flower arrangement, Ikenobō Sen'ō (fl. 1532–55), asserted that he discovered Sendenshō in 1536.[24] The postscript at the end of Sendenshō states that the text is a secret writing from the noble Sanjō family, compiled at the request of Shogun Ashikaga

Yoshimasa in 1445.[25] However, Ikenobō Sen'ō himself wrote the text as a means of authenticating his expertise.

The attribution of *Hachijō kadensho* to patriarchs of the four Yamato troupes suggests that the actual compiler(s) probably came from these groups. One of the strongest candidates is the seventh leader of the Kanze troupe, Kanze Sōsetsu (d. 1583), whose brother allegedly rediscovered Zeami's treatises.[26] References in *Hachijō kadensho* to the Kanze family as "our house" (*tōke*) and "our school" (*tōryū*) support the notion that someone affiliated with the Kanze troupe compiled the treatise.[27] According to the colophon of one of the oldest manuscripts of *Hachijō kadensho*, the so-called *Azuki Kyōdokanzō hachijōbon kadensho*, a Kanze troupe leader, whom many believe is Kanze Sōsetsu, presented a copy of *Hachijō kadensho* that he attributed to Zeami to the shoulder-drum player Kō Tadayasu (d. 1579).[28] Sōsetsu is also known to have forged Zeami's name on the colophons of manuscripts that he himself wrote.[29] Moreover, Sōsetsu and his brother Jūrō are said to have given copies of Zeami's *Fūshikaden* and other "secret" writings to the warlords Tokugawa Ieyasu and Hosokawa Yūsai (d. 1610).[30] If Sōsetsu's aim was to curry favor with powerful patrons, then it is plausible to assume that similar motives may have been behind the compilation and selective dissemination of *Hachijō kadensho*. He would not have been the only artistic master of the period to have undertaken such activities. In 1554 Miyamasu Yazaemon presented his *Kotsuzumi kudenshū* to his patron, the *shugo* of Kawachi, Hatakeyama Takamasa (d. 1576).[31] Masters in fields of study ranging from renga poetry to Zen Buddhism to swordsmanship similarly created secret writings for their patrons and were well rewarded for doing so.

This does not, however, mean that Kanze Sōsetsu was the sole creator of *Hachijō kadensho* as it exists today. Unlike modern, printed texts that represent knowledge in closed form, handwritten manuscripts, as Walter Ong has explained, encourage the reader's dialogue with the text through glossing. Ong writes that it was only with the rise of print culture that notions of plagiarism and the internal sanctity of the text became firmly established.[32] In their overview of sixteenth-century noh treatises, Omote Akira and Takemoto Mikio similarly note that copiers often interjected comments and revised the source manuscripts, especially in treatises about drums and flutes.[33] *Hachijō kadensho* reveals a comparable pattern.[34] The question of the identity of the compiler of *Hachijō kadensho*, however compelling and important, thus should not be viewed as the same as the issue of authorship in the modern sense of the term, with the author marked as the person ultimately accountable for the meaning of the text. But this circumstance should not prevent us from asking larger questions about medieval noh treatises, including who gained by their creation and circulation. To clear the way for a consideration of such questions, we may first analyze the grounds for the argument against the view that Kanze Sōsetsu was the primary "author" of *Hachijō kadensho*.

The current scholarly consensus on the authorship of *Hachijō kadensho* holds that it is a pastiche of Yamato troupe treatises and that the mixture of artistic styles found in the text indicates that the compiler was an "amateur," someone who, unlike Kanze Sōsetsu, did not make a living by performing noh full-time. This argument rests on the supposition that a "professional" such as Sōsetsu would adhere to one artistic style and not espouse the practices of other Yamato noh troupes. In this context "amateur" and "professional" are not understood in the modern sense that opposes avocation and vocation. Instead, they are used to indicate differing degrees of familiarity with noh practices. As evidence that the compiler was an amateur, Nakamura Itaru pointed to the many instances in which *Hachijō kadensho* interweaves performance techniques typical of the Kanze and Hōshō troupes (*kamigakari*) with Konparu and Kongō (*shimogakari*) traditions. The description of the dance of Okina in Chapter 1, for example, follows the *shimogakari* practice of having a kyōgen actor takes the role of Senzai. (In the *kamigakari* tradition a *shite* actor takes that part.) Chapters 5 and 6, on the other hand, describe *kamigakari* customs regarding costumes and dances. Although the text generally uses *shimogakari* treatises and terminology, it also incorporates *kamigakari* technical terms. Nakamura interpreted this eclecticism as carelessness on the part of the "amateur" compiler and as proof that he lacked direct knowledge of the traditions he discussed.[35]

However, this notion of professionalism is too narrow for sixteenth-century noh. Modern standards of performance do not tolerate a mixing of the artistic styles of, say, the Konparu and Kanze schools, and the five modern schools of *shite* performers use different choreography, costuming, and methods of singing. Professional members of these schools thus cannot readily perform together. However, in the late sixteenth century, the division between the various artistic styles of the Yamato troupes was not so clear-cut. Many treatises on singing (*utai*) and musical instruments from this period defy simplistic categorization by artistic style. No doubt late medieval Yamato troupes frequently shared expertise. For one thing, they were closely related to one another. According to *Yoza yakusha mokuroku*, the mid-seventeenth-century genealogical record of noh performers, Kanze Sō-setsu's younger brother, nicknamed Little Hōshō (KoHōshō), became head of the Hōshō troupe. KoHōshō later married a daughter to the son of Kongō Sōsetsu and then adopted this new son-in-law as his successor to the headship of the Hōshō troupe. Thus Kanze Sōsetsu's brother led the Hōshō troupe, and a cousin by marriage led the Kongō. Sōsetsu had even stronger ties to the Konparu troupe through his mother, who was the daughter of Konparu Zenpō. Kanze Sōsetsu and the sixtieth leader of the Konparu troupe, Konparu Yoshiteru (fl. sixteenth c.), were thus first cousins.[36]

These blood ties between the four Yamato troupes translated into a close familiarity with styles of performance associated with the different troupes and the exchange of artistic techniques at the individual and the group level. This acquaintance with the performing styles of the other groups allowed the four troupes to perform together on occasion, as they did when Toyotomi Hideyoshi ordered the leaders of the Kongō, Hōshō, and Kanze troupes to sing together as his supporting chorus for a performance at the imperial palace in 1593.[37] The compiler of *Hachijō kadensho* may have been an "amateur," but he had access to an impressive collection of noh treatises and possessed a command of many facets of performance. On the other hand, if a "professional" like Sōsetsu did indeed compile the work, the blending of styles might better be attributed to the incorporation of noh writings obtained through his close contacts with relatives who led the other three Yamato troupes. In that case, *Hachijō kadensho* can also be seen as a device for coping with the challenges confronting the four Yamato troupes in the latter part of the sixteenth century.

The Four Yamato Troupes and Their Rivals

Of the many groups of noh performers active in the capital region in the fifteenth century, the so-called four Yamato troupes of Konparu, Kanze, Hōshō, and Kongō are the best known today. Since the fourteenth century, these troupes enjoyed the patronage of Kōfukuji temple and Kasuga shrine in Nara, where they enacted the yearly festival noh in return for benefits and protection. The troupes were also sustained by close links to the Ashikaga shogun and *shugo*. As noted in the previous chapters, two of noh's greatest dramatists and theorists, Zeami Motokiyo and Konparu Zenchiku, came from the Yamato tradition.

The four troupes faced many difficulties in maintaining their livelihood in the sixteenth century. By mid-century, the shogunate and many of the *shugo* houses who had sustained the troupes had disintegrated into competing factions and no longer had the financial means to support noh theater except on rare occasions. The Yamato actors were forced to leave the capital region to find new supporters among the rising provincial warrior powers. The Kanze, who had been most favored by the Ashikaga shogun, sought the patronage of Tokugawa Ieyasu in Suruga. Hana Kongō took his troupe to Kai province (Yamanashi prefecture) to perform for Takeda Shingen (d. 1573), and the Hōshō sought the backing of the Hōjō family in Odawara.[38]

In the same period, the relationships between the Yamato troupes and Nara religious institutions were disrupted. In 1541 a quarrel between Hana Kongō and the leader of the Konparu troupe over precedence in seating at the Wakamiya festival noh at Kasuga shrine in the eleventh month provoked three of the four troupes to refuse to take part, leaving only the Kongō to continue the festival. When the conflict was settled in the favor of the Konparu troupe three years later, the Kongō left the festival, and the Konparu performed by themselves. In 1560, 1569, and 1570, none of the four Yamato troupes came to the Wakamiya festival, and the noh had to be canceled. Oda Nobunaga (d. 1582) summoned the four troupes to the traditional torch-lit noh in the second month of 1576, but they returned together to the Wakamiya festival only in 1593 on the orders of Toyotomi Hideyoshi.

In the sixteenth century the Yamato troupes faced not only the challenge of finding new sources of economic support but also competition from a variety of other theatrical groups. A few of these were led by women, such as Chiho *tayū* (n.d.), who performed for Hideyoshi.[39] Others featured attractive boys in starring roles. Members of the warrior class and townspeople formed their own noh groups, referred to as *tesarugaku* troupes. Several of these groups, such as the Shibuya and the Toraya troupes, continued for several generations and enjoyed the patronage of the imperial court. By Hideyoshi's time, the Toraya and Shibuya could claim nearly a century of performances as well as a distinct flair for exciting productions. Honganji temple in Kyoto had its own noh troupe, which starred one of the top performers of the era, Shimotsuma Shōshin, who instructed Hideyoshi's ill-fated nephew Hidetsugu (d. 1595) in noh. Even more threatening to the Yamato troupes were other regional groups of noh performers such as the Umewaka from Tanba and the Yamazaki from Ōmi, which could trace their heritage as far back as any of the four Yamato troupes. In the time of Zeami, the Umewaka performed at the imperial court, and by the mid-sixteenth century they were receiving the patronage of Oda Nobunaga. The Yamazaki later took up residence in Hideyoshi's Nagoya castle in Hizen province (modern Saga prefecture), and their number included Hideyoshi's personal noh teacher, Kurematsu Shinkurō (n.d.).

However, the Yamato troupes' major competitor was the Ōmi Hie. Perhaps because the Yamato eventually triumphed over the Hie and subsumed them, historians know comparatively little about them.[40] Yet the Hie played a critical role in the development of noh theater. Zeami identified the Ōmi Hie as one of the three troupes serving Hie shrine at the base of Mount Hiei, part of the religious complex of the Enryakuji temple. As such they were situated to obtain the patronage of one of the largest landowners and most powerful political forces in medieval Japan. In Zeami's period, another Hie group from Tanba province received the patronage of Retired Emperor GoKomatsu, and by the sixteenth century had achieved great success in Kyoto.[41] Both Hie troupes were able to take advantage of their bases in nearby Ōmi and Tanba provinces to secure commissions to perform at religious institutions and benefit noh in the capital.[42]

The records of the Ise family, whose members served as stewards (*shitsuji*) in charge of protocol and ceremonies for the Muromachi bakufu, show that the Hie troupes also enjoyed close contacts with the bakufu in the late fifteenth and sixteenth centuries. The writings of Ise Sadayori, in particular, suggest that in the early sixteenth century the Hie troupes received favors from the shogun comparable to those obtained by the Kanze. Sadayori was a keen observer of noh. As mentioned in the preceding chapter, his *Tadasugawara kanjin sarugaku nikki*, an account of Kanze On'ami's benefit performance at Tadasugawara in Kyoto in 1464, is one of the most detailed descriptions of a noh performance during the medieval period.[43] In *Nenjū jōreiki*, his account of annual bakufu ceremonies, Sadayori noted that the Kanze troupe made its New Year's greeting to the shogun on the fourth day of the first month and that the Hie troupe received gifts of silk after their New Year's greeting three days later.[44] No mention was made of other troupes participating in the New Year's festivities, an indication of the privileged position of the Kanze and the Hie troupes. Sadayori's *Sōgo ōzōshi* (ca. 1528), which covers etiquette at the Muromachi bakufu and the protocol used for noh performances, offers further evidence of the prominence of the Hie troupes. It notes that whenever noh was performed at the Muromachi bakufu, two actors from the Hie troupes and a few *dengaku* performers were ordered to provide commentary on the play for the shogun. At the end of this text, Sadayori listed the great noh performers of his day, ranking actors from the Hie troupe immediately following the Kanze and omitting reference to any of the other three Yamato troupes.[45] Clearly the Hie held a significant place in shogunal patronage of noh in the late fifteenth and early sixteenth centuries.

The records of benefit noh performed in the capital in the late sixteenth century by the Tanba Hie troupe attest to the strength of the Hie troupes in the period when *Hachijō kadensho* was compiled. Six of the fourteen references in diaries to the Tanba Hie troupe from 1573 to 1595 mention their holding benefit noh in the capital. This compares with five conducted by the Umewaka troupe and a few by *tesarugaku* troupes.[46] During this period the departure of the Yamato troupes from the capital to seek patrons in the provinces had reduced the number of groups. Nevertheless, such records point to the continued popularity of the Hie troupes.

The disdain with which the Yamato troupes regarded the Hie troupes' popularity is suggested by an episode involving an actor of the Tanba Hie adopted into the Kongō house. In 1587, when the leader of the Kongō troupe died, this actor, renamed Kongō Yaichi (n.d.), succeeded him as head.[47] The year following Yaichi's appointment, the Kongō resumed performing the torch-lit festival noh in Nara, and the new troupe leader enacted the ceremonial dance of Okina. The other three Yamato troupes refused to perform with the Kongō that year, because of the large number of "amateurs" (*shirōto*) in the Kongō troupe's ranks. Yamato antagonism toward the Hie, even after one of the Hie had joined and rose to a position of authority within their own ranks, is apparent. Later chroniclers of the Kongō troupe apparently felt equally ambivalent about Kongō Yaichi and omitted him from the troupe's genealogies and histories.[48]

Despite their continued popularity, the Hie troupes in Kyoto were, like the Yamato troupes, hard hit by erosion of their traditional economic base in the late sixteenth century. In 1571, Oda Nobunaga destroyed their traditional institutional basis of support when he reduced the monastic establishment on Mount Hiei to ashes in his campaign against Enryakuji. As Yamaji Kōzō has pointed out, the Hie troupes also suffered the consequences of the cadastral surveys conducted by Toyotomi Hideyoshi and daimyō in the following decades. Noh performances at village shrines and other religious institutions, he argues, had been a major source of sustenance for the Hie troupes. The surveys deprived such institutions of proprietary rights rooted in the estate (*shōen*) system of landholding and left them without the resources to support noh troupes. This, in turn, forced the Hie troupes to seek affiliation with larger troupes that received stipends from the warrior elite.[49]

The situation resulted eventually in the absorption of the Hie actors by the triumphant Yamato troupes. As *Sarugaku dengi*, a mid-Edo-period collection of stories about noh troupes, put it, "During the period of Nobunaga, Hideyoshi, and the beginning of the present [Tokugawa] era, the Hie were heralded as skilled and were at the peak of their art; yet most of their descendants died out except for a few remaining Hie heirs." *Sarugaku dengi* located these heirs among the chorus members of the Kanze and Hōshō troupes; they retained the Hie name but had otherwise become part of the Yamato troupes.[50] This development did not take place immediately, however. In the late sixteenth century, the Yamato troupes were trying to consolidate ties with potential patrons such as Hideyoshi or Ieyasu, and the Hie groups remained significant rivals. The circumstances are reflected in *Hachijō kadensho*. In it the compiler(s) sought both to promote noh as something worthy of support by ambitious rulers and to establish the pre-eminence of the Yamato over the Hie tradition.

Retelling Noh's Myths

One way in which *Hachijō kadensho* sought to establish the superiority of the Yamato troupes was through its account of the origins of noh. Comparison of the *Hachijō kadensho* version of these legends to that found in Zeami's *Fūshikaden* shows clearly how the compiler tried to elevate the status of the Yamato troupes at the expense of the Hie.

Zeami was the first noh performer to record the history of noh and to link contemporary practices to the roots of the art in the age of the gods. To what degree his discussion was his own creation or reflected the oral legends of the Yamato troupes is uncertain. It is evident, however, that his written account of the origins of noh was meant only for his descendants and most trusted associates. The polemical tone of *Hachijō kadensho*'s version of noh's origin, by contrast, indicates that it was aimed at a wider audience. The compiler was not preaching to those already committed to the Yamato tradition but trying to shape the views of readers, especially potential patrons, from outside the world of noh.

Fūshikaden begins with an explanation of the genesis of noh (*sarugaku*).

In searching for the origins of *sarugaku* and *ennen*, some say they came from India, and some say they have been handed down since the age of the gods. Yet as time moves on and those ages grow remote, any proper skill is lacking to learn the ancient ways precisely. The origin of the nō, which we all enjoy today, goes back to the reign of the Empress Suiko when Prince Shōtoku commanded Hata [Hada] no Kōkatsu (some say for the peace of the country, some say to entertain the people) to create sixty-six public entertainments, which were named *sarugaku*. . . . Later, the descendants of Kōkatsu inherited this art and served at the Kasuga and Hie shrines.[51]

Zeami integrated the history of the troupes associated with the Hie shrine in Ōmi with the legacy of the Yamato troupes serving the Kasuga shrine in Nara. Privileging neither his own Kanze troupe nor the Yamato troupes over those serving at Hie shrine, he stated that both the Hie and the Yamato groups were descended from Hada no Kōkatsu and that both continued Kōkatsu's legacy.

Zeami's son Motoyoshi wrote glowingly about the Hie troupe in *Sarugaku dangi*. Since Zeami helped edit the work, it probably expresses his views as well. *Sarugaku dangi* praised Dōami (d. 1413) of the Hie troupes for having reached the "highest flower" of the art and included him among the "four great founders of the Way" of noh.[52] Two other of the four founders were not even noh actors but *dengaku* performers. By including noh performers from different geographical regions and troupes along with actors from other genres of performing arts as the "ancestors" of noh, *Sarugaku dangi* proclaimed the breadth of noh's heritage and acknowledged that it could be performed well even by actors outside the genre of noh. *Sarugaku dangi* borrowed Zeami's unambiguous remark in *Fūshikaden*: "[The noh from] Yamato and Ōmi as well as field music have completely different styles and forms, but in all of these, the flower of fascination shines through."[53]

To say that *Hachijō kadensho* took a far less sanguine view of the Hie and a more sectarian view of noh than did Zeami and Motoyoshi is an understatement. It excluded the Hie altogether from the mainstream history of noh, which it associated only with the Yamato. Although Dōami was one of greatest noh actors in the fifteenth century, eclipsing even Zeami at times, he received no mention. *Hachijō kadensho* also severed the common bonds of blood and artistic tradition between the Hie and Yamato troupes drawn by Zeami and Motoyoshi. Whereas Zeami stated that Hada no Kōkatsu, the creator of the first sixty-six noh, was the ancestor of both the Yamato and Hie, *Hachijō kadensho* contended that the first sixty-six noh were created by Takeda and Hattori, the direct ancestors of the Yamato troupes:

An inquiry into the origin of noh reveals that His Highness [Prince Shōtoku] commanded Hada no Kōkatsu to create interesting performances that would ensure peace and entertain the populace. Kōkatsu took this order to heart, and he created the first thirty-three noh. However, these lacked the essence of noh today: the performers recited one waka poem, were accompanied only by percussion instruments, and danced only one noh at a time. These noh were performed only at small parties. But later on, two famous performers called Takeda and Hattori revised these pieces. These two men created sixty-six noh and made many different types. Today, these are known as Kasuga noh. Takeda is the ancestor of the Konparu family, and Hattori is the ancestor of our [Kanze] family.[54]

By emphasizing the role of Hattori and Takeda, surnames used by leaders of the Konparu and Kanze troupes, respectively, in the medieval era, *Hachijō kadensho* put the Konparu and Kanze lineages and their Kasuga noh at the center of the history of noh; simultaneously it omitted the role of the Hie troupes.

Hachijō kadensho continued the effort to distance the Hie from the Yamato by using different Chinese characters to refer to Yamato and Ōmi noh. According to Zeami's explanation in *Fūshikaden*, Prince Shōtoku decided that the style of dance he commanded Hada no Kōkatsu to create should be written with the Chinese character "to speak" (*shin/mōsu*, 申), one of the elements in the word deity (*kami*,

神) in the term "divine music" (*kagura*, 神楽), the dance art said to date to the age of the gods, when the deities of the High Plain of Heaven performed before the Sun Goddess Amaterasu. Zeami explained that this style of dance was called *sarugaku* (申楽) because the character *shin* was read *saru* in the context of the calendar, where it referred to the zodiacal sign "monkey." He added that the same characters could also be interpreted as "speaking for enjoyment."[55] This explanation was designed to dissociate noh from the more popular way of writing *sarugaku* with the character for "monkey" (*saru*猿), which had inelegant if not derogatory connotations. (Although monkeys were believed to have magical powers to ward off evil, in medieval folk tales they were also a common metaphor for people trying to ape something beyond their capacity.)[56] Since Zeami held that *both* Yamato and Ōmi noh could be traced to Hada no Kōkatsu and the *kagura* of the gods, he did not differentiate the terms used for the two forms of noh.

Hachijō kadensho, in contrast, reserved Zeami's method of writing *sarugaku* only for the noh performed by the four Yamato troupes and claimed: "Since the era of Hada no Ujiyasu, the term 'speaking for enjoyment,' has been used to designate the four [Yamato] troupes."[57] Ōmi *sarugaku*, by comparison, the compiler pointed out, was written with the characters meaning "monkey music." According to *Hachijō kadensho*, the founders of Ōmi *sarugaku* had learned their craft from the monkeys living on Mount Hiei, who imitated the *kagura* dances of the deity Kuni no Tokotachi no Mikoto.

The god [Kuni no Tokotachi no Mikoto] amused himself by performing various noh called *kusemai*. The monkeys living deep in the mountains watched the noh that the god created and imitated him. This is the origin of the *sarugaku* of the three Hie troupes. These three troupes are called the Hie, the Sakada [Sakaudo], and the Yamashina.[58]

Hachijō kadensho was not the only work of the time to make such associations. The late Muromachi-period *Teikin ōraichū*, an annotated version of *Teikin ōrai*, a widely used collection of model letters, also differentiated Yamato from Hie noh on the basis of how the word *sarugaku* was written. "Writing *sarugaku* as 'monkey music' is the style of the Hie school. Writing *sarugaku* with the character for 'monkey' denotes Ōmi *sarugaku*." *Teikin ōraichū* linked this designation with the fact that the Hie troupes served the mountain deity Sannō as *saru-*

gaku performers in the same way that the monkeys of Mount Hiei served Sannō as divine messengers. Another annotation described the presumed founder of the Hie troupes, Hie *tayū*, as creating *sarugaku* after spying on the divine monkeys in the service of Sannō.[59] *Teikin ōraichū* further presented the Hie as an offshoot of the Konparu, via the third son of Hada no Ujiyasu, Takeda Mitsutarō.

One day, Mitsutarō had a disagreement with the Konparu and thus left Yamato and went to the province of Ōmi, where he started Sannō *sarugaku* and took the name Hie *tayū*. He adapted the practices of the Konparu, changing the singing, the music, and even the rhythm into the Ōmi style. When Mitsutarō gained the forgiveness of the Konparu and returned to Yamato, he left his younger brother in Ōmi to serve as the head performer of the Hie troupe belonging to the Konparu school.[60]

A similar story of the Hie troupe's originating from the Konparu appeared in *Sarugaku kikigaki*, completed in 1599 by an author writing in support of the Konparu troupe.[61] Like *Teikin ōraichū* and *Hachijō kadensho*, *Sarugaku kikigaki* used the term "monkey music" to designate Ōmi *sarugaku*; it also implied that the Ōmi groups were "amateurs" of more recent origin than the Yamato troupes. *Hachijō kadensho* played on such associations of the Hie troupes with "monkey music" to mark them as performing an inferior type of noh compared with that produced by the Yamato troupes, who, it claimed, represented the art's true traditions.

Whoever compiled *Hachijō kadensho* cast a wide net for aesthetic and religious ideas to frame noh but ultimately held firm to the premise that theory should be applicable to the actual conditions of performance. According to *Hachijō kadensho*, noh was more than a profound artistic and spiritual accomplishment or a skill that almost anyone with talent could develop to perfection, as Zeami and the early noh theorists had held. It was instead a hereditary profession endowed with a body of specific techniques equally suited to providing casual entertainment, supplying background music for ceremonies, and serving as a device for furthering effective governance. It was, in other words, a commodity to which performers invoking myths of bloodlines and history could lay claim and, in turn, market. Although many factors contributed to the triumph of the four Yamato troupes, the demise of independent noh troupes such as the Hie, and the professionalization of noh in the Edo period, the rhetoric of *Hachijō kadensho* illuminates the strategies pursued by the Yamato troupes to secure their place in a new social and political order; it also helps explain why military hegemons such as Hideyoshi and Ieyasu found noh and the four Yamato troupes worthy of support.

Writings and Standardization

Besides promoting the legitimacy of noh, treatises supplied specific technical information and thereby contributed to the standardization of noh from the late sixteenth century. Sixteenth-century noh manuscripts, for instance, describe dance forms in much more concrete detail than their predecessors. Chapter 5 of *Hachijō kadensho*, for example, contains long lists of the appropriate masks for plays. It also provides diagrams of dance patterns for specific plays that sketch the locations dancers should occupy on the stage. The chapter concludes with diagrams of the sitting and standing postures appropriate to different male and female roles (see Fig. 3.1).

Such detailed notations were the antecedents for a new class of manuscripts that described all the dance and song movements for a given play. In noh, as in the martial arts and tea ceremony, extended movement patterns are broken down into discrete parts called "forms" (*kata*). *Kata* are the building blocks of noh dances. By the late sixteenth century, noh performers had created a new category of writing called *katazuke*, or "form-added," which listed the correct dance and song forms next to the text of the play, allowing the performer to know precisely which movement coordinated with which passage of the text, how to sing that passage, and how the movement should be integrated with the vocal and musical parts. Shimotsuma Shōshin, the renowned noh performer of Kyoto's Honganji temple, authored several collections of *katazuke*, which were disseminated in manuscript form during his life and available in print from the 1640s.[62] Shimotsuma was not a member of one of the four Yamato troupes. His writings suggest that standardization involved many different noh performers working independently toward a common goal of defining a professional commodity.

This trend toward standardization has been well documented in terms of the greater definition of performance practices in written texts, but in the historiographical literature standardization has been

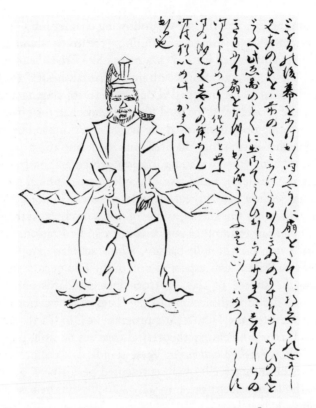

Fig. 3.1 Illustration of a posture for the play *Tōru* from the Ōtsukibon *Kadensho*, the oldest extant manuscript version of *Hachijō kadensho*. Late Muromachi period. The end of each volume bears the signature Zeami, but a colophon attributes the work to the four leaders of the Yamato troupes. Courtesy of Waseda University Theatre Museum.

The text reads: "For the second half of the play *Tōru*, when the curtain is raised, the fan is held upright in this manner like an officer's staff (*shaku*). The left hand is held firmly above the belt that holds the edge of the folded outer robe (*kariginu*) just as in this picture. Just before the singing finishes, change the position of the fan to its usual place and sing the opening phrase (*deha*) in the area of the *shitebashira* [where the bridge joins the main stage]. The latter approach is not very unusual, but depending on the circumstances one can try to make it so. When the dance of the officer's staff is over, take the fan and hold it as before to exit" (*Hachijō kadensho*, p. 603).

attributed not to the proliferation and acceptance of these writings by actors but to warrior patronage and performers' resulting complacency. Yokomichi Mario has argued that once noh actors began receiving stipends from the Edo bakufu (see the following chapter for a description of this system), they lost interest in thinking creatively about entertaining audiences and turned instead to writings like *katazuke* to formalize their art. The result was to turn noh into a "ritual theater" (*shikigaku*). Writings like *katazuke* that spelled out methods of singing and movement and the properties to be used for noh plays had the effect of consistently creating noh that pleased the actors' warrior patrons, but they also meant that actors lost the freedom to decide these matters for themselves.[63] This view of standardization, which emphasizes its hegemonic characteristics, is indicative of the historiographical notion that noh theater became "ritual theater" under the sway of the Edo bakufu. Chapter 7 examines this theory as one of noh's modern myths, but this section studies one example of performance standardization, that of the New Year's noh for the Edo bakufu, which scholars happen to consider the most "ritualized" aspect of noh in the Edo period, in order to determine the source of these performance standards and to judge whether noh did indeed succumb to the tastes of its warrior masters.[64] The precedents for the New Year's program at Edo Castle date to fifteenth- and sixteenth-century theoretical treatises on noh, popularized in texts such as *Hachijō kadensho*. These standards were not particular to noh for the military elite but represented performers' attempts to create methods for selecting noh for any audience on the basis of popular customs and beliefs.

What was once called pine-music—an art the Kanze troupe adopted from the *shōmonji* in the fifteenth century—had by the Edo period taken the name "first songs" of the New Year, *utaizome*.[65] According to the records of first-song performances at Edo Castle, which survive from the year 1664 on, the program for the shogun became standardized by the latter half of the seventeenth century.[66] By that time, the four Yamato troupes and the Kita troupe shared responsibility for the New Year's performances at Edo Castle, following a rotation system established in 1663.[67] Every year, the leaders of the Kanze and Kita troupes were joined in Edo by a leader of either the Kongō, the Hōshō, or the Konparu troupe. The two troupes that did not perform at Edo Castle participated in the Nara festival noh instead.

The Kanze leader began the performance with the opening song, "Waves of the Four Seas" ("Shikainami"), from the play *Takasago*. Next, he sang a selection from the play *Oimatsu*. Then, the leader of the Kita troupe took his turn to sing a portion of *Tōboku*. Finally, a leader of the third troupe in attendance sang another part of *Takasago*. For all four of these songs, the actors remained seated and sang only the main passages of the plays in a style called "seated songs" (*ibayashi*). When all the selections were finished, the performers received sleeveless robes (*kataginu*) as gifts from members of the audience. The only dance in the program, "Yumiya tachiai," followed. "Yumiya tachiai" is a short piece, and all three of the leaders of the noh troupes in attendance danced the same part simultaneously. The day's performance concluded with the shogun and the daimyo bestowing more robes on the leaders of the troupes.

The Edo bakufu's first-song program incorporated two selections from *Takasago*. In *Takasago*, a wandering priest asks an old couple at Takasago Bay (in Hyōgo prefecture) about the famous pine tree there. The priest inquires about an old poem in the tenth-century imperial anthology *Kokinshū* which states that the pine tree of Takasago is married to a pine at Sumiyoshi Bay and wonders aloud how this "marriage" was possible because the two pine trees are leagues apart. The old man replies that true love overcomes any distance or physical obstacle. The priest then discovers that the old man and woman are the spirits of the two pine trees.

Takasago and *Oimatsu* were classified as "celebrational" (*shūgen*) noh as early as Zeami's lifetime.[68] As a verb, *shūgen* means "to celebrate," "to pray," or "to marry"; as a noun, it can also refer to a marriage ceremony and even the consummation of a marriage. *Takasago* has been sung at weddings since at least the sixteenth century.[69] Today, most programs of noh plays conclude with a brief song sung by the chorus after the last play called the "added celebration" (*tsuke shūgen*). The song most frequently sung as an added blessing is another portion of *Takasago* called "Senshūraku." This song was so closely associated with felicitous endings that in the Edo period the term *senshūraku* was used to refer to the final day of a theatrical performance or a sumo tournament in order to close an event on a positive note.

Takasago apparently became a standard part of first-song performances beginning in the late sixteenth century. Chapter 3 of *Hachijō kadensho* provides information on noh songs appropriate for different festivals and occasions and cites *Takasago* specifically for first songs at the New Year. "The noh song 'Takasago' invokes the pine tree. This song celebrates the practice of the pine tree on the Day of the Rat. . . . Consequently, since *Takasago* is a noh that heralds the bountiful virtues and majesty of the pine tree, in the New Year it is called the first song (*utaizome*)."[70] "*Takasago* invokes the pine tree," according to *Hachijō kadensho*. In the first half of the play the chorus sings the praises of the pine tree while the character of the old man dances.

> Yet of all the trees the pine is lord
> Endowed with princely dignity.
> Changeless from age to age,
> In fadeless green endures a thousand years.[71]

The pine was the chief symbol of the New Year's holiday in the medieval era, and *Hachijō kadensho* referred to the New Year's custom of decorating dwellings with pine branches on the Day of the Rat. In short, the central image of the pine tree in the play *Takasago* provided the rationale for singing the work at New Year's since the pine tree fit the season.

A review of the definitions of *shūgen* found in the treatises of Zeami, Zenchiku, and Konparu Zenpō reveals that certain noh may be classified as *shūgen* because they express sentiments of celebration. For these theorists noh were not inherently "celebrational" by their own nature; rather, these plays evoked feelings of felicity by borrowing from auspicious imagery, such as the New Year's pine tree. The distinction between the relative nature of celebration found in the noh as opposed to the absolute quality of celebration in the holiday itself is important. A review of the theories behind celebrational noh demonstrates that the use of these noh at ceremonial events, such as the bakufu's New Year's performances, drew attention to the inherent auspiciousness of the holiday; the songs themselves did not magically create an air of celebration.

Zeami was the first to apply the term *shūgen* to noh theory. In his most comprehensive text on noh music, *Various Matters Concerning the Five Modes of Musical Expression* (*Go'ongyokujōjō*), he described five categories of noh music, the so-called five modes (*goi* or *go'on*): namely, celebrational music (*shūgen*), elegant music (*yūkyoku*), music expressing romantic longing (*renbō*), mournful music (*aishō*), and musical works requiring virtuosity (*rangyoku*). Zeami compared the qualities of the five modes to trees: the pine tree for *shūgen*, the cherry tree for *yūkyoku*, an autumn maple for *renbō*, a winter tree for *aishō*, and a cedar for *rangyoku*. For each example, Zeami included an appropriate poem.[72]

Zeami prefaced the discussion of *shūgen* by citing a long-life poem (*ga no uta*) by the priest Sosei (n.d.) from the tenth-century *Kokinshū*.

Yorozuyo o	Ten thousand years for you
Matsu ni zo kimi o	Is my prayer to the pine
iwaitsuru	Hoping to be the crane
Chitose no kage ni	Living for a thousand years
sumamu to omoeba	In your shadow.[73]

Zeami commented: "Without a doubt, the pine is a sacred tree. Its color is constant, appearing unchanged for a thousand autumns. Its image alone fills our senses with the nature of the universe. The music of *shūgen* closely resembles the pine as the mode evoking the joys of peace on earth."[74]

Although the long-life poem Zeami selected did not refer directly to the New Year, the wording recalls the greetings and sentiments of that holiday. According to the introduction to this poem in *Kokinshū*, Sosei's salutation of "ten thousand years [of life] for you" was directed to the daughter of Yoshimine Tsunenari (n.d.) on her fortieth birthday. Yet such references to ten thousand years and one thousand years also evoke the greetings typically used during the New Year's holiday. One such greeting common in the late medieval period was *gyokei senzu banzai*—"May your pleasures and joys last a thousand autumns and ten thousand years."[75] The medieval performing art *senzumanzai*, which can be translated literally as "one thousand autumns and ten thousand years," expressed similar sentiments and was a favorite entertainment to celebrate the New Year. Although Zeami did not mention the New Year's holiday specifically in his reference to *shūgen*, his discussion of the five modes follows the change of seasons, with the pine tree representing *shūgen* preceding the spring cherry tree. Therefore, we can conclude that Zeami associated the pine tree closely with the celebration of the New Year's holiday and used these correlations to inform his definition of *shūgen*.

Konparu Zenchiku linked *shūgen* more explicitly with the New Year in two of his treatises on music, *Go'on jittei* and *Go'on sangyokushū*.[76] A passage in the latter reads:

[The mode of *shūgen*] is similar to the auspicious words (*shūgen*) of the New Year, spoken when we go to the residence of the nobles and say, "Congratulations this year" and "May you have happiness for one thousand autumns and ten thousand years." An old poem reads:[77]

Kasugano ni	In the fields near Kasuga
wakana tsumitsutsu	I am gathering fresh herbs;
yorozuyo o	Ten thousand years of joy for you,
iwau kokoro wa	This gesture of prayer
kamizo shiruran	The gods surely recognize.[78]

Zenchiku referred to the custom at the imperial court of collecting fresh herbs (*wakana*) for presentation to the emperor at the New Year. This practice occurred on the first Day of the Rat—the same day commoners decorated their homes with pine branches for good luck.

Zenchiku's grandson Konparu Zenpō borrowed the same poem for his discussion of *shūgen* in two texts on music, *Ongyoku go'on* and *Go'on no shidai*, both of which found their way in corrupted form into *Hachijō kadensho*. In *Go'on no shidai*, Zenpō succinctly wrote: "*Shūgen*—the joy of the New Year, similar to wishing someone one thousand autumns and ten thousand years (*senzumanzai*)."[79]

In summary, from the perspective of fifteenth- and sixteenth-century noh theorizing, the use of *Takasago* and other *shūgen* noh at the New Year recognized the sentiments inherent in the season. The same seasonal references were the inspiration for the meaning of the mode of *shūgen* in noh theory. *Shūgen* noh celebrated the holiday, but they did not create the reason for that celebration: the New Year's was naturally a time of celebration and required music that acknowledged that fact. *Hachijō kadensho*, which popularized these ideas, did not rely on the complex theories found in the treatises of Zeami and Zenchiku, instead it presented the rationale for selecting appropriate noh plays for certain occasions, and its anonymous compiler chose plays for the New Year whose central image was the pine tree.

For the New Year, *Hachijō kadensho* stated that there were "many noh about the great virtues and dignity of the pine" that would be appropriate, and the play *Venerable Pine* (*Oimatsu*) certainly belonged in this list.[80] As in *Takasago*, the *shūgen* play *Oimatsu* features a dance by the spirit of a pine tree. However, in *Oimatsu*, a plum tree shares the limelight with the pine. A traveler from the capital arrives at Anrakuji temple in Kyūshū where an old man and woman show him a famous pine and a noted plum tree. The old couple explain that the plum, named Kōbaidono, and the pine, named Oimatsu, are deities. The spirit of the aged pine appears in the second half of the play and dances. In some variations of the play, the spirit of the plum joins the dance.[81]

In the next play in the bakufu's program, *Tōboku*, a plum tree serves as a site for the meeting of a priest with the spirit of the Heian poet Izumi Shikibu (b. 976?). Izumi Shikibu is credited in the play for planting the plum tree long ago at Tōboku-in temple, and her spirit emerges from the tree in the second half of the play. *Hachijō kadensho* clarified the association of the plum flower with New Year's using the example of the play *Naniwa*, which bears many similarities to *Tōboku*. *Hachijō kadensho* refers to *Naniwa* by the alternative name *The Plum of Naniwa* (*Naniwa no ume*) to emphasize the centrality of the plum tree in the work. "The plum is a tree noted for its spirit (*kokoro*). In poetry as well, it is called the older brother of the cherry blossom [since it blooms earlier]. The plum is also the leader of all flowers. But, in any case, the plum is the flower selected for the New Year. There-fore . . . *The Plum of Naniwa* is sung for first songs."[82] A court official meets an old man and a youth beneath a famous plum tree associated with the Emperor Nintoku. The old man and youth disappear and in the second half reveal themselves to be the Emperor Ōjin and the fe-male spirit of the plum.[83] Although a selection from *Tōboku* and not *Naniwa* was performed at the Edo bakufu's *utaizome*, the distinction between the two plays is minor since both plays are variations on the same theme of plum flowers. Moreover, *Tōboku* refers specifically to the New Year's holiday in the opening phrase declaimed by a monk and his attendants (*waki* and *wakitsure*) hurrying to Kyoto, the "flow-ery" capital (*miyako*).

> The New Year ushers in the spring.
> The New Year ushers in the spring.
> Let us hasten toward flowery Miyako.[84]

When the monks arrive in the capital, they marvel at the plum flow-ers in full bloom at the New Year.

The most distinct piece in the *utaizome* program at Edo Castle was "Yumiya tachiai." The dance is not part of a noh play, nor is it usually performed in programs of noh. Today, "Yumiya tachiai" is only regu-larly performed at the yearly Wakamiya festival at Kasuga shrine in Nara by actors of the Konparu school. This limited performance of the dance seems to have been a general rule since the medieval period. Actors performing "Yumiya tachiai" occasionally wear Okina masks. Yet, in terms of sanctity, it ranks beneath Okina.[85] For the perform-ance before the shogun, Okina masks were omitted, and "Yumiya tachiai" seems to have served as a competition piece, since all three noh leaders danced the same role simultaneously. *Tachiai* literally means "standing together," and from Zeami's day the word referred to actors from the same or different troupes performing alongside one another in competition. In other words, "Yumiya tachiai" allowed the audience the unique chance to compare the abilities of the leaders of three noh troupes. It also gave the actors the chance to compete for immediate rewards, namely, the rich robes offered by the members of the audience.

The appearance of "Yumiya tachiai" at the conclusion of the bakufu's *utaizome* program highlights the spectacle value of the piece in the performance and discounts its use as a ritual. Today, as in the medieval period, Okina is performed only at the start of a program of noh plays. When Okina is not performed, a *shūgen* noh, such as *Takasago*, is typically used. In the bakufu's New Year's program, "Shikainami" from *Takasago*—a song used for many celebrational occasions—began the performance—the most sacrosanct position in the program. "Yumiya tachiai" concluded the program with a flourish. The excitement of the dance derived from its glorification of martial virtues, cast in awkward religious verbiage, as indicated by the dance's opening lines: "The merits of a mulberry wood bow and mugwort arrows are truly blessed. Rejoicing, rejoicing, we, too, study the skills of the bow transmitted from the famed archer Keiyō, so that our honor, in defending the warrior houses of the bow and arrow, will shine with the elegance of a 'crescent-bow moon' above the clouds."[86] The song continues by expressing images of warfare within a bizarre religious framework. Shakyamuni Buddha, for example, is mentioned as he "draws his bow of compassion and looses the arrows of wisdom to wake humanity from the sleep of the three poisons" of craving, wrath, and ignorance. Although the martial theme of the dance was unrelated to the earlier part of the bakufu's *utaizome* program, the subject of "Yumiya tachiai" likely appealed to samurai audience, who were poetically addressed as the "families of the bow and arrow" in the song. According to the research of Amano Fumio, "Yumiya tachiai" was sometimes performed before battles in the sixteenth century, with the actors donning armor and wielding real weapons.[87] Therefore, it must have been able to rouse the spirits of warriors before combat and was surely an exciting conclusion to the shogun's *utaizome* program.

The first-song performances at the Honganji temples in Kyoto in the Edo period bear a close resemblance to those at Edo Castle, and the descriptions indicate that these followed historical precedents initiated and sustained by performers, not warriors. First-song performances at Honganji date to the early sixteenth century, predating the division of Honganji temple into Western (Nishi) and Eastern (Higashi) factions. The tenth head of Honganji temple, Shōnyō (d. 1554) recorded in his diary, *Temmon nikki*, the first mention of *utaizome* performances at Honganji. Sake cups circulated between the performers and audience as the songs were sung. Performances of Okina and three noh enacted by Honganji monks followed.[88] Later in the sixteenth century, the ceremony moved to the fifteenth day of the first month, and Honganji monks were accompanied by professional actors invited for the occasion. Pine-music became a public event at both Honganji temples in the first century of the Edo period.[89]

Annual performances at the Eastern Honganji began in the first decade of the seventeenth century and continued for the first half of the century, when the frequency of performances grew inconsistent. According to a program from 1661, after drinks and food were served, two Honganji monks sang an opening song. The performance included works typical of the New Year, such as *Takasago* and *Naniwa* as well as portions of *Yumiyawata*, *Tama no i*, and *Taema* for the first round of singing. Another round of drinks and food followed, and then the second round of noh songs, which could include works such as *Yōrō*, *Daie*, *Tsurukame*, and *Kureha*. On the same day, Higashi Honganji monks also performed "pine-music" consisting of Okina followed by several noh plays and kyōgen. Different groups of the temple's clerics took responsibility for parts of the performance. For example, retainers (*jishū*) played musical instruments to accompany the monks (*bōzushū*) who danced the parts of Okina.[90] The tradition of first songs had apparently ended at the Eastern temple by the middle of the Edo period.

The monks of the Western Honganji temple also combined their performances of first songs and pine-music into a single day. The performance of first songs included noh sung by the monks themselves. The pine-music that followed featured Okina with three noh and two kyōgen. Okina was performed by the same group of monks who had sung the first songs. Other monks acted and sang in the noh, which sometimes included lay people from outside the temple as musicians. More noh, termed pine-music, followed this performance and was enacted by troupes from outside the temple. Records are scarce, and the practice may have been suspended in the early seventeenth century, but performances of first songs at the Western Honganji appear to have continued until the end of the Edo period.[91]

Kyō habutae oridome, a sightseeing guide to Kyoto published for tourists in 1689, mentioned the pine-music performances on the second day of New Year at both Honganji temples.[92] A seventeenth-century chronicle of yearly festivals in Kyoto, *Hinami kiji* by Kurokawa Dōyū (d. 1691), provides more details about the seasonal context of these performances.

The houses of both nobles and warriors hold pine-music today. This is a custom of our province, from the third day to the fifteenth day of the New Year. Noh songs are chanted, and there are dances with drums. This custom of our province, called pine-music, is celebrated by collecting pine branches and praying for longevity. Today, three noh are performed at the Western and Eastern Honganji temples. Priests from branch temples wear costumes and perform. Afterward, professional noh actors perform in what are called the "subsequent noh."[93]

This description gives the impression that both temples had ceremonies coinciding with similar performances at the homes of warriors and nobles. The lengthy explanation of pine-music in this guide for tourists indicates that the custom may have been unfamiliar to many visitors to the capital.

In addition to the pine-music and first songs, Western Honganji hosted noh on the fourth day of the New Year, in the so-called New Year's music (*gosechibayashi*), beginning in 1613. Priests and outside professionals began the performance with Okina; this was followed by as many as eleven noh. After 1651, the performance was opened to the public with complimentary sake, soup, and sweets served. The most frequently performed plays at these New Year's noh in the eighteenth and nineteenth century were *Takasago*, *Oimatsu* and *Yōrō*, the first two of which were also included in first-song program for the shogun.[94]

Although the performances of first songs at the two Honganji temples showed wider variation than the version enacted for the shogun, there was also a continuity in the preference for *shūgen* plays such as *Takasago* and *Oimatsu*, a choice that suggests the salience of these works at the New Years. As the previous discussion of early noh theory argues, performers not warriors formulated these aesthetic guidelines in writings whose dissemination facilitated the popularization and acceptance of these performance standards.

Konparu Yasuteru and the Last Noh Treatise

As the preceding discussion has indicated, actors from the late sixteenth century on operated in a much more defined performing ethos that specified the types of plays for certain occasions as well as the masks, costumes, dance forms, and vocal patterns. Although standardization might be seen to limit the freedom of artists to create, it is absolutely essential for professionalization, as Magali Larson has argued, since it creates stable criteria for evaluating professional competence. Larson explains that "the standardization or codification of professional knowledge is the basis on which a professional 'commodity' can be made distinct and recognizable to the potential publics." In other words, when members of an occupation employ standards, they create a product recognizable to consumers. This, in turn, fosters a sense of group identity, according to Larson, and this in turn creates a "cognitive dimension" for a profession: the shared assumptions and methods that serve as a common bond for the profession's members. "Cognitive commonality, however minimal, is indispensable if professionals are to coalesce into an effective group," notes Larson.[95] For noh, standardization made possible by wider dissemination of noh writings including *Hachijō kadensho* through the medium of print heightened "professional" self-consciousness among Yamato noh performers, as the subsequent chapters describe.

The heyday for secret noh treatises reached its peak in the sixteenth century and declined with the advent of the printing industry beginning in the 1590s. Significantly, the last major noh theorist, Konparu Yasuteru (d. 1621), dates from this transitional period. Yasuteru was the head of the Konparu troupe and a descendant of Zenchiku and Zenpō. He was also the last theorist in the manner of Zenchiku and Zeami and speculated on the nature of art and the philosophy of the actor's "flower." Yet, his treatises had only minimal impact on the noh world, due to their limited dissemination. However, it is doubtful that they would have had much greater resonance if they had had a wider readership. As described in this chapter, the trend in noh manuscripts of the sixteenth century was away from theory and toward concrete descriptions applicable to performance. Noh performers after Yasuteru continued to write texts, but secret treatises of the theoretical type that Zeami authored were no longer created, in part because standardization left less room for philosophical speculation and in part because secret manuscripts offering obtuse theories no longer held the unchallenged symbolic power that they once did after they appeared in print. The medium of print not only made secret manuscripts more available and thereby furthered standardization and professionalization but also fundamentally altered the playing field in the noh world by redefining the relationships between writing and orality, text and practice, and authority and authorship, as the next chapters examine.

CHAPTER 4

Bloodlines

"My teacher's blood is my blood, my teacher's flesh is my flesh, our deep blood bond is a relationship that transcends that of parent and child."
—Takabayashi Ginji

The transition from the chaos of civil war in the sixteenth century to the establishment of the early modern state at the beginning of the 1600s brought fundamental changes to noh theater, especially for the four Yamato troupes under the patronage first of the hegemon Toyotomi Hideyoshi and later of the Tokugawa shoguns. This chapter traces the impact of warrior rule on noh theater through the lens of genealogy. The warlords that unified Japan in the late sixteenth century envisioned a world ordered by the principle that social status and occupation were determined by patrilineal descent. This provoked the development of a discourse on genealogy. From the seventeenth century on, the Tokugawa shoguns demanded genealogies from warrior families and from noh performers, while keeping their own family's history a state secret.[1] The profusion of noh genealogical writings that started in the seventeenth century reflected the efforts of performers to justify their social standing to the bakufu and come to terms with the new political system. In addition, the discourse on genealogy presented actors with a new medium for constructing authority, denigrating rivals, and building walls around their occupation. Noh was not unique in respect to this heightened focus on genealogy. The Edo period witnessed the spread of the use of terms such as "blood relation" (*ketsuen*) and "bloodline" (*kettō*) to describe lineage and generational succession.[2] The structures that emerged from this discourse centered on myths of great ancestors as "founders," whether Zeami in noh or Rikyū in the world of tea or even the bakufu's deified founder, Ieyasu. Authority depended on family lineage and the proximity of one's blood connection to the lineage's patriarch as well as claims to knowledge and other powers received from that figure. This chapter examines noh's discourse on heredity first from the broad context of noh troupes and then from that of a lineage within one troupe.

The Medium of Genealogy

Although the Edo period witnessed a boom in the creation of genealogies, these writings originated earlier. Genealogies were a time-honored method of constructing authority, dating to the eighth-century *Nihon shoki* and *Kojiki*, which described the heritage of the imperial court. As the anthropologist Takie Sugiyama Lebra has noted of early Japan, "tradition, precedents, and especially ancestry or genealogical orthodoxy served as the principal sources of legitimacy for state authority."[3] For medieval warriors, genealogies served as the primary means of establishing a noble pedigree. Consequently, the temptation for those of humble origin to embellish or create genealogies must have been great. The falsifying of genealogical records among the powerful but non-noble emerged during the era of the first warrior government, the Kamakura bakufu, in the late twelfth century. In this period, genealogies were used to prove descent from a noble house, to secure ranks at the imperial court, and to claim rights to a benefice such as the income derived from a landholding. Similarly, proof of membership in the Minamoto clan, and hence an affiliation with the founder of the Kamakura bakufu, Minamoto Yoritomo (d. 1199), brought access to the bakufu's court system and its powers to adjudicate disputes, certify wills, and confirm appointments. By the Warring States period in the sixteenth century, the falsification of genealogies became a typical procedure of warriors for securing political legitimacy. As Herbert Plutschow has noted, "any person assuming power needed to claim descent from an illustrious ancestor."[4] Proof of a noble lineage allowed the claimant to receive appointments from the imperial court, which lent sanctity to military power. Tokugawa Ieyasu, in his climb to power, garnered a string of court titles from minister of the right (*udaijin*) to chief of the Minamoto (*Genji no chōja*), and, finally, to the office of shogun.[5] However, Ieyasu's claims were not always recognized. In 1566, the imperial court denied him the governorship of Mikawa province on the grounds that his genealogy and his claims to the name Fujiwara Ieyasu were both spurious. Ieyasu later justified his claim to the position of shogun by "discovering" Minamoto bloodlines.[6] Earlier, Toyotomi Hideyoshi had asserted his descent from the Taira family, as had his predecessor, Oda Nobunaga. Later, Hideyoshi had himself adopted into the noble Fujiwara house in order to qualify for the high office of regent (*kanpaku*) in 1585. Subsequently, Hideyoshi's authorized biography, *Tenshōki*, claimed that he was the illegitimate son of an emperor![7]

The concept of heredity also informed the efforts of Hideyoshi and the Tokugawa regime to bring order to society. Specifically, the Toyotomi and Tokugawa regimes fostered social distinctions based on heredity and occupation, and they introduced measures to curb social mobility. The best known are Hideyoshi's efforts to separate the peasantry and samurai by making the former a class of cultivators and the latter a class of full-time warriors. His policy created a distinction between agriculturalists and warriors, two categories that had in many instances been blurred on the local level because some medieval warriors engaged in farming just as some peasants occasionally took up arms to fight. In 1584 Hideyoshi forbade peasants from leaving the land they cultivated. Four years later he ordered a sword hunt to disarm the peasantry. In 1590, he enacted a legal distinction between peasants and warriors: the duty of the peasants was to till the soil, and the obligation of the warriors was to fight. In the following year, he prohibited changes of occupation. Hideyoshi's countrywide cadastral survey (1582–98) established and registered proprietorship of land, created a tribute rate for each parcel of land, and further bound the peasantry to the soil. The intent of his 1591 census (*hitoharai*) was to drive the remaining masterless samurai (*rōnin*) and other "outsiders" from villages, where they might interfere with agricultural production or foment rebellion. Hideyoshi's policies demarcated society into status divisions based on occupation. He distinguished roughly 80 percent of the population as peasant cultivators, bound to the land they farmed. As for the warriors, approximately 5 percent of the total, Hideyoshi attempted to remove them to castle towns and out of the countryside.

Although Hideyoshi died in 1598 and the Tokugawa eliminated his heir in 1615, the Tokugawa administration owed much to Hideyoshi's attempts to freeze the social system. Like Hideyoshi, the Tokugawa bakufu wanted to prevent anyone from rising above the station of their birth. Historian John Hall characterized the administration of law in the Edo period as "rule by status."[8] Ostensibly, society was divided into four status groups—samurai, peasants, craftsmen, and merchants—although there were many hierarchies within these divisions and many, including noh and other performers, the court, and the clergy, that did not fit into this schema. Nonetheless, the bakufu interpreted the law and meted out punishments according to this social hierarchy, typically exacting penalties not only on the offender but also on the offender's relatives, heirs, and sometimes entire family line.

Separating people into status categories was an ongoing process for the Tokugawa regime, for it had to work against the economic and social forces that threatened to blur these lines. The historian Wakita Osamu has noted that the mid-seventeenth century saw the beginning of what scholars term a "discourse on status" (*mibunseiron*), articulated by the bakufu as a reaction to growing social contradictions: the impoverishment of warriors, the growing economic strength of merchants, and the increased division of labor.[9] Ideologues such as Hayashi Razan (d. 1657) mustered scholarly and moral arguments to naturalize the bakufu's policy of rule. Razan, who served as a consultant to the first four Tokugawa shoguns and whose descendants enjoyed government sponsorship, wrote, "The separation into four classes of samurai, farmers, artisans and merchants . . . is part of the principles of heaven and is the Way which was taught by the Sage (Confucius)."[10] Taking concrete steps to distinguish social groups, the bakufu enacted sumptuary laws beginning in the second half of the seventeenth century that stipulated appropriate styles of clothing, hairstyles, food, transportation, and domiciles for each status group.[11] The persecution of groups on the margins of society—most notably the historically discriminated non-people, *hinin*, who engaged in livelihoods viewed as impure, and the defiled ones, *eta*, who were perceived as outcasts—intensified in the Edo period through prohibitions against intermarriage with the general population and restrictions on the location of residence.

Genealogy also served the bakufu in its relations with the feudal lords, the daimyō. The bakufu directly controlled the major cities of Edo, Kyoto, and Osaka as well as a large proportion of the arable land in Japan. Three types of daimyō controlled the remaining territories: those who were relatives of the Tokugawa (*shinpan*) house; hereditary vassals of the Tokugawa house (*fudai*), who had fought or whose ancestors in the patriline had fought on Tokugawa Ieyasu's side at the decisive battle of Sekigahara in 1600; and "outside lords" (*tozama*), daimyō who joined the Tokugawa ranks after Sekigahara and their descendants. To preserve the hereditary distinctions between the types of daimyō, the bakufu prohibited intermarriage among these groups. Daimyō could not marry without the consent of the bakufu, as stipulated in the Laws for Warrior Houses (*Buke shohatto*) issued in 1615. The bakufu insisted on knowing the identity of every daimyō's principal wife and heirs, and later it ordered these individuals to live permanently as hostages in Edo. Daimyō were obliged to divide their time between Edo and their home domain. Finally, the bakufu commanded that daimyō provide genealogical records of their families, which it then compiled into a massive genealogy in 1643 titled *Kanei shoka keizu den*. Besides charting each family's background, this genealogy described any hereditary links with other daimyō, the shoguns' highest vassals (*hatamoto*), and the Tokugawa family.[12] Genealogical information proved crucial from the bakufu's perspective because heredity alone determined who qualified to fill government posts, influenced the outcome of judicial decisions, and provided guidelines for shaping the power structure at the macro- and micro-levels of society.

The bakufu's attempts to regulate society through heredity reinforced the primacy of patrilineal descent. In the medieval period, a warrior might pass his headship to his most talented son or another favorite heir rather than his first-born son, but primogeniture had become the norm among samurai by the Tokugawa period. The bakufu institutionalized this norm among daimyō both by demanding the public declaration of the name of the daimyō's heir and by reserving the right to confirm that appointment. The bakufu declared that a daimyō must designate an heir before his death, and these designations required the bakufu's sanction.[13] If a daimyō died without designating an heir, the bakufu might confiscate his lands. It made no exceptions even for relatives of the Tokugawa family. Tokugawa Ieyasu's fourth and fifth sons died heirless, and the bakufu seized their landholdings in Owari and Hitachi provinces. The scholar Ōishi Shinzaburō has illustrated the prevalence of primogeniture in early Tokugawa Japan with the case of the heirs of Tokugawa Ieyasu. Ieyasu passed the office of shogun to his son Hidetada (d. 1632), and he later designated Iemitsu (d. 1651), Hidetada's first-born son, as heir. Ōishi pointed out that

Ieyasu's choice of Iemitsu was not automatic for many, including their mother, Oeyo, who considered Iemitsu's younger brother Tadanaga (d. 1633) better suited for the position. Shortly after making his decision, Ieyasu sent a letter to Oeyo explaining his rationale: "Daimyō view the eldest son with special regard. Younger sons are considered to be akin to servants. . . . For the second son to have greater influence than the older is the root cause of family troubles."[14] Beyond the warrior class, primogeniture became the norm for households (*ie*) throughout Tokugawa society, regardless of social standing.

The discourse on heredity facilitated the deification of Tokugawa Ieyasu as an ideological linchpin for Tokugawa domination. Under the direction of his grandson Tokugawa Iemitsu, Ieyasu received the posthumous title Great Avatar of the Eastern Sunlight (*tōshō daigongen*). The regime claimed that Ieyasu was an incarnation of a buddha, and his appointment as "sun god" placed him on par with the Sun Goddess Amaterasu, the divine founder of the imperial line. Shogun Iemitsu rebuilt Ieyasu's mausoleum at Nikkō in 1634, and the shrine received the same ranking as the imperial shrine for Amaterasu at Ise. Subsequent shoguns paid homage to Ieyasu at Nikkō, as did daimyō at local Tōshōgu shrines throughout Japan.

According to the historian Herman Ooms, the bakufu's deification of Ieyasu constituted a new image of personal authority premised on the development of a discourse that supported the ruler's efforts at self-deification and the popular acceptance of this belief. Ooms noted that other groups, such as peasants later in the Edo period, appropriated the bakufu's tactics to glorify their martyrs.[15] Other examples of the glorification of founding patriarchs are to be found among occupational groups and in most performing arts in the Edo period. The "Southern Barbarian" (Nanban) school of gunnery in the Edo period claimed its founder was a foreigner named Haburasu, and the Ōtsubo school of horsemanship traced itself back to the great hero Yamato Takeru, glorified in the *Kojiki* and *Nihon shoki*.[16] In the case of tea ceremony, the seventeenth century witnessed a "return" to the teachings of "the founder" Sen no Rikyū (d. 1591). The late seventeenth-century resuscitation of Rikyū accompanied a renewed interest in his "teachings" (some spurious, such as the *Nanpōroku*) and the popular acceptance of the idea that Rikyū had created the tea ceremony. Pivotal to the glorification of Rikyū were the three Sen families, Omotesenke, Urasenke, and Musashi Kōji Senke, who claimed descent from him. The Urasenke family even constructed a private chapel called the Rikyūdō in Rikyū's honor in the seventeenth century.[17] The veneration of Zeami and On'ami in noh theater, described below, also crystallized in the seventeenth century and falls into this same pattern. Noh exemplifies how occupations, particularly the performing arts, adapted to the early modern social system by embracing the state's discourse on genealogy and patriarch veneration to build their own structures of domination in their respective spheres.

Noh Theater Genealogies

The bakufu provided the impetus for noh performers to write genealogies as a means of gathering information useful for controlling them. In short, genealogies were a method of observation and domination and must be viewed alongside the other ways in which the bakufu regulated noh. The chief means of control was financial. The bakufu followed Toyotomi Hideyoshi's practice of paying stipends to noh troupes. Hideyoshi began this practice in 1593 by granting stipends of tribute rice as well as landholdings to the leaders of the four Yamato troupes. He allotted the generous sum of 1,000 *koku* to the leaders of the Kongō troupe and Hōshō troupe. The Konparu and Kanze troupes were rewarded 400 and 200 *koku*, respectively, to augment their income from rights to lands (*chigyō*) in Nara and Kyoto. Thus, Hideyoshi designated approximately 1,000 *koku* to each troupe, paying the performers out of the pockets of his daimyō vassals. Hideyoshi also extended his largesse to individual actors who were not members of the four Yamato troupes. For instance, he granted rights to lands worth 700 *koku* to a hip-drum player.[18] However, in contrast to these one-time gifts to performers, the stipends for the leaders of the four Yamato troupes were annual disbursements. After a brief hiatus, the Tokugawa bakufu resumed the grants to the Yamato noh troupes and later the newly formed Kita troupe and, from 1618 on, requisitioned contributions from daimyō for this purpose.[19]

In 1647, the bakufu issued a formal statement regarding its expectations of noh performers entitled "Rules for Sarugaku Troupes." These regulations are representative of the Edo bakufu's measures to freeze society along hereditary lines by prohibiting social mobility and enacting sumptuary laws.

Rules for Sarugaku Troupes

Actors should not neglect the arts transmitted in all their families, and they are not to perform arts inappropriate to their status. They must solely uphold the old ways of their family's occupation. They must follow the orders of the troupe leader (*tayū*) in all matters. If there is a lawsuit, an actor's request to government officials ought to be made through his troupe leader. When there is a matter of some dispute, the troupe leader ought to report directly to the same officials.

Furthermore, on occasions of performances of noh, if actors are summoned on the day prior to the performance, they will assemble at the residence of the troupe leader and practice diligently. Actors should not fail to attend on these occasions. There should be no mistakes on the following day.

Without being at all extravagant, actors should be frugal in all matters. Their dwellings, clothing, food and other items ought to be plain and should suit their station. It is prohibited for them to leave their family's profession and study the warriors' arts, which are inappropriate to their status. Aside from the costumes and properties for noh, they should not accumulate worthless goods.

When actors play the roles of daimyō and lesser lords, they must conduct themselves in an appropriate and sober manner. They must not take meals with daimyō and other men of rank when they are in their attendance.

Also, there are tales of the many generations of fame of the Konparu troupe. However, the present troupe leader, although already mature, is unskilled in the art. From this point forward, he must devote himself to his art. One of the older members of the Hada troupe ought to advise him carefully. Hereafter any further negligence would be immoral.[20]

The first section makes it clear that the bakufu considered noh a hereditary occupation, and it urged actors not to forget that. Accordingly, it sought to prevent performers from taking up other livelihoods, especially martial training restricted to the samurai. In fact, edicts issued later in the seventeenth century prohibited noh actors from wearing two swords like samurai. These edicts also repeated the bakufu's demands that performers maintain themselves in a manner fitting their station and continue their original livelihoods.[21]

Besides exhorting noh performers to preserve the skills handed down in their families and to live morally, the bakufu asserted its rights to arbitrate the content of noh's traditions. The public reprimanding of the head of the Konparu troupe is particularly telling in this regard. To add injury to insult, the bakufu later commanded that the leaders of all four Yamato troupes study under the guidance of Kita Shichidayū I (d. 1653), who had won bakufu patronage when he broke away from the Konparu to form his own troupe. The bakufu's decree may have resulted from Tokugawa Iemitsu's fondness for the Kita school.[22] In any case, it demonstrated that the bakufu would take steps to regulate not only the behavior of actors but also their artistic product. Fortunately for noh performers, such demands proved the exception rather than the rule.

Subsequently, rather then define noh's traditions itself, the bakufu commanded actors to demonstrate their artistic heritage by submitting genealogies. Beginning in the mid-seventeenth century, it ordered all the leaders of the five noh troupes that received stipends to create *kakiage*, "presented writings." The bakufu's demand for *kakiage* from performers followed the precedent of its decree that samurai and daimyō submit *kakiage*. These documents provided information on a family's origins, honors that members of that family had received, and other details useful to the government in allocating offices. Noh performers' *kakiage* additionally supplied troupe histories, listed the troupe's performance repertoire and famous possessions, and gave details about noted former leaders. An early example is *Onōgumi oyobi kyōgengumi* (ca. 1661), which described the repertoire and secret expertise (*naraigoto*) of twenty-one noh and kyōgen families.[23] The 1721 *Kyōhō rokunen kakiage*, examined below, is the most comprehensive of the extant early genealogical writings submitted by actors in terms of the numbers of entries and the amount of detail. It also provides a picture of how performers co-opted this genre of writings to authenticate themselves and their art through the medium of genealogy.

On the fourth day of the sixth month of the sixth year of Kyōhō (1721), the Junior Elder (*wakadoshiyori*) Ōkubo Narihiro assembled representatives from the five noh troupes at his residence and ordered them to submit documents to the bakufu about noh and their family's histories. On the seventh day of the next month, the lead members of lineages of musicians, *waki*, and kyōgen players were called to the home of another junior elder and told to provide similar reports. Both junior elders acted under the command of the eighth Tokugawa shogun, Yoshimune (d. 1751), in their capacity as supervisors of tradesmen and professionals. The documents that they assembled from noh performers formed the basis for *Kyōhō rokunen kakiage* (hereafter *Kyōhō kakiage*).[24]

Kyōhō kakiage represented an orthodox—though not necessarily truthful—telling of the traditions of the various noh troupes. The reports submitted by the five troupes bore the names of the troupe leader, except for the one prepared by the Kanze. (Kanze Konjūrō, the brother of the Kanze troupe leader, responded for his brother, who was ill). The junior elder had ordered each leader to write about the origins of noh, the history of his family, the authorship of plays, and details about stage conventions, including differences between present and past practices, as well as information about famous mask-carvers, any treasures held by their family that had been bequeathed by a previous shogun, and a list of plays that the troupe did and did not perform. All these factors constituted the legacy of the troupe as seen through its history, genealogy, and past accomplishments. Not surprisingly, the troupes responded to these questions in the manner most flattering to themselves. The following sections compare how the Konparu and Kanze leaders invoked two rival visions of the history of noh to construct the authority of their respective troupes.

The Konparu and the Rediscovery of Hada no Ujiyasu

Since the time of Zeami, the Konparu had claimed to be the oldest noh group and traced their lineage to the Hada clan in the era of Prince Shōtoku in the seventh century. Zeami's *Fūshikaden* credited Prince Shōtoku and Hada no Kōkatsu with devising the sixty-six entertainments that were the forerunners of noh and praised both men as demigods and credited Kōkatsu's descendant, Hada no Ujiyasu, with revising the sixty-six entertainments into the three principal works of the *shikisanban* including Okina.[25] However, after the era of Zeami and Zenchiku, Ujiyasu's name disappeared from the history of noh. Subsequent writers ignored him and credited others with creating Okina and noh from the sixty-six entertainments. The late sixteenth-century *Hachijō kadensho* stated that the performers Takeda and Hattori, the ancestors of the Konparu and Kanze families, had adapted Prince Shōtoku's entertainments into sixty-six noh plays. The mid-seventeenth-century critique *Bushōgoma* similarly omitted Ujiyasu and credited Zeami with fashioning the first sixty-six noh. Kanze

Motonobu (d. 1666), who authored a private genealogy of noh troupes in the mid-seventeenth century, *Catalog of Actors of the Four Noh Troupes* (*Yoza yakusha mokuroku*), mentioned Hada no Ujiyasu as the teacher of both the Konparu and the Kanze. According to Motonobu, the founder of the Kanze school, Kan'ami, created the first noh.[26]

In the midst of these competing claims over the creator of noh, the Konparu reasserted Ujiyasu's pivotal role to strengthen their own authority. The Konparu troupe's contribution to *Kyōhō kakiage* stated that Ujiyasu was the originator of what would be called noh, although his descendant Konparu Zenchiku was the first to give those entertainments that name.[27] By affirming Ujiyasu's role as an early architect of noh and reasserting his connection with their better-known patriarch Zenchiku, the Konparu leaders credited their lineage with the creation of noh and thereby claimed supremacy over its legacy.

The Konparu family's renewed fascination with the early history of noh and the Hada lineage of Kōkatsu and Ujiyasu may have arisen from the erroneous belief that Kōkatsu, whom some believed was Ujiyasu's father, had authored some of Zeami's and Zenchiku's writings. One seventeenth-century Konparu troupe leader, Konparu Hachiemon (d. 1661), added colophons to Zeami's *Shūgyoku tokka* and Zenchiku's *Go'on sangyokushū*, attributing both texts to Kōkatsu.[28] Hachiemon's claim ignores the fact that the manuscript in question bore Zeami's signature. Hachiemon's colophons reveal the efforts of the Konparu family elite to look beyond the era of Zeami and Zenchiku and even Ujiyasu to the earliest moments in the history of noh supposedly dominated by the Hada ancestors of the Konparu troupe.

The Konparu family also asserted their connections to the Hada lineage by using the Hada clan name in public documents. The author of the Konparu's submission to *Kyōhō kakiage*, Ujitsuna (d. 1784), claimed to be the sixty-ninth head of the Konparu house descended from Kōkatsu. He also attached the surname Hada in the list of names of all the leaders of the Konparu troupe and stated that there were "no breaks in the Konparu lineage's bloodline,"[29] although he conceded the lack of written records prior to Zenchiku's father.[30] He further documented his connection to the Hada by asserting that his family still owned a flagstaff and Buddhist relics inherited from Prince Shōtoku and passed down the Hada line. Ujitsuna's list of valuables included a curtain from Hōryūji temple, which Shōtoku had established, masks of Okina and Sanbasō crafted by Prince Shōtoku himself, and a "mask of heaven" that had supposedly fallen from the sky in Shōtoku's time.[31]

The highlight of Ujitsuna's portrait of the Konparu troupe's historical legacy and links with the Hada was his retelling in *Kyōhō kakiage* of the story of the miraculous appearance of Kōkatsu. Ujitsuna retold the story, first recorded in Zeami's *Fūshikaden*, of the discovery of Kōkatsu as a baby floating in a jar on the Hase River in Yamato province. Ujitsuna added that a written genealogy was found inside the jar with baby Kōkatsu—a reflection of the importance of such documents in Ujitsuna's era.[32] The genealogy stated that the infant was the second son of the first emperor of China, Qin Shi Huangdi. Rather than simply claim that Kōkatsu was a reincarnation of the first Chinese emperor, as Zeami had three centuries earlier, Ujitsuna's version of the tale made the assertion that the Hada and the Konparu were the legitimate descendants of the first emperor of China and cited a written genealogy to authenticate the claim! (Ujitsuna was apparently unaware that the Chinese emperor predated Kōkatsu by some 700 years.) Nevertheless, through his embellishment, Ujitsuna magnified the glory of the Hada line and deepened its connection with the cultural and historical legacy of ancient China, thereby claiming for the Konparu a mandate to dominate noh.

A comparison of Ujitsuna's documentation of the Konparu troupe's past with other Konparu troupe genealogies reveals that the deep interest of the Konparu troupe in its early history was not historical, in the sense that it was based on previous documents; nor were the genealogical claims consistent. Genealogists of the Konparu troupe suffered what Takie Sugiyama Lebra has referred to as "genealogical amnesia," ignoring or forgetting the earliest historiographical records of their troupe, particularly the first family tree, the *Genealogy of the Enman'i Troupe* (*Enman'i keizu*), created by Zenchiku in the fifteenth century (see Fig. 4.1).[33]

Zenchiku's genealogy recorded only the number of generations of troupe leaders before Ujiyasu and the names back to Zenchiku's great-grandfather Bishaō Gon no Kami. Zenchiku claimed that he was thirty generations removed from Ujiyasu—a conclusion that corroborated Zeami's calculation in *Fūshikaden*.[34]

Edo-period genealogists of the Konparu troupe ignored Zenchiku's calculations and tabulated the generations differently. *Kyōhō kakiage*

Fig. 4.1

Konparu Zenchiku's *Genealogy of the Enman'i Troupe*
(the figures in parenthesis indicate position in
the sequence of leaders after Ujiyasu)

stated that Zenchiku was thirty-nine generations from Ujiyasu and forty from Kōkatsu. *Kyōhō kakiage* identified Ujiyasu as Kōkatsu's second son.[35] Other Edo-period genealogies of the Konparu calculated the generations differently. *Yoza yakusha mokuroku* characterized Ujiyasu as a distant relation of Kōkatsu, not his son.[36] Other genealogies placed Zenchiku fifty-seven generations from Hada no Kōkatsu and named seventeen generations of actors between Kōkatsu and Ujiyasu.[37] All these sources ignored the information in Zenchiku's *Genealogy of the Enman'i Troupe*. In another puzzling move, *Kyōhō kakiage* referred to Zenchiku's father as Motokiyo—as in Zeami Motokiyo—not Yasaburō.[38] In other words, *Kyōhō kakiage* appears to have mistaken Zeami for Zenchiku's father or at least greatly confused Zenchiku's paternity by conflating his biological father, Konparu Yasaburō, and the man who was in many respects his inspiration and artistic father, Zeami.

Although these Edo-period genealogies differed in the details, all of them shared a concern to clarify the history of the Konparu house by connecting noh's earliest beginnings as told in its origin stories of Kōkatsu and Ujiyasu with the received historical tradition that began with Zenchiku. The Edo-period authors attempted what Zenchiku did not; namely, to bridge the mythic past with the historical present by constructing a family line and filling it with names. The lists of actors from Ujiyasu to Zenchiku did more than simply fill a blank space: the litany of names alongside the records of relics from Shōtoku's era demonstrated the unbroken lineage of the Konparu. The Konparu troupe leaders' bloodlines enacted the transmission of the art from the distant past to the present and legitimated the current troupe leaders at the end of that line.

Kanze Genealogies
and the Lost Leader Motomasa Jūrō

The Kanze troupe faced similar difficulties in constructing a seamless genealogy connecting their origins with the beginnings of noh and culminating in its current leadership. Instead of venerating ancestors from the rival Hada lineage (which Zeami had once done), however, the Kanze claimed that its three early patriarchs—Kan'ami, Zeami, and On'ami—were responsible for creating noh. But the Kanze troupe first had to surmount the problem of explaining the connections between these three figures. Zeami was Kan'ami's son, but, as we have seen in earlier chapters, the relationship between Zeami and On'ami was more complicated. Although Edo-period genealogies of the Kanze troupe show On'ami as the third troupe leader and Zeami's successor, modern historians have concluded that relations between Zeami and On'ami were strained. Zeami meant his natural son Motomasa, known as Motomasa Jūrō in the Edo period, to be his successor, and the son did take over the Kanze troupe in 1422. On'ami had formed a Kanze rival troupe by 1429 that competed with Zeami and his son's group until Motomasa died and Zeami was exiled. On'ami then claimed undisputed mastery over the Kanze legacy. Although Zeami says little about On'ami, his *Kyakuraika* contains a powerful eulogy to Motomasa:

The deepest mysteries of our vocation, whatever I have received from my father or garnered in my own life until this extremity of age—I have entrusted every last one of these to my heir, Motomasa, and have merely been waiting for the last event of life; but now without warning Motomasa is dead, our vocation thus brought to an end and our troupe already destroyed.[39]

Zeami's final testament to Motomasa revealed both that his affection for his son was great and that he never considered On'ami the successor to his family or his art.

The current understanding of the relations between Zeami, On'ami, and Motomasa is based on modern interpretations of Zeami's treatises and other primary sources, but Edo-period authors drew their own conclusions. Some writers assumed that On'ami was Zeami's biological son. Majima En'an, who wrote under the pseudonym Shūsen'o, stated in his mid-seventeenth-century noh critique *Bushōgoma* that the first three leaders of the Kanze were Kan'ami, Zeami, and On'ami.[40] The Edo-period genealogy *Kanze fukuda keizu* identified On'ami as Zeami's son, as did a contemporary Hōshō troupe genealogy.[41] Yet, Kanze school genealogists such as Kanze Motonobu, author of the 1646 *Yoza yakusha mokuroku*, discovered otherwise. Motonobu wrote that On'ami was Zeami's nephew, whom he later adopted, and that Motomasa Jūrō was Zeami's biological son.[42] During a period in which primogeniture was valorized, this conclusion raised troubling questions about rightful succession in the Kanze lineage: namely, Why did On'ami succeed instead of Motomasa? The chief task of Kanze genealogists in the Edo period was to acknowledge Motomasa Jūrō but explain why On'ami succeeded to the headship of the Kanze troupe.[43]

The Kanze lineage began with Kan'ami. According to *Kyōhō kakiage*, Kan'ami's parents had moved from Iga province (modern Mie prefecture) to Yamato, where they placed their son and his two brothers in the charge of the Kasuga shrine in Nara as performers. After the first two sons died of illness, Kan'ami's father visited Hase Kannon temple, where a monk informed him that if he renamed his surviving child after the Bodhisattva Kannon, he would survive. That son, renamed Kan'ami, did survive and became a noh performer.

Kyōhō kakiage credited Kan'ami with helping to create noh. Specifically Kan'ami, it claimed, wrote the first noh songs (*utai*) based on several different sources, including the *kagura* songs from Okina. The author of the troupe's contribution to *Kyōhō kakiage*, Kanze Konjūrō, referred readers to the appended list of plays by Kan'ami for examples.[44] Kanze Konjūrō then recognized Zeami's contribution to noh's evolution and wrote that Zeami had standardized the format of noh plays and of vocal music (*utai*).[45] Zeami eventually passed this knowledge to Konparu Zenchiku, a claim that implies that Zenchiku's contribution to noh results from Zeami's instruction in dramaturgical techniques. Konjūrō, however, left the precise nature of Zeami's teachings to Zenchiku unspecified.

Turning to the question of On'ami, Kanze Konjūrō stepped lightly over the question of Zeami's successor. He acknowledged that Zeami

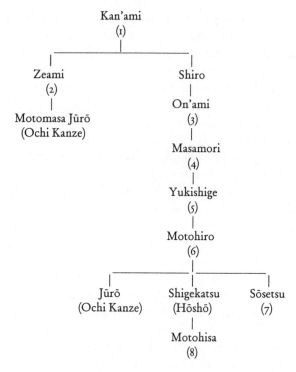

Fig. 4.2
The Kanze Lineage as Understood in the Edo Period
(figures in parentheses indicate position
in the sequence of leadership)

had a son named Jūrō and that Jūrō had formed a troupe in Ochi in the southern part of Yamato province. (Jūrō's full name was Kanze Motomasa Jūrō, but nowhere in *Kyōhō kakiage* is his full name given.) Jūrō inexplicably removed himself from the succession process, and, Konjūrō explained, Zeami adopted On'ami, the son of his younger brother Shirō, as his heir.[46] Konjūrō left the reason for Jūrō's departure for Ochi ambiguous, and that allowed him to justify Zeami's adoption of On'ami out of his need for an heir. On'ami thus became the third head of the troupe (see Fig. 4.2).

Other genealogists felt the need to explain in great detail why Jūrō left for Ochi and did not succeed to the family headship after Zeami. According to Motonobu's sketch of Zeami's life in *Yoza yakusha mokuroku*, Motomasa left for Ochi after a disagreement with Zeami, taking a younger brother named Kanze Shichirō Jirō with him.[47] Together, the two brothers formed the Ochi troupe, which lasted only a few generations. Motonobu blamed Zeami for Jūrō's departure, stating that he cared more for Konparu Zenchiku than his own son and that this misplaced affection prompted the shogun to exile Zeami. Even so, Motonobu proclaimed On'ami a worthy successor and his talent the equal of Zeami's: "On'ami was in no less degree a noted performer than his adoptive father, Zeami."[48] Eighteenth- and nineteenth-century genealogies of the Kanze troupe such as *Profound Words on the Secrets of Noh* (*Shinkyoku shōmyō higen*; 1756) by Bokkai Mohee (n.d.) and Asano Eisakū's (also known as Asano Yoshitari; b. 1782) *Lineage of the Kanze Family* (*Kanshi kafu*) further embellished the story of Motomasa. Both authors contended that Zeami disinherited Motomasa, chose On'ami as the next leader of the troupe, and forced Motomasa to leave the capital for Ochi.

The twentieth-century scholar Kobayashi Shizuo has argued that the confusion in the Edo period about Zeami and his relationship to Motomasa and On'ami stemmed from a misunderstanding of the date of Motomasa's death. Bokkai and Asano recorded that Motomasa died in 1459 at age sixty-five, but Kobayashi clarified that Motomasa had died twenty-seven years earlier in 1432. Kobayashi concluded that the story of Zeami's disinheritance of Motomasa developed to explain On'ami's succession to the headship of the Kanze troupe during Motomasa's lifetime, since Motomasa was thought to have lived much longer.[49] However, this explanation does not answer the question why the earlier *Kyōhō kakiage* and *Yoza yakusha mokuroku* versions of the story, which do not provide a death date for Motomasa, nonetheless omitted him from the lines of succession.[50] Accordingly, it seems that the effort to write Motomasa out of the Kanze lineage was intentional and not based on mistaken information: Motomasa's presence muddled the presumption of the unbroken bloodlines and artistic teachings in the Kanze house that its genealogists attempted to construct.

For *Kyōhō kakiage*, Kanze Konjūrō made up for the lack of detail about On'ami's succession to the leadership of the troupe by citing his many accomplishments. In fact, he dwelled much longer on the development of benefit (*kanjin*) noh by On'ami than on Zeami's legacy. Even before he recounted the history of his troupe, he mentioned documents pertaining to On'ami's famous benefit noh at Tadasugawara in Kyoto in 1464 that he had appended to his account. Benefit noh provided the chance to perform for a large audience, with the prospect of considerable financial gain from admission revenues. In the Edo period, the bakufu allowed only the Kanze troupe the special right to perform one extended benefit noh performance during the lifetime of each Kanze troupe leader. *Kyōhō kakiage* provided a rationale for this unique privilege by citing On'ami as the creator of benefit noh. To further embellish On'ami's glory, Konjūrō enumerated the many artifacts presented to On'ami. He claimed the Kanze troupe still owned a parasol given to On'ami by Shogun Ashikaga Yoshimasa and a lacquered mask-box for Okina masks given on the occasion of On'ami's famous benefit noh at Tadasugawara.[51] Curiously, Konjūrō did not mention any treasures in the Kanze family that had once belonged to Zeami.

The Hegemony of the Konparu and Kanze Myths

The bakufu's command to create genealogies gave each noh troupe the opportunity to explain the development of noh solely in terms of the family history of their own troupe leader. By valorizing their connection to such prominent figures as Prince Shōtoku and Zeami, the Konparu and the Kanze troupes succeeded in mustering the most convincing evidence to support their versions of noh's past; hence their interpretations of noh's history became the dominant ones in the Edo period, to the extent that other noh troupes cited them as authoritative. Another crucial factor supporting the dominance of the Kanze and Konparu was the perception that most of the plays performed at that time were attributed to authors affiliated with these troupes. As Kanze Motonobu summarized in *Yoza yakusha mokuroku*: "A great proportion of the noh songs (*utai*) that are beloved and in circulation in society now are the creations of Zeami. The noh created by the Konparu are fewer than those created by the Kanze. There are only a few noh produced by the Hōshō and Kongō."[52]

The dominant position of the Kanze and Konparu troupes in noh discourse was reflected in the genealogical writings of the Kongō and Hōshō troupes. Both troupes interwove their family genealogies into the Konparu and Kanze troupes' narratives. The Kongō troupe's submission to *Kyōhō kakiage* explained that the troupe had lost part of its family genealogical records in a fire in 1657. Nevertheless, the Kongō, like the Konparu, claimed descent from Hada no Ujiyasu. The

Kongō troupe's account further endorsed the Konparu troupe's version of the creation of noh by crediting Konparu Zenchiku with devising noh dramaturgy.[53] The Hōshō troupe traced its ancestry to the Kanze by claiming that the founder of the Hōshō, Ren'ami, came from the same family as Kan'ami. This familial connection was invoked to explain why the Hōshō sang in the same style (*kamigakari*). The lineages of the Kanze and Hōshō troupes were viewed as interrelated in Zeami's time, as *Sarugaku dangi* noted. However, the same treatise made no mention of Ren'ami, the "founder" of the Hōshō troupe.[54] In fact, the genealogical records of the Hōshō troupe presented in *Kyōhō kakiage* cannot be verified prior to the fifth leader of the troupe, Kanze Shigekatsu KoHōshō (d. 1572), who was son of Kanze Motohiro and was adopted into the Hōshō troupe as its successor (see Fig. 4.2).[55] Still, the Hōshō troupe did not look solely to the Kanze for their legitimacy since their account asserted that the ancestors of all four Yamato troupes had contributed to the structure of noh performance and music.[56]

As the newest troupe, the Kita could not make much of a claim to the ancient legacy of the four Yamato troupes other than noting that their founder, Kita Shichidayū, had studied with both Kongō and Konparu masters.[57] Consequently, the Kita declared in *Kyōhō kakiage* that the origins of noh were unknown; their account instead concentrated on enumerating Shichidayū's accomplishments. For example, they borrowed from the legacy of Toyotomi Hideyoshi to lend prestige to the troupe by professing that Hideyoshi gave Shichidayū ("seven-year-old troupe leader") his name in recognition of that prodigy's gifts as an actor.[58]

Genealogy and Social Organization

Another ramification of the genealogical turn in noh discourse was the institutionalization of the primacy of the leader of the noh troupe as the lineal descendant of ancient patriarchs. By virtue of his hereditary connection with a founding patriarch, the troupe leader held authority over the other members of his lineage as well as non-relatives in the troupe, all of whom were incorporated in the familial structure of the school (*ryū*).

The word *ryū* can be translated as "school" when it refers to an institution and as "style" when it describes the modes of production particular to that organization. The Edo period witnessed a profusion of schools in the arts, occupations, and religious traditions. Over a dozen schools of firearms vied with one another for prominence in the Edo period, with the Inatomi, Tsuda, and Nanban eventually winning out. Zen Buddhism was represented by three schools in the Edo period—Sōtō, Rinzai, and Ōbaku. Schools even proliferated in areas such as ceremonial food preparation (*shiki hōchō*) with the revival of the Shijō, Ōgusa, and the Shinji schools, which began in the Muromachi period, and the creation of new schools such as the Ikama.[59] The term *ryū* was first used in reference to the Kanze and Konparu noh troupes in the late sixteenth century and was extended to the other three major noh troupes (Hōshō, Kongō, and Kita) by the mid-seventeenth century.[60]

The organizational basis of a school resembled an extended family with the house of the leader functioning as "main house" (*honke*) at the core. The main house lent its name to the school, and the head of the main house exercised hereditary control over the school as its top teacher. The leader of the school, called the "family head" (*iemoto*) by the eighteenth century, served as the chief arbiter of the school's style, top manager of its affairs, and sole owner of its highest teachings, which were typically passed on only to the next family head. The families that dominated schools benefited from the ideology of the Tokugawa bakufu, which sought to define heredity as the sole determinant of power and status. This legacy is seen today in, for example, the Urasenke school of tea ceremony, as described by Jennifer Anderson: the authority of the headmaster of the Urasenke depends on his hereditary descent from a great master, Sen no Rikyū, and on exclusive access to the highest secret teachings.[61]

Kanze Motonobu's *Yoza yakusha mokuroku* provides a case study of how one performer understood the constitution of noh schools in the mid-seventeenth century and power relations within and among them. In the century that Motonobu composed his text, noh had slowly transformed itself from a guild (*za*) system into the more complex structure of interlocking schools. A performer belonging to one of the four Yamato troupes or the newer Kita group would also be a member of a school of a performance specialty. Thus, Kanze Motonobu was both a member of the Kanze troupe and one-time head of the Kanze Shinkurō lineage of shoulder-drum performers. In describing both groups, he presented schools structured by lineages that were themselves constructed from patrilineal descent lines, marriage alliances, and master-disciple relationships verified by the transmission of professional knowledge. Motonobu's text reveals the way in which the organizational concept of school came to dominate the noh profession, as well as the contribution of genealogy to the solidification of these institutions.

Catalog of Actors of the Four Noh Troupes

Motonobu conceived of *Yoza yakusha mokuroku* as a two-part reference work on the lives and achievements of performers from the distant past to his time. The first part presents biographies of performers from the late fourteenth century to the mid-sixteenth century. The second part, entitled "A List of Actors from the Four Troupes in Recent Times" ("Kindai yoza yakusha mokuroku"), offers biographies beginning from around the year 1560. Motonobu presented the first part as a revision of older writings and the second part as his own handiwork. He completed the first draft of both volumes in 1646. After further revisions, he presented the manuscript to his son in 1651, although the final version of the text dates to two years later. Motonobu cautioned his son to keep the writing secret. "This work should not be shown to outsiders or reproduced other than for the one son who will succeed to the headship of our family of shoulder-drum players."[62] However, Motonobu subsequently gave a copy of his text to the son of his older brother. A few handwritten copies of *Yoza yakusha mokuroku* exist, and the work never saw wide dissemination or publication in the Edo period. Nevertheless, by the late Edo period *Yoza yakusha mokuroku* became prized as an authoritative reference by noh scholars such as Asano Eisoku, and modern scholars still mine the text for biographical information. Although the second part has proved to be more historically accurate than the first, both parts are equally polemical in their efforts to substantiate the superiority of the Yamato troupes as a whole and Kanze Motonobu's family line in particular.[63]

Motonobu stated that he had compiled the information for the first part of his text from earlier writings, chiefly *Yoza no yakusha mokuroku* by Jiga Kunihiro (d. 1580), a stick-drum player and a distant relative.[64] Motonobu wrote that he utilized his great-uncle Kanze Shigenari's (n.d.) copy of Kunihiro's text and claimed to have made only a few revisions.

Jiga Yozaemon Kunihiro wrote the first part of this text, and he recorded the actors of the four troupes from long ago. The leader of the Kanze troupe, Shigenari, copied this text. Jiga Yozaemon added red circles to the names of the talented and famous, and Shigenari copied these as well. I added parts of the text that had been left unspecified such as individual names, the dates when performers flourished, and their age, which I took from the writings of Kanze Motoyori Nobumitsu. I also appended the stories of Miyamasu Yazaemon related by my grandfather Sōsatsu, which my late father, Kanze Shigetsugu, often told me. I did this to make the text a primer for our Way.[65]

Motonobu insisted that he merely fleshed out Jiga's work by including a few more names and details derived from the works of his ancestors: texts by Nobumitsu (d. 1516) and oral histories transmitted within his family. According to Motonobu, Jiga's manuscript provided only the names of the leaders of the Kanze and Konparu troupes and omitted those of the Kongō and Hōshō leaders.[66] Besides adding information, he decided to include stories told by his father, Shigetsugu (also known as Kanze Matajirō Shigetsugu; d. 1627), and grandfather Kanze Sōsatsu (also known as Kanze Kurō Toyoji; d. 1585) about the great shoulder-drum player Miyamasu Yazaemon.

Motonobu's decision to add stories about Yazaemon provided an opportunity to secure his lineage's legitimacy as leaders in the world of noh and experts in the shoulder-drum. Although he owed his family name of Kanze to his descent from Kanze On'ami's son Nobumitsu, Motonobu traced his family's expertise with the shoulder-drum outside the Kanze line to Yazaemon. He contended that his grandfather, who had founded the Kanze Shinkurō house of shoulder-drum, was Yazaemon's top student. Motonobu's father, Shigetsugu, was the second-generation head of the house. Motonobu's elder-brother Kanze Sōya (also known as Kanze Shinkurō Toyokatsu; d. 1646) succeeded to the family headship, and the post passed to Motonobu when his older brother fell ill in 1632. Motonobu later relinquished the post of family head to his older brother's son Toyoshige (d. 1688) in 1646, the year he completed the first draft of his manuscript.

Motonobu's put the finishing touches on *Yoza yakusha mokuroku* after retiring to Kyoto, and his text reflects his surroundings. With a population of 400,000, Kyoto was nearly the size of Edo in the mid-seventeenth century and still its economic rival. Kyoto also dominated culture in the early Tokugawa period. Despite the fact that the leaders of the noh troupes lived in Edo, noh remained especially strong in Kyoto, where performers had tested and matured their art for several centuries. A popular introduction to noh theater published in 1687, *Nō no kinmō zui*, listed 274 noh performers in the Kyoto-Osaka area compared with 117 in Edo.[67] In contrast to Edo, where most performers worked for the bakufu and daimyō, in Kyoto, the noh world included actors associated with the five dominant noh troupes as well as groups linked with religious institutions and independent troupes that had performed there for several generations. According to a guidebook to Kyoto published in 1689, Kyoto residents could enjoy the performances of these various groups almost every month.[68]

In retiring to Kyoto in 1646, Motonobu followed in the footsteps of other performers of his era who gave up their official stipends in Edo for life in the capital. A contemporary of Motonobu with the family name of Hiyoshi relinquished his place as a secondary actor (*tsure*) in the Kanze troupe to return to the Kyoto region and become lead performer at the Hie shrine in Ōmi, where the Hiyoshi, also known as the Hie, had long performed.[69] Also in the seventeenth century, the eldest son of the Shindō school of *waki* gave up his appointment as head of his lineage to teach noh chanting (*su'utai*) to amateurs in Kyoto.[70] Motonobu's motivation for relocating to Kyoto may have been to join his family there. In 1632, his older brother, Sōya, relinquished the headship of the family and left Edo for Kyoto on the grounds of illness, but this may have been an excuse to leave service in Edo because he continued to perform and teach in the Kyoto-Osaka region. Whatever his reason, moving to Kyoto brought Motonobu into contact with performers outside the four Yamato troupes. *Yoza yakusha mokuroku* expressed his desire to establish the pre-eminence of the four Yamato troupes collectively against these "outsiders" as well as to delineate power relations within the Yamato troupes.

Structural Changes: The Case of the Kanze

Yoza yakusha mokuroku sheds light on the organizational changes that occurred in noh troupes from the medieval to early modern period. Unfortunately, little is known about the structure of noh troupes in the medieval period and how they evolved in the early modern period. The size and constitution of noh troupes is also a mystery, since medieval records of performances typically mention only the name of the troupe leader. *Sarugaku dangi* offers a few details about the Kanze troupe in the early fifteenth century (see Chapter 2), but the lack of other sources frustrates comparison. *Yoza yakusha mokuroku* likewise needs to be used with care as a historical source because the author's portrait of the history of noh was intended to increase the prestige of his own lineage. Consequently, although we know comparatively more about the Kanze troupe, we do not know if the Kanze troupe was typical.

A few conclusions can be drawn from the history of the Kanze troupe. First, around the time that noh performers became literate in the late fourteenth century, heredity replaced seniority as the primary determinant of power and status within a troupe. Second, greater specialization is evident by the late sixteenth century. Whereas in medieval troupes hierarchies were based on age with little differentiation according to role, early modern troupes are affiliations of different lineages, each responsible for distinct parts in a performance. Third, the organization of the troupes became more complex beginning in the seventeenth century. Compared with their medieval counterparts, troupes in the early modern period were much larger, with members spread throughout Japan. As a consequence of the troupes' larger size, relationships among members became less personal and more bureaucratic in the Edo period. In the absence of close contact, genealogy allowed the members to map the structure of their troupes and elucidate each performer's role and his relationship with all other members of the troupe. The following analysis relies on *Yoza yakusha mokuroku* to trace these changes and examines the role of the early modern discourse on genealogy in facilitating them.

As noted in Chapter 2, heredity replaced seniority as the most important determinant of authority within troupes in the late fourteenth century when the lead performer (*tayū*) displaced the elder (*osa*) as the leader. At the same time, the position of *tayū* became hereditary, and the Kanze and Konparu adopted the family name of their lead performer as the name of their troupe. The *tayū* may have gained more prestige not only through his acting ability but also through his role as the author of plays that cast himself as the lead performer. Writing centuries later, Kanze Motonobu depicted the post of *tayū* as the backbone of the medieval noh troupe. "Long ago, the head of a troupe (*tayū*) had ability in all aspects of the arts of performance. He created noh himself; then he created the *tsure*, *waki*, hip-drum, shoulder-drum, flute, stick-drum, and *aikyōgen* parts, and he taught these parts to the people in the troupe." In the "old days," according to Motonobu, the *tayū* "served the function of having to continue the headship (*sōryō*) of the family," but in his era the situation had reversed, and the hereditary head of the family called himself, de facto, *tayū*.[71] Motonobu's critique was less an attack on the institution of hereditary succession than on the practices of rival families who tried to appropriate titles he believed they did not deserve.

According to Motonobu, the post of chief attendant (*gon no kami*) was determined by seniority and talent in the medieval period but became an appointed position in the early modern era. In *Yoza yakusha mokuroku*, he defined the "chief attendant" as the second oldest member of the troupe, who acted as the assistant to the troupe leader.[72] In the past, "the chief attendant served as the representative of the head of the troupe. Consequently, since ancient times the term 'chief attendant' was written as 'temporary protector' (*kari ni mamoru*)." Motonobu stressed that ability and age were prerequisites for the title of chief attendant. He wrote: "No one can become a chief attendant without being famous and having a comprehensive understanding of secret expertise (*narai higoto*) in great detail for all the parts."[73]

In the medieval era, membership in the troupe depended on affiliation with the troupe leader either through blood or by a personal or contractual bond. According to Kanze Motoyoshi, the author of *Sarugaku dangi*, outsiders with the requisite talents had to pay to join the Kanze troupe, and paid dearly—Motoyoshi said the cost of membership was 1,000 *mon*.[74] Presumably, full membership gave a performer a greater share of the revenues and additional rights.

Membership in medieval troupes probably fluctuated and depended on the composition and skills of the members of the leader's family, the troupe's personnel needs, and the deals it could strike with outside performers. The troupe leader took the lead role (*shite*) in most of the plays that the troupe performed, and he cast members of the troupe in other parts depending on their skills and age. To give one example, during the Kanze troupe's large benefit performance at Tadasugawara in Kyoto in 1464, the sixty-six-year-old On'ami performed the lead role in five plays over the course of three days. His son and successor Masamori performed the lead role in nineteen other plays. Ise Sadayori's records of the performance list the names of two kyōgen actors who performed: Usagi Dayū and Saburō Shirō.[75] Kanze Motonobu mentioned these two as members of the Kanze troupe in *Yoza yakusha mokuroku*, but they may have joined On'ami only for that one performance.[76] Records indicate that On'ami had six other sons besides his heir, Masamori, and a few of these became noted musicians and may have performed at the famous 1464 noh. According to *Yoza yakusha mokuroku*, On'ami apprenticed two of his sons to study musical instruments. Sōkan went to study with the stick-drum player Konparu Kan'a. Another son, Nobumitsu, trained in the hip-drum from On'ami's brother, Kanze Ren'ami.[77] The examples of Sōkan and Nobumitsu are indicative of the ways in which a troupe leader could adjust the size and composition of his company by adopting out some sons and training others in needed roles.

A lack of role specialization allowed medieval troupes to function without having to employ specialists since one performer could take different roles as needed. For instance, drummers in the medieval period typically played all three types of drums. Similarly, an able singer from the chorus usually filled the role of side-actor, *waki*, which was not distinct from the chorus until the Edo period.[78] This flexibility disappeared in the first century of the Edo period with the establishment of schools of experts in the various roles. Kanze Motonobu's *Yoza yakusha mokuroku* was written during this transition and indicates the role of the genealogy in shaping the structure of the troupe. Thus, Motonobu presented an anachronistic view of medieval noh by dividing medieval actors by the specialties of *waki*, shoulder-drum, hip-drum, and stick-drum. Instead of reflecting medieval reality, this move facilitated the construction of lineages and a history for each of these arts. It also reveals the new importance of heredity in professional prestige.

The Kanze troupe grew much larger in the Edo period, first, by subsuming other noh troupes, and, second, by establishing branch families. The Umewaka and Hie, which had been active in Kyoto since the fifteenth century, joined the Kanze troupe in the seventeenth century, most likely for financial reasons. The Umewaka family's pedigree rivaled that of the Kanze's, and in the early decades of the seventeenth century they overshadowed the Kanze.[79] Nevertheless, the bakufu's lucrative stipend system and the chance to perform for the ruling elite proved strong incentives for performers like the Ume-

Table 4.1
The Kanze Troupe in the Late Edo Period

Role	Family	Origin
Shite	Kanze *iemoto*	Kanze main house
(and chorus)	Kanze Tetsunojō	Kanze branch house
	Hie, Umewaka, etc.	Independent troupes
	Katayama, Hayashi, etc.	Disciples of *iemoto*
Waki	Shindō, Fukuō	*Tesarugaku*
Flute	Kasuga, Morita	Independent performers
Shoulder-drum	Kanze, Kō	Kanze family, independent
Hip-drum	Kadono	Independent
Stick-drum	Kanze	Kanze family
Kyōgen	Sagi	Independent

SOURCE: Based on Yokomichi and Koyama, *Nōgaku no densho to geiron*, p. 23.

waka to join one of the four Yamato troupes. Thereafter, the Umewaka became an important lineage of lead performers (*shite*) within
the Kanze troupe. Many formerly independent noh troupes like the
Hie and Umewaka that became lineages within the Kanze assumed responsibility for different performance specialties; these sub-schools
within the troupe took form in the Edo period (see Table 4.1).

Only two of the lineages in the Kanze troupe besides the *iemoto*
bear the name Kanze and trace their roots to the main family through
sons of On'ami: the Kanze lineages of shoulder-drum and stick-drum.
Apart from disciple houses like the Katayama, the remainder of the
lineages in the troupe claim descent from troupes and performers once
independent of the Kanze. The ancestors of the Fukuō and Shindō,
for example, were *tesarugaku* performers who joined the Kanze in the
seventeenth century. The Kasuga lineage of flute players claimed descent from Ogiya, an independent performer active from the middle
of the sixteenth century. Kanze Motonobu listed the Morita lineage as
"amateurs" in *Yoza yakusha mokuroku*, an indication that their position in the Kanze troupe as flute players was not firmly established
until after the mid-seventeenth century. The Kō house originated as a
troupe from Uji but became shoulder-drum players under the tutelage
of Miyamasu Yazaemon and began performing with the Yamato
troupes in the sixteenth century.[80]

In the Edo period, the Kanze troupe also trained disciples in the
role of lead performer (*shite*), and these, in turn, formed their own

lineages. Thus, the founder of the Katayama family began his career with the Kanze as a disciple of the troupe leader in the eighteenth century, and his descendants became the troupe's chief representatives in Kyoto in the latter half of the Edo period. Marriage and adoption were often used to strengthen bonds between the Kanze and these disciple houses. In a recent example, the twenty-fourth leader of the Kanze family, Kanze Sakon (d. 1939), was born in the Katayama house but adopted into the main line of the Kanze family as the heir. Such an arrangement is also typical in schools of tea ceremony. For instance, the Urasenke tea school consists of the Sen Sōshitsu family as the main line (*honke*) and several subsidiary families, the Ōtani, Naya, Izumi, Iguchi, Shiotsuki, and Sakurai houses, who might provide an heir if the main house needs one.[81]

In the Kanze troupe each of the lineages responsible for a performance role became associated with a distinct school (*ryū*) of performance, which referred both to the troupe as a whole and to subdivisions within it. That is, the term "noh school" is most closely associated with the five *shite* schools of Kanze, Konparu, Kongō, Hōshō and Kita, but all the other roles have their own schools as well. For instance, the Shindō and Fukuō lineages, which once performed both in the chorus and as *waki* for the Kanze troupe, practiced a style of noh chanting (*utai*) in the Edo period that differed from that used by the Kanze and were considered schools in their own right despite being members of the Kanze troupe.[82]

Kanze Motonobu's *Yoza yakusha mokuroku* documents the evolution of both troupes and lineages of performance specialties within the troupes as schools, although his foremost concern was to provide evidence of his own family's heritage. Since both the troupe and lineages within it espoused their own styles and organizational structures, Motonobu's concern was to reveal the relationship between the two and demonstrate that the troupe's authority was greater than that of its parts. His reliance on genealogy to diagram these relationships is apparent in his treatment of the Shindō and Fukuō lineages. Although both lines derived from rival performance traditions outside the Kanze, Motonobu presented these lineages of *waki* as the artistic descendants of Kanze Nagatoshi (d. 1541), whom he mistakenly thought

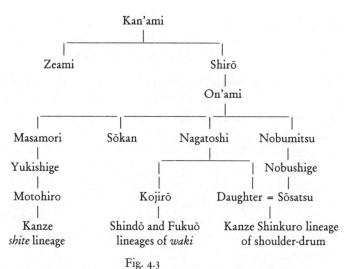

Fig. 4.3
Waki and Shoulder-Drum Lineages in *Yoza yakushu mokuroku*

was a son of On'ami (see Fig. 4.3).[83] (Nagatoshi was Nobumitsu's son and On'ami's grandson.) This move was meant to establish the Shindō and Fukuō as subsidiary to the Kanze.

Motonobu also used the genealogy to delineate the power relations among the lineages in a troupe. By constructing Nobumitsu and Nagatoshi as brothers, not father and son, Motonobu could distinguish their respective "descendants" as separate, collateral groups. Since he recognized members of Nobumitsu's lineage as drummers and Nagatoshi's descendants as *waki* performers, he could present Nobumitsu as a great musician and Nagatoshi as a consummate *waki* performer. His portrait of Nagatoshi is especially problematic since the *waki* did not become a distinct part until the end of the sixteenth century, well after the lifetime of Nagatoshi; yet, Motonobu listed Nagatoshi as one of the first *waki* performers in the Kanze troupe. Similarly, Nobumitsu's categorization as a hip-drum player was also anachronistic since drummers in Nobumitsu's lifetime played more than one instrument. In short, Motonobu wrote backward from his own era to concoct lineages of performers, fabricating both anachronistic performance specialties and fictitious familial relationships to diagram contemporary power relationships among lineages within the Kanze troupe and to demonstrate the subordination of performance specialty to lineage.

Ostracizing "Amateurs"
and Defining "Professionals"

Motonobu used lineages both to unite and to divide performers; his major categorical distinction opposed the hereditary professionals against the amateurs. Motonobu equated professionalism and status as a noh actor (*yakusha*) with hereditary membership in one of the four Yamato troupes. From Motonobu's perspective, any performer outside one of the four Yamato troupes—including the entire Kita troupe—were amateurs (*shirōto*). He defined amateur by affiliation not livelihood; thus, all the performers that Motonobu listed as amateurs made a living by performing noh, and many came from families that had done so for several generations.[84] Motonobu's definition of amateur and professional also reinforced the prejudice that amateurs lacked talent. Although he claimed to base many of his evaluations of performers on the pronouncements of his father and grandfather, in nearly every case Motonobu judged so-called amateur performers as unskilled in comparison with their Yamato school counterparts. This use of the word "amateur" reflected a mentality about social organization and heredity that mirrored the ideology of the Edo bakufu, for Motonobu sought to distinguish the professionals of the four Yamato troupes from amateurs in the same way that the bakufu wanted to separate discriminated groups from commoners: to use heredity to turn arbitrary pronouncements about occupations into social reality. Before we turn to the particulars of Motonobu's text, this larger discourse on heredity and its connection with social marginalization deserves further attention.

As described earlier, the policy of rule by status formulated by Toyotomi Hideyoshi and perpetuated by the Edo bakufu was predicated on the enactment of distinctions among groups. The Edo bakufu endeavored to make occupational differences such as samurai, peasant, craftsmen, and merchant more pronounced through sumptuary legislation and by gauging punishments according to nuances of status. The bakufu further reified status as a category of social identity by constantly pronouncing on the differences among groups. It has been argued that the Edo bakufu created its subjects by identifying their opposite: constituting the good people (*ryōmin*) by enforcing discrimination against the bad—masterless samurai, kabuki actors, prostitutes, and outcasts (*eta*).[85]

The bakufu's role in the establishment of Buddhist sects and in the persecution of Christians offers an especially revealing case of the way it fostered group identification through marginalization. The bakufu undertook the organization of Buddhist sects hand-in-hand with the persecution of Christians; the same bakufu appointee set the direction for both policies. The bakufu's depiction of Christianity as a threat to the social order that needed to be rooted out allowed it to develop mechanisms of persecution and control, beginning with the organization of Buddhist sects and culminating in inquisitorial councils. The effort began in the seventeenth century with the organization of temples into sects. First, the bakufu ordered the registration of all Buddhist temples and monks; then, it required that each temple and all its members be incorporated in a hierarchical organization through affiliation with a main temple (*honji, honzan*) or branch temple (*matsuji*) of the same sect. Finally, it stipulated that all families register with a local temple or shrine. These local religious institutions maintained records about birth, death, occupation, residence, and travel for all the members of their parish.[86] The resulting system meant that everyone in Japan was registered with a religious institution, which was itself part of a larger hierarchy of subtemples or subshrines under the control of a main temple or shrine.

The connection between the creation of this hierarchy of temples and the persecution of Christianity is seen in the figure of the abbot of Nanzenji temple in Kyoto, Ishin Sūden (d. 1633), the bakufu appointee responsible for receiving the names of all the registered temples. He was also a strong advocate of suppressing Christianity, and in 1614 he petitioned Shogun Hidetada that Christian missionaries be expelled, citing Christianity's malevolence and its potential to undermine native religious beliefs. Most foreign missionaries left after Hidetada made Sūden's memorial into law in the same year.[87] By that time, missionaries, who had first arrived in Japan with the earliest European visitors in the mid-sixteenth century, had enjoyed some success. Estimates place the number of Japanese Christians in the late sixteenth century as high as 300,000, including six daimyō. Persecution of Christians, however, predated Hidetada's edict. Although Hideyoshi welcomed foreign trade and maintained personal contacts with several Jesuit missionaries, the rise of Christianity among the peasantry was especially worrying for him. Fearing that Franciscan missionaries were attempting a popular uprising, Hideyoshi ordered the expulsion of missionaries in 1597 and executed six Franciscans and twenty Japanese converts in Nagasaki that same year. The Edo bakufu viewed Christianity with comparable suspicion as a threat to political order; as the historian George Elison remarked, "The Tokugawa indeed felt that Christianity was a disease which infected their subjects with disloyalty."[88] Yet, full-scale persecution of Christianity did not begin in earnest until Sūden's edict. As many as 6,000 Christians were executed between 1614 and 1640, when the bakufu created a Board of Examination of Sects (*Shūmon aratame*), which ordered the populace to register annually at Buddhist temples and implemented the use of tests such as the forced desecration of Christian icons at checkpoints to uncover hidden believers.[89] Probably only a few thousand Christians survived the first four decades of bakufu rule, and they maintained their faith in scattered and isolated communities. A further result of these moves was social control; as George Elison has noted, "Forced registry of all of the people's lands in Buddhist temples made of Buddhism an instrument applied to the elimination of religious heterodoxy."[90]

Research on medieval Europe that posits the coevolution of the oppression of marginal groups and the development of mechanisms of social control offers a point of comparison for understanding the Tokugawa bakufu's motivation for anti-Christian persecution and the ordering of Buddhist temples into sects. Jeremy Cohn has probed how Dominican and Franciscan friars in the thirteenth century oversaw nearly all the church's anti-Jewish activities.[91] According to Cohn, the orders of Dominican and Franciscan monks that were created to confront heresy and decadence in the clergy wanted to define a universal church by denying Jews a legitimate place in society. Robert Ian Moore has made a stronger argument about the use of discrimination by secular and religious institutions to strengthen their domination of society. In *The Formation of a Persecuting Society*, Moore contended that marginalization and oppression served as expedient means for secular rulers and the church to consolidate power. He found that the increased marginalization and oppression of Jews, heretics, lepers, and prostitutes in twelfth-century Europe derived from the ruling elite's tactics of political competition and became institutionalized through state and church mechanisms of inquisition and punishment. Persecution required that certain vulnerable groups be identified as antisocial and anti-Christian. Moore noted that the dominant images of Jews, heretics, and lepers in the twelfth century were interchangeable: all were the children of the devil, malicious, impious, and unwashed.[92] Anti-Semitism and other forms of discrimination may not have begun with the medieval church, but the researches of Cohn and Moore suggest that the religious and secular rulers persecuted vulnerable groups to engender larger mechanisms of social control. Similarly, although both anti-Christian sentiment and the persecution of outcast groups in Japan predate the seventeenth century, the virtual obliteration of Christianity and the increased marginalization of outcasts such as the "defiled ones," *eta*, and "non-people," *hinin*, under the aegis of the Tokugawa bakufu facilitated the implementation of the bakufu's policy of rule by status, in general, by naturalizing the social system as "pure" in contrast to "impure" groups, and, in particular, as a catalyst for the consolidation of religious institutions to register and control the populace.

Kanze Motonobu's rhetoric in *Yoza yakusha mokuroku* about amateur noh performers needs to be viewed against the backdrop of the persecution of marginal groups in the seventeenth century. Although Motonobu continued an earlier polemical tradition of denigrating rivals, prior authors were neither as thorough in their usage of the term "amateur" nor as venomous as Motonobu. Like the Tokugawa bakufu's policy toward Christians (or the medieval Church's actions against Jews), Motonobu used the negative connotations of "amateur" as a means of consolidating and legitimating the structure of the four Yamato troupes while ostracizing anyone else. Motonobu thus translated the bakufu's policies for controlling society into a rationale for fashioning a profession.

Motonobu's diatribe against amateurs also needs to be viewed against currents in seventeenth-century noh. He composed *Yoza yakusha mokuroku* during a transitional period in noh history that witnessed the end of independent troupes and the consolidation of noh performers into five large, country-wide organizations. Although independent groups still performed in Kyoto in Motonobu's lifetime in competition with other regional groups such as the Hie troupe from Ōmi, this eclecticism ended shortly after his death. Motonobu's rhetoric may not have contributed directly to the demise of independent troupes, but his text reflects the belief in the natural superiority of certain performers through their affiliation with special lineages and the abhorrence of individuals outside this system. The naturalization of such ideas in the Edo period contributed to the ruin of independent performers.

Most of the performers whom Motonobu classified as amateurs came from the ranks of *tesarugaku*. *Tesarugaku* literally means "skilled noh"; the term originated in the fourteenth century in reference to noh performed by people who did not belong to a troupe (*sarugaku za*) affiliated with a religious institution.[93] The prefix *te* means "hand" and by derivation "skill." Consequently, *tesarugaku* originally did not have negative connotations and implied that the players were in fact talented. The term was applied to a wide variety of noh performers in the fifteenth and sixteenth centuries, including troupes composed largely of women (*onna sarugaku*), children (*chigo sarugaku*), and the *shōmonji*.[94] *Tesarugaku* groups were often a match for the four Yamato groups. As noted in Chapter 2, the *shōmonji*'s popularity in Kyoto in the fifteenth century made them a target for the Kanze and Konparu troupes. In another example, Prince Sadafusa, the author of *Kanmon gyoki*, favorably compared the skills of an all-woman's group from Shikoku with Zeami's troupe.[95]

Tesarugaku enjoyed a boom in Kyoto in the late sixteenth century and early seventeenth century. The upswing in popularity of *tesarugaku* began when Oda Nobunaga entered Kyoto in 1569 and peaked in the 1580s, when the names of famous *tesarugaku* players became household words.[96] Townspeople in Kyoto could watch *tesarugaku* performers in benefit performances and at religious festivals. For impecunious nobles and warriors, *tesarugaku* players were a much less costly alternative to the actors from the Yamato schools since *tesarugaku* troupes typically cost one-tenth the amount to hire.[97] Over time, *tesarugaku* performers began to win patrons in the highest levels of society. To celebrate his rise to the office of regent (*kanpaku*), Hideyoshi hired the Horiike *tesarugaku* troupe. When Hideyoshi enthusiastically began to learn noh himself, his first instructor was the *tesarugaku* performer Kurematsu Shinkurō.[98] The Toraya was another *tesarugaku* noh troupe with status and important patrons. They received the patronage of the noble Konoe family in the late sixteenth century and later the Shimazu daimyō house in the Edo period.[99] The Shimazu's patronage of the Toraya gave them close contacts in the court and bakufu: two places where the Shimazu house, as an outside (*tozama*) daimyō, was supposed to have little influence.[100] The Shibuya, whose history predates the Toraya, likewise had intimate (sometimes scandalously intimate) relations with members of the elite.[101] They were famous for their innovative staging techniques, ranging from the construction of the first indoor noh stage in Kyoto in 1530 to audience-pleasing acrobatics.[102]

Despite the talent, inventiveness, and popularity of many *tesarugaku* troupes—or more likely because of these factors—in the discourse of the Yamato troupes the term *tesarugaku* became associated with the word "amateur" (*shirōto*). In many instances *tesarugaku* performers such as the Toraya and Shibuya troupes were labeled "amateurs" even though they performed noh as their sole livelihood and had done so for generations. *Tesarugaku* groups no doubt resisted this derogatory appellation. Both *shōmonji* and non-*shōmonji tesarugaku* performers identified themselves collectively as troupes (*za*), and their leaders used the title *tayū*. By the late sixteenth century, however, the word *tesarugaku* had become a politically charged designation, especially as used by the Yamato troupes. Konparu Yasuteru, leader of the Konparu troupe, denigrated the Hie troupes from Ōmi as *tesarugaku* performers. He also criticized "amateur" noh, complaining that "amateurs believe that gaudy noh is good noh."[103] Yasuteru's near-contemporary Kanze Sōsetsu, the leader of the Kanze troupe in the late sixteenth century, criticized amateur performers in his *Sōsetsu shimaizuke* as "lacking tradition."[104] *Hachijō kadensho*, which offered a scathing condemnation of the Hie, similarly portrayed noh players outside the four Yamato troupes as "amateurs." Claiming the dance of Okina as the legacy of the Yamato troupes, *Hachijō kadensho* declared that this dance "should not be taught to amateurs."[105]

So close was the association of amateur and *tesarugaku* that the term *tesarugaku* disappeared from the lexicon in the first decades of the Edo period to be replaced by the word "amateur" as the general nomenclature for performers outside the Yamato troupes.[106] Amateur came to be defined not on the basis of occupational status but as anyone (including the Kita troupe patronized by the shogun) who lacked an association with the four Yamato troupes and knowledge of their traditions.

Shūsen'o's mid-seventeenth-century noh critique *Bushōgoma* is the most blatant example of the display of contrived tradition to denigrate performers outside the Yamato troupes. Since Shūsen'o was an eye doctor, not a full-time performer, he concocted most of the traditions he mentioned in *Bushōgoma*. (Ironically, modern noh scholars call him an "amateur" for that reason.)[107] Shūsen'o lauded the trained noh actors (*nōshi*) of the Yamato troupes who had secret expertise (*narai*) and derided amateurs who lacked such wisdom. In one instance, he borrowed the analogy of warfare to portray the combat between an ill-prepared amateur and a veteran Yamato performer.

In the art of war, a man who is ignorant cannot be victorious. Everyone may say that there are cases when even an amateur's prowess triumphs in the art of war, but by no means does that constitute true skill. A great man who gradually masters the fundamental transmission will accumulate honors as the years pass. He will gain an extraordinary victory replete with miracles. Even if that warrior is injured, he will not be defeated.[108]

Shūsen'o's formulation of the qualities of the amateur and professional and his directness in attacking his foes were two themes that also appeared in Kanze Motonobu's *Yoza yakusha mokuroku*.

Motonobu's bifurcation of amateur and professional is reflected in the structure of his text. The first two parts of his work describe actors of the past and present from the four Yamato troupes; "amateur" performers outside these groups appear at the end. His list of sixty "amateurs" included many famous actors such as Shimotsuma Shōshin. He remarked that Shōshin performed noh "in the style of an amateur," and he classified this famous actor from Honganji temple in Kyoto as an "amateur."[109] Yet, Shōshin was considered the equal of the greatest performers of the four Yamato troupes during his lifetime and served as noh instructor to Hideyoshi and his nephew Hidetsugu. Under the Tokugawa regime, Shimotsuma won Ieyasu's favor as well. He wrote many influential books of notations for performances (*katazuke*) such as *Tōbushō* (ca. 1596) and treatises on stages and properties, which were published and became popular references in the seventeenth century. Motonobu's criticisms of performers the caliber of Shōshin reveals that his desire to promote the four Yamato troupes took precedence over an accurate representation of the accomplishments of other groups.

Another way that Motonobu discredited "amateur" performers was by attributing their successes to a relationship with the Yamato troupes. Thus, whenever Motonobu praised an actor from outside the four Yamato troupes, he invariably mentioned that performer's debt to a member of the Yamato troupes. He cited Kanze Sōsetsu as the teacher of Shibuya Sōun of the Shibuya troupe, for example, even though Sōun was thirty-six years Sōsetsu's senior.[110] Nonetheless, Motonobu declared that, despite his tutelage by a great teacher, Sōun's "noh was not good."[111] In other instances, he incorporated independent noh performers into the medieval Yamato troupes as a way of co-opting their legacy. For example, he included the famous kyōgen actor Hiyoshi Yauemon as a member of the Kanze. Scholars note that Yauemon may have performed on occasion with the Kanze, but he remained a member of the Tanba Hie troupe.[112] By locating Yauemon within the Kanze, Motonobu assimilated him into the Kanze troupe's legacy, just as the four Yamato troupes were in the process of absorbing once-independent troupes and actors in the era Motonobu was writing. Motonobu's project supplied historical justification for the Yamato troupe's aspirations to incorporate rival noh groups and persecute outsiders.

Constructing Lineages

Besides delineating the basis for the broad distinction between amateur and professional, heredity determined the hierarchy of lineages within the Yamato troupes. Looking out from the perspective of his own family, Motonobu saw a complex landscape that described relationships among the performers of the four Yamato troupes. He sought to explicate these conditions to his descendants, and his decision to compile a genealogy of the four Yamato noh troupes revealed the degree to which heredity determined power and status in his era.

Motonobu organized *Yoza yakusha mokuroku* by classifying performers first by role type (*shite, waki,* musician, kyōgen) and then by the name of the noh troupe with which each performer was affiliated. Accordingly, he began with *waki* and listed all the *waki* actors chronologically in each of the four Yamato noh troupes. For instance, in Part I of *Yoza yakusha mokuroku,* Motonobu listed three *waki* who performed with the Konparu.

Chronology of Waki *Actors in the Konparu Troupe*

○ Hiyoshi Yojirō. He was the first *waki* in the Konparu troupe and the father of the lead performer of the Miyaō troupe. Yojirō was son-in-law by marriage to Konparu troupe leader Konparu Yoshiteru.

○ Meichi. It is said that Meichi studied with Toragiku Saburō. There were other successors to Hiyoshi Yojirō and Meichi. Later, Meichi lived in Uji.

○ Jūniyosaburō. He served as the substitute *waki* for Hiyoshi Yojirō.[113]

This list provides another example of how Motonobu's description of medieval noh reflected an early modern reality. The Hiyoshi (Hie) and Miyaō were noh troupes active in the late sixteenth century.[114] Motonobu's assertion of a marriage tie between Hiyoshi Yojirō and the leader of the Konparu is particularly telling because, as described below, marriage ties provided a convenient rationale for linking two different lineages. In both cases, according to Motonobu, the legacies of the Hiyoshi and Miyaō troupes had been subsumed by the Konparu.

Motonobu's biographical entries are terse. In most instances he noted the performer's familial relations and teachers, although in a few cases he gave only the performer's name. Longer entries run several lines and include anecdotes about a performer's career. He drew red circles by the names of famous performers to distinguish them, such as the three *waki* actors listed above. He also provided birth and death dates and posthumous Buddhist names when he could.

Kanze Motonobu intended *Yoza yakusha mokuroku* as a guide for his descendants to their family's past and as an aid in deciphering power dynamics in the noh world. Although he followed the genealogical turn in noh discourse and endorsed patrilineal descent as the most important factor in legitimating authority, Motonobu also detailed other strategies performers used to forge alliances and establish their pedigrees. Other legitimation strategies such as marriage, master-student relationships, and the transmission of unique secret teachings could prove a workable substitute for the legitimacy granted by primogeniture.

Problematic Patriarchs

As stated above, Motonobu traced his family's lineage to Kanze Nobumitsu, whom he recorded as On'ami's seventh son (see Fig. 4.3), and he signed *Yoza yakusha mokuroku* as the "fifth-generation descendant of Kanze Nobumitsu."[115] On'ami's first son, Kanze Masamori, inherited the leadership of the Kanze troupe. Motonobu traced the careers of three other of On'ami's sons. Sōkan (n.d.) studied the stick-drum with Konparu Kan'a (n.d.). As mentioned above, Nagatoshi apprenticed under Kongō Motomasa (also known as Sakamoto Shirōjirō Motomasa and Kongō Shirō Gon no Kami; n.d.) and became a *waki* performer, and Nobumitsu studied the hip-drum with On'ami's brother Ren'ami.[116]

There are several historical inaccuracies in Motonobu's genealogy that provide clues to how he constructed it. First, he followed the long tradition of deploying the names of great performers of the past as founding patriarchs. Both Kanze Ren'ami and Konparu Kan'a, whose names sounded authoritative and whom Motonobu listed as teachers of On'ami's sons, are of dubious historicity.[117] Second, as noted above, Motonobu misconstrued the relationship between Nobumitsu and Nagatoshi. Nobumitsu and Nagatoshi were not brothers, as Motonobu claimed, but father and son. Motonobu traced his lineage to Nobumitsu through a son named Nobushige.[118] He probably created this Nobushige as a link between the illustrious Nobumitsu and his descendants in the same way that those who created genealogies writing for *Kyōhō rokunen kakiage* filled gaps in their family trees. However, the later genealogy of the Kanze house of shoulder-drum players included in *Kyōhō rokunen kakiage* omitted Nobushige.[119]

What accounts for Motonobu's confusion about his own ancestors? Why did he view Nobumitsu and Nagatoshi as brothers? Judging from his descriptions of these performers, he apparently wanted to distinguish them as the founders of two different performance lineages, *waki* and shoulder-drum respectively. His portrait of Nobumitsu as a consummate musician reinforced his authority as a patriarch of the shoulder-drum: Nobumitsu possessed a "clear understanding of all aspects of the art and wrote many noh himself."[120] Moreover, Nobumitsu "was granted unprecedented favors from the gods, more than any other famous performer in the four troupes." He further claimed that Nobumitsu won the title of chief attendant, a rank second only to the leader of the troupe in proficiency and authority.[121] For Motonobu, Nobumitsu could only be the founder of a lineage of great musicians, whereas Nobumitsu's "brother" Nagatoshi was the patriarch of all *waki* performers (see Fig. 4.3).

Mythical Marriages

Motonobu also cited marriage as a rationale for the close relationships between actors in separate lineages, but these marriages may also have been fabrications. Although performers of the Yamato troupes frequently married the daughters of other performers, Motonobu's only purpose in mentioning marriages (and women) in *Yoza yakusha mokuroku* was to join lineages of performers who otherwise would have no connection. For instance, Motonobu postulated a link between the lineages of Nobumitsu, the patriarch of all drummers in the Kanze troupe, and Nagatoshi, the progenitor of the troupe's *waki*, in the form of a marriage between Nagatoshi's unnamed daughter and Nobumitsu's grandson, Sōsatsu (see Fig. 4.3).[122] However, the lineage chart that the Kanze lineage of shoulder-drum performers presented to the bakufu seventy years later in *Kyōhō rokunen kakiage*, which correctly recognized Nagatoshi as Nobumitsu's son, recorded a marriage between Kanze Sōsatsu and the daughter of Miyamasu Yazaemon.[123] In short, the later genealogy transformed the master-disciple relationship described in *Yoza yakusha mokuroku* into a marriage relationship to make the bond between the two performers and the lines of succession more concrete. This move simplified the connections between the most important patriarchs in the Kanze shoulder-drum lineage.

Creating fictitious marriages in genealogies seems to have been a useful method of linking unrelated performers. Other problematic examples of marriage appear in *Yoza yakusha mokuroku*. According to Motonobu, Nobumitsu married the daughter of his teacher, Kanze Ren'ami, who had married the daughter of his teacher, Yukimatsu Saburō (n.d.). Likewise, Jiga Yozaemon married the daughter of the head of the Kanze troupe, Motohiro, who in turn had married the daughter of the leader of the Konparu troupe leader, Zenpō. In each of these instances, Motonobu used marriage bonds to construct a close relationship between actors from unrelated lineages. Motohiro's marriage to Zenpō's daughter explained the close connection between Zenpō's son Sōtan and Motohiro's son Shigekatsu.[124] It was important for Motonobu to establish a link between Sōtan and Shigekatsu since it explained how he and his lineage held secret teachings about consummate rhythm (*ranbyōshi*) from the Konparu house (see below). Whether these marriages actually occurred did not matter since they still might serve a convenient way to establish familial bonds among performers when written into a genealogy.

One marriage mentioned by Motonobu deserves special attention: namely, the reputed marriage of Zeami's daughter to Zenchiku. Most modern noh scholars believe that Zenchiku did indeed marry Zeami's daughter. Noel Pinnington, for example, wrote that there was "no reason to doubt it."[125] Although Zenchiku's grandson Konparu Zenpō referred to Zeami as his "great-grandfather" in one of his treatises, there is no contemporary evidence from Zeami's or Zenchiku's writings or other sources that confirms this marriage.[126] Zenchiku was said to have been born in 1405, when Zeami was around forty years old, and chronologically the marriage is plausible. Yet, it is uncertain that Zeami even had a daughter. In the era in which Motonobu wrote, the question of Zeami's daughter served as a focal point of ideological contention between the Kanze and Konparu troupes and their competing claims about the history of noh and the roles of Zeami and Zenchiku in that history. In his submission to *Kyōhō rokunen kakiage*, the leader of the Konparu troupe used the marriage as a means of personifying Zenchiku's reception of Zeami's complete teachings. The author, Konparu Ujitsuna, further claimed that Zenchiku had developed the art of noh beyond his father-in-law, Zeami. In the Kanze contribution to *Kyōhō rokunen kakiage*, the marriage of Zeami's daughter to Zenchiku implied that the Konparu school's noh derived from Zeami's ideas.

Motonobu took a different view. In *Yoza yakusha mokuroku*, he credited Zeami's favoring of Zenchiku as leading to his downfall. "Zeami displeased the will of the shogun by favoring his son-in-law Konparu Zenchiku over his own son, and so he was exiled to the island of Sado."[127] Motonobu's reference to "Zeami's son" was not to his real son Motomasa but to On'ami, whom Zeami had adopted and asked to lead the Kanze troupe after his relationship with Motomasa supposedly soured, according to Motonobu. Thus, Motonobu faulted Zeami for turning his back on On'ami in favor of Zenchiku. Cognizant of the symbolic importance of marrying a daughter to a designated successor, Motonobu attributed Zeami's banishment to Sado to his failure to support his rightful successor, On'ami. In summary, Motonobu implied that Zeami's exile was punishment for not marrying his daughter to his rightful heir, On'ami. Since Motonobu is incorrect about the relationship between Zeami and On'ami, his claims of a link by marriage between Zenchiku and Zeami might also be unreliable.

Knowledge from Teachers

Motonobu portrayed his lineage as empowered by both heredity and transmitted knowledge. His grandfather, Sōsatsu, founder of the Kanze school of shoulder-drum, personified the confluence of bloodlines and expertise. On the one hand, Sōsatsu descended from On'ami's son Nobumitsu. On the other hand, he acquired his mastery of music from the great Miyamasu Yazaemon, whom Motonobu described as an accomplished performer in all aspects of noh. Yazaemon had earned the honorary title *tayū* during his lifetime, a testimony to his mastery of all facets of performance. Evidence of Yazaemon's prestige in the Edo period is the fact that both the Kanze and the rival Kō lineage of shoulder-drum viewed him as their patriarch. Kō Tadayasu, who established the Kō house, studied with Yazaemon. Although Motonobu admitted this fact, he also noted his grandfather Sōsatsu had received several secret writings from Yazaemon and that Kō Masayoshi had not.[128] He presented other evidence that demonstrated that his grandfather was Yazaemon's chosen successor. This "evidence" reveals Motonobu's method of constructing authority via genealogy. In the first line of his grandfather's biography, Motonobu wrote:

He was the sole authorized disciple of Miyamasu Yazaemon and his adopted son. When Yazaemon passed away, Sōsatsu received the secret writings [held by Yazaemon] of Chief Attendant Minō and texts authored by [Yazaemon's brother] Yashichi, totaling three works of great importance. Sōsatsu received a complete exposition of the detailed knowledge of the shoulder-drum from these texts.

Motonobu claimed that Sōsatsu was the son of a *waki* performer named Nobushige, who is credited with no other major accomplishment in *Yoza yakusha mokuroku*. As noted above, his name was excised from subsequent genealogies of the Kanze lineage of shoulder-drum. Sōsatsu's artistic legacy derived from his apprenticeship with Miyamasu Yazaemon, who adopted him briefly and gave him the name Miyamasu Kyūrō. Although Sōsatsu returned to the Kanze, he maintained a close relationship with Miyamasu as suggested by his inheritance of Miyamasu's collection of secret writings and other personal effects, which included a short sword, a box for a shoulder-drum, aged skins for drumheads, and some treasured garments. Motonobu added that his family preserved all these relics. Sōsatsu also received a license (*sōden no inka*) from Yazaemon that attested that Sōsatsu had received knowledge of the highest oral teachings. Motonobu recognized the importance of the license and all the other objects as signifying his grandfather's succession to Yazaemon.[129]

Besides glorifying Miyamasu Yazaemon, Motonobu brought to light all the great performers of the past who had instructed members

...sō mask, 16.9 cm × 13.9 cm × 6.3 cm (Muromachi period). Attributed to
Designated an Important Art Object by the Japanese government. Cour-
Mitsui Bunko.

of his family. He identified notable actors in his text with red circles
above their names, but the performers he most admired and whom he
claimed had the greatest significance for his family he ranked as chief
attendants. Motonobu listed four chief attendants who had special
links with his family in an appendix to *Yoza yakusha mokuroku*.[130] The
first was Kanze Nobumitsu, the founder of his family's lineage. The
second, Kongō Motomasa, taught Nobumitsu's "brother" Nagatoshi
the art of *waki*. The third, Yogorō Yoshihisa (n.d.) was a hip-drum
performer and the teacher of Nobushige and of Miyamasu Yazaemon.
Finally, Konparu Kan'a was a stick-drummer and step-uncle to the
Kanze lineage of shoulder-drummers through marriage of his daughter
to Sōsatsu's brother, Sōi. Motonobu positioned these four performers
in orbit around his family line.

Motonobu's Family Secret: Ranbyōshi

Through these connections with the great masters of the past, Motonobu was able to make one further claim to fame for his lineage: that
they possessed secret teachings on consummate rhythm (*ranbyōshi*).
The term *ranbyōshi* derives from the term "consummate music" (*rangyoku*), which refers to passages in plays that require special skill, secret knowledge, and spiritual energy to perform properly. *Ranbyōshi*
has become synonymous with the distinct and complicated shoulder-
drum passage of the play *Dōjōji* that precedes the lead actor's leap into
the suspended bell (see Color Fig. 7), but in the Edo period it was also
associated with the plays *Higaki* and *Sōshi arai Komachi*. In *Dōjōji*, the
long passage requires precise timing between the dancer's slow foot-
work and the shoulder-drummer's vocalizations and percussive blows.
Today, an actor typically performs *Dōjōji* as a "graduation piece"
marking the completion of training and entrance into the professional
world. Due to its complexity, the *ranbyōshi* section of *Dōjōji* is said to
require secret knowledge to master.

In his account of *ranbyōshi*, Motonobu defied the conventional
understanding that the leaders of the Kanze troupe had created or
inherited special teachings on *ranbyōshi*. Instead, he argued that his
family possessed secret teachings on *ranbyōshi* from the Konparu. He
further insinuated that the Kanze leader stole that information from
his lineage. He recounted that Shogun Ashikaga Yoshiteru commanded Miyamasu Yazaemon to give oral transmissions (*sōden*) to

the Kanze troupe leader Sōsetsu on *ranbyōshi*. On account of this precedent, Shogun Tokugawa Hidetada forced Motonobu's older brother, Sōya, to perform *Sekidera ranbyōshi* and teach the piece to the leader of the Kanze.[131] Motonobu's tacit criticism of the Kanze troupe leader was made possible by the fact that he was writing for members of his lineage and not for the audience of the Kanze troupe.

The importance of the story of *ranbyōshi* was not to denigrate the Kanze leader, instead it was the final evidence of the authority of Motonobu's lineage. He depicted amateur performers and his competitors as either mishandling or misunderstanding *ranbyōshi* and berated members of both the Ōkura and the Kō schools of shoulder-drum for their inability to play it. According to Motonobu, Miyamasu Yazaemon had chastised the founder of the Kō lineage, Tadayasu, for his failings at *ranbyōshi*. Tadayasu's son, Masayoshi (d. 1626), was even willing to teach the *ranbyōshi* for *Dōjōji* for money, and that was a much worse travesty in Motonobu's opinion. He taught *ranbyōshi* to a courtesan named Tamon from the pleasure quarters of Shimabara in Kyoto as well as to a maker of Buddhist surplices and a kettle maker.[132]

Kanze Motonobu's *Yoza yakusha mokuroku* exemplifies the use of genealogy in early modern noh discourse and the ways in which the myth of heredity was invoked as the principal logic to organize institutions and give a familial order to knowledge. Although Motonobu might fault a few past leaders of the Kanze and Konparu troupes, he could not deny that these leaders had a special expertise, because the same assertion underlay his own authority as head of his lineage of shoulder-drum. Motonobu's *Yoza yakusha mokuroku* utilizes the logic of heredity, first, to contrast professional and amateur performers and, second, to justify the pre-eminence of his lineage through claims of close ties with the greatest performers of old and the possession of specialized knowledge. By translating the bakufu's techniques for political control through the medium of genealogy to the context of his professional world, Motonobu articulated one of the first and most extensive organizational theories of a school as both a style and an institution.

1. Okina (*Hakushikijō*) mask, 19 cm × 16 cm × 9.? tributed to Nikkō. Designated an Important Art C ment. Courtesy of Mitsui Bunko.

2. Sanb
Kasuga.
tesy of

1. Okina (*Hakushikijō*) mask, 19 cm × 16 cm × 9.2 cm (Muromachi period). Attributed to Nikkō. Designated an Important Art Object by the Japanese government. Courtesy of Mitsui Bunko.

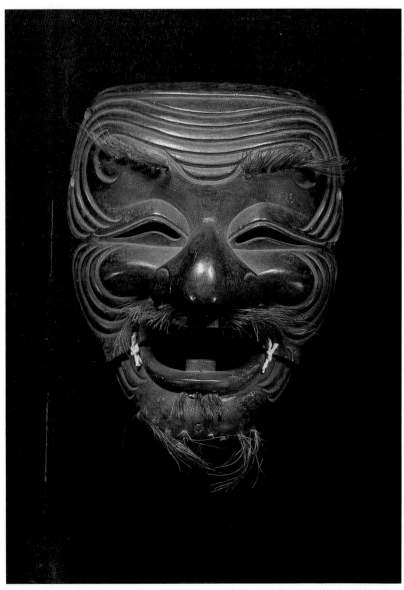

2. Sanbasō mask, 16.9 cm × 13.9 cm × 6.3 cm (Muromachi period). Attributed to Kasuga. Designated an Important Art Object by the Japanese government. Courtesy of Mitsui Bunko.

3. *Ko'omote* mask named "Flower," 20.8 cm × 13.2 cm × 7.2 cm. (Muromachi period). Attributed to Tatsuemon. Designated an Important Art Object by the Japanese government. Courtesy of Mitsui Bunko.

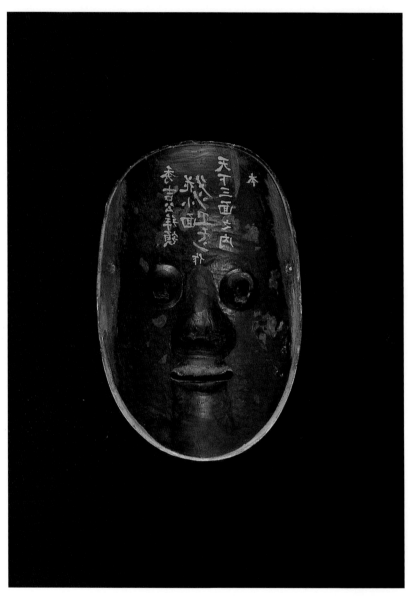

4. Reverse of the *ko'omote* mask "Flower." The attribution in gold paint reads: "Received from Lord Hideyoshi, the *ko'omote* Flower, carved by Tatsuemon, among the three best masks in the world, an original." Courtesy of Mitsui Bunko.

5. *Fudō* mask, 21.1 cm × 17 cm × 8.3 cm (Muromachi period). Anonymous. Designated an Important Cultural Property by the Japanese government. Said to have the blood stains of "Nose" (Hana) Kongō Ujimasa on the back. Courtesy of Mitsui Bunko.

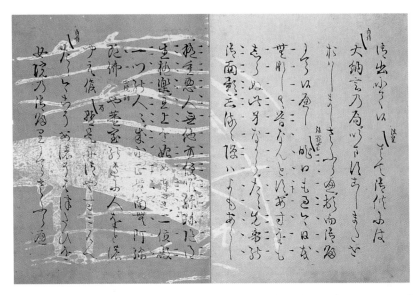

6. Page from an *utaibon* by Hon'ami Kōetsu of the play *Ohara gokō*. Courtesy of the Hōsei University Institute of Nōgaku Studies.

7. *Ranbyōshi* section from *Dōjōji* performed by Urata Yasuchika. Photo by Kin no Hoshi Watanabe Shashinjō. Courtesy of Watanabe Shin'ya.

8. Dance selection (*maibayashi*) from *Taihei shōjō* performed by (*from left*) Urata Yasuhiro, Urata Yasutoshi, and Urata Yasuchika. Photo by Ushimado Shashin-kobō. Courtesy of Ushimado Masakatsu.

CHAPTER 5

Mass-Produced Mystery

The composition of vast books is a laborious and impoverishing extravagance. To go on for five hundred pages developing an idea whose perfect oral exposition is possible in a few minutes! A better course of procedure is to pretend that these books already exist, and then to offer a résumé, a commentary.

—Jorge Luis Borges

In the medieval period, authority in noh and many other occupations was constructed around icons, first masks and then secret manuscripts. In both cases, physical objects fostered group identity and claims to expertise and legitimacy. Even if the ancient masks were never shown and the secret text never consulted, their presumed existence and the legitimacy they epitomized could still be invoked.

In the early modern period, authority became much more abstract and less dependent on physical objects. As we saw in the preceding chapter, a discourse on heredity that paralleled the government's rule by status empowered groups of actors by virtue of their relationship to certain lineages. However, the turn toward genealogy—and the evolution of a more abstract notion of authority—was also a function of the advent of the printing industry, the subject of this chapter.

The medium of print, after its introduction in the late sixteenth century, almost immediately affected noh. Secret noh texts such as *Hachijō kadensho* and the libretti of noh plays (*utaibon*), such as the beautiful example by the studio of Hon'ami Kōetsu (d. 1637) depicted in Fig. 6 in the section of color illustrations in this book, were among the first printed books available. *Utaibon* in particular became bestsellers that saw countless reprintings. Other books were written

Fig. 5.1 Scene from *Diagrams of Noh* (*Nō no zushiki*) depicting the play *Shun'ei*, published in 1697. Courtesy of the Hōsei University Institute of Nōgaku Studies.

specifically to introduce the costumes, staging, and repertoire of noh to new audiences, such as the illustrated guides *Nō no kinmōzui* (1687) and *Nō no zushiki* (1697; see Fig. 5.1) By making available secret texts on noh, the nascent publishing industry turned private intellectual traditions into public commodities. This had two results for noh's ethos. First, it affirmed the importance of "secret" treatises and other writings as essential references for artistic production and reception. Second, it cast a new spotlight on the authors of these texts.

In the first case, the popularization of knowledge about noh through print was a two-edged sword for performers. On the one hand, the dissemination of writings about noh created a better-educated and more receptive audience. Amateur study of noh blossomed in the Edo period partly because of the greater availability of noh libretti and other texts, not to mention the interest sparked from reading them. On the other hand, the availability of once-secret texts threatened actors' claims to authority based on their ownership. When everyone knows a secret, that secret, as Zeami long ago noted, becomes nothing special. When the contents of a performer's secret library are available at the corner bookshop and anyone who can afford them can purchase, read, and interpret them, what authority remains with the actor? Performers' interest in genealogy was one reaction to these changes, since the authority generated by genealogy did not rely on the possession of objects like secret manuscripts. Performers also reconfigured the relationship between orality and literacy as they related to professional knowledge. Giving more weight to privately and orally transmitted expertise than to written—and now published—secrets ensured that noh masters retained ultimate authority over their art.

The second result of the advent of the print industry was a focus on the author, and this, too, reinforced the discourse on heredity and rendered authority independent of the text or object. Just as noh genealogists identified the patriarchs of their lineage as having formative roles in noh's creation, print facilitated the identification and idealization of the "authors" of writings as great patriarchs of ways of knowledge. Print helped to make the names of Zeami in noh, Sen no Rikyū in tea ceremony, and Dōgen in Zen synonymous with their fields of knowledge. Indeed, these authors became more symbolically important as authorities than did the texts attributed to them. Rather than invoke a secret text, discussions turned to "Zeami's" or "Rikyū's" text and eventually to Zeami's or Rikyū's legacy.

The writings of the mid-seventeenth-century noh critic Shūsen'o (Majima En'an) offer one perspective on the changing construction of authority in noh in the seventeenth century. Shūsen'o is remembered for his publication *Bushōgoma* in which he critiqued a benefit performance by the Kita troupe, substantiating his vilification with citations from "secret" noh treatises, which, it turns out, he had fabricated. Although he made his argument through references to secret manuscripts, he did not premise authority solely on the possession of such writings. Instead, the rationale of *Bushōgoma* was that ultimate knowledge transcended any text, for it was located in the actor's bloodlines, his body, and his speech. Shūsen'o thus turned the logic of medieval authority upside down: instead of arguing that certain actors were authorities because they owned icons like texts, he based the authority of texts on their owner-performers' bloodlines, which he took for granted as authoritative.

The Rise of the Printing Industry

Before the seventeenth century, religious institutions dominated the production of printed texts, and these works consisted mostly of religious tracts and images. Jesuit missionaries brought the first movable-type printing presses to Japan in the sixteenth century. Yet the new technology was not applied in earnest until similar presses were brought back to Japan from Korea after Toyotomi Hideyoshi's campaign there in the 1590s.[1] Ultimately, woodblock printing proved a less expensive and faster method than movable type, and the boom in commercial publishing in the Edo period grew out of the use of woodblocks.

In the early Edo period, publishing was a small-scale operation because the same workshops printed and then sold books. Printer, publisher, and book seller did not become distinct occupations until the late nineteenth century in Japan. Kyoto dominated the publishing industry until the eighteenth century, and it was not until late in that century that Edo finally surpassed Kyoto and Osaka to become Japan's publishing capital.[2] The names of approximately 1,200 Edo-period publishers are known. Of these, 506 operated in Kyoto and 375 in Edo. Although concrete figures on print runs for different books are unavailable, no more than several hundred copies were printed for most books at a single time, but popular books were frequently reprinted. For example, in the seventeenth century, movable-type editions (*kokatsuji*) of *Hachijō kadensho* were published in the Keichō (1596–1614) and Genwa (1615–24) eras, followed by woodblock versions in 1624, 1650, 1657, and 1665 (see Fig. 5.2). Popular books were the frequent targets of pirating: publishers might duplicate the work of their competitors or buy the woodblocks to republish a book under their own name. The version of *Hachijō kadensho* published by Hiranoya Sahyōe (fl. 1660–1715) of Kyoto in 1665 became the mostly widely copied edition in the Edo period. Soon after Hiranoya printed it, another Kyoto publisher, Yamamori Rokuhyōe (n.d.) bought the woodblocks,

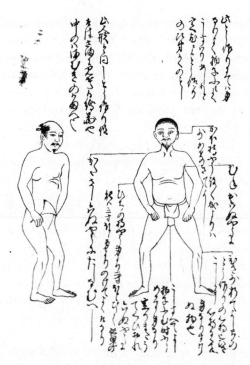

Fig. 5.2 Illustrations of a posture for a male role from an edition of *Hachijō kaden-sho* titled *Kadensho. Vol. 1* (*Kadensho kan dai ichi*), an early moveable-type (*koka-tsuji*) version, early seventeenth century(?). Courtesy of Waseda University Theatre Museum.

The text reads: (*figure on right*) "This posture is perfect since the appearance is good as is the stance with its lowered hips and firmly placed feet. The way to a good posture is just like this. The head is straight forward and tilted slightly upward. The chest is not thrust outward. The knees are slightly bent like the image of a drawn bow. Attention is paid to the knees and hips in order to create a good appearance. The hips are set well, and they remain motionless when stamping the feet. The appearance is stable, since the forearms and neck remain straight. The elbows are bent and are about six centimeters away from the torso; but, for de-mon roles, they should be about nine centimeters away from the torso. The shoulders are not hunched, but relaxed with poise.

(*figure on left*) "This is the same posture as the previous one facing forward, but this one is illustrated in profile" (*Hachijō kadensho*, p. 597).

changed only the name of the publisher to his own, and turned out his version. Later, when Yamamori published a few tourist guides to Kyoto that proved popular, Hiranoya quickly came out with his own versions of these works by the same trick.[3] Such cases provide evidence of the popularity of certain books even when concrete data about print runs are unavailable. Without enforceable copyright laws, publishers banded together in guilds (*shorin nakama*) to police themselves and appealed to the bakufu to prohibit pirating of texts, but both attempts to enforce publication rights were unsuccessful.[4] *Hachijō kadensho* continued to be published throughout the Edo period, an indication that demand for the book never subsided.

The price of books can be determined by consulting lists of publications (*shoseki mokuroku*). Nakamura Itaru examined four such lists for the years 1681, 1696, 1709, and 1716 and determined that the price of *Hachijō kadensho* in those years was, respectively, twelve, nine, nine, and twelve *monme*. In terms of the cost of rice in the Kyoto-Osaka area at the time, Nakamura determined that these prices were equivalent to the cost of 0.158, 0.086, 0.138, and 0.1 *koku*.[5] Considering that a *koku* of rice was a year's supply for one person, a price equal to that of about one-tenth a *koku* was quite high, but not higher than the market would bear. In concrete terms, a pornographic story cost about two weeks of meals, the charge for a romantic tale could supply a person with food for one month, and technical works were several times those amounts. Yet books need not always be purchased to be read; they could be rented at a tenth the original cost.[6] Many later Edo-period manuscript copies of *Hachijō kadensho* can be traced to the 1665 printed version. Copyists rented or borrowed a printed text and then laboriously handcopied a version for their own libraries.

Impact of Print on Occupational Discourse

The publishing industry changed intellectual discourse by disseminating formerly private writings. This popularizing of information reinforced an institution's claims to knowledge in its field, as the case of *Sendensho* in the world of flower arrangement illustrates. As noted in Chapter 3, *Sendensho* played a pivotal role in the transformation of the art of flower arrangement, first as a secret manuscript and later as a published work. The founder of the Ikenobō school of flower arrangement, Ikenobō Sen'ō, asserted that he had discovered *Sendensho* in 1536 when in fact Sen'ō himself wrote the text as a means of legitimating his expertise. When *Sendensho* was published in the seventeenth century, the prestige of the Ikenobō school grew in proportion.

After the first printed versions of *Sendensho* appeared in 1643, the theories of the Ikenobō school came to dominate the world of flower arrangement, and the number of Ikenobō teachers and students increased accordingly. So successful was the Ikenobō school that competing schools of flower arrangement soon "discovered" and published their own secret writings that proved that their school was even older than the Ikenobō.[7]

Reformers in the Sōtō school of Zen similarly saw the publication of the writings of their founder, Dōgen Kigen, as a catalyst for strengthening their efforts to effect institutional changes. Indeed, the popular recognition of Dōgen as a great Zen intellectual dates to the initial publication of his writings in the Edo period.[8] The monks of Eiheiji temple under the direction of Abbot Kōzen (d. 1693) published the ninety-five books of Dōgen's masterwork, *Treasury of the True Dharma Eye (Shōbōgenzō)*. Edo-period Sōtō sect reformers then began citing Dōgen's writings in an effort to change succession practices in Sōtō temples.

According to the tenets of Sōtō Zen, religious attainment was transmitted from master to student. Lineage charts visually depicted the succession of enlightened teachers from the time of the historical Buddha through the patriarchs in India and China to teachers in Japan. However, in the medieval period, Sōtō practices deviated drastically from this rule. For example, succession to a lineage was more often determined by the lineage of the temple in which a monk resided than by the lineage of that monk's teacher. Succession documents, likewise, showed great variations. Keizan (d. 1325), the fourth-generation leader after Dōgen, described an episode in his *Denkōroku* in which Dōgen's teacher in China, Rujing, showed Dōgen several succession documents. Dōgen queried him about the differences between these documents and earlier genealogies he had seen: "Why are there differences in the schools of Zen? If the succession is continuous from India to China, how could there be differences?" Rujing replied that all the patriarchs were buddhas; therefore, such differences did not matter.[9] Although Rujing mollified Dōgen with this response, Sōtō sect reformers of the Edo period were greatly concerned with rectifying the succession process. Manzan Dōhaku (d. 1715), the abbot of Daijōji temple in Kaga province, cited passages of *Shōbōgenzō* to argue for rationalizing the rules governing succession to clarify that a disciple could claim succession only from one master. Manzan and his colleague Baihō Jikushin

(d. 1707) proposed this policy to the bakufu in 1700. The bakufu accepted Manzan's proposal three years later and entrusted Manzan and Baihō with supervising all the Sōtō temples in Eastern Japan. The bakufu further ruled that the Sōtō sect should base all its policies on the writings of Dōgen.[10]

However, publication of Dōgen's writings did not resolve disputes about their correct interpretation within the Sōtō community. In 1722, at the request of Sōtō leaders, the bakufu prohibited the copying and printing of *Shōbōgenzō*. Sōtō intellectuals still recognized Dōgen's writings as authoritative, but few could concur on their meaning. Tenkei Denson (d. 1735), for instance, cited *Shōbōgenzō* to contradict Manzan and edited a commentary to Dōgen's writings entitled *Shōbōgenzō benchū* in which he argued against Manzan's ideas.[11]

As the examples of Ikenobō Sen'ō's *Sendensho* and Dōgen's *Shōbōgenzō* reveal, authors became as much symbols as creators of knowledge, since they bespoke the authority of a group associated with a body of texts. Print affected how texts symbolized knowledge. The perception of *Sendensho* as a "secret" manuscript "discovered" by Ikenobō Sen'ō differed from the perception of it in published form centuries later, because the symbolic value of the text had changed. With the text more readily available, the authority gained from possessing it came to mean less than the authority to interpret it, which had to be demonstrated by other means, chiefly heredity.

Authorization

One approach to judging how the symbolic value of texts changed with their increased availability is to consider the strategy of what can be called "authorization." Authorization refers to the relationship between the ascription of authorship to a written text and the construction of authority of those who claim possession of it. As Michel Foucault noted, the author is the name invoked to implant unities, coherence, and links with reality into the troublesome language of texts.[12] Assigning authorship is a hegemonic strategy intended to ascribe meaning and establish control. In the case of *Sendensho*, for example, Sen'ō felt that his text would acquire more authority if he attributed it to someone else. How, then, did print effect authorization?

Given the high value placed on documents in the medieval period, false authorization—what would be termed "forgery" today—proved an expedient method of establishing individual authority. Falsely ascribing *Hachijō kadensho* to the four archetypal leaders of the four Yamato troupes enabled the compiler of this sixteenth-century noh treatise to assert the rights of the Kanze, Konparu, Hōshō, and Kongō troupes over their rivals, the Hie. But forgers in the early modern period did not enjoy as much leeway as their medieval predecessors had in the strategy of authorization. Specifically, forgers in the fields of the performing arts in the Edo period faced three constraints that limited their ability to authorize. First, the Tokugawa bakufu's attempt to freeze the occupational order gave primacy to heredity as the principal determinant of social standing and power. This made individual social mobility through the creation of a spurious paper trail much more difficult than in the past. Second, early modern forgers in the fields of noh, tea ceremony, and flower arrangement worked in a context in which certain lineages already held sway over fields of knowledge on the basis of heredity: namely, the four Yamato noh troupes, the Sen families in tea ceremony, and the Ikenobō house for flower arrangement. The dominance of these institutions over discourse in their respective fields made it more difficult for upstarts to challenge them. Third, thanks to the publishing industry, the literate public could amass information much more readily than in the past. Anyone could purchase published "secret" writings and avoid the costly and time-consuming initiation into the private world of a field of intellectual or artistic endeavor. Thus, forgers needed to reconcile their claims to knowledge in an environment in which the public was better informed by virtue of their (potential) access to printed texts.

For these reasons, early modern forgers tended to ascribe their writings to better-known figures in the fields of the performing arts such as Zeami and Rikyū. Indeed, as described below, Zeami and Rikyū become widely known in their respective fields in the seventeenth century, thanks in part to two texts falsely attributed to them. In a study of the history of the book in Japan, Peter Kornicki has described how the name of a well-known author could positively affect the retail value of a text and boost sales beginning as early as the seventeenth century. This, too, prompted many writers and publishers to ascribe their books to famous people. More important, Kornicki notes that by the eighteenth century, the bakufu mandated that the names of the "real" author and publisher appear first in the colophon and later in the title of a book, an indication that it viewed both parties as responsible for the contents of a work.[13]

The Popularization of Zeami

Thanks to the publishing industry, Zeami became recognized widely in the seventeenth century both as an author of plays and as a noh theorist. Certainly, Zeami was widely recognized in the Edo period as a prolific author of noh plays. *Kyōhō rokunen kakiage* (1721) lists twenty-four plays by Zeami working alone and twelve collaborations with his father, Kan'ami, and his son Motomasa, more than by any other playwright.[14] His recognition as a theorist was based on his purported authorship of *Hachijō kadensho*. Although Zeami's name was added to a few early handwritten copies of *Hachijō kadensho*, his association with the manuscript developed later when publishers appended his name to printed copies in the latter half of the seventeenth century, most notably the widely circulated woodblock version of 1665, which included Zeami's signature at the end of every chapter.[15] Most printed versions of *Hachijō kadensho* after the second half of the seventeenth century bore Zeami's name. And, "Zeami's *Kadensho*" was cited in writings ranging from *jōruri* puppet theater to the famous Kabuki treatise *Yakusha rongo* to the first treatise on the aesthetics of kyōgen, *Waranbegusa*.[16] As noted above, except for the corrupted versions of two of Zeami's treatises that appear in *Hachijō kadensho*, the remainder of his theoretical writings remained widely unknown until rediscovered in the early twentieth century. In short, before the rediscovery of the historical Zeami in the twentieth century, the name of Zeami reappeared in noh discourse in the seventeenth century as a symbol of noh's legacy.[17]

Also in the seventeenth century, Sen no Rikyū's name became to the world of tea ceremony what Zeami's name stood for in noh, again thanks in part to an apocryphal manuscript. Forged treatises on the tea ceremony boomed in the seventeenth century, and most were attributed to Rikyū. These texts confirmed Rikyū as the grand patriarch of the way of tea (*chadō*). The intent of these forgeries was to assist their authors in establishing tea ceremony dynasties that claimed Rikyū as founding teacher. However, Rikyū never wrote lengthy theoretical works on tea. The first writings on tea ceremony, which date from the sixteenth century, such as *Matsuya kaiki* and *Tennōjiya kaiki* are simple records of the proceedings of tea parties. Nevertheless, the writings that appeared a century after Rikyū's death marked a "return to Rikyū," as writers claimed that their knowledge derived from the practices of the long-dead master. Yamada Sōhen (d. 1708), for instance, who established the Sōhen school of tea in Edo, claimed that his writings were based on Rikyū's ideas. He presented his *Chadō yōroku* as an oral transmission from Rikyū.[18]

The most famous "rediscovery" of Rikyū, however, was *Record of Nanpō* (*Nanpōroku*), said to be a journal of Rikyū's oral instructions (*kikigaki*) dutifully recorded by Nanpō, a hitherto unknown and historically suspect "top student" of the master. Tachibana Jitsuzan (d. 1708) declared that he discovered *Nanpōroku*, exactly 100 years after Sen no Rikyū's death. According to Jitsuzan, the text was so secret that even Rikyū's descendants did not own a copy! Like the Edo-period version of *Hachijō kadensho* with Zeami's name at the end of every volume, each of the seven volumes of *Nanpōroku* bore a postscript by Rikyū certifying their authenticity and accuracy. The text is surely a forgery by Jitsuzan. First, there is no evidence that someone named Nanpō ever studied with Rikyū or even lived in Rikyū's time. Second, prophetic passages in the text attributed to Rikyū offer clues that Jitsuzan was the author. For example, *Nanpōroku* attributed this declaration to Rikyū: "A person will appear in a later age who understands this way of tea . . . and even if a hundred years have elapsed, my bones will be invigorated, my spirit will be filled with joy, and I will surely become the patron deity of *chadō* (the way of tea)."[19] Jitsuzan no doubt created *Nanpōroku* to authorize his own way of tea. Although he did not disseminate *Nanpōroku* widely, after his death his descendants produced more copies as a step in founding their own school of tea ceremony, which they dubbed the "Nanpō school." Publication of the writings of other famous tea masters, such as Kobori Enshū (d. 1647) and Furuta Oribe (d. 1615), followed the appearance of *Nanpōroku*. Dissemination of these texts through print furthered the efforts of leaders of their respective schools in popularizing their school's practices.[20] Yet, ultimately, none of these newer schools rivaled the standing of the three Sen families who descended from Rikyū: Omote, Ura, and Musashikōji.

The previous examples suggest some of the changes brought by print to occupational discourse. The most profound of these was the denaturing of secrecy. Even as the printing of secret manuscripts spread information about an occupation, it destroyed the secrecy surrounding these texts, not only changing traditional patterns of reception but also threatening the mechanisms that had reinforced the authority of a text, its owner, and the occupations associated with it. It is no coincidence that at the same time the notion of "secret" manuscripts was being made obsolete by printing, these same writings began to be attributed to "great men" like Rikyū and Zeami. Precisely because a text lost legitimacy because of exposure, it needed to acquire authority through another means. Attribution to a great author served admirably well. Elizabeth Eisenstein, in her study of the effects of printing in early modern Europe, has noted this shift in authority: "New forms of authorship and literary property rights undermined older concepts of collective authority. . . . Veneration for the wisdom of the ages was probably modified as ancient sages were retrospectively cast in the role of individual authors."[21] One further effect of the popularization of the texts supposedly authored by great men was that these writings testified more to the authority of institutions than to that of the people who actually wrote them. An analysis of Shūsen'o's *Bushōgoma* supports this observation and reveals how occupations handled the crises brought about by the denaturing of secrecy, not by abandoning either secrecy or writing but by reasserting the primacy of extra-textual, orally transmitted secret knowledge over the written word.

A Hidden Author

Bushōgoma is a critique of a five-day benefit noh performance in 1658 by the Kita troupe in Kyoto, witnessed by an author who called himself the "Old Man of the Autumn Noh Fan," Shūsen'o. As noted above, the Kita was the only new troupe able to rival the four older Yamato troupes and, like them, receive a stipend from the bakufu. However, the Kita did have their detractors, and the author of *Bushōgoma* was certainly the most outspoken one.

Shūsen'o's text is constructed as an attack on the Kita in the form of a "critical writing" (*hyōbanki*), a genre popular in the Edo period. In *hyōbanki* the author evaluates the members of a group and their skills; the usual targets were kabuki actors and geisha. *Bushōgoma* was the only *hyōbanki* about noh theater published in the Edo period. The text has three parts. The first two parts offer a critique of the Kita troupe's five days of performance, play by play. The final part is an invective against the second leader of the Kita troupe, Jūdayū (d. 1665).

Bushōgoma was Shūsen'o's second censure of the Kita. He also wrote a critique of Jūdayū's performance at Kanda Myōjin shrine in Edo in 1653 entitled *A Critique of the Jōō Era Noh at Kanda Myōjin Shrine* (*Jōō shinji nō hyōban*). Shūsen'o referred to this earlier review in *Bushōgoma*, but only two copies of the earlier text exist today, and the work was never published in the Edo period.[22] In both works Shūsen'o claimed deep knowledge of noh and the right to say something about its performance. He demonstrated an even greater dislike for the Kita school and its chief actor Jūdayū.[23]

Shūsen'o introduced himself in *Bushōgoma* as a lifelong fan of noh in a brief preface in which he also set out his goals for the text.

Will the roots of the pine at Takasago hold firm? Will the pure source for the ceaseless rush of the Kamo River flow without end? I am an old man who has seen many years. From the time I wore my hair like a child until the age of forty, I have enjoyed noh. I was asked about the famous people of the way of noh; so I composed a short book about the great legacy of actors of the past and the terrible state of current performers. I called this work *Bushōgoma*, which means "lazy top." If a top is turned well, it will spin, but if it's spun poorly, it will not spin at all. Another meaning of this title is brought out by the fact that adults should not want to play with children's toys. In truth, I provide advice about the greatness of the noh of the past, which were modeled on sound examples, and I chastise the mistakes of following bad precedents.[24]

Takasago and Kamo are poetic place-names and central images in two noh plays by the same name: the pine tree in the play *Takasago* and the Kamo River in *Kamo*. Shūsen'o's allusions to two famous plays positioned him at the headwaters of the "sources" of noh, where he could begin a nostalgic journey backward to its roots. He returned to this imagery at the end of his preface, where he answered the question he posed at the outset about noh's origins and continued vitality. After probing the roots of noh and viewing its present course, he found noh in dire need of assistance. He offered to help single-handedly: "I must prop up the roots of Takasago and walk to the source of the Kamo River."[25]

Comparing the way of noh to a top that had needed to be spun correctly on its point, Shūsen'o titled his text *Bushōgoma*. The pun is revealed in the Chinese characters for the title. In place of the characters meaning "lazy top" (不精独楽), the author wrote a four-character homonym that means "dancing correctly, speaking with eloquence" (舞正語磨). According to the preface, the author's expertise derived from years of watching noh. He disclosed that his deep comprehension of noh's old ways would form the basis of his critique.

But Shūsen'o was not who he pretended to be. According to Omote Akira, its mysterious author was not an expert in noh but none other than an eye doctor from Osaka named Majima En'an.[26] The journey to that conclusion took Omote several decades of research. While editing *Bushōgoma* for publication, Omote recognized the great similarities between *Bushōgoma* and a noh treatise called *Writings on the True Mirror* (*Jikkanshō*). *Jikkanshō* was believed, even by some twentieth-century scholars, to be the work of Kanze On'ami, the third leader of the Kanze troupe. Shūsen'o cited *Jikkanshō* by name at several places in his text. However, Omote found that one-third of the examples Shūsen'o attributed to *Jikkanshō* could not be found in extant versions of that text. Omote then tried to trace the other sources cited in *Bushōgoma* to their original writings. Some sources cited by the author did not seem to exist, and quotations from treatises did not match the originals. Moreover, all examples of "ancient precedents" (*kojitsu*), which Shūsen'o attributed to a variety of writings, came from *Jikkanshō* alone.[27] Omote began to entertain the possibility that the author of *Jikkanshō* had copied from *Bushōgoma*, but he eventually concluded that the reverse was true. He discerned that the great similarity between *Bushōgoma* and *Jikkanshō* was due to the fact that the same person had authored both texts: Shūsen'o was the pseudonym of Majima En'an.[28] Thus, the same author wrote two critiques of noh performances (*hyōbanki*) including *Bushōgoma* and notations to dances (*katazuke*) under the pen name of Shūsen'o. But, when he wrote *Jikkanshō* and a few other "secret" noh manuscripts sometime during the Kanei and Kanbun periods (1624–73), he posed as a copyist using his real name of Majima En'an and ascribed these writings to one of the most revered actors of the past, Kanze

On'ami.[29] Consequently, anyone living in the seventeenth century who read *Bushōgoma* and then somehow acquired *Jikkanshō* or another noh manuscript forged by Majima En'an would have no idea from the texts themselves that these texts had been written by the same author. *Bushōgoma* was Shūsen'o's only writing to see publication during his lifetime. Yet, given the tremendous energy Shūsen'o put into his bogus secret manuscripts, he meant them to be read and believed, and he may have hoped to sell them. The constant references to secret manuscripts in *Bushōgoma* served as advertisements to develop a market for secret noh writings that the real author could supply under a different name. Read alongside each other, the two types of writings illuminate the differences between the nature of public knowledge presented in printed texts like *Bushōgoma* and the type of private expertise usually available only by oral transmission but purportedly reproduced in Shūsen'o's forgeries of secret manuscripts like *Jikkanshō*.

Where did Shūsen'o's knowledge of noh come from? He claimed that his expertise derived from experience and secret writings. Clearly, he was an amateur noh performer with some knowledge derived from his experience and from published sources. Omote Akira has concluded that Shūsen'o either read *Hachijō kadensho* or that many of *Hachijō kadensho*'s ideas had become standard knowledge by the time that Shūsen'o wrote *Bushōgoma*.[30] Shūsen'o, however, never referred to *Hachijō kadensho* or any other published texts by name.[31]

Interestingly, the Kita troupe's response to *Bushōgoma* did not counter the logic of Shūsen'o's methodology or uphold Jūdayū's greatness solely on the basis of his natural talent. Instead, the anonymous rebuttal, *Sarugutsuwa*, cited secret manuscripts said to belong to the Kita to defend the school's lineage. However, the Kita school's texts *Jitteishō* and *Kagetsushū* were as much forgeries as Shūsen'o's sources for *Bushōgoma*.[32]

The Kita Troupe

Shūsen'o articulated his motivation for writing *Bushōgoma* as an effort to clarify old knowledge; his chosen means for doing this was to denigrate the Kita troupe. His earlier critique, *Jōō shinji nō hyōban*, had a similar purpose of slandering Kita Jūdayū. Why did Shūsen'o select the Kita and Jūdayū as targets?

The Kita offered a convenient whipping post for Shūsen'o because of their success and relative newness. Jūdayū was the son of the founder of the Kita, Shichidayū. Shichidayū gained affiliation with the Kongō troupe at an early age and performed as a Kongō actor at age ten at the torch-lit noh of Kōfukuji temple in Nara in 1595. He then became the adopted son of the leader of the Kongō troupe and the leader of the troupe in 1605. He left the Kongō troupe in 1619 and began calling himself Kita Shichidayū in 1627. The four Yamato troupes plus the Kita troupe were the only noh groups chosen by the Tokugawa bakufu to receive stipends. However, when the payment system to actors first began, Kita Shichidayū received his share from the Kongō family, since he had been their former head.[33]

The novelty of the Kita troupe left its leadership open for criticism from the Yamato troupes. In 1634, Shogun Tokugawa Iemitsu punished Shichidayū by placing him under house arrest for making a mistake in a performance of *Sekidera Komachi* at the retired emperor's residence, the Sentō Palace. The jealousy of the lead actors of the Yamato schools likely provoked such an unusual punishment, since the leaders of the Yamato troupes were the authorities called by the bakufu to give their opinions on the case.[34] But the incident did not tarnish Shichidayū's reputation for long. As noted earlier, in 1647, the bakufu issued an order chastising the noh troupes for their lack of respect for old customs and for their extravagance. At the same time, it commanded the leaders of the four Yamato troupes to study under Shichidayū—in effect to learn about traditions of noh from the Kita leader. The heir of the leader of the Kanze troupe studied the play *Dōjōji* with Shichidayū, and the Kongō and Hōshō troupes also sent representatives to study with him.[35] Given Shichidayū's fame, Shūsen'o reserved his vitriol in *Bushōgoma* for Shichidayū's son, Jūdayū, who became second head of the Kita troupe in 1653 after his father's death. Shūsen'o even praised Shichidayū, but only to cast aspersions on Jūdayū. For instance, he contrasted Shichidayū's skill at dancing with Jūdayū's posturing, which Shūsen'o found reminiscent of kabuki.[36]

Although he did not rival his father, Jūdayū was nonetheless a respected actor in his day. He became a favorite of Shogun Tokugawa Ietsuna (d. 1680) and performed for the shogun more than any other actor. On the fourth day of the eighth month of 1653, Jūdayū accomplished the extraordinary feat of dancing lead role in twelve noh plays for the shogun.[37] In the Kyoto-Osaka region, the Kita troupe enjoyed great support and popularity in the time of Jūdayū. Apart from a few actors of the Kongō school, all the actors who performed for the retired emperor in the Sentō Palace were Kita performers. Outside Kyoto, Kita actors received stipends from some of the largest domains during Jūdayū's tenure as leader, including Kii (a domain of 555,000 *koku*), Mito (350,000 *koku*), Kaga (125,000 *koku*), Sendai (620,000 *koku*), Hiroshima (426,000 *koku*), Tōsa (172,600 *koku*), Tokushima (257,000 *koku*), and Kumamoto (540,000 *koku*).[38] Shūsen'o's condemnation of the Kita troupe and its leader reflected more of his dislikes, as well as the prejudices of the Yamato troupes, than an impartial critique of Jūdayū's merits. Unable to deny the Kita troupe's strength and talent, Shūsen'o repeatedly emphasized the importance of heredity, specifically the unbroken lineages of the Yamato troupes. He also exalted the secret wisdom of the Yamato, which he argued came from the gods.

Narai, *the Increasingly Abstract Vocabulary of Secret Knowledge*

As described above, the publication of secret writings represented a double-edged sword to occupations like noh, since printing divulged knowledge to a large audience. On the one hand, teachers of noh or any other art might win adherents when more people became aware of their school's traditions. On the other hand, if the text functioned as the sole source of truth, then anyone purchasing the text could claim authority. Therefore, actors and other professionals needed new methods to legitimate themselves as authoritative interpreters of texts and of their fields of expertise.

Consequently, the printing of once-secret manuscripts was accompanied by the development of means to distinguish relative knowledge—such as information in its printed form—from absolute knowledge, which was possessed solely by the masters of a given art. Differentiating levels of knowledge allowed members of the performing arts to retain authority while still disseminating information. The crudest distinction between relative and absolute knowledge lay between what scholars term "complete transmission of the secrets" (*kanzen sōden*) and "limited transmission" (*fukanzen sōden*).[39] Since the authority of occupations depended on a monopoly of expertise, only the top masters were privy to the complete transmission, which marked the revelation of all the secrets of the art. Everyone else who studied the art received only limited transmission, the kind of knowledge also found also in printed books.

In addition, notions of hierarchies of secret knowledge in the performing arts gained currency by the end of the seventeenth century. To illustrate this point, the modern scholar Nishiyama Matsunosuke quoted the diary of village headman Kawachiya Yoshimasa from Daigatsuka Village (in modern Osaka prefecture). The citation is particularly revelatory of the vocabulary brought to bear to codify knowledge in the relative (public) and absolute (private) sense.

Knowledge (*denju*), oral traditions, and secret knowledge exist in all the arts. The nō, in particular, has many secret transmissions. Such things often appear to be useless, but this is not so. These transmissions impart a great respect for the Way and strengthen one's resolve to practice. Thus these secrets are in fact the supreme teaching. Secret pieces (*naraigoto*) and transmissions (*denjugoto*) are highly principled. One must learn them from one's teacher with reverence.[40]

Knowledge came to be organized according to a hierarchical pyramid, and once-secret writings that became public knowledge through publication fell to the bottom layer of the pyramid. At the intermediate level were "secret pieces" (*naraigoto*) and select "transmissions" (*denjugoto*) available only to initiated students, transmitted orally from a teacher. At the pinnacle was the most profound category of knowledge, available only to top masters and the head of a school.

Naraigoto or *narai* are classifications of secret knowledge, and like this village headman, Shūsen'o posited these as central to noh discourse and to any performer's authority. *Narai* are still the key units for qualifying secret knowledge in noh. Today, the word can refer to a play or part of a play that requires special knowledge to learn and perform.[41] Plays in this category include such revered works as *Shakkyō*, *Dōjōji*, *Sekidera Komachi*, *Higaki*, *Obasute*, and *Sotoba Komachi*. The designation of what constitutes a *narai* depends on the particular school of noh. A *narai* in one school may be just an "ordinary matter" (*hiramono*) for another school. *Narai* are said to mark advanced or difficult plays or portions of plays that require extraordinary ability on the part of the performer and necessitate special—therefore secret— knowledge.[42] *Narai* today are ranked according to their level of difficulty or sanctity in terms of "initial," "intermediate," and "profound" (*shoden*, *chūden*, and *okuden*) or "small," "medium," "great," "profound," and "separate" (*konarai*, *chūnarai*, *ōnarai*, *omonarai*, and *betsunarai*). The highest level of *narai* are the most restrictive, occasionally limited to one actor per generation in a school or family. For example, a noted kyōgen actor, the late Nomura Manzō VI (d. 1978) bypassed his first son, Mannojō (b. 1930, now called Manzō), and taught only his second son, the current Nomura Mansaku (b. 1931), the play *Tanuki no haratsuzumi*.[43] (The two brothers are still feuding over who is their father's legitimate successor.) *Narai* were traditionally the mark of professional status in noh and presented only to actors of certain lineages or chosen heirs; today, however, amateurs can learn *narai* after purchasing a license from the family-head of their school through their teacher.[44] Of course, the more important the *narai*, the more expensive the license.

Viewed historically, the development of *narai* as a category of secret knowledge was a response to the increased dissemination of noh writings. Zeami did not make much of the term *narai* in his writings, at least in the modern sense of the word.[45] Although he differentiated between oral knowledge (*kuden*) and secret treatises (*hidensho*), he intended all his knowledge to be maintained as restricted secrets. For Zeami, the distinction between *narai* and other types of occupational expertise was unnecessary. As noh manuscripts became more widely disseminated in the sixteenth century, noh treatises began to devote more attention to *narai* and to discuss them in concrete terms, as the mid-sixteenth century *Hachijō kadensho* illuminates. In that text, *narai* approximate reminders not to forget crucial aspects of a given piece. Volume 5 of *Hachijō kadensho* offers a few *narai* for specific dances. One of the most detailed descriptions of a *narai* included is for the play *Kantan*. In *Kantan* the main character (*shite*) dreams he has become the emperor of China. The first part of the *narai* for *Kantan* cues the actor to give the appearance of drifting off to sleep.

In the play *Kantan*, at the point in the song "lying down on the pillow," be sure to lie down on the pillow. It is important to give the appearance of falling asleep and of sleeping. If the actor does not close his eyes, it will not look as if he is sleeping. The *narai* is for the actor to close his eyes.[46]

The *narai* for Kantan is a simple reminder to the actor to perform an appropriate action at the correct time. At first glance, in contrast to the modern notion of *narai*, this *narai* does not require great technical skill or spiritual prowess to execute. Yet, the actor playing the lead role in *Kantan* would be wearing a mask and might forget to adjust the mask slightly downward to give the appearance of sleep at the appropriate time. Still, the teaching is just common sense. The passage evokes Zeami's observation about the mundane quality of secret knowledge: "When these so-called secret things are revealed openly, they often appear to be nothing special."[47]

The concept of *narai* as a category of secret knowledge took form in the Edo period. In contrast to earlier noh writings, there are three changes in Shūsen'o's use of the term that show this development. First, Shūsen'o declared that *narai* were central not auxiliary to noh. In Shūsen'o's words, "There can be no art without *narai*."[48] Second, he surrounded *narai* with mystery by classifying them without discussing their contents. Thus, in contrast to *Hachijō kadensho* and to his own forged manuscripts, which detailed the contents of *narai*, Shūsen'o's published writings made *narai* sound mysterious and profound without revealing what they actually were. Third, he described *narai* as a function of the genetic inheritance of the Yamato troupes, ultimately equating the possession of expertise with the bloodlines of a few noh lineages, particularly the Kanze.

A story in *Bushōgoma* attested to the value of *narai* for noh.

It is written in *Jikkanshō* that in years past Hiyoshi Matagorō came to a meeting of the Kanze troupe near Higashiyama [in Kyoto], where he called upon Kanze Sukemasa to ask him a question. Matagorō asked, "What is this talk about musical modes? I created a dance based on new principles. So, can you create some effects for my dance that will match the rhythms that I will play? I will reward you if you assist me." Sukemasa retorted, "How can I create an effect for something that has neither precedent nor sense of propriety? In this family, there is established knowledge (*naraimono*) created by the three generations of Kan'ami, Zeami, and On'ami. You surely must be joking!"[49]

Here, Shūsen'o described an encounter between the head of the Kanze troupe and an actor from the Hie/Hiyoshi troupe, or perhaps a musician by the name of Hiyoshi working for the Kanze. (Neither Hiyoshi Matagorō nor Kanze Sukemasa appears in other historical sources; and, both seem to be characters of Shūsen'o's invention.) Following precedents in texts such as *Hachijō kadensho*, Shūsen'o deployed the name of Hie/Hiyoshi as a foil to the mainstream Yamato tradition, depicting the Hie as ignorant of noh's true heritage. The point of the anecdote is that artistry must be based on established traditions like *narai*. This assertion equated *narai* with the traditions guarded by the Yamato troupes. Moreover, this conceptualization of *narai* disallowed any effort to reinterpret the noh repertoire except by using *narai* known only to the leaders of the Yamato troupes.

Jikkanshō, Shūsen'o's manuscript that he falsely credited to Kanze On'ami, is a collection of *narai* for different plays. It reveals his conception of *narai* in relationship to other types of secret knowledge. Shūsen'o offered "established *narai*" (*sadari no narai*) for the plays *Takasago*, *Naniwa*, and *Seiganji*. He also discoursed on *narai* for "performing indoors" (*zashikimai no narai*) and for the proper method of walking on the stage (*suriashi no narai*). His description of the *narai* for the play *Dōjōji* includes diagrams illustrating how the lead actor should stamp his feet. The colophon to this manuscript contrasted *narai* with other types of secrets available to noh performers in the Kanze family.

In our family, there are two things: *narai* and "great matters" (*daiji*). *Narai* are, needless to say, the words to songs, the requirements for noh, and the correct execution of matters of protocol. Great matters are not made by mortals: each one was the creation of a buddha or else the secrets of the deities. Great matters also include precedents (*reishiki*) established by the likes of Prince Shōtoku, wise sages, learned scholars, and upright priests.[50]

This passage reveals that the ubiquitous *narai* are the work of mortal actors as opposed to the more highly revered "great matters," which were created by deities and sages long ago. The example Shūsen'o provided of a "great matter" was "consummate rhythm" (*ranbyōshi*), imparted by the Bodhisattva Kannon to the founder of the Kanze line, as described below.

Shūsen'o used a variety of other mysterious artistic terms in *Bushōgoma* that he claimed formed the basis for noh's aesthetics.

Until the time of Kanze Kan'ami, only one verse was performed at a time, but in the generation of Zeami, the sixty-six noh of today were created, based on the five laws, the three elements, introduction-break-fast (*jo-ha-kyū*), the five postures, the seven modes, six elements, and seven paths. Since the so-called source is the same for all of the four troupes, there are no other family customs. Anything else is an individual fabrication entirely, and these practices are not incorporated into noh.[51]

Some of these terms, such as "introduction-break-fast" (*jo-ha-kyū*), can be found in Zeami's writings because they predate noh theater. Most of the other terms, such as the "six elements" and the "seven paths," were either Shūsen'o's creations or his reworkings, and he did not define their meaning in *Bushōgama*.[52] On the one hand, the lack of concrete definition reveals the meaninglessness of these terms for noh performance practices. On the other hand, the same lack of definition coupled with the mysterious aura the author conjured to surround these secrets gave them life.

Shūsen'o paraded these secrets to "stage" their meaning; therefore, his could be called a "simulated secrecy." His deployment of secrets—hinting at them in his printed works and even manufacturing "secret" manuscripts—mirrors how the mass production of texts through printing changed the nature of secrecy. This change in the nature of secrecy can be characterized as a shift from "representation" to "simulation," to borrow Jean Baudrillard's terms. Whereas representation stems from the principle of the "equivalence of the sign and the real"—for instance, the equivalence of a secret manuscript with the fact that it remained secret—"simulation" is representation that has given way to the reproduction of copies of copies (simulacra) that have no original—in the same way that a secret text becomes secret in name only when it was printed multiple times and could be purchased at the local bookshop. The availability of secret knowledge through printed texts like Shūsen'o's marked the mass production and consumption of information at the same time that it denatured secrecy. Seshūno's writings move one step further toward simulation by the way he plays at secrecy, evincing what Baudrillard has called a "strategy of the real."[53] That is to say, although his writings may not be simulacra in the fullest sense, since he copied some of his ideas from earlier manuscripts that he misquoted or failed to cite, his texts mask the absence of medieval practices of secrecy that had once enshrouded knowledge. They reveal what Baudrillard calls a "sorcery" playing at appearances.[54] This play with secrecy allowed Shūsen'o to walk the thin line between fabrication and being discovered at it.

Shūsen'o's simulation of secrecy contrasted with medieval practices of secrecy, which were dependent on controlled dissemination of the secret manuscripts. *Hachijō kadensho*, for instance, warned readers not to share any of the instructions with outsiders and amateurs.

There are thirty-seven sections of writings here about the beginning of noh and the Okina dance recorded exactly as they were conveyed to me. Since every part of this treatise is about the Way of the Gods, the details should be treated with reverence and discretion. People who do not maintain this knowledge carefully will be punished by the gods.[55]

Hachijō kadensho's injunction to secrecy covered the contents of the entire manuscript. Consequently, the information in it had the aura of prestige associated with the work's controlled availability—not to mention the threat of divine punishment for disclosing this information. Since the entire manuscript was supposed to be secret, the contents could be more explicit. Shūsen'o, in contrast, wrote *Bushōgoma* as a book to be printed for a public audience; therefore the entire work could not be construed as a secret manuscript. Instead, he continually invoked an aura of secrecy within the text itself to leave the contents of his secret information a mystery. For example, where the *Hachijō kadensho* clarified Okina, Shūsen'o obfuscated it. As described in the following section, Shūsen'o hinted at complex knowledge, such as twelve *narai* for Okina, but did not divulge it.

Blood, Body, and Knowledge

The chief revelations of *Bushōgoma* were the existence, not the contents, of secret knowledge along with the equation of that knowledge with the four Yamato troupes. Actors outside these troupes who might appear to dance and sing proficiently only performed superficially and never drew on noh's mystical core teachings, according to the author. Shūsen'o demonstrated this notion in his description in *Bushōgoma* of Jūdayū's performance of Okina on the first day of the troupe's benefit performance. He began by noting that Jūdayū omitted all of the *narai* requisite for the dance.

There were none of the traditional practices in Okina. There are twelve *narai* pertaining to the Way of the Gods, from the time of entering the stage to the end of the dance, including those in the greenroom beforehand. However, none of these were performed. Moreover, Jūdayū did not even bow after appearing on stage. He did not make a mudra when he moved his mask. When he sang "peace in the world," he omitted the *narai* of alpha-omega (*a-un*). The dance is called Okina precisely because there are such customs. As a rule, all alterations in Okina or in the *waki* noh that follow are detestable. It is said that "one must perform rites as if

the gods were present." For instance, consider the attendance of rites on
the first day of the New Year, abbreviations are never allowed in those
proceedings. In the same way, for what is called noh, when actors wear
the appropriate court hats and formal dress and perform in ceremonial
robes [for Okina], omitting customs is all the more despicable. Precisely
because these practices were established in the remote past, they are laud-
able and felicitous.[56]

At the outset, Shūsen'o noted twelve *narai* that Jūdayū left out of his
performance, but provided no more details. The single *narai* he cited
by name, the so-called "alpha-omega" (*a-un*) *narai*, he also left unclari-
fied, noting only its absence.[57] Readers knowledgeable about esoteric
Buddhism might infer that *a-un* refers to two letters of the Sanskrit
alphabet, but Shūsen'o never explained what they meant to noh. In
his earlier critique of Jūdayū's performance at Kanda shrine in Edo in
1653, Shūsen'o was a bit more forthcoming about the twelve *narai* for
Okina but was equally vague about the contents of the *narai*.

The chant of Okina is composed of a mixture of Buddhist prayers (*darani*)
and Shinto verses. Consequently, the part "the color of the sun tomor-
row" is the place where there is a *narai* about fulfilling the prayer for
such a day, but Kita Jūdayū forgot it and did not sing it. Therefore, he did
not appease the deity Myōjin. It is said that "if one does not act truthfully,
one will be punished by the gods."[58]

Here, he located the precise place where Jūdayū forgot to enact the
"correct" *narai*, but he provided no details about its contents. As with
the *a-un* mantra, the "prayer for such a day" suggests possible depths
of meaning without saying anything concrete. In both instances,
Shūsen'o simply used the words as jargon and implied that the meaning would be self-evident to anyone who knew noh secrets. Such a
person would also recognize that restricted information could not appear in print. And, he left the true necessity of *narai* beyond doubt by
calling down divine punishment on those ignorant of them.

Shūsen'o had to be careful to concoct traditions about noh unknown to his readers. Consequently, he favored arenas such as the
backstage ceremonies before an Okina performance that were hidden
from the eyes of the audience. For example, in the description of Jūdayū's dance of Okina in *Bushōgoma*, he referred readers to his earlier,
unpublished critique of Jūdayū's performance of Okina at Kanda

shrine. In this work, he detailed what was supposed to occur back-stage before a performance of Okina.[59]

First, in the mirror room, sake is offered to Nikkō and Gekkō [the masks of Okina and Sanbasō], and there are Buddhist mantras, sacred spells, and divine verses that are intoned. This occurs at the beginning of the program. Then the actors wearing formal robes sit in a row and partake of the sake. Beginning with the lead actor, all the actors chant mantra and intone sacred verses. At the raising of the stage curtain, everyone in the mirror room rises. The lead actor makes the sign of creation and chants a mantra. While reciting sacred verses, he points his fan with the pivot facing outward at the curtain, and draws Sanskrit letters in the air. In addition, there are twelve *narai* pertaining to the Way of the Gods that are carried out from the time of entering the stage to the end of the dance, including those in the greenroom beforehand.[60]

The account of the rites in the greenroom is evocative for its details, but the relationship between this description and the performance by Kita Jūdayū is uncertain. Since the Okina rites occurred backstage, not in front of the audience, how did Shūsen'o, who was sitting in the audience, know if they took place or not? Moreover, how would his readers know about the execution of unseen rites? This absence proved an opportunity for Shūsen'o to stage his own knowledge.

Shūsen'o's recounting of the mysteries of Okina reflect his assumption that his readers knew something about the dance and how it was performed. Therefore, he focused on the hidden world of backstage rituals, which he presented as the true meaning of Okina. Accordingly, the pre-performance ceremonies described in *Bushōgoma* was much more elaborate than those mentioned in *Hachijō kadensho*, which prefaced its remarks on Okina with this warning:

This section provides instructions for the dance of Okina. The secrets conveyed here are the most restricted knowledge of *sarugaku* and contain many things that inspire awe. These matters derive from the customs of deities, and seven days of purification are required to perform Okina. Consequently, these secrets are not something to be spoken about lightly and should not be taught to amateurs.[61]

Hachijō kadensho stipulated seven days of purification to perform Okina but offered nothing comparable to the pre-performance rituals that obsessed Shūsen'o in *Bushōgoma*. *Hachijō kadensho* was encyclo-pedic in its range of sources, and had such pre-performance rites existed in the era of its compilation, the text might have made some mention of them. In any case, the dearth of information about what occurred before the performance of Okina gave Shūsen'o opportunity to write what he wished.

In *Jikkanshō*, Shūsen'o could disclose more secrets about Okina. Accordingly, the putative author, Kanze On'ami, issued a much more complicated warning about teaching these secrets. This warning revealed that the absolute truth of Okina was to be found not in the relative meaning of any text or the superficialities of a performance but in the physical body and blood of the performer.

Concerning giving instruction in Okina, perform seven days of purification and abstinence; maintain a separate fire (*bekka*) from women [for cooking and bathing] . . . wear the nine protective signs. Do not transmit these matters to anyone but one heir. You can teach the verses to your students as usual. Do not read about giving instructions to Okina when your body is impure. In addition, never sing the verses to Okina in a lewd manner without a sense of spiritual decorum. This must remain secret.[62]

In addition to seven days of sexual abstinence and purification, Shūsen'o stipulated that someone about to transmit knowledge about Okina to his successor should avoid sharing the same fire with a woman. Modern noh performers report that they maintain the practice of "separate fire" (*bekka*) before a performance of Okina. For as long as seven days, actors avoid eating food cooked by women or using the same bathwater for fear that the fire used to heat food or water might transmit "female" contaminants. Shūsen'o portrayed the custom of "separate fire" as a necessity for the master about to teach Okina to his successor, although he did not link the custom to the performance itself.

If uninterrupted by female contamination, Shūsen'o imagined the secrets of noh would flow like blood from generation to generation of male performers. In fact, he told the history of noh in *Bushōgoma* to draw a close connection between patrilineal bloodlines and knowledge.

The story of *sarugaku* and *ennen* has it that they were the creation of Prince Shōtoku and that they were started by the Konparu. What are termed noh today came through the revelations of Hase Kannon and began with the Kanze troupe. Thus, the founders of *sarugaku* are the Konparu, and the progenitors of noh are the Kanze.[63]

Retelling the familiar story of the origin of noh allowed Shūsen'o the opportunity to state with finality how noh's aesthetic principles were both divine and the property of only certain bloodlines, namely, the leaders of the Kanze and Konparu troupes and, by extension, their relatives, the Hōshō and Kongō. Their patrimony testified to their primacy over their "amateur" contemporaries.

Shūsen'o's fascination with the body of the performer and with physical purity was a function of his emphasis on genealogy, and here he owed a debt to the dominant ideology of the Tokugawa regime. The discourse on genealogy described in the previous chapter informed the Tokugawa shogunate's equation of blood with identity as seen in its prohibition of the intermarriage of different status groups. On the one hand, such rules sought to solidify the social system by inhibiting social mobility. On the other hand, the bakufu's laws also aimed to prevent the commingling of the outcast *eta* group with the rest of society. Shūsen'o employed a similar logic, which premised purity on heredity and blood, in his writings. In the case of his description about teaching Okina, Shūsen'o (in the voice of Kanze On'ami) emphasized that physical defilements caused by contact with women, however remote, might interfere with patrilineal transmission of secret expertise. The warning in *Jikkanshō* against potential pollution from women articulated the linkage between genealogy and blood in negative terms: patrilineal transmission could be corrupted unless purification rites and barriers against pollution were erected.

Blood and Consummate Knowledge

Shūsen'o drew a positive correlation between patrilineal bloodlines and expertise about noh theater in *Bushōgoma*, and he adduced the concept of *rangyoku* as concrete evidence of the transmission of knowledge in the patrilineal bloodlines of the Kanze house. *Rangyoku* has been translated as "consummate music"—*ranbyōshi* is the rhythm appropriate for that music.[64] Zeami coined the term *rangyoku* in the context of his discussion of the five modes (*shūgen, yūgen, renbō, aishō,* and *rangyoku*) in two treatises, *Five Modes* (*Go'on*) and *Go'ongyoku jōjō*. In contrast to the other four modes, which are based on feelings, consummate music is based on artistic virtuosity. Plays that fall into the category of "consummate music" require a high level of skill and have unique passages.[65] Consequently, Zeami wrote *ran* in the compound word *rangyoku* with the Chinese character meaning "to excel" (*takeru*). In the current repertoire, there are certain plays associated with *rangyoku* qualities such as the *ranbyōshi* in *Dōjōji* mentioned in Chapter 4. There are also about fifty *rangyoku* works, such as the plays *Matsura monogurui* and *Shimameguri*, which are no longer part of the repertoire but from which highlights are still performed.[66] In terms of the modern classification system, *rangyoku* are synonymous with *narai* and require special knowledge, training, and permission from the leader of a noh school to perform. The transformation of *rangyoku* from works that required talent to pieces that required access to secret knowledge and the permission of the troupe leader to perform occurred in the Edo period. A comparison of the discussion of the concept of *rangyoku* in the sixteenth-century *Hachijō kadensho* with that in *Bushōgoma* makes this clear. In Shūsen'o's noh discourse, *rangyoku* combined the concept of private secrets, *narai*, with the genealogy of the Kanze family to locate profound knowledge within bloodlines.

The definition of *rangyoku* in *Hachijō kadensho* resonates with Zeami's idea that "consummate music" depended on the talent of the actor for success. In the first place, *Hachijō kadensho* used the same Chinese characters as Zeami did to write *rangyoku*. The definition of *rangyoku* in *Hachijō kadensho* also conformed with Zeami's. *Rangyoku* is called "advanced music" (*kono kyoku wa takeru kyoku nari*).[67] *Hachijō kadensho* also followed the established convention in noh writings beginning with Zeami of comparing the five modes to different trees. *Rangyoku* takes the form of an aged cypress, marked by an unusual and beautiful shape that developed naturally over the years. The cypress tree serves as a metaphor for the ability of a mature actor to draw from his experience and perform difficult works. An inexperienced performer assaying the same work would be like a young pine tree intentionally bent out of shape in a vain, unnatural attempt to create something beautiful.

People who lack sensitivity will marvel at the shape of something like a garden pine that was made to look interesting by stretching the shrunken parts and twisting the straight parts. This is not something done in our Way. Because we can perceive the tree's artificiality, it is not at all interesting. A pine tree that grew naturally from a small sprout will gain many peculiarities of its own as the years pass, and this tree is truly interesting.

This is how *rangyoku*, too, when sung will surpass the other four types of music.[68]

By the definition in *Hachijō kadensho*, *rangyoku* were naturally excellent because of the performer's years of accumulated experience and inherent talent.

Shūsen'o told a different tale in *Bushōgoma* about *rangyoku*; for him *rangyoku* are linked to secret knowledge about *ranbyōshi* possessed only by the Kanze family.

The *ranbyōshi* of the Konparu school is modeled after a variation of Okina. The point in this dance where there is a disjointed rhythm is called a *ranbyōshi*, or chaotic rhythm. This is maintained as a secret teaching among the three troupes and even those actors who do not have official stipends (*musoku*). It was transmitted in detail to Hanazaki Sakyō and Asai Kinosuke.[69] However, the *ranbyōshi* of the Kanze is from the fortieth ruler of our land, Emperor Temmu. The emperor, while sojourning beside the Yoshino River, was playing the koto. When he played the song "Yūran," five heavenly maidens came down from the firmament, singing five songs, and fluttering their robes.

Then all of them ascended to the heavens, where the emperor learned their dances, like saints dancing on the clouds. This is the origin of the five modes. Following the example of the song "Yūran," the name *ranbyōshi* was coined and was later danced by the courtesan Higaki. Since there were five heavenly maidens, there are five dances.[70]

According to this explanation, most troupes followed the tradition of *rangyoku* derived from a variation of Okina, and only the Kanze was heir to the *ranbyōshi* taught to Emperor Temmu (d. 686) by five angels, which made its version authoritative.

The link between *rangyoku* and the Kanze family becomes clear later in the story with the introduction of a messenger from the Bodhisattva Kannon. According to Shūsen'o, Higaki passed the secrets of *ranbyōshi* to a female entertainer named Chishū. Shūsen'o informed his readers that Chishū added poetry (*waka*) to the *rangyoku* dance. Yet, she feared to teach anyone the dance, lest she incur divine punishment.[71] Centuries later, according to *Bushōgoma*, Kan'ami, the founder of the Kanze troupe learned about *rangyoku* from a mysterious, elderly female entertainer. The passage is reminiscent of a noh play when the aged women reveals herself to be the famed dancer of old who has become an agent of the Bodhisattva Kannon after her death.

When Kanze Kan'ami went down from the capital to Higo province, on the evening of the seventeenth day of the eighth month in the sixteenth year of Ōei [1409], Kannon spoke to him from the door of the cave [where he was sleeping] in the middle of the night. Suddenly an old woman appeared from out of nowhere, saying that she had not spoken to someone from the capital for a long time and that she had earned her living as a *shirabyōshi* long ago. She said to Kan'ami that he was the person to receive the revelation of Hase Kannon and that she was the bodhisattva's messenger. She told Kan'ami that she had arrived to transmit the knowledge of *ranbyōshi* to him.[72]

The mysterious stranger offered to teach Kan'ami if he promised that he would pass the knowledge on only to one child in his family, lest he, too, suffer divine punishment. After imparting this knowledge, Kan'ami's benefactor disappeared. He passed these secrets only to his son Zeami, who used the *ranbyōshi* for his play *Higaki*.[73] (Kan'ami died in 1384, long before the events Shūsen'o offered in this story.)

Shūsen'o's conclusion that the divine *ranbyōshi* formed the basis for Zeami's play *Higaki* is a telling ending to his legend. Significantly, he noted after the story that the secret knowledge to *Higaki* was recorded in a text by Kanze Motohiro (d. 1522) written for the warlord and artistic genius Hosokawa Yūsai.[74] But the writing to which Shūsen'o referred was not an actual work by a sixteenth-century master, instead, it was a text that Shūsen'o wrote, *Annotations to Higaki* (*Higaki katazuke*).[75] In other words, the long description in *Bushōgoma* of the uniqueness of the Kanze school's version of *rangyoku* was an advertisement for a text purporting to offer the secret notes to that play written by Shūsen'o himself!

Although Shūsen'o's annotations for the play *Higaki* never saw publication, his depiction of *rangyoku* and other secrets in *Bushōgoma* had a much more lasting impact on noh discourse. His contribution to the discourse on noh theater was his revelation to the public of varying qualities of privately held knowledge about noh and his mythologizing of bloodlines as the primary vehicle for the transmission of that secret information. The irony of his contention that hierarchies of secret knowledge formed the basis for noh lay in the fact that he had to create this secret knowledge himself.

In deploying the names of bogus texts and hinting at tantalizing secret *narai* in *Bushōgoma*, Shūsen'o reversed the accepted use of secret writings dating from the era of Zeami. Whereas Zeami and the compiler of *Hachijō kadensho* cloaked their manuscripts with secrecy, Shūsen'o simply cited the existence of secrets without disclosing their substance. He imagined secret writings as testimonials to abstract knowledge wedded to genealogy. Thus, his veneration of secret knowledge was not a tactic to protect private knowledge, as it had been for medieval noh theorists, but a strategy to authorize his writings. However, in reaffirming the supremacy of the Yamato troupes on the basis of their bloodlines, Shūsen'o made the secret writings of the sort that he could offer relative truths. In contrast, the full transmission of noh's secrets occurred within the Kanze family's blood. Perhaps that is why Shūsen'o's forgeries never came near the printing press.

CHAPTER 6

Print and Order

Utaibon are the guiding laws of our school.

—Fujinami Shisetsu

The organization of occupations as schools (*ryū*) in the seventeenth century began to engender new institutions in the second half of the eighteenth century and led to what scholars have termed "family-head systems" (*iemoto seido*). Today, the term "family head" is synonymous with traditional performing arts such as the tea ceremony, Japanese dance, noh, and flower arrangement. But in the Edo period *iemoto* could be found in pursuits as diverse as swimming, "Dutch learning" (*rangaku*), the martial arts, and cooking. Besides the family head, who is esteemed as the supreme practitioner and teacher of the art, the system depends on lower-ranking professionals, who serve as teachers, and amateur students, whose tuition fees, gifts, and purchases of licenses are the chief revenues for the school.

The development of the prerogatives of the family head marked the defining moment in the foundation of noh and other arts as professions deriving significant revenues from teaching amateur students. Professionalization, as Magali Larson defines it, is a "process by which producers of special services . . . [seek] to constitute and control a market for their expertise."[1] In the Edo period, schools created family-head systems as a way both to optimize their control of expertise and to merchandise knowledge to amateur students.

The chapter examines the role of printed texts in the formation of family-head systems in schools in the eighteenth century. For noh, the availability of printed *utaibon* helped to popularize the art of unaccompanied noh chanting, or *su'utai*, in which a seated chorus in an unstaged performance chants and sings the play. *Su'utai* dates from at least the era of Zeami, and it became an amateur pastime among the nobility and warrior elite when these groups gained access to manuscript copies of noh plays in the sixteenth century. In the Edo period, the publishing industry made *su'utai* an accessible hobby for the rest of society by printing *utaibon*. The popularization of *utaibon* enabled performers to earn a large part of their income by teaching amateur students, who in turn contributed revenues crucial to the development of the *iemoto* system. A further step toward a family-head system occurred when the *iemoto* gained control over publication of *utaibon* and created standardized versions of the noh repertoire. The fifteenth head of the Kanze school, Kanze Motoakira (d. 1774), played a major role in standardizing noh play-books.[2] Motoakira and other noh *iemoto* used publishing to assert their authority not just over *utai* but also over every aspect of their school's performance style. Thus, publishing was crucial to standardizing noh and consolidating the power of the family head.

The Development of Iemoto *and the Ordering of Knowledge*

Institutionally, the family-head system grew out of the various schools that developed in the seventeenth century; ideologically, the system preserved the dominant myth that authority derived from hereditary control of secret knowledge. As we saw in the previous chapter, the tendency to link heredity with expertise intensified in the Edo period under the aegis of the Tokugawa bakufu's policy of rule by status. In the seventeenth century, many occupations developed into schools and emulated the structures of extended families with a main house (*honke*) and branch families. The main house asserted its dominion over the branches by claiming exclusive access to the most profound knowledge in its field because of its direct descent from a great patriarch. The names of such patriarchs—Zeami, Sen no Rikyū, and Ikenobō Sen'ō, to name a few—became household words in the Edo period thanks to the publishing industry, and this publicity contributed to the dominance of the Kanze, Sen, and Ikenobō families over their respective artistic fields. This institutional and intellectual foundation proved the nucleus for the development of the family-head system when the leader of the main house began to assert his absolute authority over the activities of his school.

Family-head systems preserved the hegemonic notion that authority depended on bloodlines and mastery of secret knowledge; however, from the late 1700s the family heads at the pinnacle of their occupations began to interpret their mandate in a new manner. Rather than simply venerate the past or display their family's traditions for a largely passive audience, *iemoto* packaged their received knowledge and aggressively marketed their traditions to amateur students. The motivation for *iemoto* and other members of a school to encourage amateur involvement was predominately financial—to control the revenues brought in by tuition fees, purchases of texts, and licensing. The instruments that family heads used to regulate amateurs also assisted them in tightening control over the activities of professionals in their schools by clarifying hierarchies of power and knowledge that confirmed *iemoto* as supreme.

The scholar Nishiyama Matsunosuke dates the earliest use of the term *iemoto* to 1757.[3] The novelty of the *iemoto* system in the eighteenth century becomes apparent when we look at a leader of a school who lived a century earlier. Kanze Motonobu (d. 1666), the author of *Yoza yakusha mokuroku*, would today be called an *iemoto* since he held the highest hereditary position in the Kanze school of shoulder-drum and had access to the most profound knowledge in his occupation. However, calling Motonobu by this title is anachronistic for two reasons. First, he lacked the power to change the modes of production in his school. Second, he did not recognize the potential for marketing his specialty to amateur students.

Although Motonobu detailed every shred of evidence that supported his lineage's authority on the basis of hereditary descent from famous performers and its reception of the highest expertise from the greatest masters of the past, he made no effort to transfer the authority that he ascribed to his lineage to himself. To judge from *Yoza yakusha mokuroku*, Motonobu's foremost concern was not to demonstrate his supremacy but to equip his descendants with knowledge of their family line in order to ensure the pre-eminence of the Kanze house in the field of shoulder-drumming. In short, Motonobu lacked the pluck and vision of *iemoto* a century later who sought single-handedly to re-craft the received tradition for their own benefit. Motonobu's near-contemporary, Shūsen'o, the author of the noh critique *Bushōgoma*, demonstrated the audacity of later *iemoto* in his marketing of secret noh knowledge to an amateur audience. Yet, as an outsider to the noh world, he lacked the institutional backing to realize his hope of selling the secret noh writings that he attributed to others.

Second, Kanze Motonobu cannot be considered an *iemoto* because he disavowed amateur participation in the noh world. Motonobu used the term "amateur" (*shirōto*) as a mark of derision for performers outside the four Yamato troupes. For him, the dissemination of knowledge to "amateurs" was a heinous offense and a mark of unprofessionalism. Family-head systems, in contrast, developed because of attempts to cultivate amateur involvement through the marketing of an occupation as a hobby, a possible vocation, and a form of spiritual cultivation.[4] Motonobu was concerned more with who knew what in the professional world than with the question of how "professional" knowledge should be packaged for sale to outsiders.

Licensing

Schools became family-head systems when they developed mechanisms to market expertise to amateurs, and this required the development of a licensing system. Nishiyama Matsunosuke has traced the practice of granting licenses to Kūkai, the founder of the Shingon Buddhist sect in Japan, who granted certificates to his advanced students to acknowledge their religious attainments.[5] For noh, the earliest antecedents to licenses were secret writings and other treasures transmitted to select students, which confirmed hierarchies within troupes and empowered relationships between a master and his heir or chief disciple. In the medieval period, Zen Buddhism recognized that a variety of objects could signify the transmission of enlightenment from master to disciple, but by the end of the medieval period documents called "seals of enlightenment" (*inkajō*) became the primary signifiers of religious authenticity. Leading noh performers started granting comparable certificates to their professional disciples by the seventeenth century.[6] Whereas religious masters might grant one certificate to a few top students to recognize their complete mastery of certain expertise, family-head systems created a series of licenses that distinguished many levels of attainment. The tea masters Joshinsai (d. 1751) of the Omotesenke school of tea and his younger brother Ittō

(d. 1771), the eighth-generation master of Urasenke, are credited with transforming their schools into family-head systems by their initiation of a system of seven grades of proficiency. These tea masters issued different licenses for each of the seven levels of training in recognition of students' mastery of the tea procedures (*temae*) appropriate to that level.[7] The Shino school of incense appreciation created nine ranks, each with an appropriate level of transmission from introductory (*nyūmon*) to full initiation (*kaiden*). The school's record, *Shinoryū kōdō monjinroku*, which covers the period from the early eighteenth century to 1846, reveals that only a small number of students advanced to the highest level. Nearly 2,500 people received the introductory transmission, but only fifty-seven attained the highest rank. Besides motivation, commitments of time, energy, and financial resources no doubt restricted access to the higher levels of licenses.[8]

Licensing systems resolved several dilemmas for schools in marketing their expertise to amateur students. First, by offering a series of licenses, schools created a standardized curriculum that they could use to attract students and sustain their interest. Second, licensing empowered schools with a means to regulate the dissemination of secret knowledge. Students received only the knowledge appropriate to their level of training and their ability to pay. Thus, by controlling amateur access to secret knowledge, professionals preserved their own authority and ensured that they monopolized their school's highest wisdom, although students who earned the final license might qualify as teachers and be able to instruct their own students and thus have an incentive to restrict dissemination of knowledge. Further study might win higher advancement in the school. But the position of *iemoto* was always hereditary and not licensed, and the *iemoto* usually retained the exclusive right to grant licenses to students and teachers. Finally, licensing provided schools with significant income. As a rule, the higher the rank, the more expensive the license. Besides being a source of revenue for the head of the school, selling licenses help the noh teacher to augment the money earned from students' monthly fees, which today constitute the main source of income for professional noh performers.

The first amateur students of noh in the Edo period came from the ranks of the Tokugawa bakufu's hereditary retainers (*gokenin*), but the growing popularity of *su'utai*, facilitated by the publishing industry's creation of inexpensive *utaibon*, made study with a professional teacher possible for people in other sectors of society.[9] Although *utaibon* were readily available, learning to sing them required study with an accomplished teacher who taught students to read the musical notation and dispensed his professional wisdom for more challenging works. As in the other performing arts, schools of *su'utai* granted their highest knowledge to only a few disciples. The noh play *Sekidera Komachi*, for instance, was one of the most exalted works for performers of *su'utai* because it confirmed the performer's personal mastery. Kanzawa Teikan (d. 1795), the author of a collection of essays called *Okinagusa*, wrote that *Sekidera Komachi* could be performed only with the permission of the head of the school: "It is a fact that performing *Sekidera Komachi* requires a license from the *iemoto* for the right to perform it and for six additional *narai* pertaining to the work."[10]

As mentioned above, Kanze Motoakira has been viewed as a pivotal figure in establishing the family-head system for noh through his publishing activities, most notably his standardization of *utaibon*. Motoakira's *Revised Book of Noh Plays of the Meiwa Era* (*Meiwa kaisei utaibon*) published in 1765 provided an authorized version of the scripts to 210 noh and systematized the techniques for performing these plays. The crystallization of the family-head system in noh has been dated to the first decades of the nineteenth century when other leaders of noh troupes began to publish standardized *utaibon*, following the lead of Motoakira.[11] To understand Motoakira's accomplishments, we need to place his efforts in the context of the noh world of his time to follow the linkages between the publication of *utaibon*, the growth of amateur interest in studying *su'utai*, and the rise of professional *su'utai* teachers.

Su'utai *and* Utaibon

The art of *su'utai* dates from the late fourteenth century, but it did not become widely popular until the advent of published *utaibon* in the Edo period.[12] In that period, practitioners of linked verse and other genres of poetry studied noh songs to gain familiarity with classical literature. The philosopher Ishida Baigan (d. 1744) recommended the study of noh performance along with the tea ceremony to his disciples.[13] However, the study of *su'utai* spread far beyond a small coterie of literati. Even children studying in temple schools (*terakoya*) learned the basics of *su'utai*.

Popular interest in *su'utai* can be gauged by the numbers of *utaibon* published in the Edo period. Medieval students of *su'utai* relied on handwritten copies of noh texts, and a few collectors managed to amass several hundred *utaibon* manuscripts.[14] The advent of the printing industry in the late sixteenth century made *utaibon* available to a wider audience. Upward of a thousand different *utaibon* editions were published. *Utaibon* represented a good investment for publishers since they were best-sellers throughout the Edo period. An *utaibon* might consist of only one noh song or several hundred. Thirteen *utaibon* published during the years 1670 to 1692 included 100 selections. Typical print runs of *utaibon* ran from 200 to 300 copies.[15] Publishers even created small-size volumes for travelers so that they could take their hobby with them on the road. Professionals accumulated large libraries; the head of the Fukuō school, for instance, claimed in 1721 to own 800 *utaibon*.[16]

The popular excitement over *su'utai* and the revenues to be gained from selling *utaibon* created a market for new plays. According to one calculation, some 2,000 noh were written in the Edo period to be sung as *su'utai*.[17] Some of these embraced subjects far from the typical conceptions of noh, such as unabashed advertisements for restaurants or patent medicines. The Pure Land, Zen, and Nichiren sects penned noh as aides in proselytizing.[18] Other authors created humorous *utai* by inserting off-color puns in works from the traditional repertoire. Educators such as the compiler of the mid-Edo period *Easy to Use Noh Songbook (Ben'yō utaibon)* touted the value of learning noh songs as mnemonic devices for studying other disciplines. This text included fifteen *utai*; three of these were complete noh, and the remainder were short songs. Topics ranged from discourses on arithmetic, religion, and calendars to a catalog of street names in Kyoto, chapter titles in the *Tale of Genji*, and facts about Chinese medicine.[19]

As is clear from Konparu Zenpō's writings, noh performers had taught *su'utai* to amateurs since at least the early sixteenth century, but the specialized profession of *su'utai* teacher crystallized in the Edo period.[20] Kyoto was the center for *su'utai* singing, and the most successful *su'utai* teachers were affiliated with the Shindō and Fukuō schools.[21] The Shindō and Fukuō families, who took the lead in developing the market for professional *su'utai* teachers, were once-independent (*tesarugaku*) noh performers who had joined the Kanze troupe in the early seventeenth century. Although both families were members of the Kanze, each maintained its own distinct interpretations of the Kanze style, a fact that warrants calling them the Shindō and Fukuō schools (*ryū*). Initially, the Shindō had the most success as teachers of *su'utai*, perhaps because of the popularity of their published *utaibon*, which were the versions most frequently published during the mid-seventeenth century. One member of the Shindō school appears to have worked as a *su'utai* teacher in the late 1630s in Kyoto.[22] Later in the century, the Fukuō school achieved dominance over *su'utai* in the Kyoto region and overshadowed its rivals. So powerful was the Fukuō school in the capital that later histories erroneously credited an early master of the Fukuō with creating the art of *su'utai* and bringing it to Kyoto. The Fukuō, who remained part of the Kanze troupe, ultimately fell under the sway of the Kanze family head, whose efforts to control noh in Kyoto spelled an end both to the autonomy of the Fukuō and to the distinct performance-style of Kyoto noh. This process began with Kanze Motoakira.

Noh Theater's First Iemoto—Kanze Motoakira

Kanze Motoakira's chief contributions to the development of the family-head system in noh were his publications, especially *Meiwa kaisei utaibon*.[23] With the Tokugawa bakufu's sanction, he created the earliest and most comprehensive standardized versions of noh plays accompanied by notes on their performance. He thereby asserted the right of the *iemoto* to dictate the content of the received tradition. *Meiwa kaisei utaibon* was not without its critics, but the text served as the basis for subsequent *iemoto* to gain control over the publishing of plays and thereby determine the standards of performance for amateurs and professionals in their school.

Motoakira invoked Zeami's name to justify *Meiwa kaisei utaibon*, although his motivation for publishing the work was more pragmatic. In the introduction to the text, he cited a passage from Zeami's treatise *Sandō*, in which Zeami called for someone to amend the errors in previous texts and create standardized versions. Although Motoakira's audience may not have heard of that particular treatise by Zeami, most would have recognized Zeami as a great playwright and as one of the founding patriarchs of the Kanze troupe. Motoakira made the same reference to Zeami in a published list of the authors of 210 plays, *Nihyakujūban utai mokuroku*. To give Zeami greater importance as a playwright, Motoakira attributed seventy-three plays to him—about forty more than Zeami is believed to have composed. Motoakira also included plays by Zeami that were no longer performed in his Meiwa-era *utaibon*, such as *Akoya no matsu*, *Furu*, and *Matsura*. By documenting Zeami's great impact on the Kanze repertoire, Motoakira cast his efforts to edit noh texts as an act of filial piety to his great ancestor and reminded his readers about the wellspring of his authority. Motoakira evoked Zeami as the consummate troupe leader that he himself strove to become, someone who had mastery over both the private (esoteric) expertise of the profession and what can be termed its "exoteric" performance practices—the public demonstration of expertise. Motoakira had the fortune and political savvy to employ this image of leadership as a means to consolidate his control over the Kanze.

Simply on the basis of their secrecy alone—a product of their limited dissemination—Zeami's manuscripts served as excellent tools for Motoakira to authenticate his mastery over noh's esoteric teachings relative to other members of his troupe. By selecting only top disciples to receive secret writings, Motoakira designated a number of people as worthy of sharing in classified information, an act that helped him reinforce hierarchies and alliances within his troupe. However, what differentiated Motoakira from previous troupe leaders who had likewise used secret writings to trade prestige for arcane knowledge was his special respect for Zeami's treatises. Motoakira not only distributed Zeami's treatises but also added copious notes based on his training in philology, which he gained from study with national learning, *kokugaku*, scholars such as Tayasu Munetake (d. 1771). One of the first texts he allowed to circulate selectively was Zeami's *Learning the Way* (*Shūdōsho*), a treatise which argued that the leader of the troupe possessed the most skill and authority; Motoakira published this text in 1772. He also prepared a version of *Fūshikaden* for publication but died before it appeared in print. Amid the longstanding practice of venerating secret writings solely because of their secrecy and against the general preference for texts devoted to concrete hints on noh performance, *katazuke*, Motoakira's scholarly efforts marked an important step in identifying and explicating Zeami's theoretical ideals. He offered these annotated versions of Zeami treatises to top disciples and to the public, not simply to promote Zeami but so that his authority over noh would be acknowledged.

Motoakira likewise attempted to display mastery over what can be called noh's "exoteric traditions," the nuggets of expertise demonstrated before an audience. He worked hard to popularize noh in the Edo period and revived the practice of holding large, outdoor "benefit" performances. His fifteen-day performance in Edo in 1750 was the first such show in a century and featured the exciting play *Shakkyō*, which piqued popular interest in noh and the Kanze school. Sixty years later, Sasaki Haruyuki, author of *Traces of Unaccompanied Noh Chant Through the Ages (Su'utai yoyo no ato)*, described this event as a seminal moment in the history of noh.[24]

For his revised collection of *utaibon*, which he intended to contain authoritative versions of plays, Motoakira succeeded in obtaining financial backing from the bakufu, which provided him with several loans and the use of its official print shop—a publisher that had never before published a collection of plays. He also enlisted the assistance of prominent *kokugaku* scholars and poets, including his teacher Tayasu Munetake, the poet Katō Enao (d. 1785), and the noted philologist and *Manyōshū* expert Kamo no Mabuchi (d. 1769). Motoakira's team studied the original poems and literary works that were the sources for plays to correct the wording of cited passages. They used red ink to indicate corrections and notations, and added pronunciations to the texts of 210 plays. After Motoakira completed his task, he and his younger brother proceeded to Edo Castle on the twenty-first day of the six month of 1765 to receive a reward from the shogun.[25]

Financial gain has been suggested as an important factor in Motoakira's reason to publish *Meiwa kaisei utaibon*. The Kanze troupe faced economic difficulties in the early eighteenth century, and Motoakira borrowed money from the Tokugawa bakufu several times in the years 1736 to 1740. By publishing an authoritative collection of noh plays, he could capitalize on the renown of his family name and garner a percentage of the lucrative market for *utaibon*. In the Edo period, the most frequently printed *utaibon* followed the style of the Kanze school, yet unlike today, when the head of the Kanze school controls the copyrights to these texts, anyone with a press could print Kanze *utaibon*.[26] The power of Motoakira's office proved a further advantage over the other compilers of noh texts: he could and did order members of the Kanze school to use *Meiwa kaisei utaibon* in place of other texts.[27]

Motoakira had his changes to the plays printed boldly in red ink, and these marks bear witness to his view of his mandate to reinterpret noh's traditions. His revisions consist largely of corrections of noh plays based on older scripts, as well as notes on the correct pronunciations of certain words. In some instances, these changes in pronunciation appear to be purely arbitrary. For instance, he changed the well-known opening words of noh's most famous dance, Okina, from *dō dō tarari* to *tō tō tarari*. The older version is still used by the Konparu, Kongō, and Kita schools.[28] By exchanging one set of (meaningless) syllables for another in noh's most revered work, Motoakira demonstrated that his authority extended into the most ancient and exalted reaches of noh's traditions. Beyond making corrections, Motoakira also rationalized the notation system used to indicate how plays were to be sung. For each play he dictated the appropriate costumes to be worn, the proper masks, the dimensions of the props, blocking, and choreography. He even included the *aikyōgen* part, in which a kyōgen actor appears halfway through a play to recapitulate the plot for the audience.[29]

Motoakira's standardization of variations (*kogaki*) to noh plays in *Meiwa kaisei utaibon* had a great impact on fixing the parameters for artistic interpretation. *Kogaki* are renditions of noh plays that include deviations from the customary costuming or choreography. *Kogaki* help both to demarcate the level of dignity (*kurai*) of a play and to define normative elements. For example, a play usually calling for a dark-colored cloth over a stage property might have a *kogaki* in which a white cloth is used to lend greater gravity to the play. Motoakira listed 250 variations for the 210 noh in *Meiwa kaisei utaibon*, with between one and three variations for each play. He presented nine variations for *Okina* alone. Many of Motoakira's variations had precedents in earlier performance techniques. Others, such as the *kogaki* for the play *Matsukaze*, were his inventions and added to the number of accepted variations employed by the Kanze.[30] Motoakira attached names to all the *kogaki* in *Meiwa kaisei utaibon*, new and old.[31]

The increase in the number of variations disguised the fact that Motoakira fixed the canon of possible renditions of noh plays: defining *kogaki* provided a way to rationalize his control over their use. Heretofore *kogaki* had usually demanded knowledge of one or more *narai*, the vital, secret teachings relating to performance and could only be performed by special dispensation from a teacher, if not from the *iemoto* himself. Noh teachers had been issuing licenses for *narai* since at least the seventeenth century, but Motoakira's systematization of *kogaki* and *narai* created a hierarchy for these esoterica. This hierarchy culminated in ten special *narai* plays, eight of which Motoakira attributed to Zeami, and all of which required the troupe leader's permission to perform.[32] This innovation formed the foundation for the modern licensing system, which ranks plays, *kogaki*, and *narai* according to level of difficulty and dignity and demands increasingly exorbitant amounts from amateurs the higher the level. Motoakira's systematization of *kogaki* variations provided a technology for structuring the hierarchical ranks within the Kanze school by restricting the right to determine a performer's use of a *kogaki* variation (and usually to perform certain plays in the first place) to the *iemoto*. After Motoakira's time, Kanze school performers seeking to make a significant change in a given play had to choose from the variations named by Motoakira for that work.

The drastic narrowing of the noh canon in the Edo period to the modern repertoire, which consists of only a few hundred plays, was yet another legacy of Motoakira's *Meiwa kaisei utaibon*—one that his contemporaries strongly protested. Kanzawa Teikan, himself an amateur student of *su'utai*, singled out the arbitrariness of Motoakira's new collection of noh plays for disapproval. He challenged Motoakira's assertion that he as *iemoto* was correcting the noh handed down from his ancestors, and he pointed to the hundreds of plays not included in *Meiwa kaisei utaibon*, noting that the Fukuō school in Kyoto owned 500 different noh texts. Motoakira's selections were idiosyncratic, Kanzawa pointed out, particularly his inclusion of the play *Ume*, which Motoakira himself had written. He concluded there would be innumerable more noh in the canon if Motoakira had permitted new works.[33]

Despite the voices of protest, Motoakira's rules for noh performance facilitated professionalization by standardizing practices in a manner comparable to the licensing systems in schools of tea ceremony and incense appreciation. The standardization of occupational expertise is in Magali Larson's view a defining moment in the creation of a professional product and a community of professionals: "The standardization or codification of knowledge is the basis on which a professional 'commodity' can be made distinct and recognizable to the potential publics." In the case of noh theater, Motoakira's rules clearly

designated the product of the Kanze school. For each play, only specific costumes, masks, and staging techniques were allowed. As Larson
further notes, professional institutions socialize their members to
identify with the hierarchies and sets of standards upon which their
community is established, and these "homogenizing and unifying effects depend on a standardized body of knowledge."[34] By designating
the *style* of performance created by the Kanze school, Motoakira forti-
fied the construction of a group identity for the members of the
Kanze school as professionals adhering to shared principles. Although
not everyone agreed with Motoakira's innovations—after Motoakira's
death in 1774, the new head of the Kanze troupe ceased publishing
Meiwa kaisei utaibon because of opposition to the work within the
school—later members of the Kanze school adhered to Motoakira's
rules for performance and showed allegiance to the role of the family
head in defining those rules. Motoakira's legacy today is the rigid
world of noh in which a narrow canon of several hundred plays is enacted according to strict rules interpreted according to the views of the
family head.

Iemoto *and Mask Discourse*

Motoakira's efforts to codify the Kanze school's style through his
work on *utaibon* parallel those of his contemporary Kita Hisayoshi
(d. 1829) to standardize masks. Hisayoshi undertook the same goal of
standardization for the Kita as Motoakira had envisioned for the
Kanze. In 1776, he became the first leader of the Kita troupe to issue
utaibon in his name. Hisayoshi may have found his inspiration in
Motoakira and also in schools of incense appreciation, since he had
studied in the Shino school, collecting many of that school's secret
writings and even penning his own treatises on incense appreciation.[35]

Hisayoshi wrote two treatises on masks, *Notes on Masks* (*Kamenfu*)
and *Treatise on Mask Connoisseurship* (*Men mekikigaki*).[36] The first he
intended for a general readership, publishing it in 1797. The second
was completed in the same year as a more detailed, private reference
for himself and later leaders of the Kita school. Both texts recapitulate
older myths about masks, but *Men mekikigaki* is written with more
skepticism in its attempts to reconcile earlier, diverse accounts. In
each text, Hisayoshi presented a definitive list of mask carvers,
grouped according to the categories of divine masters, ten masters, six

masters, masters of the middle period, and masters after the middle period. He also included genealogies of the mask-carving families, the Izeki, Kodama, and Deme. Read together, these two texts provide insight into Hisayoshi's private and public discourse on masks: what he wanted the public to know and what he intended only for a few members of his school, chiefly his successors as family head.

In *Kamenfu*, Hisayoshi restricted himself to a discussion of the genealogy of mask-carving families, but his aim was to challenge the lore carvers told about their profession. He attempted to place mask carvers in chronological order by category, but the work offers little information about the work or styles of individual craftsmen. It begins on a skeptical note, with Hisayoshi explaining that in his fifty years of professional experience he had seen only ten ancient masks (*kosaku*) out of a thousand; moreover, masks from the "middle period" (*chūsaku*), dating to the late fifteenth century, were also relatively rare. He then provided lists of mask-makers and introduced divergent views about them, questioning, for example, whether the carvers Fukurai and Ishiōhyōe were different people, or why the patriarch of all the schools of mask carving, Sankōbō, should be included among the "ten master carvers." He entertained these theories in order to dispel them—Ishiōhyōe and Fukurai were the same person, and Sankōbō belonged among the later six masters not the top ten. Hisayoshi's opportunity to speak definitively about masks enabled him to demonstrate his authority on the topic in this published work.

At the same time that Hisayoshi was proving his expertise about masks to the public, he and the other family heads of noh schools were establishing rules governing the use of masks in performance. As noted above, Kanze Motoakira's *Meiwa kaisei utaibon* specified the precise masks allowed for each play. Innovative actors of the twentieth century as exemplified by Kanze Hisao still lament these rules, which they say limit the actor's ability to change the mood of the performance by selecting any mask.[37] The family head claimed this prerogative for himself: mask use became an expression of the school's artistic style, which he alone claimed the right to determine.

Another element of mask discourse that allowed the family head to strengthen his authority within his school was in his distinction between "original masks" (*honmen*) and copies. By the era of Motoakira and Hisayoshi, almost all the noh masks in the collections of the top troupes were attributed to the greatest carvers, the so-called ten masters (*jissaku*). Yet the historicity of these masks was sometimes questionable. A Sanbasō mask in the former collection of the Kongō troupe (see Color Fig. 2) was long attributed to the carver Nikkō, although some scholars today date it to the Edo period.[38] Whether the leaders of the Kongō troupe in the Edo period considered this mask to be authentic is an interesting question. The early seventeenth-century biography of Toyotomi Hideyoshi, *Taikōki*, as mentioned in Chapter 1, exclaimed that no one could tell the difference between the five ancient masks copied for Hideyoshi by the carver Sumi no Bō and the original masks belonging to the Konparu and Kanze troupes.[39] Similarly, copies by the fourth leader of the Ono Deme house, Deme Tosui (d. 1729) of two *zō'onna* masks, one belonging to the Kanze troupe and the other to the Kita troupe, have been noted for their faithfulness to the originals.[40] The distinctiveness of these two masks demonstrates Tosui's skill as a master replicator; his own works would be practically undetectable if not for evidence such as a signature or seal on the back. Tosui is representative of carvers of the Edo period who no longer created new types of masks but concentrated instead on carefully replicating every detail of older models. It is easy to imagine how skilled carvers who made a living from their ability to copy older models faithfully might become expert forgers; this posed a direct threat to noh family heads or anyone else who sought to use "original masks." Thus, at the same time noh performers claimed to own vast collections of authentic masks by the ten masters, they showed tremendous anxiety about the ability of mask carvers of later periods to replicate these same models and hence about the authenticity of the masks in their own collections.

The term "original mask" (*honmen*) developed in response to the increased homage paid to older masks against the backdrop of the corresponding proliferation of copies. *Honmen* were supposed to be prototypes, designed when the corresponding role in a play was first created. Consequently, only the oldest masks attributable to the ten masters and perhaps the six masters could be said to qualify as "originals." Possession of original masks testified to a direct link to a school's early history and the foundation of noh as a whole; even today the family head's *honmen* are often the object of veneration and considered sacred.[41] John Berger—with reference to Walter Benjamin—spoke to a similar revaluation of originals and copies with the advent of photography and the availability of reproductions of paintings: "The unique-

ness of the original work now lies in it being the original of a reproduction. It is no longer what its image shows that strikes one as
unique; its first meaning is no longer to be found in what it says, but
what it is."[42] Value of the original, in other words, depends on its authentic uniqueness.

Anxiety over originals and copies was not simply the effect of the
growth in the mask carvers' skills or of the parallel development of
printed copies of "secret treatises"; it also reflects the rise of the power
of the family head to determine authoritative customs and authenticity, as well as the competing claims of rival troupes to ownership of
"original" masks. The Kita troupe claimed to own the original *zō'onna*
mask, attributed to Tatsuemon (late 14th c.?), even though Zōami
(ca. 1400) allegedly invented this mask and named it. This meant that
the Kita "original" predated the invention of the mask. Kanze Motoakira attempted to catalog all the original masks held by the five noh
troupes in his 1771 *Shoke menme roku*, and he came up with a total of
seventy-five masks. His list exposed the arbitrary nature of the designations of certain masks as "originals," a product of the lack of consensus regarding them.[43]

Hisayoshi intended *Men mekikigaki* to be a guide for his heirs in
disentangling the competing claims of performers and mask carvers
about masks. To that end, he detailed points of mask connoisseurship,
discussed techniques for mask carving, painting, and lacquering, and
tried to reach definitive conclusions about the style of certain mask
carvers, all with the aim of empowering his heirs by giving them the
acumen to judge real masks from copies. Hisayoshi even revealed the
methods that mask carvers used to age masks artificially by using
agents made from soot and oil.[44] In *Men mekikigaki* he also embarked
on more wide-reaching discussions that challenged the dominant notions about mask traditions, the same traditions that he had presented
to the public in *Kamenfu*. For example, as if to show the constructed
nature of categories of mask carvers, in *Men mekikigaki* Hisayoshi
bent the rules of accepted categorization he had set forth in *Kamenfu*
by including seventeen mask carvers in his list of the so-called six masters. Hisayoshi preserved the grouping of Prince Shōtoku, Fujiwara
Fuhito, Kōbō Daishi, and Kasuga in the category of "divine masters,"
but he almost completely dismissed the works attributed to these
greats in this private text:

The aforementioned works [by the divine masters] are rarely seen and difficult to distinguish. On careful inspection it is difficult to determine their authenticity. That being said, the reverse sides of these masks are unusually rare and different from ordinary works. But does that make these works real? The painting on all of these works should not be taken as original, but considered as having been retouched later. In spite of the fact these were repainted, none are later than works of the middle period (*chūsaku*) [fifteenth century].[45]

Hisayoshi backed away from completely dismissing the attributions of masks to the divine masters, but he affirmed that these works had been retouched by later hands and suggested that they may even be the products of later ages.

Challenging accepted classification schemes for old masks was only one step away from dismissing the authenticity of the old masks themselves. Hisayoshi stated bluntly that most masks said to be ancient were in fact later copies, and he instructed his successors to make *Men mekikigaki* their guide in separating original masks from copies. Hisayoshi made that claim more explicitly later in the text when he asserted that masks attributed to Prince Shōtoku were often the work of Tokuwaka instead and that Himi may have created masks attributed to Nikkō and Miroku. Indeed, he attributed most of the masks reputed to be ancient masterpieces to the leaders of the Deme and Izeki families and dated them to the late sixteenth and early seventeenth centuries. He gave examples of misattributions for almost every great carver, and he wrote that many of the masks said to be by Shakuzuru and Sankōbō were actually by Izeki Chikanobu, the founder of the Ōmi Izeki house. Similarly, masks attributed to Tokuwaka and Ko'ushi (also read as Kōji) were actually done much later by Chikanobu's successor, Izeki Jirō. He cautioned readers to look for the name "Izeki" on the back of the mask or for special marks appearing just above the nose that would indicate a later period than that of the ten masters.

With mask attribution and use depending largely on the claims of mask carvers and the leaders of noh troupes, Hisayoshi wanted to clarify which versions members of the Kita school should follow. Thus he dispelled two theories held by the Konparu school: the claims that Ippen was another name for Shakuzuru and that the Magojirō mask belonging to the Konparu had been carved by Bōya Magojirō, one of the six masters. In another instance, Hisayoshi presented the definitive methods the Kita school should use to differentiate masks made by Shimotsuma Shōshin and how the origin of the mask used in the play *Kumasaka* should be explained. For Hisayoshi, standardization of mask traditions depended as much on learning the truth about masks as it did on finalizing definitive interpretations for the subsequent leaders of his school to follow.

Images of Iemoto *in the Histories of* Su'utai

The publications of Kanze Motoakira and Kita Hisayoshi illustrate the self-consciousness of these two leaders of their powers as family head in the eighteenth century; other sources reveal how other noh actors interpreted the role of the family head in this period. Sasaki Haruyuki's *Su'utai yoyo no ato*, a short history of the art of performing *utai*, offers such a perspective on the institution of the family head. Although written by an amateur student on behalf of his teacher, the work justifies one family's transference of allegiance from one family head to another.

Sasaki Haruyuki stated in the preface to *Su'utai yoyo no ato* that his teacher had requested that he serve as an objective author and write the work.[46] Sasaki's teacher was a professional *su'utai* teacher in Kyoto named Asano Eisoku (also known as Asano Yoshitari; b. 1782). Eisoku was the eighth-generation head of the Asano family and an early historian of noh. Sasaki mentioned in his preface that he had used many of Eisoku's scholarly works, including *Transmission of Unaccompanied Noh Songs* (*Tomogara jujuden*), as references in composing *Su'utai yoyo no ato*. Eisoku apparently viewed the composition of the work as a delicate but essential project that required a seemingly unbiased author but one armed with the right information. The work was intended to explain why Asano Eisoku's family left the Fukuō subschool and become directly affiliated with the Kanze *iemoto*. The text itself was published seven years after the Asano joined the Kanze school in 1811.[47] *Su'utai yoyo no ato* affords a glimpse at what noh professionals, particularly Asano Eisoku, valued in a family head and the reasons one could use to condemn one *iemoto* and support another.[48]

Some have concluded that *Su'utai yoyo no ato* was written to defend the rights of the Fukuō family head against the Kanze, but that appraisal considers only one dimension of the text's argument.[49] The text does explicate that the Fukuō family's rights as *iemoto* of *su'utai* in the Kyoto region preceded those of the Kanze. However, the initial glorification of the Fukuō leaders was not a clear mandate for their control of noh in Kyoto, as the subsequent relationship between the Fukuō and the Kanze portrayed in the text reveals. Specifically, the text's portrait of the Fukuō school is initially quite glowing, but the author's tone gradually darkens as he describes later Fukuō leaders. The work is vague about the reasons the Fukuō school lost its momentum in later decades, but the author's contrast of the greatness of the Fukuō school's early leader, Sōha (also known as Hattori Sōha; d. 1703), with the arbitrary character of later *iemoto* such as Sōseki (d. 1721) provided ample justification for the Asano's decision to leave the Fukuō. The fact that the work was printed in Kyoto meant that it was intended for a local audience, probably of *su'utai* students who might be curious about an inside history of the art, the relations between the Kanze troupe and the Fukuō school within it, as well as the background of their local teachers' decisions to affiliate themselves more closely with the Kanze school.

Sasaki Haruyuki's portrait of Fukuō Sōha presents an idealized *iemoto*. Sōha enjoyed all the hereditary prerequisites of a grand master as the son of the younger brother of the ninth leader of the Kanze troupe and the son-in-law of the second head of the Fukuō family.[50] Sasaki wrote that after resigning the leadership of the Fukuō school, Sōha retired to Kyoto, taking the family name of Hattori, an early name of the Kanze family. *Su'utai yoyo no ato* explained that both Sōha and his son and heir Sōseki were referred to by the name Kanze during their lifetimes because of their blood relation to the Kanze. The Fukuō also lived in a Kyoto mansion belonging to the Kanze family.[51]

From Sasaki's perspective, an *iemoto* must be a consummate artist; consequently, his main technique for lauding Sōha was to praise his mastery of the art of *su'utai*. He credited Sōha with the creation of *su'utai* and its longevity, calling him the "father of the art."[52] He wrote: "From the time when Hattori Sōha came to Kyoto in the eighth year of the Kanbun era [1668] to the time when Sōseki assumed leadership, fifty-four years passed. Even though Sōha has passed from the world, how could the art of *su'utai* ever come to an end? Now, even a century later, this art is still transmitted continuously."[53] In Sasaki's view, the art of *su'utai* continued because of Sōha's greatness—and despite the mediocrity of Sōha's descendant, Sōseki. As a further illustration of Sōha's prowess, Sasaki retold anecdotes in which Sōha triumphed

over other performers. In one, the young Sōha was summoned to accompany a famous drummer named Kadono.[54] Kadono bragged that
he could play any song that Sōha could sing. In retaliation for Kadono's arrogance, Sōha began singing *Sarashina no kusemai*, a specialty
of his school. Kadono did not know the tune, and he could not play a
single beat. The crestfallen drummer later wrote a letter to Sōha to
apologize. Sasaki noted that the letter was still in the possession of the
Fukuō family and that the same story could be found in Kanzawa
Teikan's *Okinagusa*. Sasaki concluded his portrait of Sōha to suggest
that Sōha's spirit continued to guide the development of the art after
his death.[55]

Sōha's artistic legacy may have continued a century after his death,
but Sasaki took a less flattering view of Sōha's heirs. He recorded the
words of one of Sōha's top students, Takemura Sadakatsu (d. 1698),
lamenting Sōha's passing since he had no qualified successor. Sasaki
explained that Takemura could not become the student of Sōha's heir,
Sōseki, for three reasons: Sōseki was too young, was not an established performer, and had a difficult temperament.[56] *Su'utai yoyo no
ato* also narrated Takemura's many conflicts with Sōseki, which pre-
cipitated Takemura's eventual dismissal from the Fukuō school in
1694. Sasaki faulted Sōseki's arrogant demeanor for Takemura's dismissal, not to mention the school's many other problems.

Sasaki's portrait of Sōseki defined the model family head through a
negative example. Ideally, an *iemoto* was supposed to be like Sōha—
someone who had the talent and charisma fitting to his hereditary position. Although Sōseki could claim the hereditary right to the highest
post in the Fukuō school, he lacked the maturity and ability required.
From Sasaki's perspective, Sōha's chief disciples were the real
torchbearers of his artistic legacy. He illustrated this point by describing Takemura's establishment of a monthly *su'utai* recital at Kyoto's
Sōrinji temple in Sōha's honor.[57]

Sasaki explained that other former students of Sōha also challenged
the legitimacy of Sōseki and gave different rationale for doing so. Sōseki expelled another disciple, Ogawa Toyoyuki, for publishing a text
of 100 *utai* in 1701.[58] Ogawa asked Sōseki's permission to publish his
text in 1699, but Sōseki, who had published a collection of seventy-two
plays the previous year, prohibited Ogawa from publishing. Ogawa,
for his part, sought to bypass Sōseki's authority by offering the following tale. As Ogawa was enjoying the recuperative waters at Arima hot

spring in Settsu, he fell asleep. A voice came to him in a dream praising his singing ability. When he awoke, he discovered a manuscript beside his pillow with the name of the founder of the Fukuō lineage, Fukuō Moritada, written on it.[59] Ogawa grew excited when he realized that no similar text existed in the library of the Fukuō family. Sasaki Haruyuki, who retold this tale in *Su'utai yoyo no ato*, conceded that Ogawa's fame grew because of this "discovery."[60] Although Sōseki could enforce his control over the publication of the school's texts by banishing offenders like Ogawa, his actions revealed his failure to rule by example not force. By reciting these incidents, Sasaki laid the groundwork for presenting the reasons why his teacher's family, the Asano, chose to leave the Fukuō to join the Kanze.

Besides listing reasons why professionals might turn against an *iemoto*, Sasaki described the positive ways in which professionals benefited from close contact with the family head. Blood ties with the *iemoto*'s lineage were an important way to build prestige for *su'utai* teachers, as they had long proved to be for noh actors. Sasaki mentioned that his teacher's family, the Asano, had ties by marriage to both the Kanze and the Fukuō houses.[61] Performing with the *iemoto* was another way that bonds between the head of the school and its members were forged and maintained. The Fukuō school and its rivals conducted monthly recitals in temples in Kyoto. *Kyō habutae oridome* (1689), a guidebook to Kyoto for tourists, lists several such monthly *su'utai* performances. On the seventeenth day of each month, for instance, the students of the Shindō school assembled at Kōdaiji temple for a monthly concert.[62] Programs for the Fukuō school's monthly performance at Sōrinji temple were sold in teahouses in Kyoto's entertainment quarter of Gion.[63] The recitals gave students the chance to showcase their talents and *su'utai* teachers the opportunity to increase their reputation locally and possibly attract more students.

Professionals might perform *su'utai* monthly with the Fukuō *iemoto* in small, public concerts such as these, but these events could not compare with the renown garnered by taking the stage with the leader of the Kanze troupe in an outdoor performance of several full-length noh plays complete with costumes, musicians, and a large audience. *Su'utai yoyo no ato* presented a lengthy account of a 1702 performance by the thirteenth leader of the Kanze troupe, Kanze Shigenori (d. 1716), in Kitano in northern Kyoto to show that performing with the Kanze troupe leader convinced many Fukuō school professionals to switch to the Kanze.[64] The performance lasted for four days, and Sasaki listed the names of the important actors who came with the Kanze troupe leader from Edo and the twenty-four performers of the Fukuō who accompanied them. Many of the players on the Fukuō side who took positions in the production in the chorus later became Kanze Shigenori's students—Inoue Jirō, Hayashi Konomu, and Iwai Shichirō.[65] Significantly, all these families later left the Fukuō school and transferred their allegiance to the Kanze, and the Asano, Inoue, Hayashi and Iwai houses, along with the Sono, became the dominant Kanze school teachers of *su'utai* in Kyoto, the so-called five Kanze houses of Kyoto (*Kyō Kanze no goken'ya*). Curiously, in his narrative of Kanze Shigenori's grand Kyoto performance in *Su'utai yoyo no ato*, Sasaki failed to mention what the Fukuō *iemoto*, the great Sōha, did during that event and chose instead to focus on the future disciples of the Kanze *iemoto*.

Studying with the *iemoto* provided an even stronger link with him and implied access to important knowledge that could increase one's professional status. Sono Kyūbee, for instance, traveled to Edo to study with Kanze Motoakira in 1764. The Katayama family, who later succeeded the Fukuō as the leading representatives of the Kanze school in Kyoto, owed their high status to their direct apprenticeship with the Kanze *iemoto*. The founder of the Katayama house, Katayama Toyosada (d. 1728) moved to Kyoto from Katayama village in Tanba province and became an amateur noh performer.[66] Toyosada's son and grandson both went to Edo to train with the fourteenth Kanze *iemoto*, and their apprenticeship proved their key to fame.[67] In 1759 the Katayama became the Kanze school's chief lieutenants in Kyoto when Fukuō Sōseki's widow, Chisei, died in 1759.[68] The Katayama family maintains this post to this day.

To judge from *Su'utai yoyo no ato*, the Kanze *iemoto* also mediated disputes among actors, something that the Fukuō leader did not do. After Sono Kyūbee returned to Kyoto from studying with Kanze Motoakira in Edo, he planned to stage a *su'utai* performance. Inoue Jirō, Hayashi Konomu, and Iwai Shichirō promised to perform with Sono, but failed to show up. When Sono reported the incident, Motoakira expelled all three of the offenders from the Kanze school. Inoue and Hayashi made a special trip to Edo to beg Motoakira's pardon. Iwai waited until Motoakira came to Kyoto in 1772 and received a pardon.[69] The incident reveals the negative consequences of not conforming to professional etiquette, the importance of membership in the Kanze school, and the right of the *iemoto* to define and enforce the parameters of professional behavior, which professionals could not ignore.

Power in a profession, writes Magali Larson, is the "contents of [professional] knowledge and the legitimate conditions of access to it."[70] The *iemoto* system served both functions for noh by providing a final authority on the art in the person of the family head and a method by which professionals could gain knowledge and prestige by building a relationship with that leader. The interaction between the *iemoto* and other professionals could become a purely top-down relationship if the *iemoto* attempted to consolidate all powers for himself. However, *iemoto* like Fukuō Sōseki who acted arbitrarily faced challenges from other professionals in their school. Although Kanze Moto-akira received his share of criticism for altering the Kanze school's repertoire with his publication of the *Meiwa kaisei utaibon*, he had a much firmer claim to authority in his school relative to the Fukuō, given the superiority of his lineage. All *iemoto* had to be able to mediate between their disciples, and their ability to do so depended on the strength of their personal relations with the members of their school. Personal ties not founded on heredity or marriage could be constructed through apprenticeship and joint performances.

Epilogue—The Demise of the Kyoto Kanze

The Asano family's shift of allegiance from the Fukuō to the Kanze was a short-lived victory, for the family's demise illustrates the extent of the powers assumed by the Kanze *iemoto* in the twentieth century. Shortly before Sasaki completed *Su'utai yoyo no ato* in 1818, the Asano family had joined the ranks of other former top disciples of the Fukuō school—the Hayashi, Inoue, Sono, and Iwai—as the top practitioners of the Kanze school in Kyoto. In this capacity, the five Kanze houses benefited from the prestige derived from their association with the Kanze *iemoto*. At the same time, their geographic separation from the Kanze *iemoto* in Edo granted them a degree of autonomy in setting their own standards of performance. Although full members in the Kanze school, the five Kanze houses preserved styles of singing different from that of Edo. The noh historian Nonomura Kaizō wrote that when he lived in Kyoto in 1908, Kyoto audiences still identified not only a distinct Kyoto-Kanze sound but also the unique styles of the Iwai and Sono families.[71] This diversity ended in the early twentieth century, when the Asano and the other Kanze school performers in Kyoto faced increased pressure from the Kanze *iemoto* to conform to the "standard" modes of singing used in Tokyo. When Kanze Moto-yoshi (also known as Kanze Hisashi; d. 1920) first performed in Kyoto, the audiences in Kyoto scorned his manner of singing *utai*.[72] After be-ing adopted into the Katayama house in 1892, Motoyoshi reacted by waging a campaign aided by his brother, the twenty-third Kanze *iemoto* Kiyokado (d. 1911), to promote the Tokyo method of singing *utai* as the sole standard for the Kanze school, and he tried to convince the Haya-shi, Inoue, Ōe, and Ōnishi families in Kyoto to abandon the distinct Kyoto style of singing in favor of his "standard" interpretations.

Motoyoshi's son Kanze Sakon became *iemoto* in 1911 and continued his father's crusade against the Kyoto style of singing.[73] In 1920, in the school's magazine, *Kanze*, Sakon stated: "My aim is to standardize the *utai* of this school, like drinking the same brand name of beer from the same brewery." Toward that end, Sakon continued Kiyokado's practice of sending loyal Kanze disciples from other parts of Japan to Kyoto, such as members of the Sugiura, Urata, Yamamoto, and Ueda families. He himself made monthly trips to Kyoto to make certain that the Kanze school members were conforming.[74] Sakon's role model in all of this could have easily had been Kanze Motoakira, as it could have been his father, for like Motoakira, he revised the school's *utaibon* to facilitate the standardization of performance practices.[75] In his memoirs, Sakon made specific mention of his admiration for Mo-toakira's *Meiwa kansei utaibon*, and he even annotated Motoakira's text on noh masks in the same work.[76] Also, like his great predecessor, Sakon gathered an impressive array of intellectuals for his *utaibon* pro-ject, enlisting top noh scholars including Nonomura Kaizō, Nogami Toyoichirō, Nose Asaji, Kobayashi Shizuo, and Miyake Noboru. Sa-kon's aim in his *utaibon* project, as his student and collaborator Fuji-nami Shisetsu described it, was to make changes to the words of the plays and also to how they were performed.[77] He explicitly designated the sound level (*onkai*) for sung passages and added further notations designating pronunciation (*furigana*). He also ordered for the first time that all the 210 plays included in the work be fit into the five-category schema for categorizing plays. Sakon succeeded in forcing

Kyoto actors to conform to his standards by invoking his authority on the basis of his mastery of ancient writings in his possession.[78] Before a performance of the play *Fujito* in Kyoto in 1938, Sakon briefly discussed the technicalities of singing the play in which he made reference to his authority. He exclaimed, "The basis of this discussion derives not from some decision about the way things should be. . . . I, Kanze Sakon, perform this and interpret it this way as a result of my research in numerous writings as head of the Kanze school; therefore, I speak with confidence in describing what constitutes the Kanze school and the art of the school's top master."[79] In asserting the supremacy of the Kanze family's style of performing noh, Kanze Sakon established that the Kanze family head was the final authority, notwithstanding any regional differences or customs. The *utaibon* that Sakon published are still used by the Kanze school today. Of the five "Kyoto Kanze families," only the Hayashi adopted the style favored by the *iemoto*. And only it survives; the remainder disappeared.[80] In retrospect, the trend toward standardization and adherence to the authority of the *iemoto* to set these guidelines did apparently bring order to the professional product of the members of the Kanze troupe but at the sake of the loss of individual and local interpretations of that style.

CHAPTER 7

Rituals

Actors and scholars today are just as apt to compare noh to a ritual as they are to another performing art. The slow pace, the highly codified gestures used in acting and dancing, the low-pitched chanting of the chorus, and the drummers' howling calls all evoke a "ritualistic" feel, to the point that the term "ritual" has become a cliché for noh, as have the words "ceremonial," "liturgical," and "hypnotic."[1] The close associations between noh and ritual are seen as more than metaphors. Some have suggested that noh originated in the shaman's trance or in the ceremonies enacted at medieval religious institutions. However, as Chapter 3 described, noh and ritual became most closely associated with the Edo period, to the point that the noh performed during that era is called "ritual theater" (*shikigaku*). This ritual theater is said to be the product of the warrior government's patronage of noh: in return for receiving stipends from the Tokugawa bakufu, actors performed in a style pleasing to their patrons and changed their modes of performance and their repertoire. The legacy of these changes, it is argued, are still visible in the refined noh drama seen today.

In modern noh discourse, the term "ritual" is also closely associated with the dance of Okina. Okina has been important to noh since the days of Zeami in the late fourteenth century, and its exact relationship to noh and its meaning have been debated since then. The so-called ritual aspects of the dance are reversals of the typical dramaturgical conventions of noh: secret ceremonies before the performance, the donning of masks onstage in full view of the audience, and distinct forms of performance. Many consider Okina the historical basis of noh drama, and Okina is a familiar point of comparison for delineating the salient features of noh. Okina is both noh's origin and its difference.

Okina and the noh performed for the Edo-period shoguns and at other occasions may indeed have had "ritualistic" features, but the concept of noh as a ritual theater is a modern one, created decades after the fall of the Tokugawa bakufu during a period of institutional crises for noh and of social transformation for Japan. An "invented tradition" of the Meiji (1868–1912) period, ritual was invoked as noh's past and mediated how noh was to be understood in the present.[2] Remaining undefined, the concepts of noh theater and ritual were played off each other to produce meaning, first as a medium of ultranationalism in the service of the modern state and, then in the post–World War II era, as a myth in the service of the noh profession.

Ritual/Theater

The Japanese term for noh as a ritual theater is *shikigaku*, which the *Kōjien* dictionary defines as "an entertainment used in ceremonies." This definition offers little information about what *shikigaku* looked like as a performing art compared to noh, except that it was somehow more "ritualistic." The dictionary further notes that "the term generally refers to noh and kyōgen performed for the Edo bakufu."[3] This definition assumes that the audience is the primary catalyst for the ritualization of noh and that noh became a ritual theater in the Edo period under the aegis of warrior government.

Based on such a definition, a history of ritual theater would begin with the establishment of warrior patronage of noh. The dean of modern historical studies of noh, Nose Asaji, set the course for this mode of analysis in his monumental *Thoughts on the Origin and Development of Noh* (1938), which traces the development of noh up to the sixteenth century. Nose identified what he believed were the antecedents to Tokugawa-era ritual theater, and he presented his findings in a short chapter titled "*Sarugaku* as the Ritual Theater for Warriors." According to his chronology, noh served religious institutions in the Heian and Kamakura periods and survived due to their patronage. The Muromachi shoguns and powerful warrior houses began to sponsor actors in the fourteenth century, and their patronage gradually changed noh.

All the [medieval] daimyo had their own favorite noh actors. For example, the Akamatsu family liked the Kongō troupe. The Hosokawa favored the Kanze troupe. The Hōjō family at Odawara, likewise, supported the

Hōshō troupe. Similarly, the Konparu troupe, through its marriage connections to the Kanze troupe, was subsequently employed by warrior
houses. Each of the *sarugaku* troupes sought daimyo as patrons. Therefore,
we can imagine that the *sarugaku* troupes were increasingly able to improve their art as a result.[4]

By the Edo period, Nose concluded, noh existed solely because of the
patronage of the warrior class and served the warriors' needs for a ritual performing art.[5] He associated the ritualization of noh with the establishment of a patronage system that began with Toyotomi Hideyoshi's provision of stipends to the leaders of the four Yamato noh
troupes.

Although the basic dynamics of the patronage system are known,
how warriors may have influenced the aesthetics of noh is uncertain.
Ritual theater is considered the by-product of warrior patronage, perhaps an expression of the warrior's artistic tastes or an attempt to secure authority through philosophy or mysticism. Omote Akira and
Amano Fumio, in their authoritative history of noh, dub the Edo period the "age of ritual theater" (*shikigakuki*). Like the compilers of the
Kōjien dictionary, they equate *shikigaku* with noh and kyōgen performed for the Tokugawa shoguns.[6] Although the authors briefly
problematize their portrait of the age of ritual theater by noting that
some actors employed by the warrior elite did not perform ritual
theater and that others active in Osaka and Kyoto had no relation to
ritual theater, they devote most of their history of noh in the Edo period to the study of Tokugawa patronage. This approach does provide
details about what happened at the shogun's castle, but no space is devoted to the roles of the performers in shaping the meaning of their
work and the ability of audiences to interpret a single play in different
ways.[7] As the authors admit, Edo Castle was only one venue for noh
performance in the Edo period, and the ritual-theater thesis does not
encompass the large, outdoor benefit performances (see Fig. 7.1),
smaller "street-corner" (*tsuji*) shows, the noh enacted regularly at festivals, and the extremely popular pastime of *su'utai*.[8] Not only does
the ritual-theater theory deny the diversity of Edo period noh, but it
also ignores variations in noh style, such as the pronounced regional
differences in singing noh even within the same school.

Other scholars define "ritual theater" more specifically, but these
definitions are equally as problematic. Donald Keene has suggested

Fig. 7.1 Scene from the 1848 scroll *Subscription Noh of the Kōka Era* (*Kōka kanjin nō emaki*) depicting a performance in Edo by the Hōshō school of the play *Funa Benkei* on the seventh day of a fifteen-day performance. This was the last subscription noh in the premodern era. Courtesy of the Hōsei University Institute of Nōgaku Studies.

that the Edo bakufu imparted "Confucian" elements to noh: "The shoguns, devoted to Confucian doctrines, considered rites and music to be essential elements of government . . . the gravity and stately movements of noh won favor at the shogun's court, which was run according to the decorum imposed by the Confucian code."[9] Keene, however, does not mention the specific "Confucian codes" that the Edo bakufu used to mold noh into ritual theater.

More problematic is his chronology of the development of ritual theater. Keene dates the origin of ritual theater to the reigns of the first shogun, Tokugawa Ieyasu, and his three successors (1603–80). Yet, as Herman Ooms's research has illuminated, the first four Tokugawa shoguns paid little attention to Confucianism and did not favor it.[10] Ooms's study also contradicts the similar conclusions of the scholar Nakamura Yasuo: "Noh became the official ceremonial art (*shikigaku*) of the Tokugawa bakufu, just as Confucianism became the official philosophy of the bakufu-clan system."[11] It appears that the ambiguity of the term "ritual theater" in prior historiography and the wealth of implications of the word "ritual" have fed fantasies about a ritual theater and what that may have looked like in the service of the state. The historical record does not, however, sustain these visions.

Shikigaku may be associated with the Edo period, but the word itself dates only to the end of that era, at the earliest. *Shikigaku* does not appear in any major Tokugawa-era dictionaries, including the *Nippo jisho* published by Portuguese missionaries in 1604; *Wakun no shiori*, edited by the *kokugaku* scholar Tanikawa Kotosuga (d. 1776) and published in 1777; the nineteenth-century *Gagen shūran*, compiled by Ishikawa Masamochi (d. 1830); and *Rigen shūran*, edited by Murata Ryōa (d. 1843).[12] The early twentieth-century noh historian, Ikenouchi Nobuyoshi, whose monograph on Edo-period noh remains the standard reference, wrote that he could find no instance of the term *shikigaku* in primary sources about noh for the Edo bakufu.[13] Consequently, although *shikigaku* is synonymous with Edo-period noh today, it does not appear to be a technical term in use in the legal or intellectual discourse of the Edo period. This makes it a historiographic, not a historical term, for the Edo period.

As a historiographic term, the usage of *shikigaku* is imprecise and provides an example of a *différance*, a term coined by Jacques Derrida and described by Pauline Rosenau as "a structuring principle that suggests definition rests not on the entity itself but in its positive and negative references to other texts [in which] meaning changes over time, and ultimately the attribution of meaning is put off, postponed, deferred, forever."[14] In other words, "ritual theater" joins together two ill-defined terms to apparently create a new meaning, which is itself ultimately not defined. On the one side, is the word "ritual," a term coined in the nineteenth century whose meaning has been debated ever since.[15] As Richard Schechner has noted, "Even to say it in one word, ritual, is asking for trouble. Ritual has been so variously defined—as concept, praxis, process, ideology, yearning, experience, function—that it means very little because it means too much."[16] One might also define "theater" in a number of ways. Certainly, as the present work explores, what constituted "noh theater," for instance, has been a politically charged and contested matter throughout noh's six-hundred-year history. Consequently, the study of the historiography of ritual theater should begin by examining when and why these terms came to be joined together and the meanings that were generated as a result of this union.

The Invention of a Ritual Theater

The origins of ritual theater, if they are to be found, lie in the late nineteenth century not the seventeenth. Ritual theater was a tradition invented in the Meiji period: a concept that gradually developed through the combined effort of government agencies, aristocrats, and scholars, first, in an effort to emulate Western opera and, second, to transform noh into a medium supporting ultra-nationalism and militarism. That is to say, ritual theater makes its appearance at the moment that it was said to have disappeared.

The notion of ritual theater surfaced at a time of seminal transition for noh and for Japanese society as a whole. After the Meiji Restoration in 1868, noh performers lost their government stipends and their most generous patrons. Like the samurai who lost their status and salaries in the early years of Meiji, many performers were forced to seek other employment and became tobacconists, druggists, priests, and gardener's helpers. A few performers, such as Hōshō Kurō XVI (d. 1917) and Umewaka Minoru I (d. 1909), predicted the extinction of their art.[17] However, unlike the samurai who had lost not only their status but also the rationale for their existence with the formation of a modern conscript army in 1873, noh performers had skills that were still in demand, providing they could be marketed in the changing social setting.

Two groups came to the aid of noh in the Meiji era, and these two groups formulated the invented tradition of noh as a ritual theater. The first group was the Meiji government, beginning with individual officials, chiefly members of the court nobility, and later the Imperial Household Ministry (Kunaishō), the government office that managed the ceremonial, official, and personal affairs of the emperor and imperial family. The Household Ministry became the most important financial patron of noh in the Meiji period, and its top officials headed the main organizations supporting noh. The second group pivotal in forming the myth of ritual theater consisted of scholars, including historians in the direct employ of the state and scholars of literature active in the noh associations under the Household Ministry's shadow.

The catalyst for the Meiji government's interest in noh was its experience dealing with the West. In 1871, Minister of the Right Iwakura Tomomi (d. 1883) and other top members of the government embarked on an eighteen-month tour of America and Europe to improve diplomatic relations and scrutinize Western society. The historian Kume Kunitake (d. 1931), one of the fifty people accompanying the mission, served as Iwakura's personal secretary. According to Kume's account, during its visit to Paris in 1872, the Japanese contingent was escorted to a large hall, which they at first assumed was a palace. They were astounded to learn that they had been led to a theater to witness the performance of an opera. Iwakura was no doubt relieved to learn that this was not an insult but the French government's custom for entertaining foreign delegations.[18]

The visit to the opera made a strong impression on Iwakura, who concluded that, like France, Japan must provide a suitably refined entertainment for foreign dignitaries. He decided that noh was the closest performing art to Western opera, and he lobbied for government support. Why did Iwakura choose noh? The conservative scholar of literature and self-proclaimed expert on ritual Akabori Matajirō explained in 1920 that the ancient court music, *gagaku*, was considered too old-fashioned and the *shamisen* music used in the rambunctious Kabuki theater too crass. Western theater was inappropriate because, like Westerners themselves, it "reeked of butter." Classical noh was the obvious choice, according to Akabori.[19]

Iwakura had the chance to try a noh performance out on a foreign audience at his own residence during the visit of former U.S. President Ulysses S. Grant to Japan in 1879. By all accounts, Grant enjoyed Hōshō Kurō's performances of *Mochizuki* and of the *Earth Spider* (*Tsuchigumo*), and he urged Iwakura to preserve noh.

Iwakura realized that if noh were to rise to the level of Western opera, it would need government aid. Prior to the performance for President Grant, he hosted a show for the emperor at the Aoyama Palace of the Empress Dowager Eishō (d. 1897). Eishō proved a strong supporter of Iwakura's patronage of noh. In 1878, the Imperial Household Ministry funded the construction of a noh stage at her residence and sponsored annual performances for the imperial family and select members of the nobility. However, the location of the stage in the imperial residence meant that it was ill-suited for hosting performances for foreign dignitaries.

With assistance from the Imperial Household Ministry and a grant from the empress dowager, Iwakura worked to open a noh theater in Shiba Park in Tokyo in 1880. He visualized the members of the Meiji nobility as the chief patrons and audience for this theater. And he sought to recruit them for his new Noh Theater Society (Nōgakusha). A document entitled "The Proceedings for the Establishment of the Noh Theater Society" ("Nōgakusha setsuritsu no tetsuzuki") advocated state support for noh and its use to entertain foreign dignitaries.[20]

In another step to justify this project and win support, Iwakura employed two influential historians, Kume Kunitake and Shigeno Yasutsugu (d. 1910), to conduct research on historical precedents for state sponsorship of noh and for its use as a theater suitable for government functions. Kume, Iwakura's former secretary, had found employment in the state-sponsored College of Historiography, the precursor for the Historiographical Institute now at Tokyo University. Shigeno headed this same body of historians, who had been ordered by the government to compile a national history.[21]

The history of noh written by Kume and Shigeno is little more than an overview, which is probably what Iwakura wanted, because he incorporated it into public announcements about the founding of his noh society. Their work is especially important for understanding the beginnings of the historiographical concept of noh as ritual theater, *shikigaku*. According to this history, noh became *shikigaku* under the patronage of the warrior elite during the Edo period. As a ritual theater of state, noh not only achieved greater artistic refinement but also came to express the virtues of Confucian filial piety and respect for hierarchical relationships. Kume and Shigeno ended their history of *shikigaku* with the fall of the Tokugawa regime and the warning that noh needed to be restored to its former greatness, lest it, too, disappear.[22]

This argument, which presented civil ritual and state service as an integral part of the history of noh, was an invented history, as embodied by the authors' use of the newly coined word *nōgaku*, which replaced the older and more problematic term *sarugaku* noh, which some still rendered in writing as "monkey music." Thus, the modern term *nōgaku* emerged against its invented premodern equivalent, *shikigaku*; this development inaugurated a structured dialogue between ritual and theater and ensured that noh was something more than an entertainment but not a full religious rite. This Meiji-period myth of *nōgaku* as the modern counterpart of a traditional, ritual theater (*shikigaku*), supposedly created by the Edo shoguns and embodying Confucian principles, became the dominant historiographical view.

Iwakura had been the chief financial supporter of the noh society, and it fell on hard times after his death in 1883. The Imperial Household Ministry attempted to reorganize the society in 1890 and renamed it the Nōgakudō. But the group's financial problems continued, and the theater in Shiba Park was forced to billet troops during the Sino-Japanese War of 1894–95. After the war, the Household Ministry attempted to resuscitate the society. The chief minister of the Imperial Household Ministry, Hijikata Hisamoto (d. 1918), became the new head of the society, and in 1896, with another grant from his ministry, he helped to transform the society into the Noh Association (Nōgakukai). The new group broke with custom and admitted members from outside the Meiji aristocracy. Wealthy merchants provided a much-needed financial boost to the group, with the Mitsubishi and Mitsui families each contributing the then-substantial sum of 500 yen.[23]

Even though wealthy industrialists were allowed to join the nobility as the society's patrons, the association preserved the earlier society's vision of noh as an elite and ritual theater. The association's charter called for the support of noh and for performances specifically for members of the nobility. It also promised to sponsor further research into the history of noh and of other "ritual performing arts" (*shikireigaku*). The society then took steps to "re-create" noh in its true ritual form, not as an imitation of Western opera but as it was imagined to have been presented before the Tokugawa shoguns. In November 1896, the Nōgakukai held its inaugural performance, hosting what it termed a "ritual" (*shiki*) noh. The society's literature described the performance "as in the formal style of the age of the Tokugawa bakufu." Hijikata Hisamoto, in his capacity as the chief minister of the Imperial Household Ministry and as leader of the noh association, advocated that similar ritual noh be performed for the three major civil holidays of the year: New Year's, the Emperor's Birthday, and Empire Day.[24]

Iwakura had planned to use noh as a national theater for entertaining foreign guests, but after his death the Imperial Household Ministry saw two further reasons for supporting noh. First, noh and particularly the command performances attended by the imperial family could serve that ministry's goal of manufacturing a perceived closeness between the emperor and the people, which became an aim of government-sponsored ceremonies from the 1890s.[25] Second, as noh pundits argued in publications, identifying noh as one epitome of traditional culture could stave off the malicious and disruptive effects of Western culture. Akabori Matajirō, writing in the noh periodical *Yōkyokukai*, decried the poisonous effect of Western culture on Japanese traditions, particularly the slow erosion of the links between the elite and the masses. Noh as "ritual theater" would repel Western influence and recover the time-honored moments of celebration that had once united court and populace.[26] Even the historian Kume Kunitake, who had traveled to the West and had himself been the target of conservative attacks for his academic work, argued that noh should serve as a rallying point against Western influence. In the monthly magazine *Nōgaku*, Kume criticized the West and advocated that Japan needed pure traditions such as noh and the "way of the warrior" (*bushidō*) to preserve and strengthen its native spirit.[27] The same journal carried a transcription of a speech made before a noh benefit performance in 1908 by Ōkuma Shigenobu (d. 1922), who would become prime minister in 1914. In this article, entitled "Noh as a National Theater," Ōkuma described noh as a national theater (*kokumingeki*), whose spirit (*seishin*), he claimed, would benefit both the mentally ill (*seishin byōsha*), the intended beneficiaries of this particular performance, and the greater spirit of the nation.[28]

The Noh Association's move toward ultra-nationalism was as geographic as it was ideological. In 1902 the association moved the Shiba noh stage to Yasukuni shrine, the memorial for the nation's war dead. At Yasukuni, the association gradually replaced performances of ritual noh for association members with "imperial command performances" (*gyōkei*) open to the general public.

Despite the aim of using noh as a bridge between the masses and the imperial state, association members were unwilling to associate directly with the public. In a study of state-sponsored rituals in the Meiji period, Takashi Fujitani has noted that the authorities had to impose order on groups and crowds to prevent inappropriate behavior.[29] The same was true for public performances of noh: the Noh Association and the Imperial Household Ministry stipulated that those in attendance had to behave in an orderly fashion. Both groups created rules to discipline the audience, in an attempt to define a spectatorship appropriate to the invented tradition of ritual theater. But these modern aims of creating a docile, silent, and well-behaved audience conflicted directly with older customs of noh viewing, which included eating, drinking, and conversing.

Eating during performances was an especially contentious issue and reveals the contradiction between state policy and popular practices. Conservatives viewed eating as antithetical to their image of noh as a ritual theater. Kume penned a short history of eating during noh in which he framed the practice as ill-mannered and poorly suited to formal occasions such as the modern "revivals" of ritual noh.[30] In 1907, at the first imperial command performance sponsored by the Noh Association, it inserted a one-hour lunch break in the program. At the same time, it tried to prevent disorder by dictating proper dress for audience members. Men were to wear either formal kimono (*montsuki hakama*) or Western-style "frock coats" (Prince Alberts), and women were to dress either in formal kimono, or in Western-style "visiting dresses." Still, the audience persisted in eating in the theater, and the following year the association built a dining hall adjacent to the theater. Apparently, the audience remained restless because in 1910 the Noh Association stationed police officers at the entrance to record the names and occupations of those attending a performance.[31]

The 1915 performance to celebrate the accession of the Taishō emperor represented the culmination of noh as a ritual, a medium that facilitated the juxtaposition of a timeless image of imperial rule with an idealized and ordered vision of a disciplined public. In this instance, the public consisted of the closed audience for the ceremony of succession, namely, the nobility, elder statesmen (*genrō*), foreign diplomats, chief ministers, and 100 army and civil service officers. The journal *Nōgaku* contained a review of this performance and described the actors' "tears of joy"; it declared the event the ultimate manifestation of noh's purpose. According to the author, the enthronement ceremony embodied a "quiet stillness" (*seishuku*), which noh itself was ideal in cultivating. This stillness could teach the Japanese people gratitude and respect and would prove the emetic to "vomit out" the poisons of Western culture, in the colorful phrasing of the author. Noh would serve as a timeless rite supporting an eternal institution, not to mention ensuring the health of the Japanese spirit.[32]

Complementing the development of noh as a ritual theater was the trend of creating new noh with militaristic and ultra-nationalist themes. From the period of the Russo-Japanese War on, famous poets such as Takahama Kyoshi (d. 1959) began to write noh with patriotic and bellicose themes. Takahama's plays, like many others, warned about Russian expansion into China, representing China as a young maiden about to be ravished by Genghis Khan. Other wartime plays include *Fierce Eagle* (*Arawashi*), which was composed by a naval officer, and *Imperial Warship* (*Miikusabune*).

Noh performers and scholars, like the rest of the entertainment industry in Japan from kabuki to the all-female Takarazuka Revue Theater, collaborated with Japan's militarization in the 1930s.[33] Remarks made by Kanze Sakon, the twenty-fourth leader of the Kanze school, in 1938 are typical: "I believe that in extraordinary times such as these, culture and artistic techniques must not languish; we must dedicate ourselves to the feeling of deep gratitude we have for the many people on the field of battle, and I want those of us on the home front to realize our true duties."[34] The historian Ienaga Saburō has provided a lengthy discussion of the voluntary decision of leaders of the noh schools to cease performing the famous play *Semimaru*, since the drama portrayed members of the imperial house with physical disabilities. In a more sweeping change in 1940, the Noh Professional Association (Nōgaku kyōkai) mandated more polite language for references to emperors in plays and made editorial changes to many plays.[35]

The Unmasking of Ritual Theater

Japan's defeat in World War II brought a swift end to the militarization of noh. At the same time it reconfigured noh's relationship to ritual. Because ritual noh was so intertwined with the goals of militarism, in the postwar era the term *shikigaku* acquired pejorative connotations. Postwar scholars still located "ritual theater" in the Edo period, but instead of upholding the bakufu's use of noh as a mirror for a modern state theater, the postwar noh establishment blamed feudal samurai for corrupting noh and creating an elitist, ritualized drama, two trends that in their view needed to be contested.

This change in attitude from support to condemnation can be seen in the shift in pre- and postwar scholarship in the evaluation of noh's founding father, Zeami, whose writings were rediscovered and published in 1909.[36] In prewar scholarship, Zeami's theories were viewed as the intellectual foundation for ritual theater, but in the postwar era his ideas have come to be associated with the true spirit of noh that needed to be resuscitated to overcome the problems brought about by ritualization and samurai patronage. Representing the wartime view, Matsumoto Kamematsu in 1942 argued that Zeami's theories provided the ideological catalyst for the ritualization of noh under the Tokugawa military regime and facilitated the development of a more refined art. Noh, Kamematsu claimed, would have disappeared without military sponsorship.[37] Postwar scholars still lionized Zeami, but they reached opposite conclusions on Zeami's relationship to the military and his role in ritualizing noh. Representative of postwar scholars is

Yokomichi Mario, who contrasted Zeami's populist spirit with the government-controlled ritual theater of the Edo period, which he viewed as elitist and ossified. Yokomichi announced: "Zeami was a man who lived over six hundred years ago, but I believe that after the war noh has returned to the ideals of noh that Zeami created."[38] Yokomichi did not explore the implications of his argument, but his statement is an admission that ultra-nationalism and militarism in the twentieth century were the true reason for noh's difficulties and the changes in its aesthetics. Militarism for Yokomichi is a force that duped and manipulated noh for three centuries, a view that ignores the role of performers and academics in supporting modern militarism and ultra-nationalism.

The rejection of ritual theater coincides with a change in attitudes toward the past that occurred in the Occupation period, As historian Carol Gluck has noted, after World War II "the bad parts of the past, Tokugawa and imperial Japan included, were labeled 'feudal' and rejected."[39] One of the chief ways noh performers came to terms with their wartime experiences and Japan's defeat was to re-evaluate their traditions, especially those surrounding Zeami. For noh scholars and performers of the postwar era, Zeami symbolized noh's fundamental spirit, an essence that had been lost or obscured and had to be recovered. Zeami's writings represented the potential to rescue noh from the perils of militarism and state control, a conflict played out not in the more recent experiences of World War II but in the changing attitudes toward ritual theater and the Edo regime. Some noh performers, chiefly the brothers Kanze Hisao and Kanze Hideo (b. 1927), participated in academic study groups on Zeami's writings in the 1950s and then, inspired by Zeami's ideas, created ensembles such as the Renaissance Group in 1950 and the Flower Group (Hana no kai) as a means to expunge "feudal" elements from noh, which they attributed to ritual theater.[40] Whereas the noh establishment in the Meiji and prewar periods invented the tradition of ritual theater to find a place for noh in the service of the modern state, in the postwar era the concept of ritual theater retained its close association with the Edo period but became a target of resistance. This tactic psychologically distanced the noh community from the events of World War II and, by extension, exonerated it of culpability in furthering militarization and ultra-nationalism.

Okina—A Ritual That Is and Is Not Noh

In the postwar period, with "ritual theater" upheld as an aberration, the dance of Okina became the new medium of noh's *différance*, an anti-theatrical opposite to noh that at the same time contained its spiritual core. At present Okina is called a ritual; it is one of the "three rites."[41] When actors talk specifically about what makes Okina a ritual, they note the features that distinguish it from typical noh drama. Even though Okina is performed on a noh stage by noh actors, it departs from noh's theatrical conventions. It is usually performed on special occasions, such as New Year's, and it is always the first work on the program.[42] Three other characteristics mark Okina as different. First, Okina begins with elaborate ceremonies enacted backstage. Second, Okina lacks identifiable characters, a plot, and setting—to name the most outstanding differences. Finally, during the performance of Okina, the actor dancing the role of Okina is not said to be representing a god as in a play; rather, he is said to magically become (the) god.

The interpretation of Okina as a ritual act of apotheosis, or shamanistic possession, as described below, is a modern replacement for previous explanations. In the premodern era, Okina and the rest of the dances of the *shikisanban* were viewed as representations of the divine. Premodern views of Okina were based on contemporary religious beliefs, whereas the modern interpretation was created after these modes of thinking came into dispute. Consequently, the modern version can also be termed an "invented tradition," a myth that testifies to the authority of the noh profession while masquerading as a ritual re-enactment of an ancient spiritual rite.

Acting Ritually

The audience can catch a quick glimpse of the rites occurring backstage before a performance of Okina when one of the performers momentarily parts the curtain separating the greenroom from the stage and strikes a flint and steel together. This provides the audience with the only visible indication that ceremonies of purification and worship are occurring in the liminal area of the backstage in the mirror room (*kagami no ma*), where performers customarily don their masks and contemplate their dramatic personae in a large mirror before a play. The location of these rites in an area accessible only to the performers, as opposed to the public space of the stage, reinforces the notion that the performers are engaged in an act of worship as opposed to merely *acting worshipfully* for the audience.

The audience is not allowed to witness the backstage ceremonies, but the curious can easily find information about the ritual preparations for Okina in performers' memoirs (*geidan*). The backstage rites are often preceded by several days of sexual abstinence and purification. Experts in the subject note that the length of the period of purification has changed historically and is different for each school of noh.[43] Modern performers also disagree about how long this period once was, is now, or should be. Kanze Sakon stated that performers once maintained their austerities for a period lasting from twenty-one to thirty-seven days, but after the Meiji Restoration the time was reduced to one day.[44] The noted noh flute player Morita Mitsuharu (d. 1992) wrote that performers usually maintain three days of ritual purification before performances.[45] The Ōkura school kyōgen actor Shigeyama Sensaku II (d. 1950) wrote that actors used to practice seven days of purification and that his father had an exorcism conducted in the home during that time.[46] Nomura Manzō VI, a kyōgen actor in the Izumi school, agreed that a week of purification was needed but added that performers should also practice rigorous "cold water purifications" (*mizugori*) and avoid speaking with women or people in mourning before the date of performance.[47] The Kita school actor Takabayashi Kōji (b. 1935) said that the pre-performance rites lasted for a week to ten days for his school, and the late head of the Kongō school, Kongō Iwao II (d. 1998), claimed that actors in his school still practiced a week of austerities.[48]

Regardless of its length, the period of ritual purification has two aspects. First, actors are supposed to follow a special—but unspecified—diet. Second, as noted above, they are to avoid contact with women to the point of refraining from using bathwater or eating food prepared by women, for fear that women might transfer "impurities" to the actor through the fire used for cooking or heating the bathwater. Performers follow a practice called "separate fire" (*bekka*), and a special heating source is reserved expressly for the actor who will perform Okina. A few actors, such as members of the Shigeyama family, have abandoned the practice of *bekka*. Jonah Salz notes that the Shigeyama family "have not practiced this custom since the war. They consider it a distasteful reminder of feudal sexism and [it] holds little practical significance with the advent of gas stoves." As Salz also reports, one kyōgen family decided to forgo *bekka* after one of its younger members said he would eat instant "cup-noodles" when he had to prepare to perform in the *shikisanban*.[49] Few—if any—Japanese still cook over open fires unless a gas stove counts as such. In the present age of microwaves and hot running water, some noh performers have acknowledged the impossibility of maintaining a "separate fire," even if they wanted to.

The absence of detailed descriptions of "separate fire" rites for the earliest period makes it difficult to determine their history.[50] The concept of *bekka*, as explicated in seventeenth-century writings such as *Jikkanshō* and *Bushōgoma* by Shūsen'o, was applied to noh at a time when performers began clarifying bloodlines and writing genealogies to strengthen the hereditary boundaries of their profession (see Chapter 5). Women were mentioned in genealogies as daughters or wives or like goods exchanged in marriage to solidify bonds between two unrelated males, especially between a master-teacher and his chief successor. The concept of *bekka* deploys sexuality in the same way as the genealogy: as a means to mark vertical and horizontal unions among male performers. By indicating the absence of women, *bekka* thereby calls attention to the bond among male performers. *Bekka* also draws attention to the fact that professional expertise in noh is still constructed as flowing patrilineally from father to son, or from a male teacher such as the "family head" (*iemoto*) to a (male) disciple. Since World War II, women have been allowed to become professional noh performers, but only men may participate in Okina. Noh actors stigmatize women as a way of setting themselves apart, not just from women but also from the rest of society, by virtue of their "purity" mediated by esoteric rites.

Morita Mitsuharu's description of the backstage rituals for Okina is especially detailed. Morita wrote that on the day of the performance of Okina, a small altar is erected in the mirror room. The altar serves as a temporary place of enshrinement for the two masks used in the play, the white mask of Okina and the black mask of Sanbasō. The props used in the performance such as Sanbasō's bell-stick (*suzu*) are also placed on this altar along with offerings of consecrated rice, sake (or water), and salt in a ceremony called the *okina kazari*.[51] All the performers assemble in the mirror room, with the actor who will play

Okina sitting closest to the altar. The actor playing the role of Senzai, the actor performing Sanbasō, and the stage assistants (*koken*) take their places in that order, with the remainder of the performers seated behind them. When all the performers are seated, the actor who will perform Okina rises, approaches the altar, bows, and returns to his seat. Then one of the stage assistants rises and takes the offerings and an earthen drinking cup and presents them to the Okina actor. The actor takes the shallow cup and receives water (or sake) from another stage assistant. Sipping three times, the actor then takes rice, which he "purifies" with a wave of his hand. Then he places a little of the rice into his left sleeve. The assistant offers the sake or water to the other performers in order, which they receive and drink.[52] Komparu Kunio added that after "consuming the ritual meal," the performers are purified by a "fire ritual," the sparks made from steel and flint. The curtain is drawn upward and the actors take the stage one by one, beginning with the actor dancing the role of Senzai. As the actor playing Okina passes through the curtain, he utters a final incantation called the *okina watashi*.[53] When he reaches center stage, the other performers pause for a moment on the bridge (*hashigakari*) that leads from the greenroom to the main stage. Okina makes a full bow—some say to the audience, others say to the North Star; perhaps the bow is a survival from the period when feudal lords patronized noh.

There are many unique points about the performance of Okina that distinguish it from noh plays. First, the staging for Okina is distinctive, since the chorus lines up behind the musicians, as opposed to their usual position at stage-right of the main stage. Three shoulder-drum players perform in Okina, when usually only one performs. Finally, for performances of Okina, the customary dress of the chorus and musicians, a kimono and trousers (*hakama*), is replaced by formal dress (*suōkamishimo*) complemented with *kariginu*, a loose cloak with a round collar and flared shoulders worn over the kimono. The actors wear courtiers' hats (*eboshi*) and long-legged trousers (*nagabakama*) to complete their formal dress.

The Okina dance is one of the "three rites," a program consisting of a series of dances by separate actors in the roles of Senzai, Okina, and Sanbasō. Okina is performed by an actor from one of the five *shite* schools, and Sanbasō is danced by a kyōgen performer. Depending on the school of the *shite* actor, Senzai is danced either by a kyōgen or a *shite* actor, and it is the only role performed without a mask.[54]

The dances are performed in the order Senzai, Okina, and Sanbasō, but the discussion here focuses on Okina, since it is the focus of modern noh discourse. One of the high points of the performance occurs halfway through Senzai's dance, when the actor playing Okina dons his mask in view of the audience. This point is said to mark the actor's transformation into a deity. The actor Takabayashi Kōji gave an account of this metamorphosis: "Once I wear the mask I am in communion with the god inside me, with the universal part that transcends the mundane. That part of me which is godlike dances and that same universal god resides in the mask; therefore both mask and performer are god."[55] Instead of "getting into character" and representing a deity or any other figure as in a noh play, the actor performing Okina becomes or unites with a higher power.

The second highlight of the performance occurs when Okina utters his famous, incomprehensible lines, the so-called god-song (*kamiuta*), just before his own dance. The god-song is impenetrable even in written form, since it consists of strings of syllables threaded around auspicious verses, some taken from medieval ballads: *imayō* and *saibara*. The version used in the Kanze school is:

> OKINA: Tōtō tarari tararira, tarari agarirararitō.
>
> CHORUS: Chiriyatarari tararira, tarari agarirararitō.
>
> OKINA: Dwell here for a thousand generations,
>
> CHORUS: We will serve you for a thousand autumns.
>
> OKINA: For the life span of the crane and tortoise,[56]
>
> CHORUS: Happiness will rule our hearts.
>
> OKINA: Tōtō tarari tararira.
>
> CHORUS: Chiriyatarari tararira, tarari agarirararitō.[57]

Scholars have suggested various meanings for some of the opaque words. Some have proposed that they are magical incantations, vocalizations of musical instruments, or even classical Tibetan.[58] Perhaps the god-song is meaningless. Frits Staal, in his discussion of the 3,000-year-old Vedic Agnicayanna ritual, argued that the inherent meaninglessness of the ritual verses accounted for their preservation and allowed for a multitude of interpretations.[59] Whether the lack of a clear meaning has helped preserve the god-song of Okina is uncertain, but the

absence of stable meaning has allowed performers and scholars to im-
pute many different interpretations. This is not to say that performers
consider the drama of Okina meaningless. In fact, the modern interpretation resists the meaninglessness of Okina in favor of a definition
that substantiates the rights of professional performers. The apparent
meaninglessness of these lines is presented as a hidden mystery that
the audience simply cannot access, but one that professional performers know intimately.

Describing Okina as a mysterious ritual may absolve modern noh
performers from having to explain the full meaning of the dance;
however, the religious meanings of the dance have changed historically. The oldest form of the three rites, which predates Zeami, originally had two other roles: the masked character of the old man
Chichinojō and his young, unmasked counterpart, Enmeikaja.[60] The
oldest surviving version of the text for this part is found in the sixteenth-century *Hachijō kadensho*.

CHICHINOJŌ: What do we pray for, young lord? Oh young lord, Shakyamuni Buddha.

ENMEIKAJA: My father is King Jōbon. My mother is his wife Maya, the
daughter of Zengaku Chōja. I was born in the heaven of Tōriten.[61] I lived
in the flower garden there. Chichinojō is here with me. Let's pray together as father and son. The young lord has arrived again.

CHICHINOJŌ: Under heaven, the old man [Okina] gathers the winds, and
the people boast of the paradise of the five lakes. He is the old man with
the body of heaven. He lives without change, longer than the Kirin's
horn, living since the creation of heaven and earth, older than the five
emperors and three kings of China. He is the one. Blessings and celebrations. He holds the pine branch, *aritōtōtō*.

The setting of the dance appears to be India, and it takes the form of a
short dialogue between Enmeikaja, representing the historical Buddha
Shakyamuni, and Chichinojō, who represents Shakyamuni's father,
King Jōbon (Sanskrit, Suddhobodana).[62] One mid-sixteenth-century
explanation of the origin of the Okina dance posited King Jōbon as
the creator of the three rites.[63] From that perspective, the dialogue between Enmeikaja and Chichinojō presents both a historical-religious
vignette and a Buddhist framework for explaining these rites. Besides
the religious undertones, the scene of Chichinojō and Enmeikaja is
also more explicitly dramatic since the masked characters represent

specific figures. Their dialogue suggests that Okina is a deity. Conversely, the removal of this dialogue from most performances by Zeami's time makes Okina more abstract and mysterious.

Medieval and early modern performers posited a wide range of interpretations of the three rites in their secret treatises. Although these writings present different conclusions, they agree that the actor playing Okina represents a divinity, albeit not as specific a deity as in a noh play. Some interpretations of the three rites, such as that found in *Hachijō kadensho*, encompassed all the performers on stage including the musicians, so that the entire cast is described as representing a wide range of male and female deities, buddhas, cosmic elements, and heavenly bodies simultaneously.[64] In *Fūshikaden*, Zeami gave a Buddhist interpretation of Okina, but his contemporary Konparu Zenchiku portrayed Okina as representing a congeries of Shinto and Buddhist deities and even historical figures such as the Heian statesman and poet Sugawara no Michizane.[65] In late sixteenth-century noh writings, Okina was most often depicted as representing the Kasuga deity, but Sanbasō was variously interpreted as the Sumiyoshi deity, Amaterasu, Togakushi Myōjin, and the Kasuga deity.[66] Similar interpretations can be found in noh writings up through the end of the early modern period. In the mid-Meiji period, Kinoshita Keiken's (d. 1916) landmark work, *A Collection of Noh Secrets* (*Nōgaku unnōshū*), followed these precedents of interpretation by associating both Okina and Senzai with the deity Amaterasu.[67]

Premodern interpretations of Okina faced their first significant scholarly challenge in 1906 with Yoshida Tōgo's landmark article in the journal *Nōgaku*. Yoshida, who would win fame a few years later for publishing Zeami's newly discovered treatises, presented one of the first scholarly accounts of the history of Okina. He began with Kinoshita Keiken's analysis and proceeded to dismiss premodern views of Okina as representing a divinity.[68] Yoshida, however, did not offer a satisfactory explanation of the meaning of the dance in place of these older interpretations, beyond simply noting its antiquity and sacrality.

Yoshida's article may have challenged performers to reconcile their interpretations of Okina with modern scholarship, but performers also reacted to changes in the religious *Zeitgeist*, particularly the government persecution of Buddhism and the development of emperor-centered State Shinto in the late nineteenth and early twentieth centuries.[69] In subsequent interpretations of Okina, performers de-emphasized Buddhist, polyvalent, and syncretic interpretations, in favor of connecting Okina with the Sun Goddess, Amaterasu. This conveniently linked noh to the divine progenitor of the imperial line and the modern myths surrounding the emperor—a politic move in a period when the court and Imperial Household Ministry were key patrons of noh. Thus, the head of the Kongō school, Kongō Ukyō, explained that Okina represented Ninigi, the grandson of Amaterasu. Ukyō strengthened the connection between Okina and the imperial line by equating the box holding the Okina mask with the imperial regalia (*sanshū no shinki*).[70] The renowned actor Umewaka Minoru II (d. 1959) stated in 1935 that Okina represented Amaterasu in certain moments of the dance and at other times heaven, earth, and humanity.[71] In contrast to premodern interpretations that viewed many, if not all, of the performers as representations of the divine, modern performers from this period on focused on Okina.

The dance of Okina shares many parallels with the dance of Sanbasō that follows. Like Okina, Sanbasō dons his mask on stage. Yet, with the exception of writings by *kyōgen* actors, Sanbasō does not receive much attention in modern noh discourse, since only the actor who takes the role of Okina "becomes the divinity." The stick-drum (*taiko*) performer Komparu Kunio clarified this point: "The actor who performs the role of the mystical, old, godlike Okina must become the god."[72] Lacking the religious worldview that once had grounded interpretations of the figures portrayed on stage, modern actors marked a moment of one actor's apotheosis into a kind of divinity. Hence the focus in modern noh discourse on the point of transubstantiation when the actor dons the Okina mask. Although Shinto and Japanese new religions have many examples of living deities (*ikigami*), which are "permanent living divine presence[s]," the apotheosis in Okina is closest to Japanese shamanism, since it creates a temporary transformation.[73]

The view that Okina preserves a form of shamanistic possession is an invented tradition dating from after World War II and seems inspired by the academic field of folklore studies (*minzokugaku*). Carol Gluck has illustrated the impact of the research of folklorists such as Yanagita Kunio (d. 1962) and Orikuchi Shinobu on the field of Japanese history. Their work provoked historians to search for the people's place in the historical past. In a similar spirit, postwar scholars of the performing arts turned to folklore, Western anthropology, and the scholarly study of folk performing arts (*minzoku geinō*), to theorize about noh's origins and the early history of theater. These scholars were particularly fascinated by Okina and suggested that the Okina mask enshrined a deity (*goshintai*) and that the dance revealed noh's possible beginnings as an agricultural rite.[74] In a 1948 study, the influential noh scholar Nogami Toyoichirō compared noh with classical Greek drama and noted the universality of the origin of theater in ritual. He explained that in primitive societies a dancer representing a deity in an act of worship frequently becomes associated with that divinity in the eyes of the audience.[75] His argument was more than just a nod to the supposed origins of theater in ritual in the West, for it bore strong similarities to the theories about the relationship between ritual and drama accepted by contemporary Western scholars including Lucien Levy-Bruhl and Mircea Eliade—part of Western scholarly discourse about masks since the late nineteenth century according to Henry Pernet. In a 1968 work, Eliade made a general observation about mask wearing in so-called primitive societies, arguing that mask wearers ritually transformed into the objects of their representation and became gods in the eyes of the primitive audience. "One becomes what one displays," wrote Eliade. "The wearers of masks are really the mythical ancestors portrayed by their masks."[76] Japanese scholars have applied this argument to the Okina ritual. Yokomichi Mario, for instance, wrote that the actor donning the Okina mask becomes a god.[77]

Performers in the postwar era became acquainted with academic interpretations of Okina through their involvement in collaborative projects, chiefly the study of the newly discovered treatises of Zeami. Although Zeami's works were published in the first decade of the twentieth century, it was not until the postwar era that performers began to read Zeami in significant numbers and with scholarly attention. Kanze Hisao was among the most enthusiastic. He attended university lectures on Zeami by Nose Asaji in 1949–50 and later helped found a Zeami study group for performers, *Zeami densho kenkyūkai*, in 1952 for the purpose of understanding Zeami's theories and applying them in performance. Prominent scholars including Nishio Minoru, Yokomichi Mario, and Omote Akira participated in these seminars. The view that Okina constituted the "foundational root" of noh dance, as Zeami described in *Kyakuraika*, and of noh chant (*utai*), as Zeami's son Motoyoshi reiterated in *Sarugaku dangi*, became buzzwords for Kanze Hisao and other actors.[78] Hisao, for instance, called Okina the "original art" (*motogei*).[79] Takabayashi Kōji expressed the same concept and revealed Zeami's influence when he proclaimed: "Okina is the source of all Noh. In Okina lies the spiritual core of Noh and from Okina stems many of the technical bases of Noh, such as the rules of choreography."[80]

If Okina was the basis for noh, it became critical for performers to reassert their claim to it. Noh performers accomplished this by abandoning views of Okina's religiosity that had been made to glorify the emperor system during wartime and embracing the scholarly discourse on Okina as an ancient ritual of shamanistic possession. But, rather than assume the passive role of informants in an academic narrative, actors portrayed themselves as the gatekeepers of the Okina tradition and offered their own testimony to Okina's power. Okina has since become the most powerful myth in the noh profession, used to designate authenticity, confer legitimacy, and define artistry.

The mantra of Okina's power is expressed in the oxymoron "Okina is and is not noh," which appears frequently in the writings of late twentieth-century performers.[81] Okina is *not* noh because it is perceived to be ritual, not drama. For it to be understood as ritual, Okina by necessity must be outside the parameters of noh, and the "ritualistic" aspects of Okina, such as the backstage rites, must transgress the dramaturgical rules of noh theater. Conversely, performers also argue that "Okina is noh" because it represents the living past and core of noh theater. Although actors such as Kanze Hisao and Takabayashi Kōji may cite Zeami to argue that Okina was the prototype for noh, nowhere did Zeami state in his writings that the actor dancing the role of Okina actually becomes a deity, nor did he call attention to the moment when the actor puts on the Okina mask.

Although Okina is now the dominant medium of noh's mythos, performers cannot make equal claims to Okina's legacy. The number of women professionals continues to increase, but women cannot take part in the Okina performance. Men, too, face restrictions based on status, age, and birth. Only senior actors are allowed to take the role of Okina, and the *iemoto* usually enacts Okina on the most important occasions.

High-ranking performers describe their privileged experience in writings and interviews, and they use these forums as bully pulpits to keep other performers in line and as opportunities to fascinate their audiences with hints of secret knowledge and paranormal experiences. Kanze Hisao, for instance, contrasted the spiritual cultivation needed to perform Okina properly with the worldliness of modern actors, condemning those who gossiped and watched television before taking the stage.[82] The sanctity of Okina has also been invoked to argue against changes in the accepted staging of plays.[83] Finally, in their descriptions of Okina, the most powerful performers make mention of knowledge to which only they are privileged. The former leader of the Kongō troupe, Kongō Iwao II, alluded to secret writings about Okina in his possession, stating: "Our hidden writings concerning Okina are contained in a book several centimeters thick. The details of the ritual include many esoteric Buddhist mantras and mudras to be done throughout the performance."[84] Such testimonials reinforce the authority of the few actors allowed to take the Okina role.

Today, Okina is said to be the source and embodiment of all of noh's authenticity and its original sanctity. Performers refer to their stage experience to impose a reading of Okina as a timeless, first-person encounter with the absolute. That only senior, male actors can dance the title role reinforces the notion that knowledge is a function of hierarchy, bloodlines, and gender. Audiences can glimpse a portion of the Okina rite, but they are said to have no bearing on its meaning. They are invited to honor the rite, not interpret it. Given the constructed nature of the Okina ritual and the meanings imputed to it, Okina ought to be viewed less as a premodern religious artifact than as a modern myth of the postwar noh profession. This myth is sustained through its re-enactment in performances and noh discourse, where it is resuscitated again and again, as a medium of power.

CONCLUSION

Noh's Modern Myths

The notion of tradition . . . is intended to give a special temporal status to a group of phenomena that are both successive and identical (or at least similar); it makes it possible to rethink the dispersion of history in the form of the same; it allows a reduction of the difference proper to every beginning, in order to pursue without discontinuity that endless search for the origin; tradition enables us to isolate the new against a background of permanence, and to transfer its merit to originality, to genius, to the decisions proper to individuals.

— Michel Foucault

This book has examined the history of noh's ethos, the evolution of a shared cognitive map that performers follow to define noh and its legitimate actors. Noh's ethos is constructed from its traditions, or what I call its "myths"; these myths are in turn expressed and structured by media. Technological changes such as the introduction of new media have been one reason for changes in noh's myths and its ethos. As secret manuscripts gave way to printed texts and heredity grew in importance with the genealogical turn in political discourse in the early modern period, these developments supported institutional changes in noh, as in most other performing arts and many vocations that developed a family-head (*iemoto*) system. New myths evolved but did not entirely displace older ones. Instead, they were subsumed into a new framework. For example, eighteenth-century performers, like their fourteenth-century predecessors, still venerated ancient masks, but the manner in which they thought about these masks was influenced by the literate culture in which they lived, especially the medium of print: whereas medieval performers used masks as a technology of memory, performers in the early modern era sought to document and verify the "original masks" (*honmen*) in their possession. Where medieval performers sought to authenticate the historical legacy of their troupe by appealing to divine mysteries, early modern performers were anxious to defend and publicize the veracity of their historical legacy in an age that had rendered the original hard to distinguish from a copy. This conclusion takes stock of the present state of the myths examined in this book and examines how these myths as an ethos help sustain the institutional and ideological apex of noh's professionalization, the family-head (*iemoto*) system.

Nostalgia for Masks

A question that preoccupied performers in the eighteenth century—the authenticity of the oldest "original masks"—intensified in the twentieth century as more reliable techniques of dating became available, scholars turned a quizzical eye on claims of great antiquity, and the age of many masks collections was questioned. As original masks have been discredited, destroyed, or lost among a proliferation of copies, mask discourse has demonstrated the truth of Jean Baudrillard's observation that "when the real is no longer what it was, nostalgia assumes its full meaning."[1] Although performers' nostalgia includes a longing for masks that have been destroyed, it also serves as a way to ignore these losses by falsely positing a continuity between the present and the past bridged by appeals to emotion and mystical yearning. The mask, both as a medium of memory for the medieval performer and as an authentic historical artifact for the early modern performer, has become an icon that reminds noh performers that only sentiment or perhaps mysticism can recover what has been lost.

The fate of ancient masks in the modern period is told in terms of loss by most noh schools. Both the Kita and Konparu schools lost nearly all their most treasured masks in the modern era. Shortly after the Meiji Restoration, financial problems resulting from the end of government patronage forced the Kita school's leaders to sell many of the troupe's oldest masks. A tragic fire in 1923 destroyed many of the remaining ones. The Konparu troupe began selling off their better masks well before World War II; the Konparu even parted with the famous mask of a young woman that the warlord Toyotomi Hideyoshi had dubbed "Snow," a companion piece to the "Flower" (*hana*) mask (see Color Fig. 3).[2] After World War II, Konparu Nobutaka sold many of his school's most treasured masks to the Tokyo National

Museum. Nobutaka's account of the sale in his memoirs reflects more nostalgia than self-incrimination; he portrayed himself as a passive "war victim" (*sensaisha*), as if the masks had been lost in a bombing raid rather than being sold.[3]

Conversely, leaders of noh schools that were able to retain their mask collections took pride in their efforts to preserve their family's tradition. In an article on masks in the noh magazine *Yōkyoku kōza* in 1926, the leader of the Hōshō troupe equated the family head's collection of original masks with the life of a noh school. Any dispersion of the masks, he wrote, would reflect a lack of filial piety to one's ancestors.[4] Kanze Sakon, in his 1939 memoir, admitted that his family had lost a few of its masks but claimed that these losses were small in view of the many more treasured masks that remained in the school's storerooms, including several mentioned in the fifteenth-century treatise *Sarugaku dangi*.[5]

The nostalgia evident in modern noh discourse on masks may be attributed less to the loss of specific masks than to the dubiousness of most claims about the surviving ones. Kanze Hisao, one of the most respected and widely published actors of the twentieth century, admitted that he had a hard time believing the claims made about ancient masks. Hisao's disavowal of these myths did not, however, constitute rejection of the masks. Instead, he affirmed the sanctity of older masks and spoke of their spiritual power. When allowed to use a mask believed to have once been used by Zeami, Hisao exclaimed: "I cannot express the deep emotion I felt when I reflected on the fact that a mask that Zeami may have worn I, too, used five hundred years later; and at the same time I knew in my heart that I wanted to realize all the power of the mask on stage without making any mistakes."[6] For Hisao and many other actors in the noh world who after World War II came to associate the core of noh dramaturgy with the philosophy of Zeami, wearing a mask that the early master may have worn allowed for a return to his ideals. For this actor who tried to revive noh in the postwar era by resuscitating Zeami's theories, wearing the mask was less a matter of historical appreciation than a sensory experience of embodying Zeami. More important than the historicity of the mask was the emotion and sensitivity that Hisao brought to his appreciation of it, not to mention his efforts to channel those feelings into his performance.

Similar first-person testaments can be found in the writings of other modern performers. The Hōshō school invokes its connection with Zeami through a mask that bears the name Motokiyo on the reverse side and is said to have been a gift from Zeami.[7] Although Konparu Nobutaka admitted selling off many of his family's most ancient masks, he nonetheless affirmed that he still possessed a few masks that predated Zeami. These, he claimed, foreshadowed Zeami's theory of grace (*yūgen*), the epitome of Zeami's artistic ideals.[8] Kongō Iwao I made this same argument earlier and more deftly: "The masks *akujō* and *beshimi* by Shakuzuru and *yamauba* [also *yamanba*] and Tatsuemon's "Snow" mask date from the era before Zeami and may have taught him about noh as they still teach us."[9]

The continued references to myths about masks reveal not only the endurance of medieval legends but also the degree to which interpretations of these media have changed. Modern noh actors would have us acknowledge the mysterious antiquity of masks while recognizing that these same masks cannot be subjected to the rigors of exact dating in the same way their early modern forebears had tried. In other words, audiences should accept the testimony of the few actors allowed to wear them and appreciate the timelessness of ancient masks as well as their latent spiritual power. The leap into mysticism over the chasm of history is best exemplified by the modern version of the Okina myth, described in the previous chapter, in which an actor donning a mask on stage in full view of the audience is said to enter a private moment of divine rapture. This flight into nostalgia occurred as attempts to rewrite the past were replaced by attempts to reduce the past to a timeless sensory experience.

Burn Secret Writings
and Institutions Will Still Stand

Although secret writings have remained valuable clues to performance techniques and a medium of authority since their inception in the time of Zeami, with the standardization of noh since the early modern period, theory has arguably taken a back seat to practical application. The most esteemed secret writings today are the private performance notes (*katazuke*) carefully disseminated by professional performers; oral instructions are valued even more. Nonetheless, the structure that

Fig. 8.1 Kongō Ukyō. Courtesy of Hinoki Shoten and
the Hōsei University Institute of Nōgaku Studies.

disseminates and interprets these secrets has grown much more authoritative than the written records themselves. The events surrounding the death of Kongō Ukyō in 1936 (see Fig. 8.1) exemplify this.

In his will, the great actor Kongō Ukyō commanded that his entire
library of secret writings be thrown onto his funeral pyre. As twenty-
third *iemoto* of the Kongō school of noh, Ukyō's library must have
included writings inherited from his forefathers, private, esoteric
works intended solely for the hereditary leaders of the Kongō school
as well as texts that recorded every aspect of the Kongō school's performance style. Since these were the most secret and sacred works of
the Kongō, it would not be an exaggeration to say that his library was
the entire written memory of the Kongō school for more than 600
years. Ukyō's command was intended not only to obliterate a pre-
cious treasury of documents but to end the Kongō school.

Ukyō's desire to obliterate the Kongō school seems incongruous
for someone in his position, since, as *iemoto*, he was ultimately

responsible for maintaining and transmitting the school's artistic style. His wish seems even stranger, given the adversity he had overcome to sustain noh in the late nineteenth and early twentieth century.[10] Ukyō suffered the early deaths of his grandfather and father, both of whom had played leading roles in the revival of noh in the Meiji era. He succeeded to the post of family head in 1884 and moved to Kyoto in 1892, where he apparently suffered from poor treatment in the Kongō Kinosuke household. Returning to Tokyo in 1915, Ukyō rebuilt the Kongō noh stage in 1922, only to witness its destruction in the Kantō earthquake less than a year later. After spending five more years away from Tokyo in Kyoto, Ukyō returned in 1927 to assume direction of the Kongō school in the capital. Two years later, Ukyō published a revised version of the Kongō school's *utaibon*, copying and annotating 200 plays in his own hand, a feat that no other family head has since attempted. Ukyō is remembered as one of the great performers of the early twentieth century, especially for his sublime execution of the distinct style of the Kongō school. But Ukyō felt the Kongō had lost more than it could ever recover, and he deemed himself the last member of his family line. Consequently, he did not designate a successor, and he sold off his family's mask collection, some examples of which are depicted in this book (see Color Figs. 1–5). The posthumous destruction of his library would seal the fate of the Kongō school, he believed. However, the Kongō school endured.

The four other *shite* schools—Kanze, Konparu, Hōshō, and Kita—deemed that Ukyō's wish to destroy the Kongō would mean an intolerable loss to the noh world, not to mention the equally unbearable headache of coping with an entire school of unemployed actors and the financial hardships of the other performers who worked with them. Contrary to Ukyō's will, a son from the Kyoto branch of the Kongō family—a family of disciples who had been granted the Kongō name in the late nineteenth century—was chosen as his successor. Kongō Iwao I became the twenty-fourth head of the Kongō school and faced the task not only of rebuilding the prestige of the school but of replacing its properties. Since Ukyō had bequeathed his entire collection of masks to Mitsui Hachirōemon Takami, the head of the Mitsui conglomerate, Iwao had to accumulate another collection. He was forced to commission copies and borrow masks from the Ōe family of Kyoto (Kanze school) until a suitable collection could be purchased.[11]

Although the Kongō school was preserved through the heroic efforts of Iwao, its survival depended on the support of the noh establishment, which viewed the loss of secret writings and masks as tragic but ultimately inconsequential to the perpetuation of the Kongō school. To survive, the school simply needed a new family head—and a new head could be appointed, against Ukyō's wishes, from a high-ranking family of disciples. The case of the Kongō school reveals the extent to which modern noh depends ultimately on the preservation of the family head, who serves as the judge of authenticity and as the highest figure in the professional world. It also reveals that even the powerful traditional concepts of patrilineal succession and pure bloodlines have in the modern period taken a backseat to the more important goal of preserving an institution.

Bloodlines and the Family Head

Although medieval noh troupes were familial operations whose members shared a common ancestry, at its beginnings in the Muromachi period, noh was a much more open occupation, with performers of various backgrounds creating impromptu groups to compete in the marketplace. Many of these groups soon disappeared, such as the women's noh (*onna sarugaku*) and noh by historically discriminated groups (*shōmonji sarugaku*) that flourished in the fifteenth century. Despite the label "amateur" (*shirōto*), *tesarugaku* groups such as the Toraya and Shibuya managed to sustain noh as their principal livelihood for several generations from the early sixteenth to late seventeenth century and proved to be keen competition for the older regional groups, particularly the four Yamato troupes affiliated with religious institutions in Nara.

As this book has shown, the four Yamato groups responded to these competitors by adapting media to their advantage. For example, they used secret treatises to distinguish their artistic product; in turn, the existence of these writings deeply changed how they perceived themselves and their relationship to the production of noh. In their secret manuscripts, the Kanze and Konparu troupes of the Yamato tradition reformulated oral legends conveyed in objects of memory such as masks to claim authority based on their connections to noh's "inventors," some from the time of the historical Buddha and others

from the era of Prince Shōtoku. Such tactics resonated with their warrior patrons, especially the hegemons of the latter sixteenth century
who also sought to secure legitimacy through invented pedigrees. Not
only did the patronage of Toyotomi Hideyoshi and Tokugawa Ieyasu
prove decisive in the four Yamato troupes' growing domination of
noh, but the policies of these warlords upholding patrilineal descent as
the sole determinant of social standing assisted the Yamato performers' efforts to draw the boundaries of their occupation with hereditary
"professionals" on the inside and "amateurs" outside. Under the Tokugawa bakufu's policy of rule by status, noh performers were forced to
resolve questions of artistic paternity conclusively by documenting
their lineages. Performers responded by creating genealogies that
framed the transmission of knowledge through patrilineal bloodlines.

At the same time, Okina developed into a mechanism to sanctify
the bloodlines of performers. In the medieval era, Okina and the
other dances of the three rites represented a host of divinities, with
each role on stage signifying a buddha or deity and sometimes several
of them simultaneously. This eclectic interpretation, evident in writings from the period of Zeami in the fifteenth century to the late
sixteenth-century *Hachijō kadensho*, allowed performers to adapt
Okina to any performance venue, through implicit or explicit connections with divinities associated with the setting. But, with the genealogical turn in noh discourse in the early modern period, the rituals
preceding the performance conducted by actors in secret backstage
gradually overshadowed the dances performed on stage. Okina became a secret rite for noh at a time when the Tokugawa bakufu was
ruthlessly persecuting Christians for their participation in similar rites
of transubstantiation. Through practices such as "separate fire," performers drew attention to their own purity by exorcising any pollut-
ants that were construed as feminine and damaging to the preservation
of patrilineal bloodlines that were the supreme channels of legitimacy
and artistic knowledge.

Noh actors, along with most other performing artists of the early
modern period, refined their genealogies to claim connections with a
few, key ancestral patriarchs in the course of constructing professional
institutions such as the school and later the family-head system. As
Maurice Halbwachs writes, "The only ancestors transmitted and retained are those whose memory has become the object of a cult by

men who remain at least fictitiously in contact with them."[12] But media also played a role in the choice of the ancestors who were remembered. In the sixteenth century, the compiler(s) of *Hachijō kadensho* invoked a pantheon that included Konparu Zenchiku, Kanze On'ami, Hōshō Ren'ami, and Kongō Sōsetsu in addition to Zeami. In the early modern period, as not only family lines became refined but also a manuscript culture gave way to a print culture, Zeami came to overshadow the others because of the dissemination of plays and publications (mis)attributed to him. Zeami became a recognized author and authority in the seventeenth century long before his theories became widely available and rigorously understood even among professional noh performers. For family heads of the eighteenth century like Kanze Motoakira, the invocation of Zeami's name as patriarch and author served his efforts to standardize noh just as the names of Rikyū and Dōgen furthered the institutionalization of the tea ceremony and Zen Buddhism by providing a figurehead whose ideas could advance the policies of their descendants. Motoakira is representative of family heads, the living patriarchs of an art, who are empowered to reformulate the received legacy by their exalted bloodlines and complete intimacy with the ultimate teachings of their profession.

Professionalization
and the Family-Head System

As the example of Kanze Motoakira illustrates, control of publishing was a key step in the consolidation of the family-head system. This observation is supported by Western sociological research, which holds the standardization of occupational knowledge is a prerequisite to professionalization. Magali Larson writes, "The standardization or codification of knowledge is the basis on which a professional 'commodity' can be made distinct and recognizable to the potential publics."[13] Although all professions maintain mechanisms to govern standards, the family-head system is distinctly authoritarian since it invests a single individual with the right to decide all the parameters of an occupation. Table 8.1 summarizes the powers enjoyed by modern noh family heads, particularly the five *iemoto* of the *shite* schools (Kanze, Konparu, Hōshō, Kongō, and Kita). The family heads of other performers, such as kyōgen actors and musicians, have comparable but

Table 8.1
Rights of Modern Noh Family Heads (*Iemoto*)

---

1. Rights over the repertoire
   A. The right to remove or include a work in the repertoire
   B. The right to permit a trial performance or public performance of a new play, and the right to exclude or add that work to the permanent repertoire

2. Rights pertaining to the production of noh
   A. The right to amend the texts to noh plays
   B. The right to amend and establish "annotations" (*zuke*) to music, dance, and other production texts
   C. The right to demand from the *iemoto* of supporting roles the revision (and adoption) of "annotations"

3. Rights pertaining to performance
   A. The right to allow or prohibit actors from performing works in the repertoire
   B. The right to allow or prohibit entire performances
   C. The right to restrict ownership of masks, costumes, and noh stages

4. Rights over performers
   A. The right to recognize performers as professionals in the school
   B. The exclusive right to prohibit school members from performing
   C. The right to disbar performers from the school
   D. The right to authorize school members to form associations to produce performances

5. Rights concerning licenses
   A. The right to establish and amend varieties of licenses
   B. The right to issue licenses and collect money for granting them

6. Rights pertaining to annotations
   A. The right to make annotations to plays, secret or public
   B. The right to publish play books (*utaibon*) and other annotations
   C. The right to revenues from publishing these annotations
   D. The right to enforce the use of standard texts among performers in the school

---

SOURCE: adapted from Yokomichi and Kobayashi, *Nō, kyōgen*, p. 304.

less far-reaching powers. The modern family head's rights extend into all aspects of production and even into the personal lives of noh performers. As the case of Takabayashi Ginji introduced at the beginning of this book exemplifies, performers have been disbarred from their profession for disagreeing with the artistic vision of their family head.

The performers in the noh world with the most authority, especially the family heads, hold their elite positions by virtue of birth. Only these actors have the clout to assay the more challenging works in the repertoire or to commission new noh plays. This means that the most revered and difficult plays as well as any experimental works are performed only by the highest echelons of the noh establishment. In other words, the actors with the most to lose because of changes in patterns of artistic production and institutional structure are the ones who set the guidelines for innovation in their profession's art. Younger performers, those from less-influential families, and any who enter the profession by circuitous routes, such as by attending a performing arts university, have little chance of affecting either the theatrical or the institutional mores of their profession. Yet, the overriding authority given to the family head has meant that other myths, such as the valorization of patrilineal bloodlines, have been de-emphasized, as the case of Kongō Ukyō illustrates. Additionally, more performers are being recruited through performing arts universities than ever before, and women, who have been allowed to perform professionally since World War II, are making strides, although they still face many constraints. Modern noh has yet to see a woman become an *iemoto*, but, then, a female *iemoto* is a rarity in most traditional arts.

What Was Lost?

In this survey of the history of noh's myth-making, one element essential to noh's growth is clearly absent from the modern noh world: namely, diverse groups performing noh. It is no accident that the fifteenth and sixteenth centuries, the period of noh's most energetic development, coincided with the era in which the widest range of groups enacted noh. The full extent of the achievements of these noh groups, who appear and then disappear, in the historical record may never be known. Yet the abilities and popularity of these rival groups prompted the four Yamato troupes to adopt new media, develop elaborate myths, and hone their talents in competition. Today, when the descendants of the Yamato have won out, their families' achievements are retold as history, their myths are accepted as tradition, and there seems little room for dissenting versions of how noh might be performed.

Because of the conservative nature of authority in noh institutions, few modern dramatists aspire to create new noh plays since there is little possibility of ever seeing the works performed as part of the regular repertoire. The Japanese government opened a National Noh Theater in Tokyo in 1983, but it does not subsidize noh the same way the Meiji government did, nor does it compel performers to stage certain plays. Gone, too, are the imperial and *zaibatsu* patrons of noh, since both of these institutions were greatly restricted after World War II, and noh today depends mostly on lesson fees and other revenues from its amateur students. Finally, only noh's *iemoto* have the right to determine which works will enter the repertoire. Since noh is dominated by a few families, performers from outside this world realize that noh offers them little chance for artistic freedom. Apparently, the only way to change noh is for outsiders to undertake the creation and production of noh themselves. Although they would surely face criticism that their art is not and can never be "noh," this group would reinvigorate an art now constrained by its own ethos. Yet, if noh's history is any guide, changes in the meaning of "noh" as both an art and as a profession will occur.

Appendix

APPENDIX

Schools and Roles

This appendix is meant as a guide to the key structures and the terminology of noh.

The fundamental unit of institutional organization in the noh world today is the noh school, since all the roughly 2,500 professional performers must belong to a school. *Ryū*, the Japanese word translated as "school," can also be rendered as "artistic style," and each school espouses a distinct performance style. Amateurs also participate in schools as tuition-paying students learning the performance style of their teacher.

The noh school is structured as an extended family. Since noh is usually transmitted from father to son, entire families of noh performers belong to the same school. For example, all the performers of the Umewaka family are members of the Kanze school. The Kanze school is made up of professional performers from many such families, as well as performers who entered the profession without prior familial connections, such as through study with professionals at a performing arts university or in the National Noh Theater's training program. Whatever their origins, all members of a noh school participate in the fictional family of the school.

The leader of the noh school enjoys the patriarchal title of "family head" (*iemoto*). Ideally, the family head is the first-born son of the previous family head, but adoptions do occur when the *iemoto* does not have a son. Today, the family head serves as the final arbiter of his school's artistic style, and the school's traditions are considered his family's art. The connection between the school and the family head is reinforced by the fact that the name of the school derives from the *iemoto*'s family name. For example, the current leader of the Kanze school is Kanze Kiyokazu. The head of the noh school exercises tremendous control over all aspects of performance. His powers (described in Table 8.1) include the right to license professionals, determine the contents of the repertoire, and receive the royalties for the publication of the school's writings.

At present, there are twenty-four schools of noh, and these schools can be subdivided according to role type.[1] The type of school a performer belongs to depends on the role that performer takes in a play. Performers specialize in only one role type and perform only in that part. For example, actors who specialize in the role of the lead performer (*shite*) in a play may act in the role of the *shite* or as a companion (*tsure*) to the *shite*. *Shite* actors can also appear in the chorus when they do not take the *shite* part. The five schools for *shite* actors are the Kanze, Konparu, Hōshō, Kongō, and Kita.

There are three schools of *waki* performers: Takayasu, Fukuō, and Hōshō. The *waki* generally establishes the setting and introduces a play. Actors who study the role of the *waki* perform only in that role or as the *waki*'s companion(s) (*wakitsure*).

Musicians specialize in one musical instrument: the noh flute (*nōkan*), shoulder-drum (*kotsuzumi*), hip-drum (*ōtsuzumi*), or stick-drum (*taiko*). There are three schools for flute (Issō, Morita, and Fujita), four for shoulder-drum (Kō, Kōsei, Ōkura, and Kanze), five for hip-drum (Kadono, Takayasu, Ishii, Ōkura, and Kanze), and two for stick-drum (Kanze and Konparu).

Finally, there are two schools of kyōgen (Ōkura and Izumi). Kyōgen actors appear in two contexts in noh theater. First, they take center stage at the halfway point in many noh plays to reiterate the plot. Second, they appear in the farces, also called kyōgen, performed between noh plays.

The cast of a noh play consists of members of six different schools of performers: one for each of the specialty roles. The *shite* and the eight-member chorus are always from the same school. Performers of the same role from different schools never appear together on stage. In other words, a Kanze *shite* would never perform with a Konparu chorus, and an Ōkura school kyōgen actor will never appear with a member of the Izumi school except in special circumstances.[2]

Today, musicians, kyōgen actors, and *waki* perform with any school of *shite* actors, but in the medieval and early modern periods the ties between the *shite* and their accompanists were much stronger.

For instance, in the Edo period, the Fukuō school of *waki*, the Morita school of flute, the Kōsei school of shoulder-drum, the Kadono school of hip-drum, and the Kanze school of stick-drum performed almost exclusively with the Kanze school of *shite* performers. This amalgamation of performers was known as the Kanze troupe (*Kanze za*)—a structure that persisted until the end of the Tokugawa period in 1868. The linkage of noh performers into troupes dates from the medieval era. Lead performers (*shite*) acted as the leaders (*tayū*) of medieval noh troupes, and the troupe derived its name from the family name of the leader. The modern leaders of the Kanze, Konparu, Hōshō, and Kongō *shite* schools trace their family lineages and art back to the leaders of the "four troupes of Yamato province" (*Yamato yoza*). Thus, the current head of the Kanze school, Kanze Kiyokazu, traces his family's artistic style back twenty-six generations to Kan'ami (d. 1384), the founder of his lineage.

Reference Matter

Notes

Introduction

1. The word *nōgaku* is a modern term that refers to both noh and kyō-gen. Another word for noh is *sarugaku*. *Sarugaku* also refers to an older performing art that predates and gave rise to noh—also called *sarugaku nō*. As Benito Ortolani (*Japanese Theatre*, p. 55) indicates, there is little scholarly consensus on the use of the terms *sarugaku*, *sarugaku nō*, and *noh* to indicate different historical stages in the art's development. He adds that noh performers might refer to themselves as *sarugaku* (*nō*) performers until recently. The present work explores nuances in terms like *sarugaku* historically, but for convenience it will refer to the art as noh theater.

2. Takabayashi, *Geidō dokubon*, p. 1. Ginji's disbarment resulted from a long-standing disagreement with Minoru over artistic matters. After the death of Roppeita in 1971, Ginji was allowed to return to the Kita troupe (Takabayashi Kōji, pers. comm., Mar. 21, 2002).

3. Takabayashi Ginji was not the only actor to be disbarred in the twentieth century. Members of the Umewaka family were forced out of the Kanze school in 1920 over their efforts to create a new school of noh. The conflict between the Umewaka and the noh establishment began in the late nineteenth century and was not resolved until 1954, with the Umewaka ultimately rejoining the Kanze (Nishiyama, *Iemotosei no tenkai*, pp. 382–86).

4. Takabayashi, *Geidō dokubon*, pp. 2–4.

5. Hobsbawm and Ranger, *Invention of Tradition*, p. 4.

6. Clanchy, *From Memory to Written Record*, p. 35.

7. Barthes, *Mythologies*, pp. 117, 142.

8. McLuhan, *Gutenberg Galaxy*, p. 40.

9. Larson, *Rise of Professionalism*, p. xvi.

10. Amano Fumio, *Nō ni tsukareta kenryokusha*, p. 16.

11. According to one scholar of noh history, "The greatest players of the early Muromachi period who are known by name . . . worked with many lesser performers who were, for the most part, coarse and illiterate, and whose main concern, like others of their class, was to ensure a living for themselves in a cruel, uncertain and often hungry world" (O'Neill, *Early Nō Drama*, p. 41). Noh is not alone among traditional institutions that have substituted a simplified version of their history for a complex and conflict-ridden past; for the case of Zen Buddhism, see Faure, *Rhetoric of Immediacy*, p. 19.

Chapter 1

1. For example, Kongō, *Nō to nōmen*, p. 107; Konparu Nobutaka, *Ugokanu yue ni nō to iu*, p. 25.

2. Konparu Nobutaka, *Ugokanu yue ni nō to iu*, pp. 127, 180. Another name for an Okina mask is *hakushikijō*.

3. *Bugaku* and *gigaku* dances had little if any narrative content; noh drew most of its theatrical inspiration from the variety art *sangaku*, the dance tradition *dengaku*, and the ballad-dance performance called *kusemai*. For a narrative of the early history of noh, see Ortolani, *Japanese Theater*, pp. 54–93. The research of Gotō Hajime (*Chūsei Kamen*, pp. 882–986) has shown in addition a strong continuity between noh masks, especially demon masks, and what he has identified as "folk" (*minzoku*) masks. In Nakamura Yasuo's (*Kamen to shinkō*, pp. 61, 68) opinion, the conventions used in carving Kamakura-period statues of Shinto divinities also influenced noh masks.

4. *Gigaku* masks are not the oldest known masks, however. Archaeologists have discovered ancient masks made from clay and shell in sites in the Kantō and Tōhoku regions of Japan dating to before 200 B.C. The possible ceremonial or theatrical uses of these masks remain unknown.

5. Nakamura Yasuo, *Kamen to shinkō*, pp. 158–59. Gotō Hajime (*Chūsei kamen*, p. 884) dated one mask of the Okina variety, a mask of Chichinojō, to 1316.

6. Gotō, *Chūsei kamen*, p. 1008.

7. Besides the *shite*, accompanying performers (*tsure*) might wear masks. Kyōgen actors also make occasional use of masks. There are some plays, such as *Ataka*, in which none of the performers wears a mask.

8. Kanze Hisao, *Kanze Hisao chosakushū*, 2: 280–81.

9. The following discussion of the categories of noh masks is based on Nishino and Hata, *Nō, kyōgen jiten*, pp. 344–48; Komparu Kunio, *Noh Theater*, pp. 230–39; and Yokomichi and Koyama, *Nōgaku zusetsu*, pp. 496–538.

10. Okina celebrates the virtues of old age and can be interpreted as a prayer for longevity. Saisōrō, however, addresses the infirmities of age; according to tradition the old dancer who takes this role will die within a year (Nishikawa, *Bugaku Masks*, pp. 48–49).

11. Nakamura Yasuo, *Kamen to shinkō*, p. 35.

12. Yoshida Teigo, "The Stranger as God," p. 93.

13. Aston, *Nihongi*, 2: 68.

14. Law, *Puppets of Nostalgia*, pp. 118–19.

15. Gotō, *Chūsei kamen*, pp. 731–32.

16. Dykstra, "Miraculous Tales of the Hasedera Kannon," pp. 117–23.

17. Gotō, *Chūsei kamen*, p. 732.

18. Gotō, *Nihon no kamen*, p. 39; idem, *Chūsei kamen*, p. 733; Ruppert, *Jewel in the Ashes*, p. 134.

19. Gotō, *Nihon no kamen*, p. 160.

20. Nakamura Yasuo, *Kamen to shinkō*, pp. 97–98.

21. Amano, *Okina sarugaku kenkyū*, p. 32.

22. Nakamura Yasuo, *Kamen to shinkō*, p. 83.

23. Many of the shrine's original documents burned in a fire in 1876, but fortunately they had previously been copied and published as *Satsuma kyūki zōroku* (Gotō, *Nihon no kamen*, pp. 93–97).

24. Nakamura Yasuo, *Kamen to shinkō*, p. 33.

25. Ibid., pp. 106–7.

26. Ibid., p. 145.

27. Gotō, *Nihon no kamen*, p. 207.

28. Nakamura Yasuo, *Kamen to shinkō*, p. 63. For a photograph and description of this *zuzuiko* and the accompanying masks, see Ōtsushi reki-shi hakubutsukan, *Nō, kyōgen no furusato*, pp. 39, 78–79.

29. Kongō, *Nō to nōmen*, pp. 17–19.

30. Clanchy (*From Memory to Written Record*, p. 38) cited medieval academic treatises from as late as the thirteenth century that described practices surrounding the transference of land. These texts indicate that in addition to recording the transfer in writing, the two parties exchanged cups, knives, swords, and sometimes even pieces of turf. Such objects not only symbolized the transfer but also served as physical reminders of the exchange.

31. Noh actors also participated in the wider practices of relic adulation as a means of describing and laying claim to religious or artistic tradition. Zeami's *Fūshikaden* stated that the Konparu owned Buddha relics (*shari*) once in the possession of Prince Shōtoku. According to the *Sarugaku kikigaki* (1599; p. 218) the Konparu troupe received ninety grains of Buddha relics, which grew or shrank in size depending on the fortunes of the troupe. The late Muromachi-era guide to letter writing *Teikin ōraichū*

(p. 102) makes the even grander claim that the Konparu also owned the Yata mirror of the imperial regalia, said to hold the reflection of the Sun Goddess.

32. Zeami, *Fūshikaden*, pp. 40–41.

33. Nakamori Hiroshi, "Ōmi to nō, kyōgen," p. 10.

34. A few noh masks, such as a *ja* mask in the former collection of the Kongō family (now in the Mitsui Bunko), are said to cause rain when worn (Miyake, *Nōgaku geiwa*, p. 212). Performers may have been reluctant to boast of the rainmaking powers of their masks since most perform- ances were held outdoors at this time.

35. Nakamura Yasuo, *Kamen to shinkō*, p. 32.

36. *Sarugaku kikigaki*, pp. 246–47.

37. Nakamura Yasuo, *Kamen to shinkō*, pp. 32–33.

38. Zeami, *Fūshikaden*, pp. 302–3.

39. Trans. from Rimer and Yamazaki, *On the Art of the Nō Drama*, p. 240.

40. Hoff, "The 'Evocation' and 'Blessing' of Okina," p. 49; Arai, *Nō no kenkyū*, p. 97.

41. Kanze Motoyoshi, *Sarugaku dangi*, p. 310.

42. Zeami, *Fūshikaden*, p. 40.

43. Kanze Motoyoshi, *Sarugaku dangi*, p. 302.

44. Ong, *Orality and Literacy*, p. 70.

45. Aston, *Nihongi*, 1: 76–77.

46. Kanze Motoyoshi, *Sarugaku dangi*, pp. 301–2, 304.

47. Nose, *Nōgaku genryūko*, pp. 1069–71.

48. For a photograph of the mask Motomasa supposedly donated to the shrine, see Nakamura Yasuo, *Noh, the Classical Theater*, p. 80.

49. For the latter, see Ruppert, *Jewel in the Ashes*.

50. Arai, *Nō no kenkyū*, p. 97; Hōshō, "Nōmen no hanashi," p. 112; Su- zuki, *Nō no omote*, p. 3.

51. See the Appendix for a discussion of the rights of the family head.

52. On the early history of writing in Japan, see Farris, *Sacred Texts and Buried Treasures*, pp. 98–99.

53. "Not only does this oral aspect of manuscript culture deeply affect the manner of composing and writing, but it meant that writing, reading, and oratory remained inseparable until well after printing" (McLuhan, *Gutenberg Galaxy*, p. 90).

54. Examples outside noh include *Nanpōroku* in tea ceremony and *Ya- kusha rongo* in Kabuki; see Moriya Takeshi, *Kinsei geinō bunkashi no ken- kyū*, pp. 259–60.

55. Kanze Motoyoshi, *Sarugaku dangi*, p. 310.

56. Ong, *Orality and Literacy*, p. 100.

57. Kanze Motoyoshi, *Sarugaku dangi*, pp. 301–2.

58. For a discussion of the dissemination of *Sarugaku dangi*, see De Poorter, *Zeami's Talks on Sarugaku*, pp. 61–69.

59. Shimotsuma Shōshin, *Shōshin kikigaki*, p. 83.

60. *Hachijō kadensho*, p. 621.

61. Oze Hoan, *Taikōki*, pp. 387–88.

62. The Deme *ko'omote* measures approximately 21 cm long by 13 cm wide by 6 cm deep. Other women's masks differed in width and depth but not length. Male masks were shorter than the *ko'omote*, but wider. The *ōbeshimi* and *shishi* masks were the thickest; the *shishi* mask measured approximately 12 cm in depth (Suzuki, *Nō no omote*, pp. 20–21).

63. Kongō, *Nō to nōmen*, p. 68.

64. *Kyōhō rokunen kakiage*, p. 230.

65. Tokuda, *Rinchū kenmonshū*, p. 10.

66. *Kyōhō rokunen kakiage*, pp. 225–26.

67. Shimotsuma Shōshin, *Sōdensho*, p. 44.

68. The text is *Himitsuroku*, a draft of Tora'akira's famous *Waranbegusa* (1660). See Yonkekura, *Waranbegusa kyōgen mukashi gatarisho kenkyū*, p. 727.

69. Goody, *Logic of Writing*, p. 12.

70. Street, *Literacy in Theory and Practice*, pp. 44–65.

71. Larson, *Rise of Professionalism*, p. 40.

Chapter 2

EPIGRAPH: Zeami, *Fūshikaden*, p. 62.

1. Cited in Kitagawa, *Zeami*, p. 31.

2. Marra, *Representations of Power*, pp. 55–56.

3. Ibid., p. 107.

4. Rabinow, "Representations Are Social Facts," p. 241.

5. Zeami, *Fūshikaden*, p. 48.

6. McLuhan, *Understanding Media*, pp. 22–23.

7. Cited in Tonomura, *Community and Commerce in Late Medieval Japan*, p. 105.

8. Zeami, *Fūshikaden*, p. 41.

9. Concrete comparisons of historically discriminated groups are difficult to make because of a paucity of sources, but *shōmonji* seemed to have fared better than other groups at the periphery of medieval society. For more information on the debate among Japanese medievalists on discriminated groups, see Hosokawa, *Chūsei no mibunsei to hinin*.

10. Larson, *Rise of Professionalism*, p. x.

11. For example, Law, *Puppets of Nostalgia*, pp. 49–88; and Marra, *Representations of Power*, pp. 55–114.

12. Fujiwara-Skrobak, "Social Consciousness and Madness in Zeami's Life and Work," p. 84.

13. As Morita Yoshinori (*Chūsei no senmin to zatsugei no kenkyū*, p. 111) has explained, this interpretation of *shōmon* derives from the Sanskrit word *śrāvaka*, meaning "someone who has heard the teachings of the Buddha. " This term gained pejorative connotations early in Buddhist discourse before it arrived in Japan. Mahayana Buddhist intellectuals applied it to their counterparts of the so-called lesser vehicle (Hinayana). In Morita's opinion, this debate informed the application of the term *shōmonji* to lower-level functionaries working at Buddhist temples who were not full-fledged monks.

14. *Ainōshō*, cited in Kyōto burakushi kenkyūjo, *Shiryō kodai chūsei*, p. 546.

15. Wakita Haruko, "Chūsei hisabetsumin no seikatsu to shakai," p. 99.

16. Wakita Haruko, "Chūsei hisabetsumin no seikatsu to shakai."

17. For a map of the locations of *shōmonji* villages in medieval Kyoto, see Kawashima, *Chūsei Kyōto bunka no shūroku*, p. 168.

18. *Tokitsugu kyōki*, Tenmon 21 (1552).10 and Tenshō 4 (1576).9; cited in Murayama, *Nihon onmyōdō shiwa*, p. 241.

19. Murayama, *Nihon onmyōdō shiwa*, p. 242; and Yamamoto, "Onmyōji," pp. 121–27.

20. Kanshō 4 (1463).11.23, Bunmei 9 (1477).5.13, in *Daijōin jisha zōjiki*, 3: 368 and 6: 276.

21. Yamaji, *Okina no za*, pp. 68–69. For general information on *kowakamai*, see Araki, *Ballad-Drama of Medieval Japan*.

22. *Ryōjin hishō*, no. 443; cited in Watanabe, *Geinōshi bunkashi jiten chūsei hen*, p. 189.

23. Inuwaka was active in Kyoto in the 1420s. Nose Asaji's discussion of *shōmonji* noh is still authoritative; see Nose, *Nōgaku genryūko*, pp. 1092–104.

24. Eikyō 5 (1433).1.12 in *Kanmon gyoki*, 2: 84. *Kanmon gyoki* is an important source for information on *shōmonji* and pine-music in the fifteenth century. The diary covers the years 1416 to 1448.

25. Kakitsu 3 (1443).1.19, in *Kanmon gyoki*, 2: 638.

26. Morita Yoshinori, *Chūsei no senmin to zatsugei no kenkyū*, p. 144.

27. In Akita prefecture costumed performers still arrive at homes during the New Year to give a blessing (Morita Yoshinori, *Chūsei no senmin to zatsugei no kenkyū*, p. 125). For a discussion of other folk versions of pine-music see Yamaji, "Matsubayashi," p. 79.

28. Ōei 23 (1416). 1. 11, in *Kanmon gyoki*, 1: 2–3.

29. The Christmas wreath may have originated from a Roman New Year's custom surprisingly similar to the Japanese practice of decorating entrances with pine branches. Tertullian (ca. 160–ca. 240) condemned this "pagan" practice in strong terms: heathens "fix on doorposts laurels which shall afterwards be burnt" (cited in Miles, *Christmas in Ritual and Tradition*, p. 269).

30. *Hachijō kadensho*, p. 538.

31. Other variants for writing *matsubayashi* include the Chinese character now read as *kanaderu*, meaning "to play an instrument," or the two characters read as *hyōshi*, meaning "rhythm."

32. A portion of the *Takanami saireizu* that depicts pine-music is reproduced in Yamaji, "Matsubayashi," p. 79.

33. Orikuchi, *Nihon geinōshi nōto*, p. 266.

34. Morita Yoshinori, *Chūsei no senmin to zatsugei no kenkyū*, pp. 168–69.

35. Ōei 18 (1411).1.15, Ōei 20 (1413).1.15, and Ōei 23 (1416).1.15 in *Mansai Jugō nikki*, 1: 7, 11, 83. *Saigichō* were a regular part of performances of pine-music, as seen from the entry for Ōei 28 (1421).1.15 in *Kanmon gyoki* (1: 284), which mentioned the burning of a *sagichō* "as usual" after the entrance of the pine-music groups from nearby villages.

36. A version of *Matsuyani (Matsu no sei)* was included in the late seventeenth-century *Kyōgenki* (pp. 61–64).

37. *Matsuyani* in *Kyōgen shūsei*, p. 471. In the twentieth century, pine-music performers in Kikuchi Village, Kumamoto prefecture, still chant, "*Matsuyani ya'ani, komatsuyani ya'ani*" (Yoshikawa Kanehira, "Matsubayashi ni tsuite," p. 84).

38. The content of *furyū* dancing varied according to the occasion and participants involved. Mary Elizabeth Berry (*Culture of Civil War in Kyoto*, pp. 248–59) provides historical background on *furyū* dancing in the sixteenth and early seventeenth century, highlighting the social and political meanings of *furyū*.

39. Ortolani, *The Japanese Theatre*, p. 70.

40. The entry for Eikyō 3 (1431).1.14 in *Kanmon gyoki* (1: 568) records a *furyū* performance of *matsubayashi* by samurai from villages under Prince Sadafusa's stewardship. Sadafusa rewarded each performer with robes. A similar record can be found for Eikyō 7 (1435).1.15 in *Kanmon gyoki*, 2: 250–51.

41. The contents of the letter (*fumi*) are not stated; it could have been a sample of calligraphy or a drawing, or more likely a letter of introduction to enable the group to perform for another noble (see entry for Eikyō 4 [1432].1.13 in *Kanmon gyoki*, 2: 4).

42. In the eighth year of Eikyō (1436), the *shōmonji* Chōa troupe turned up at the residence of Prince Sadafusa and asked to perform. Sadafusa

noted in his diary that since the Chōa lacked the shogun's permission to perform, he turned them away. (Whether *shōmonji* troupes always required the shogun's permission is unknown, given Sadafusa's later actions.) The entry in Sadafusa's diary for the following day stated that the same troupe appeared again, and he turned them away once more (Eikyō 8 [1436].1.8–9 in *Kanmon gyoki*, 2: 354). The Chōa tried twice again the following year. After dismissing them once, Sadafusa took pity on them when they appeared a second time and allowed them to perform noh. Sadafusa likely regretted this decision because he described their performance as extremely inept (Eikyō 9 [1437].1.4, 6 in *Kanmon gyoki*, 2: 439–40). When the Chōa appeared the next year, Sadafusa turned them away a final time (Eikyō 10 [1438].1.7 in *Kanmon gyōki*, 2: 507–8).

43. Morita Yoshinori, *Chūsei no senmin to zatsugei no kenkyū*, p. 125.

44. Reproduced in Yamaji, "Senzumanzai," p. 45.

45. For examples, see Geinōshi kenkyūkai, ed., *Dengaku, sarugaku*, pp. 537–39.

46. Morita Yoshinori, *Chūsei no senmin to zatsugei no kenkyū*, p. 126.

47. *Oyudono no ue no nikki* was a journal maintained by women working in the inner-apartments of the imperial palace from the years 1477 to 1820; see Morita Yoshinori, *Chūsei no senmin to zatsugei no kenkyū*, pp. 130, 136.

48. Yamaji, "Senzumanzai," pp. 42–47.

49. Kim, *Songs to Make the Dust Dance*, pp. 12–13.

50. Zeami, *Fūshikaden*, p. 21.

51. Zeami, *Kakyō*, p. 109.

52. Zeami, *Fūshikaden*, p. 47.

53. Pinnington, "Crossed Paths," pp. 204–5.

54. Klein, "Allegories of Desire," pp. 363–64.

55. Kuroda, "Historical Consciousness and Honjaku Philosophy," pp. 147–48.

56. Bodiford, *Sōtō Zen in Medieval Japan*, p. 152.

57. Ibid., p. 155.

58. Faure, *Visions of Power*, pp. 49, 56.

59. Ibid., p. 58.

60. Baudrillard, *Seduction*, p. 79.

61. Zeami, *Fūshikaden*; trans. from Rimer and Yamazaki, *On the Art of the Nō Drama*, p. 59.

62. Zeami, *Fūshikaden*, p. 62.

63. Larson, *Rise of Professionalism*, p. 14.

64. Zeami, *Fūshikaden*; trans. from Rimer and Yamazaki, *On the Art of the Nō Drama*, pp. 42–43.

65. Zeami, *Kakyō*, p. 109.

66. Zeami, *Kyakuraika*, p. 248.

67. Zeami, *Kakyō*, p. 106.

68. Stock, *Implications of Literacy*, pp. 88–91.

69. Kanze Motoyoshi, *Sarugaku dangi*, p. 300.

70. Nakamura Yasuo, "Nō no koteika to iemoto seido," p. 9.

71. Ong, *Orality and Literacy*, p. 41.

72. De Poorter, *Zeami's Talks on Sarugaku*, pp. 21–22.

73. Konparu Zenchiku, *Enman'iza hekisho*, p. 312.

74. Zeami, *Fūshikaden*; trans. from Rimer and Yamazaki, *On the Art of the Nō Drama*, p. 63. Mototsugu may be another name for Motomasa or someone else. De Poorter (*Zeami's Talks on Sarugaku*, p. 36) theorized that Mototsugu was a close relative of Zeami's: "He could have been a son, a younger brother . . . or a nephew."

75. The expression "one person per generation" *(ichidai hitori)* appears in Zeami, *Fūshikaden*, p. 64. Ironically Zeami violated his precept in the same moment that he articulated it: as we have seen, the colophon to the *Style and Flower* reveals that he gave the work to Shirō and Mototsugu.

76. Zeami, *Kyakuraika*; trans. from Thornhill, *Six Circles, One Dewdrop*, p. 17.

77. Only a few of these original manuscripts survive; see Pinnington, "Crossed Paths," p. 216.

78. Zeami damned Zenchiku with faint praise in the *Flower of Returning*: "Of course, the head of the Konparu troupe's fundamental style is correct, and he may be capable of preserving our tradition, but as of now he does not seem likely to become a great performer" (Zeami, *Kyakuraika*; trans. from Thornhill, *Six Circles, One Dewdrop*, p. 17).

79. Zenchiku took this one further step by sharing some of his own secret treatises with intellectuals outside the world of noh, even asking for comments on his *Rokurin ichiro* texts from the Tōdaiji abbot of Kaidain-in, Shigyoku, and from Ichijō Kaneyoshi (d. 1481).

80. Eikyō 3 (1431).1.11 in *Mansai Jugō nikki*, 2: 205.

81. Morita Yoshinori, *Chūsei no senmin to zatsugei no kenkyū*, p. 163.

82. Zeami's song is either an independent piece or an excerpt from a play that is no longer performed (Kanze Motoyoshi, *Sarugaku dangi*, p. 305; my translation is adapted from Rimer and Yamazaki, *On the Art of the Nō Drama*, p. 244).

83. Eikyō 2 (1430).4.28 in *Kanmon gyōki*, 1: 540. Unfortunately the entries for the first three months of 1430 are missing from this diary; it is the only source of information about Inuwaka, and it is uncertain whether Inuwaka performed during the New Year in 1430 or not. Unless otherwise noted, the following discussion of Inuwaka and Koinu is derived from Nose, *Nōgaku genryūko*, pp. 1094–102.

84. Eikyō 3 (1431).1.11 in *Kanmon gyōki*, 1: 579.

85. Eikyō 3 (1431).1.13 in *Kanmon gyoki*, 1: 580.

86. Cited in Kyoto burakushi kenkyūjo, *Shiryō kodai chūsei*, p. 536.

87. Zeami, *Fūshikaden*, p. 38.

88. Kanze Motoyoshi, *Sarugaku dangi*, pp. 299–300.

89. Eikyō 1 (1429).5.13 in *Mansai Jugō nikki*, 2: 52.

90. Hare, *Zeami's Style*, p. 32.

91. Shōchō 2 (1429).1.13 in *Mansai Jugō nikki*, 2: 9–10.

92. Goshima, "Buke sarugaku to Muromachi dono ni okeru kōgyō," p. 34.

93. Eikyō 4 (1432).1.13 in *Mansai Jugō nikki*, 2: 328–29.

94. Ise, *Tadasugawara kanjin sarugaku nikki*.

95. In the modern version performed by the Izumi school of kyōgen, gourd-beating priests, who also make tea whisks, travel to Kitano shrine in Kyoto to pray for an improvement in their business. After performing a ritual dance, the Gourd God Fukube appears and blesses them. The Ōkura school's script of the plays *Fukube no shin* and *Fukube no shin tsutome iri* are similar, but the gourd beaters are not poor, and they are on an annual pilgrimage. Both the Izumi and Ōkura texts are versions reworked in the early modern period, because the protagonists of these plays are modeled after the dancing *nenbutsu* priests of the Kuyadō in Kyoto who earned a livelihood by making tea whisks and beat gourds or bells as they danced and chanted the name of Amida Buddha (*Tenshō kyōgenbon zen'yaku*, pp. 334, 340–41).

96. Kanshō 4 (1463).11.23 in *Daijōin jisha zōjiki*, 3: 368.

97. Koyama et al., *Kyōgen no sekai*, p. 137.

98. The fact that both occupations were stigmatized is apparent from the picture-scroll *Yūzū nenbutsu engi emaki* dated to 1414, which mockingly depicted *hachitataki* and monkey-trainers dressed as beggars (see Amino, *Igyō no ōken*, pp. 25–26; the depictions are reproduced on p. 26).

99. Beards of unusual length marked outcast status, as in the case of the lower-status functionaries (*hōmen*) attached to the capital police force (*kebiishischō*) (ibid., p. 9).

100. Nose, *Nōgaku genryūko*, p. 1098.

101. Eikyō 9 (1437).1.4 and 8 in *Kanmon gyoki*, 2: 439, 440. It is uncertain whether *shōmonji* required the shogun's permission to perform, or if this was simply the shogun's endorsement.

102. Eikyō 8 (1436).1.8 in *Kanmon gyōki*, 2: 354.

103. Kakitsu 3 (1443).1.14 and 19 in *Kanmon gyōki*, 2: 637, 638.

104. Ōei 30 (1423).10.1 in *Yasutomiki*; cited in Kotaka, *Geinōshi nenpyō*, p. 25.

105. *Yasutomiki*; cited in Omote and Amano, *Nō no rekishi*, p. 63.

106. Nose, *Nōgaku genryūko*, p. 1068.

107. *Inryōken nichiroku*; cited in Nose, *Nōgaku genryūko*, p. 1099.

108. Nose, *Nōgaku genryūko*, p. 1069.

109. The aristocratic author Kanroji Chikanaga (d. 1500) recorded in his diary *Chikanaga kyōki* a visit to his residence of the *kusemai* dancers Koinu Yatarō and his son Tojirō in the third month of 1476. Koinu Yatarō may have been the son or grandson of Koinu. The names Koinu Yatarō and Tojirō continue appearing in diaries as *kusemai* performers up to the late 1480s. If Koinu had any other successors, their names are now lost (Nose, *Nōgaku genryūko*, p. 1102).

110. Genki 3 (1572).1.4 and 5 in *Oyudono no ue no nikki*, 7: 72.

111. See examples from *Tokitsugi kyōki* for the years 1544–54 (Temmon 13, 14, 15, 17, 19, 21, and 23); cited in Kotaka, *Geinōshi nenpyō*, pp. 331–64.

112. Cited in Kawashima, *Chūsei Kyōto bunka no shūroku*, pp. 90–91.

113. Cited in Hane, *Premodern Japan*, p. 119.

114. Kawashima, *Chūsei Kyōto bunka no shūroku*, p. 167.

115. Morita Yoshinori, *Chūsei no senmin to zatsugei no kenkyū*, p. 117.

116. See Chapter 7 for a description of an Okina performance.

117. Mark Nearman ("Behind the Mask of Nō," p. 40) translated *Mei-shukushū* (which he read as *Myōshuku shū*) as *Writings on the Radiant Constellations*. *Shuku* in the title refers to *shukugami*, or patron-deity. My translation of *Meishukushū* as *Writings to Clarify Okina* relies on Zenchiku's equation of *Okina* with the *shukugami*.

118. Later treatises such as *Hachijō kadensho* seem to have relied mostly on the simplified version of the Okina myth found in the preamble to the first chapter of *Fūshikaden* and not the more detailed discussion in Chapter 4, entitled "Matters Pertaining to the Gods," of that work.

119. Omote, "Zeami to Zenchiku no densho," pp. 569–71. See also De Poorter's discussion of the historical reception of *Sarugaku dangi* in *Zeami's Talks on Sarugaku*, pp. 49–50, 61–69.

120. A copy was discovered in 1964 in a storehouse owned by the family-head of the Konparu school, and the original turned up soon after in the possession of the same family (Omote, "Zeami to Zenchiku no densho," p. 581).

121. Nearman, "Behind the Mask of Nō," p. 40.

122. Zeami, *Kyakuraika*, p. 248.

123. Kanze Motoyoshi, *Sarugaku dangi*; trans. from Rimer and Yamazaki, *On the Art of the Nō Drama*, p. 172.

124. *Shikisanba* is another way of rendering the term *shikisanban* (Konparu Zenchiku, *Hichū*, *Rokurin ichiro hichū* [*bunshōbon*]: trans. from Thornhill, *Six Circles, One Dewdrop*, p. 166).

125. Zeami, *Fūshikaden*, p. 14.

126. The historical relationship between the origin of noh and *ennen* is uncertain; see Ortolani, *The Japanese Theatre*, pp. 70–73.

127. Zeami, *Fūshikaden*; trans. from Rimer and Yamazaki, *On the Art of the Nō Drama*, p. 31. "*Sakaki* (cleyera ochnacea) is a type of evergreen tree important in Shinto rites. A *shide* is a specially folded strap hung as a sacred offering" (ibid., p. 31).

128. Ortolani, *The Japanese Theatre*, pp. 6–7.

129. One important question is how Zeami understood the usage of the word *kamigakari* (read *kangakari* in Zeami's day). He apparently borrowed the passage describing Uzume from either *Kojiki* or *Nihon shoki*. Modern scholars are divided over how to interpret the word in translating the original texts. Basil Hall Chamberlain (*Kojiki*, pp. 64–65, 69), after hedging in his notes, translated the description of Uzume's dance in the *Kojiki* as "possession." But W. G. Aston (*Nihongi*, p. 44) rendered the same term as "divine inspiration" in translating the section from *Nihon shoki*. The strong point of Aston's interpretation is that it alleviates the need to explain the nature of Uzume's possession: in other words, it avoids having to answers the question what deity possessed Uzume, who was herself a deity. Zeami did not reveal his understanding of how *kangakari* should be understood, and so it seems that he copied the term but did not give it great importance. *Sarugaku dangi* records an episode of a women "possessed" by the divinity of Inari shrine, and the term used is *tsuku*, not *kangakari* (Kanze Motoyoshi, *Sarugaku dangi*, pp. 303–4). Similarly, Zeami did not comment on the fact that Uzume was a female divinity, who is described as baring her breasts and genitals in such a provocative way that Chamberlain felt obliged to render part of his translation in Latin. Finally, nowhere did Zeami or his contemporaries—nor any other performers of the premodern era—develop a theory of noh acting as divine possession.

130. Zeami, *Fūshikaden*; trans. from Rimer and Yamazaki, *On the Art of the Nō Drama*, p. 3.

131. Aston, *Nihongi*, 1: 364–65, 2: 127.

132. Zeami, *Fūshikaden*, p. 39. The translation "Great Raging God" is taken from Rimer and Yamazaki, *On the Art of the Nō*, p. 36.

133. Ibid., p. 40. No such writing by Prince Shōtoku exists.

134. Ibid., p. 37.

135. Zeami, *Fūshikaden*; trans. from Rimer and Yamazaki, *On the Art of the Nō Drama*, p. 35.

136. Zeami, *Fūshikaden*, p. 40. Modern scholarly interpretations of this passage in *Fūshikaden* equate the first two dances with the Okina and Sanbasō dances of the modern version but are uncertain about the meanings of the titles. Inatsumi no Okina may refer to Inatsumi no kimi, the

deity appearing in the festival inaugurating the reign of a new emperor (Daijōsai ōname matsuri). Scholars have had little success identifying Yonasumi no Okina; see Amano, "Okina sarugaku no seiritsu," p. 168.

137. The Essence Body (*hōsshin;* Sanskrit *dharmakāya*) is the Buddha liberated from the human state and having entered nirvana. The Fruition Body (*hōjin; nirmānakāya*) represents the Buddha as chief of all bodhisattvas. The Transformation Body (*ōjin; sambhogakāya*) is the Buddha in human form, able to preach the Buddhist Law (Saunders, *Mudrā*, p. 223). "The basis of this teaching [of the three bodies of the Buddha] is the conviction that a buddha is one with the absolute and manifests in the relative world in order to work for the benefit of all beings" (Fischer-Schreiber et al., *Shambhala Dictionary of Buddhism and Zen*, p. 229).

138. Zeami, *Fūshikaden*, p. 40.

139. Kanze Motoyoshi, *Sarugaku dangi*, p. 276.

140. Konparu Zenchiku, *Meishukushū*; trans. from Nearman, "Behind the Mask of Nō," p. 45. The brackets mark the translator's insertions.

141. Komatsu, *Kamigami no seishinsei*, p. 155.

142. Kanze Motoyoshi, *Sarugaku dangi*, p. 293.

143. Ibid., p. 272.

144. Kanze Motoyoshi, *Sarugaku dangi*; trans. from Rimer and Yamazaki, *On the Art of the Nō Drama*, p. 248.

145. Konparu Zenchiku, *Meishukushū*; trans. from Nearman, "Behind the Mask of Nō," p. 48.

146. Konparu Zenchiku, *Rokurin ichiro hichū* (*bunshōbon*); trans. from Thornhill, *Six Circles, One Dewdrop*, p. 166.

147. Konparu Zenchiku, *Rokurin ichiro hichū* (*bunshōbon*), p. 249.

148. Thornhill, *Six Circles, One Dewdrop*, pp. 175–78.

149. See Chapter 7.

150. Kanze Motoyoshi, *Sarugaku dangi*; trans. from Rimer and Yamazaki, *On the Art of the Nō Drama*, pp. 224–25.

151. In contrast to the rank of *osa*, which was earned by age, the title *tayū* was an honorific designation given to talented actors, musicians, and even kyōgen performers by religious institutions such as Kōfukuji and Tōnomine. In general usage, the word *tayū* referred to the leader of a troupe. For more details about Zeami's and Zenchiku's use of the word *tayū*, see the extensive note in Omote and Katō, *Zeami, Zenchiku*, pp. 502–3.

152. Ortolani, *The Japanese Theatre*, p. 94.

153. Amano Fumio (*Okina sarugaku kenkyū*, pp. 325–35) studied the ranks within the Konparu troupe based on Zenchiku's writings, and he noted a change in leadership within the Konparu troupe from ranks based on age, such as *osa*, to honorific titles such as *tayū*.

154. Hare, *Zeami's Style*, pp. 16–18.
155. Ibid., p. 13.
156. Konparu Zenpō, *Zenpō zōdan*, p. 506.

Chapter 3

1. Kōji 2 (1556).2.0 in *Tokitsugu kyōki*; cited in Kotaka, *Geinōshi nenpyō*, p. 373.
2. Stock, *Implications of Literacy*, p. 60.
3. Jeffrey Mass (*Development of Kamakura Rule*, pp. 154–59) has argued that the sophisticated system of justice in the Kamakura era far surpassed comparable models in medieval Europe.
4. Tonomura, "Forging the Past."
5. Clanchy, *From Memory to Written Record*, p. 319.
6. Since Zeami's *Fūshikaden* was also mistakenly called *Kadensho*, the more recent title helps differentiate the two works.
7. *Hachijō kadensho*, p. 524.
8. For a description of the contents of each chapter of *Hachijō kadensho*, see Rath, "Legends, Secrets, and Authority," pp. 172–76.
9. *Hachijō kadensho*, pp. 548, 653.
10. Omote, "Zeami to Zenchiku no densho," p. 549.
11. It should not be assumed that sixteenth-century readers knew that Zeami was the author of these two works, for even those most familiar with his writings were confused about the authorship of some of his texts. For instance, Konparu Yasuteru, one of the greatest performers of the Momoyama period, who as head of the Konparu troupe had access to nearly all of Zeami's and Zenchiku's treatises, believed that Zenchiku had written part of Zeami's *Fūshikaden* (Konparu Yasuteru, *Konparu Yasuteru denshoshū*, editors' notes, p. 290).
12. For example, sections on the appropriate training for actors at different ages from Zeami's *Fūshikaden* appear at the beginning of Chapter 8, and a passage on role-playing (*monomane*) from the same work is quoted in Chapter 6.
13. *Hachijō kadensho* also borrowed from the theories of flower arrangement. For instance, the opening section of Chapter 6 compares the lead actor in a noh play to the centerpiece in a flower arrangement and the other performers to supporting branches. "Since the lead actor is the general of the noh troupe, the centerpiece of the flower arrangement, he must do all he can to ensure that the 'subsidiary plants' are situated to show him off to his best advantage" (*Hachijō kadensho*, p. 585). On the similarities between the sixteenth-century flower arrangement treatise *Sendenshō* and *Hachijō kadensho*, see Murai Yasuhiko, *Hana to cha no sekai*, pp. 149–52.

14. *Hachijō kadensho*, p. 626. For further references to these four actors, see ibid., pp. 570, 609.

15. Nakamura Itaru, *Muromachi nōgaku ronko*, pp. 492, 512–13.

16. Little information is available about Hōshō Ren'ami, his art, and his role in the Hōshō troupe. The mid-seventeenth-century collection of biographies of noh performers, *Yoza yakusha mokuroku*, which is based on the genealogical records of the Hōshō troupe, identifies him as Zeami's younger brother and states that he transformed the Tobi troupe into the Hōshō troupe (Kanze Motonobu, *Yoza yakusha mokuroku*, p. 47). Nose Asaji (*Nōgaku genryūko*, pp. 646–61) theorized that Ren'ami was Zeami's nephew.

17. Tokuda Rinchū, *Rinchū kenbunshū*, p. 9. Kongō Ukyō (d. 1936), the twenty-third leader of the Kongō, described the notorious mask as still stained by Hana Kongō's blood (Miyake, *Nōgaku geiwa*, p. 201).

18. Kanze Motonobu, *Yoza yakusha mokuroku*, p. 40.

19. Foucault, *Archaeology of Knowledge*, p. 222.

20. Foucault, "What Is an Author?," p. 452.

21. Grapard, "The Shinto of Yoshida Kanetomo," pp. 42–50.

22. Saichō (Dengyō Daishi, d. 822) founded the Tendai sect in Japan and Enryakuji temple on Mount Hiei. Kūkai (Kōbō Daishi, d. 835) founded the Shingon sect in Japan and the temple complex on Mount Kōya. Ennin (Jikaku Daishi, d. 864) was Saichō's disciple and is credited with introducing esoteric doctrine into the Tendai sect. Enchin (d. 891) was the fifth leader of the Tendai sect.

23. Picken, *Essentials of Shinto*, p. 29.

24. Ikenobō Sen'ō forged *Sendenshō* but used his own name for *Sen'ō kuden*. These writings became the basis for the Ikenobō family's philosophy of flower arrangement. One factor hindering a determination of the date of composition of *Sendenshō* is that the oldest surviving manuscript is from the Keichō era (1596–1615).

25. Murai, *Hana to cha no sekai*, p. 146.

26. Omote, "Zeami to Zenchiku no densho," p. 549.

27. *Hachijō kadensho*, pp. 512, 619.

28. Unfortunately, this version of *Hachijō kadensho* is an early seventeenth-century copy of an older text. Nevertheless, it has been determined that it is a reliable copy of one of the earliest versions of *Hachijō kadensho* (Nakamura Itaru, *Muromachi nōgaku ronko*, pp. 521–23, 574–76).

29. Sōsetsu ascribed the treatise now called the *Muromachi makkipitsu ongyoku waka* to Zeami (Omote and Takemoto, *Nōgaku no densho to geiron*, p. 306).

30. Both Ieyasu and Yūsai owned several of Zeami's writings. Sōsetsu's brother gave Ieyasu a copy of *Fūshikaden*, and Sōsetsu himself presented

Yūsai with a manuscript called *Kadensho,* (Omote, "Zeami to Zenchiku no densho," p. 553; Nakamura Itaru, *Muromachi nōgaku ronko,* p. 528; Amano, *Nō ni tsukareta kenryokusha,* p. 36).

31. Nakamura Itaru, *Muromachi nōgaku ronko,* pp. 493–94.

32. Ong, *Orality and Literacy,* pp. 98, 131–32.

33. Omote and Takemoto, *Nōgaku no densho to geiron,* p. 343.

34. The discussion of benefit noh performances in Chapter 4, for example, modified the text of Miyamasu's *Kotsuzumi kudenshū.* Miyamasu's treatise described three consecutive days of performances. *Hachijō kadensho* (p. 558) added one more day because four days had become the norm by the late sixteenth century.

35. Nakamura Itaru, *Muromachi nōgaku ronko,* pp. 501–2, 517–20. Kanze and Hōshō performance styles were termed *kamigakari* because these troupes were based "up" (*kami*) in the capital, Kyoto. Konparu and Kongō styles were known as *shimogakari* because the performers were located "down" in the old capital of Nara. *Hachijō kadensho* (p. 635) uses these terms in Chapter 7 to note differences between Kanze and Konparu performance traditions.

36. Kanze Motonobu, *Yoza yakusha mokuroku,* pp. 32, 48.

37. Amano, *Nō ni tsukareta kenryokusha,* p. 122.

38. Omote and Amano, *Nō no rekishi,* p. 72.

39. Amano, *Nō ni tsukareta kenryokusha,* p. 90. For women's involvement in noh, see Rath, "Challenging the Old Men."

40. The Chinese characters for Hie can also be read "Hiyoshi." "Hie" appears to be the earlier reading.

41. The Tanba Hie disappear from the historical record from 1432 to 1531, but they likely continued performing at shrines in and around the capital during this period (Yamaji, *Okina no za,* pp. 288–96).

42. The relationship between the two Hie troupes is uncertain. Some scholars believe that the Tanba Hie may have originated as a branch of the Ōmi troupe and over time become more influential than the parent group (ibid., pp. 307–8).

43. Among other things it provides an often-cited diagram of a circular noh stage with a bridge in the rear, rather than stage left as on the modern noh stage (Komparu Kunio, *Noh Theater,* p. 123).

44. Ise Sadayori, *Nenjū jōreiki,* pp. 278, 280.

45. Ise Sadayori, *Sōgō ōzōshi,* pp. 561, 603.

46. Katagiri, "Sarugaku 'Hieza' kō" (1981), pp. 83–87.

47. The Yamato troupes inter-adopted, but the Kongō troupe's taking a Hie troupe actor as its leader may have been unprecedented (ibid., pp. 94–98).

48. Omote, *Kitaryū no seiritsu to tenkai,* pp. 122–31.

49. Yamaji, *Okina no za*, p. 343.

50. *Sarugaku dengi*, p. 282. The integration of the Hie into the Yamato troupes in the Edo period did not happen immediately. Performers identifying themselves by the Hie name continued performing independently of the four Yamato troupes in Kyoto through the seventeenth century, and the Hie troupe performed a ten-day benefit noh in Kyoto in 1654 and another in the Genroku period (1688–1703) (Yamaji, *Okina no za*, p. 307).

51. Trans. from Rimer and Yamazaki, *On the Art of the Nō Drama*, p. 3.

52. Kanze Motoyoshi, *Sarugaku dangi*, pp. 261, 263–64.

53. Ibid., p. 260. The text paraphrases Zeami's *Fūshikaden* (pp. 42–43), which compared the grace (*yūgen*) preferred by the noh troupes from Ōmi with the role-playing (*monomane*) that was the trademark of the Yamato troupes.

54. *Hachijō kadensho*, p. 512.

55. Zeami, *Fūshikaden*, p. 39.

56. Modern Japanese retains this notion in the phrase *sarumane*, meaning a superficial imitation of others (Ohnuki-Tierney, *Monkey as Mirror*, pp. 60–66).

57. *Hachijō kadensho*, p. 518.

58. Ibid.

59. *Teikin ōrai*, dating from the early Muromachi era and attributed to the Tendai priest Gen'e (d. 1350), is a collection of letters arranged according to the twelve months of the year, plus an intercalary month. *Teikin ōraichū* (pp. 407–8) provides an unusually long gloss to the term *sarugaku*. The title *tayū* generally indicated the leader of the troupe.

60. Ibid., p. 407.

61. *Sarugaku kikigaki*, pp. 216–17.

62. Hayashiya, "Chadō zenshū no seiritsu," p. 4.

63. Yokomichi and Kobayashi, *Nō, kyōgen*, pp. 11–14.

64. Donald Keene (*Nō and Bunraku*, p. 39) writes, "The performances of nō, especially at the New Year, were elaborate rituals believed to be capable of affecting the prosperity and welfare of the state."

65. The derivation of the term "first song" stems from the belief that ordinary activities take on a special meaning in the New Year. Similar examples include the first visit to a shrine (*hatsumode*), the first use of a bow (*yumihajime*), and the first session of linked poetry (*renga hajime*).

66. Nagao, "Gobandate no seiritsu," pp. 13–24. In the first half of the seventeenth century, the Tokugawa bakufu's performance of first songs occurred on the second day of the New Year at Edo Castle. After 1654, the bakufu moved the event to the third day, when the second day became the memorial day for Tokugawa Ietsuna's mother.

The custom of first songs began in the fifteenth century but was so short lived that we cannot say much about the contents of these events prior to the Edo period. The earliest extant appearance of the term "first song" (*utaizome*) is an entry dated 1465 in the diary of a Muromachi bakufu official, *Chikamoto nikki*. This diary mentioned a first song performance for the Muromachi shogun on the fourth day of the New Year in 1465 (Omote and Amano, *Nō no rekishi*, p. 362). The program of songs for the Muromachi bakufu's performances of *utaizome* was less structured than the later version of the Edo bakufu (Komoriya, "Honganji no nōgaku," p. 22).

67. In the first decade of the Edo bakufu, only the Kanze troupe performed the New Year's first songs. When Tokugawa Ieyasu shifted his favor to the Umewaka troupe in the early seventeenth century, the Umewaka displaced the Kanze from 1610 to 1618. The Kanze returned to dominance in the 1620s, having incorporated the formerly independent Umewaka troupe. After 1632, the Kanze, Konparu, Hōshō, and Kongō troupes performed with the newly formed Kita troupe at Edo Castle. Passing the New Year in Edo meant that the Yamato troupes found themselves unable or unwilling to travel to Nara for the required festival noh in the eleventh and second months. The Kanze troupe, for example, skipped the torch-lit noh in Nara from 1617 to 1619 and the Wakamiya festival in 1618. The other troupes sent subordinates, not their leaders. The distraught Kōfukuji temple complained of the ruination of its torch-lit noh to the bakufu. To reconcile this situation, the Edo bakufu developed the rotation system in 1663 (Omote, *Kitaryū no seiritsu*, pp. 272–79; and Omote and Amano, *Nō no rekishi*, pp. 363–64).

68. Sagara, *Zeami no uchū*, p. 49.

69. *Hachijō kadensho* (p. 539) cites *Takasago* specifically as the noh to be sung to celebrate weddings.

70. Ibid., p. 538.

71. Nippon gakujutsu shinkōkai, *Noh Drama*, p. 12.

72. Zeami, *Go'ongyokujōjō*, p. 200.

73. *Kokin wakashū*, p. 117. I am indebted to Stefania Burk for identifying the character of this poem for me.

74. Zeami, *Go'ongyokujōjō*, p. 200.

75. João Rodrigues (*This Island of Japon*, p. 146), who spent thirty years in Japan as a Jesuit missionary around the turn of the seventeenth century, recorded this New Year's greeting.

76. Konparu Zenchiku, *Go'on jittei*, p. 143.

77. Konparu Zenchiku, *Go'on sangyokushū*, p. 354.

78. *Kokin wakashū*, p. 117.

79. Konparu Zenpō, *Go'on no shidai*, p. 425.

80. *Hachijō kadensho*, p. 538.

81. In the second half of the play, the spirit of the pine calls out to the absent plum spirit, which has led some scholars to conclude that the plum spirit appeared in the original version of the play but has since been edited out (Nishino and Hata, *Nō, kyōgen jiten*, p. 34).

82. *Hachijō kadensho*, p. 538.

83. The spirit of the plum is male in the Kanze version of the play, but female in the versions performed by the other schools (Nishino and Hata, *Nō, kyōgen jiten*, p. 114).

84. Nippon gakujutsu shinkōkai, *Noh Drama*, p. 79.

85. At the Wakamiya festival today, the Okina dance has more prestige since only the leader (*iemoto*) of the Konparu school can dance it on that occasion; other Konparu actors dance in "Yumiya tachiai."

86. Sanari, *Yōkyoku taikan*, pp. 85–86. Keiyō, or Okume no mikoto, was a famed archer in the army of Emperor Jimmu, described in the *Nihongi*.

87. Amano, Okina *sarugaku kenkyū*, p. 279.

88. Komoriya, "Honganji no nōgaku," pp. 17–31.

89. The division of Honganji into Eastern and Western branches occurred at the turn of the seventeenth century in a succession dispute between the sons of the eleventh abbot, Kennyo (d. 1592).

90. Kobayashi Eiichi, "Kinsei Honganji no nōgaku," pp. 9–12.

91. The historical record indicates that Western Honganji discarded the pine-music portion of the program in 1701 but revived pine-music in the late Edo period (ibid., pp. 3–8).

92. *Kyō habutae oridome*, p. 278.

93. Kurokawa, *Yoshu fushi, Hinami kiji*, p. 5.

94. Kobayashi Eiichi, "Kinsei Honganji no nōgaku," pp. 15–16.

95. Larson, *Rise of Professionalism*, pp. 14, 40.

Chapter 4

EPIGRAPH: Takabayashi, *Geidō dokubon*, p. 6.

1. Ooms, *Tokugawa Ideology*, p. 295.

2. Nishida, *'Chi' no shisō*, p. 65.

3. Lebra, *Above the Clouds*, p. 40.

4. Plutschow, *Japan's Name Culture*, pp. 156, 158.

5. Totman, *Early Modern Japan*, p. 95.

6. Plutschow, *Japan's Name Culture*, p. 158.

7. Futaki, "Hideyoshi seiken no girei keisei," pp. 144–48.

8. Hall, "Rule by Status in Tokugawa Japan."

9. Wakita, *Genroku no shakai*, p. 31.

10. Totman, *Early Modern Japan*, p. 171.

11. Shively, "Sumptuary Legislation and Status in Early Tokugawa Japan," pp. 127–34.

12. Plutschow, *Japan's Name Culture*, pp. 153–56.

13. In 1651, the bakufu relaxed its policies regarding the designation of heirs, allowing deathbed appointments (Bolitho, "The Han," p. 208).

14. Ōishi, "The Bakuhan System," pp. 19–21.

15. Ooms, *Tokugawa Ideology*, pp. 60–62.

16. Nishiyama, *Edo Culture*, p. 150.

17. Anderson, *An Introduction to the Japanese Tea Ritual*, p. 85.

18. Morisue, "Nō no hogosha," pp. 213, 220. A *koku* is approximately 45 gallons (180 liters) and is said to be the amount of rice needed to feed one person for one year.

19. Omote, *Kitaryū no seiritsu to tenkai*, pp. 183–84. Hideyoshi's heir, Hideyori (d. 1615), continued to finance the four Yamato troupes until 1609, when Ieyasu ordered them to leave Hideyori's castle in Osaka and relocate to Ieyasu's base in Suruga. This command was part of Ieyasu's effort to undermine Hideyori's authority, which culminated in an attack on Osaka Castle in 1614 and Hideyori's subsequent death.

20. Shōhō 4 (1647).6.9, *Tokugawa jikki*, 3: 487–88.

21. Noh performers tried unsuccessfully several times to win the right to carry two swords and thus affect samurai status. In 1683, the bakufu extended its prohibition against non-samurai wearing swords to specifically include noh actors in daimyō employ. The ambiguity of the status of noh performers in the Edo period is reflected in the first census of the Meiji government, which registered them in their own category, not as ex-samurai or commoners (Omote and Amano, *Nō no rekishi*, p. 99).

22. Ibid., p. 98.

23. *Kyōhō rokunen kakiage*, p. 211.

24. *Kyōhō rokunen kakiage* survives only in fragments, and its modern editors are uncertain of the order of the documents in the original; see the "Editors' Notes," in ibid., pp. 211–12.

25. Zeami, *Fūshikaden*, p. 39.

26. Kanze Motonobu, *Yoza yakusha mokuroku*, p. 28.

27. *Kyōhō rokunen kakiage*, p. 220.

28. Zeami, *Shūgyoku tokka*, p. 196; Zenchiku, *Go'on sangyokushū*, p. 374.

29. *Kyōhō rokunen kakiage*, p. 220.

30. Ujitsuna credited the list of the leaders of the Hada/Konparu troupe to Konparu Motonobu (d. 1703) and dated it 1663, *Kyōhō rokunen kakiage*, p. 221.

31. *Kyōhō rokunen kakiage*, p. 221.

32. Thus, Ujitsuna's story of Kōkatsu's discovery is closer to the version in *Sarugaku kikigaki* (ca. 1599) than Zeami's *Fūshikaden*; see *Sarugaku kikigaki*, p. 242.

33. Lebra, *Above the Clouds*, p. 131. Konparu Zenchiku, *Enman'i keizu*, pp. 308–9; and Thornhill, *Six Circles, One Dewdrop*, p. 14. The Enman'i troupe existed by at least 1268 according to the records of Kasuga shrine (Omote and Amano, *Nō no rekishi*, p. 259). Scholars have not firmly concluded if the Konparu group was simply another name for Enman'i or if the Konparu was a branch of the Enman'i troupe.

34. Zeami, *Fūshikaden*, p. 40. Neither Zenchiku nor Zeami explicated how many generations lay between Hada no Kōkatsu (ca. 600) and Hada no Ujiyasu (ca. 960). Surprisingly, Zenchiku claimed in *Meishukushū* (p. 289) that he was 40 generations removed from Ujiyasu. Since *Meishukushū* may have been intended for a more restricted audience than the Enman'i genealogy, Zenchiku may have considered the *Meishukushū* version more authoritative, but the discrepancy is still puzzling.

35. *Kyōhō rokunen kakiage*, pp. 220–21.

36. *Kanze Motonobu, Yoza yakusha mokuroku*, pp. 27–28.

37. Omote and Itō, *Konparu kodensho shūsei*, pp. 625, 635.

38. *Kyōhō rokunen kakiage*, p. 220. Another Edo-period genealogy gave the name of Zenchiku's father as Shigekiyo (Hirose, *Nō to Konparu*, p. 420). According to Edo-period genealogies (cited in Omote and Itō, *Konparu kodensho shūsei*, p. 625), the father was named Ujikiyo. Arthur Thornhill (*Six Circles, One Dewdrop*, p. 15) noted that "moto" appears frequently in names in the Konparu troupe's genealogical records. Consequently, Zeami may have adopted the name "Motokiyo" in emulation of the Konparu.

39. Zeami, *Kyakuraika*; trans. from Hare, *Zeami's Style*, p. 36.

40. Majima, *Bushōgoma*, p. 61.

41. Kitagawa, *Zeami*, pp. 24–25; Nose, *Nōgaku genryūko*, p. 647.

42. Kanze Motonobu, *Yoza yakusha mokuroku*, p. 30.

43. The rediscovery of Zeami's son Motomasa Jūrō may have been due to research into the authorship of noh plays. *Kyōhō rokunen kakiage* (p. 216) attributed four plays to a "Jūrō" (*Matsugasaki, Morihisa, Sumidagawa*, and *Shakkyō*) and three more to the collaborative efforts of Jūrō and Zeami (*Yorobōshi, Yoshino tenjin*, and *Utaura*). Except *Shakkyō*, whose authorship is uncertain, the remaining plays are recognized today as Motomasa's works. Interestingly, no plays are attributed to On'ami in this text.

44. *Kyōhō rokunen kakiage*, p. 213.

45. Ibid., p. 215.

46. Ibid., p. 214.

47. Kanze Motonobu (*Yoza yakusha mokuroku*, p. 7) noted that Kanze Shichirō Jirō became a drummer in the Ochi Kanze troupe, but there are no contemporary historical records about a son of Zeami by that name.

48. Kanze Motonobu, *Yoza yakusha mokuroku*, p. 31.

49. Kobayashi Shizuo, *Yōkyoku sakusha no kenkyū*, p. 126.

50. In another work, *Kangon shozoku no ki*, included in his *Yūgirokushō* (1811), Asano Eisoku provided a genealogy of the Kanze troupe without giving specific death dates. In a note following the entry for On'ami, he stated: "Zeami's legitimate son was called troupe leader (*tayū*) Jūrō Motomasa. He did not succeed as troupe leader due to a disagreement with Zeami. His troupe is referred to as the Ochi Kanze and was talented. There were only one or two generations of this troupe and then it disappeared" (*Yūgirokushō*, quoted in Kanze Motonobu, *Yoza yakusha mokuroku*, pp. 194–95).

51. *Kyōhō rokunen kakiage*, p. 215.

52. Kanze Motonobu, *Yoza yakusha mokuroku*, p. 29.

53. *Kyōhō rokunen kakiage*, p. 227.

54. Kanze Motoyoshi (*Sarugaku dangi*, p. 302) stated that the founder of the Hōshō troupe was Kan'ami's older brother, whose name was Yamada.

55. Omote and Amano, *Nō no rekishi*, p. 33. Kanze Motonobu (*Yoza yakusha mokuroku*, p. 47) mentioned two leaders of the Hōshō troupe before Kohōshō—Hōshō Ren'ami and Hanadaka Hōshō—but provided almost no details about them.

56. *Kyōhō rokunen kakiage*, pp. 224–25.

57. Ibid., p. 228.

58. Omote, *Kitaryū no seiritsu to tenkai*, p. 113.

59. Nishiyama, *Edo Culture*, pp. 147, 150.

60. Omote and Amano, *Nō no rekishi*, p. 274. A Kita-style of performance (*kitaryū*) existed by the time of Kita Shichidayū's death in 1653 (Omote, *Kitaryū no seiritsu to tenkai*, p. 207).

61. Anderson, *An Introduction to the Japanese Tea Ritual*, pp. 77, 92.

62. Kanze Motonobu, *Yoza yakusha mokuroku*, pp. 173–74.

63. "Editor's notes," in Kanze Motonobu, *Yoza yakusha mokuroku*, pp. 223, 229–31.

64. The Kanze school of stick-drum ended in the generation after Kanze Kunihiro. The manuscript attributed to Kunihiro, *Yoza no yakusha mokuroku*, is included in Tanaka Makoto's annotated version of *Yoza yakusha mokuroku*, pp. 181–92. Some versions included Kunihiro's name in the postscript.

65. Kanze Motonobu, *Yoza yakusha mokuroku*, p. 59.

66. Ibid.

67. *Nō no kinmō zui*, pp. 163–76, 201–35.

68. *Kyō habutae oridome*, pp. 278–91.

69. Omote and Amano, *Nō no rekishi*, p. 108.

70. Omote, *Nōgakushi shinko*, 1: 302.

71. Motonobu added that *tayū* was once also an honorary title granted by religious institutions such as Tōnomine in recognition of a performer's accomplishments; he cited the example of Miyamasu Yazaemon, who "performed the drum beautifully at Tōnomine and was named *tayū* of the shoulder-drum." Motonobu criticized *kyōgen* actors and musicians who assumed the title of *tayū* simply because their ancestors had done so. "In the past, having a great reputation made one a *tayū*. Nowadays, without any regard even unskilled people are made *tayū*. Although they might become *tayū*, they know nothing" (Kanze Motonobu, *Yoza yakusha mokuroku*, pp. 178–79).

72. Amano Fumio noted that Kanze Motonobu's sources of information for his claim that the chief attendant was the second oldest member of the troupe were uncertain. Amano conjectured that the chief attendant may have been second in rank to the *osa* in a medieval noh troupe (see Amano, *Okina sarugaku no kenkyū*, pp. 325–26, 332–33).

73. Kanze Motonobu, *Yoza yakusha mokuroku*, pp. 177–79.

74. Kanze Motoyoshi, *Sarugaku dangi*, p. 309.

75. Ise Sadayori, *Tadasugawara kanjin sarugaku nikki*, pp. 146–48.

76. Kanze Motonobu, *Yoza yakusha mokuroku*, pp. 24–25.

77. Ibid., pp. 5, 2.

78. Fujita Takanari, *Nō no korosu*, pp. 163–99.

79. Omote and Amano, *Nō no rekishi*, p. 230.

80. Kanze Motonobu, *Yoza yakusha mokuroku*, pp. 156, 13, and 106.

81. Anderson, *An Introduction to the Japanese Tea Ritual*, p. 86.

82. The Shindō school ended in 1879 with the death of its last leader. The Fukuō continues as a school of *waki* performers.

83. Motonobu (*Yoza yakusha mokuroku*, p. 2) wrote that Nobumitsu was Nagatoshi's younger brother.

84. Katagiri Noboru ("Edo jidai shoki shirōto yakusha kō," p. 84) studied Motonobu's rationale for including these so-called amateur performers and concluded that he wrote biographies of performers only from families that he thought would continue performing noh in the future—a tacit recognition of the fact that these "amateurs" earned their livelihood from noh.

85. Hane, *Peasants, Rebels, and Outcasts*, pp. 139–43.

86. Dumoulin, *Zen Buddhism*, p. 272.

87. Ibid., p. 273.

88. Elison, *Deus Destroyed*, p. 3.

89. Dumoulin, *Zen Buddhism*, p. 293.

90. Elison, *Deus Destroyed*, p. 3.

91. Cohn, *Friars and the Jews*.

92. Moore, *Formation of a Persecuting Society*, p. 65.

93. The first reference to *tesarugaku* was to a performance by priestesses (*miko*) and lower-level priests (*negi*) at the Wakamiya festival of Kasuga Shrine in 1349 (see Geinōshi kenkyūkai, *Nihon geinōshi*, 4: 34).

94. Nose, *Nōgaku genryūko*, pp. 1092–182.

95. Eikyō 4 (1432)10.10 and 10.13, *Kanmon gyoki*, 2: 63–64.

96. Geinōshi Kenkyūkai, *Nihon geinōshi*, 3: 272.

97. Ibid., 4: 38.

98. Omote and Amano, *Nō no rekishi*, pp. 81–82.

99. Katagiri, "Edo jidai shoki shirōto yakusha kō," pp. 87–90.

100. Senga, "Toraya Ryūha to Toraya Yahe'e," p. 76.

101. The earliest records about the Shibuya troupe date from 1491; the Toraya appear in the historical record in 1548 (Horiguchi, *Sarugakunō no kenkyū*, p. 137). Hosokawa Tadaoki (d. 1645) was said to have had a sexual relationship with a leading Shibuya actor (Senga, "Toraya Ryūha to Toraya Yahe'e," p. 157). Such relationships were probably common between acting troupes and their patrons, especially in troupes that featured young boys (*chigo sarugaku*). The scandal may have arisen because an adult actor was involved, not a boy.

102. Horiguchi, *Sarugakunō no kenkyū*, pp. 141, 148.

103. Konparu Yasuteru, *Konparu Yasuteru hidensho* (*otsubon*) and *Konparu Yasuteru hidensho* in *Konparu Yasuteru denshoshū*, pp. 91, 28.

104. Yet, Kanze Sōsetsu himself adopted unconventional, crowd-pleasing dramaturgical techniques when he reportedly appeared from out of the audience to take the stage in the play *Hyakuman* (Dōmoto, *Nō, kyōgen no gei*, p. 287).

105. *Hachijō kadensho*, p. 516.

106. Omote and Amano, *Nō no rekishi*, p. 89.

107. Omote, *Nōgakushi shinko*, 1: 187.

108. Majima, *Bushōgoma*, p. 98.

109. Kanze Motonobu, *Yoza yakusha mokuroku*, pp. 159, 147.

110. Nose, *Nōgaku genryūko*, p. 1135.

111. Kanze Motonobu, *Yoza yakusha mokuroku*, p. 172. In many instances Motonobu declared that prominent *tesarugaku* performers owed their fame to their Yamato teachers: "Horiike Sōwa was a student of Kanze Motoyori, as was Yasuhara Yūsan" and "Tōji no Kojirō studied with Jiga Yozaemon but had no rhythm" (Kanze Motonobu, *Yoza yakusha mokuroku*, pp. 172–73, 163).

112. Kanze Motonobu, *Yoza yakusha mokuroku*, p. 93; Katagiri, "Saru-gaku 'Hieiza' ko" (1980), pp. 162–82.

113. Kanze Motonobu, *Yoza yakusha mokuroku*, pp. 3–4.

114. The Miyaō group was a branch of the Hie troupe from Tanba province.

115. Kanze Motonobu, *Yoza yakusha mokuroku*, p. 174.

116. Ibid., p. 2.

117. Nose, *Nōgaku genryūko*, pp. 652–53.

118. Kanze Nobushige was a *waki* actor of little accomplishment according to Motonobu (*Yoza yakusha mokuroku*, p. 2).

119. *Kyōhō kakiage*, p. 237.

120. Kanze Motonobu, *Yoza yakusha mokuroku*, p. 8. Nobumitsu authored some thirty noh plays including *Tama no i, Kuse no to, Funa Benkei, Ataka,* and *Rashōmon.*

121. Kanze Motonobu, *Yoza yakusha mokuroku*, p. 177.

122. Ibid., p. 14.

123. *Kyōhō rokunen kakiage*, p. 237. According to *Yoza yakusha mokuroku* (p. 14), Kanze Sōsatsu was Miyamasu Yazaemon's student and his adopted son.

124. Kanze Motonobu, *Yoza yakusha mokuroku*, p. 37.

125. Pinnington, "Crossed Paths," p. 214.

126. Itō Masayoshi, *Konparu Zenchiku no kenkyū*, pp. 20–22.

127. Kanze Motonobu, *Yoza yakusha mokuroku*, p. 29.

128. Ibid., p. 106. A few treatises on shoulder-drum from the first half of the sixteenth century bear Yazaemon's name, including the *Oral Teachings on the Shoulder-Drum* (*Kotsuzumi kudenshū*) which was incorporated into *Hachijō kadensho.*

129. Kanze Motonobu, *Yoza yakusha mokuroku*, p. 14.

130. Ibid., p. 178.

131. Ibid., pp. 13, 33, 81.

132. Ibid., pp. 108–9.

Chapter 5

EPIGRAPH: Borges, *Ficiones*, p. 15.

1. Chibbett, *History of Japanese Printing and Book Illustration*, pp. 67–69.

2. Ibid., p. 82.

3. Nakamura Itaru, *Muromachi nōgaku ronko*, pp. 545–48.

4. Chibbett, *History of Japanese Printing and Book Illustration*, p. 88.

5. Nakamura Itaru, *Muromachi nōgaku ronko*, pp. 551–52. I converted Nakamura Itaru's amounts into *koku*. Thus 0.158 koku is given in Nakamura as 1 *to* 5 *shō* 8 *gō*, or 10.62 liters of rice.

6. Moriya Katsuhisa, "Urban Networks and Information Networks," p. 117.

7. Hata, "Kadō ni okeru densho no seiritsu," pp. 28–32.

8. Tanahashi, *Moon in a Dewdrop*, p. 23.

9. Cleary, *Transmission of Light*, pp. 223–24.

10. Bodiford, "Dharma Transmission in Sōtō Zen," p. 449.

11. Dumoulin, *Zen Buddhism*, pp. 333–37.

12. Foucault, *Archaeology of Knowledge and the Discourse of Language*, p. 222.

13. Kornicki, *The Book in Japan*, pp. 230–32.

14. *Kyōhō rokunen kakiage*, pp. 215–16, 221.

15. Nakamura Itaru, *Muromachi nōgaku ronko*, pp. 557–58.

16. Ishiguro, *Chūsei engeki no shosō*, pp. 212–21; Yonekura, *Waranbegusa kyōgen mukashi gatarisho kenkyū*, pp. 307–10.

17. Omote, "Zeami to Zenchiku no densho," p. 549.

18. Moriya Takeshi, *Kinsei geinō bunkashi no kenkyū*, p. 280.

19. Varley, "Chanoyū," pp. 166–68; *Nanpōroku*, trans. from ibid., p. 168.

20. Moriya Takeshi, *Kinsei geinō bunkashi no kenkyū*, pp. 270–80.

21. Eisenstein, *Printing Revolution in Early Modern Europe*, p. 86.

22. Omote, *Nōgakushi shinko*, 1: 75. The text of the *Jōō shinji nō hyōban* is included in Majima, *Bushōgoma*, pp. 105–34.

23. Shūsen'o demonstrated familiarity with noh music, and he had little bad to say about the musicians performing with the Kita troupe. Consequently, Omote Akira (*Nōgakushi shinko*, 1: 112) conjectured that he may have studied noh music and performed as a musician.

24. Majima, *Bushōgoma*, p. 3.

25. Ibid.

26. Omote, *Kitaryū no seiritsu to tenkai*, p. 547.

27. Omote, *Nōgakushi shinko*, 1: 103–4.

28. Ibid., 1: 116–200.

29. Majima, *Jikkanshōkei densho*, pp. 254–55.

30. Omote, *Nōgakushi shinko*, 1: 104. For example, the premise in *Bushōgoma* that the lyrics to Okina were composed from Buddhist prayers can be found in *Hachijō kadensho*, p. 524.

31. The original attribution of authorship of *Hachijō kadensho* was to Kanze On'ami, Konparu Zenchiku, Hōshō Ren'ami, and Kongō Sōsetsu. In *Bushōgoma* Shūsen'o did not mention *Hachijō kadensho*, but he credited the same four authors with a different secret treatise that he dubbed *Kaden zuinōki* (Majima, *Bushōgoma*, p. 119).

32. Omote, *Nōgakushi shinko*, 1: 83–89.

33. Omote, *Kitaryū no seiritsu to tenkai*, pp. 183–84. Shichidayū was recognized as an independent actor from around 1620, but references to

the Kita style (*ryū*) of noh are not evident until the era of Shichidayū's death in 1653 (ibid., pp. 191–207).

34. The controversy, called the *Sotoba Komachi* incident, appears to have been over the appropriate level of formality (*kurai*) of the noh when it was performed before the retired emperor relative to an earlier performance before the shogun. However, the reasons for Shichidayū's unprecedented punishment are unclear (Omote, *Kitaryū no seiritsu to tenkai*, pp. 294–307).

35. Omote and Amano, *Nō no rekishi*, p. 98.

36. Majima, *Bushōgoma*, p. 35.

37. Omote, *Kitaryū no seiritsu to tenkai*, p. 544.

38. The *kokudaka* of these domains fluctuated in the Edo period. The amount shown is for the year 1698 (ibid., pp. 546, 597–603).

39. Varley, "Chanoyū," p. 173.

40. *Kawachiya yoshimasa kyūki*; cited in Nishiyama, *Edo Culture*, p. 188.

41. Technically speaking, entire plays that are *narai* are called *naraimono*, and a *narai* that covers only a portion of a play is termed *naraigoto*. But, the terms are used interchangeably, since most plays that contain *naraigoto* are also *naraimono*. Some schools have abandoned the practice of referring to specific knowledge or plays as *narai* (Nishino and Hata, *Nō, kyōgen jiten*, pp. 268–69).

42. A noh actor of the Kanze school, Nakamori Shōzō (b. 1928), has disclosed the contents of a few *narai* for the play *Dōjōji*; see his *Nō ga ima, oshietekureru koto*, pp. 135–40.

43. Keene, "The Iemoto System (Nō and Kyōgen)," p. 32. Recently, Mannojō asserted his claim to be his father's chief successor by adopting his father's artistic name, Manzō.

44. A noh student can purchase several licenses for a single noh play. For example, a student may purchase the license for performing the play as a noh song (*su'utai*) and then buy the license for the play as a short dance (*shimai*) and finally acquire another license for learning the *shite* part for the entire work. It is not always necessary to purchase any of these licenses for an amateur to be able to study these aspects of noh: the situation depends on the arrangements between the teacher and the student and the customs of the particular school of noh. In the past, students received licenses after completing their study of a piece, but today the licenses are purchased before study commences (Nishino and Hata, *Nō, kyōgen jiten*, p. 269).

45. Zeami used the term *naraigoto* in three instances, twice in *Mirror Held to the Flower* (*Kakyō*, p. 106) and once in *True Path to the Flower* (*Shikadō*, p. 113). In each context the word is used to refer to a body of knowledge rather than to a specific teaching. In *Five Modes* (*Go'on*, p. 208),

he wrote that performing *rangyoku* required *narai*: "There are *narai* for fully creating the quality of voice for *rangyoku*." However, his notation was just a footnote to other knowledge, as opposed to *narai* in the modern sense of a distinct type of secret teaching.

46. *Hachijō kadensho*, p. 592.

47. *Fūshikaden*; trans from Rimer and Yamazaki, *On the Art of the Nō Drama*, p. 59.

48. Majima, *Bushōgoma*, p. 87.

49. Ibid., p. 61.

50. Majima, *Jikkanshōkei densho*, p. 118.

51. Majima, *Bushōgoma*, pp. 94–95.

52. Zeami spoke of the "three elements," the seed (*tane*), the construction (*tsukuru*), and the composition (*kaku*) of a noh play, in *Sandō*. In his secret writings Shūsen'o created definitions of the five laws, the five postures and seven modes, six elements, seven paths, but he did not address Zeami's three elements.

53. Baudrillard, *Simulacra and Simulation*, p. 7.

54. "In the first case, the image is a good appearance—representation of the sacramental order. In the second, it is an evil appearance—it is the order of maleficence. In the third, it plays at being an appearance—it is the order of sorcery" (ibid., p. 6).

55. *Hachijō kadensho*, p. 524.

56. As Omote Akira (in Majima, *Bushōgoma*, p. 7) noted, the quotation is from the Confucian *Analects*.

57. The reading of *a-un* is Omote Akira's (in Majima, *Bushōgoma*, p. 7) deduction premised on an alternative way of writing the second character (*un*). Another way of reading the passage is the "*narai* of calling *a*." Either way, Shūsen'o's invented this *narai*.

58. *Jōō shinji nō hyōban* in ibid., p. 108.

59. Majima, *Bushōgoma*, p. 8.

60. *Jōō shinji nō hyōban* in ibid., p. 106.

61. *Hachijō kadensho*, p. 516.

62. Majima, *Jikkanshōkei densho*, p. 149.

63. Majima, *Bushōgoma*, pp. 94–95.

64. Hare, *Zeami's Style*, p. 293.

65. Sagara, *Zeami no uchū*, p. 206.

66. Nishino and Hata, *Nō, kyōgen jiten*, p. 335.

67. *Hachijō kadensho*, p. 544.

68. Ibid.

69. Omote Akira (in Majima, *Bushōgoma*, p. 55) identifies Hanazaki Sakyō and Asai Kinosuke as noh actors who studied with Konparu Yasuteru and Shimotsuma Shōshin.

70. Ibid., pp. 54–55.

71. Ibid., p. 55.

72. The revelation of the Hase Kannon refers to a legend of how Kanami's troupe adopted the Kanze name. Shūsen'o did not include this legend, but Omote Akira (in Majima, *Bushōgoma*, pp. 55–56) noted that the story could be found in contemporary writings such as *Yoza yakusha mokuroku*.

73. The title of the play refers to the courtesan Higaki. The play relates the tale of her love affair with the noted poet Fujiwara no Okinori. In the play, a mountain priest encounters an old woman, whom he learns is Higaki. In the second half of the play, Higaki recreates a dance she once performed for Okinori.

74. Kanze Motohiro, as Omote Akira (in Majima, *Bushōgoma*, p. 56) noted, died more than a decade before he would have had the opportunity to transmit any such treatise to Yūsai.

75. *Higaki katazuke* in ibid., p. 150.

Chapter 6

EPIGRAPH: Fujinami, *Utai rokujūnen*, p. 143.

1. Larson, *Rise of Professionalism*, p. xvi.

2. Nakamura Yasuo, "Nō no koteika to iemoto seido."

3. Nishiyama, *Iemoto no kenkyū*, p. 148.

4. Schools of performing arts such as the tea ceremony still market themselves as forms of spiritual cultivation. The tea scholar and practitioner Jennifer Anderson (*An Introduction to the Japanese Tea Ritual*, p. 90), for examples, justifies the family-head system in tea ceremony (*chanoyu*) in spiritual terms: "Tea would not require a centralized system of authority if it were merely an artistic tradition or a casual form of social intercourse. . . . Chanoyu is a highly focused form of religious practice."

5. Nishiyama, *Iemoto no kenkyū*, pp. 146–47.

6. In *Yoza yakusha mokuroku* (p. 14), Kanze Motonobu mentioned that his grandfather Sōsatsu received a certificate (*sōden no inka*) from Miyamasa Yazaemon attesting to his reception of secret oral knowledge about the shoulder-drum. Motonobu's discussion of licenses may be apocryphal, but the example demonstrates that noh performers valued licenses in the mid-seventeenth century.

7. Anderson, *An Introduction to the Japanese Tea Ritual*, pp. 68–69.

8. Nishiyama, *Iemoto no kenkyū*, p. 39.

9. Ibid., p. 291.

10. Kanzawa, *Okinagusa*, 22: 334.

11. Nakamura Yasuo, "Nō no koteika to iemoto seido," pp. 22–24.

12. Omote, *Nōgakushi shinko*, p. 280.

13. Moriya Takeshi, "Yūgei and Chōnin Society in the Edo Period," p. 52.

14. Omote, *Nōgakushi shinko*, p. 287.

15. Geinōshi kenkyūkai, *Nihon geinōshi*, 5: 188.

16. *Kyōhō rokunen kakiage*, p. 235.

17. Kobayashi Kenji, "Edo bunka no naka no nō," pp. 85–86.

18. Geinōshi kenkyūkai, *Nihon geinōshi*, 5: 124–25.

19. *Ben'yō utai*, p. 687. Nishino Haruo ("Kyōhō zengo no shinsaku," pp. 131–35) identified five categories of Edo-period *utai*: (1) stories about the historical foundations of temples and shrines created to raise money for religious institutions; (2) commemorations of famous poets and authors; (3) anecdotes about famous places; (4) songs written as literature to be read rather than for performance; (5) adaptations of *bunraku* and kabuki plays, such as a noh version of *Chūshingura*. Noh authors came from diverse social backgrounds, such as monks, doctors, members of the nobility, and poets.

20. *Zenpō zōdan* contains the Konparu troupe leader's observations about amateur involvement in *su'utai* singing. The text records Zenpō's comments to one of his amateur students. In one instance, Zenpō cautioned his pupils not to sing *su'utai* at a party unless they were invited to do so. In another, he derided the hurried methods of study employed by amateur *su'utai* singers in Sakai city (Konparu Zenpō, *Zenpō zōdan*, pp. 548, 505).

21. In Edo, "attending a *su'utai* recital" was a euphemism for a trip to a brothel. Nishiyama, *Iemotosei no tenkai*, p. 363.

22. Omote, *Nōgakushi shinko*, pp. 295, 302.

23. For an expanded discussion of Kanze Motoakira's achievements, see Rath, "Remembering Zeami," pp. 194–99.

24. Sasaki, *Su'utai yoyo no ato*, pp. 674–75.

25. Nakamura Yasuo, "Nō no koteika to iemoto seido," p. 18.

26. Nishiyama, *Iemoto no kenkyū*, p. 298.

27. Ibid., pp. 298, 31, 314–15.

28. Omote, *Nōgakushi shinko*, pp. 355–59.

29. Nishiyama, *Iemoto no kenkyū*, p. 316.

30. Nakamura Yasuo, "Nō no koteika to iemoto seido," pp. 22–24.

31. Omote and Amano, *Nō no rekishi*, p. 134.

32. *Nihyakujūban utai mokuroku*; cited in Ikenouchi, *Nōgaku seisuiki*, 1: 161.

33. Kanzawa, *Okinagusa*, 21:. 15, 21, 41.

34. Larson, *Rise of Professionalism*, pp. 40, 42.

35. Omote, *Kitaryū no seiritsu to tenkai*, pp. 666–76.

36. Both are included in Ikenouchi, *Nōgaku seisuiki*, 1: 316–48.
37. Kanze Hisao, *Kanze Hisao chosakushū*, 2: 289–90.
38. Shimazu et al., *Mitsuike kyūzō nōmen*, p. 186.
39. Oze, *Taikōki*, p. 397.
40. Kanze Hisao, *Kanze Hisao chosakushū*, 2: 288.
41. Toida, *Nō*, p. 63.
42. Berger, *Ways of Seeing*, p. 21.
43. Nogami, *Nōmen ronko*, pp. 96–109.
44. *Men mekikigaki* in Ikenouchi, *Nōgaku seisuiki*, 1: 316–40.
45. Ibid., 1: 316.
46. Sasaki Haruyuki was the second-generation owner of a bookstore on Teramachi Street in Kyoto. (The shop is still in operation.) Unfortunately, he died before completing *Su'utai yoyo no ato*. Another of Eisoku's students, Asai Tameyoshi, put the final touches on the manuscript. Sasaki's postscript dates from the third year of Bunka (1818) and Asai's from two years later (Sasaki, *Su'utai yoyo no ato*, pp. 657–58).
47. The Asano made a series of attempts over several decades to join the Kanze (Nishiyama, *Edo Culture*, pp. 194–95).
48. My discussion of the Fukuō as *iemoto* draws upon the conclusions of Nishiyama Matsunosuke presented in his *Edo Culture* and *Iemoto no kenkyū*.
49. Nishiyama, *Iemoto no kenkyū*, p. 309.
50. Sasaki (*Su'utai yoyo no ato*, p. 660) stated that Sōha studied *su'utai* with Kanze Motoyori, the son of Kanze Nagatoshi, who was credited in the Edo period as one of the founders of the art of the *waki* in the Kanze troupe. Sasaki's version corresponds with the Fukuō house's genealogy in *Kyōhō rokunen kakiage*.
51. Sasaki, *Su'utai yoyo no ato*, pp. 661, 671.
52. Ibid., p. 664.
53. Ibid., p. 681.
54. *Okinagusa*, which records the same anecdote, identifies the drummer by his full name: Kadono Shōkurō (d. 1657) (Kanzawa, *Okinagusa*, 20: 305–6). Kanze Motonobu (*Yoza yakusha mokuroku*, pp. 169–71) listed Kadono as an "amateur" shoulder-drum performer. The Kadono house became a professional family of hip-drummers in the Kanze troupe.
55. Sasaki, *Su'utai yoyo no ato*, p. 666.
56. Ibid., pp. 668, 673.
57. Ibid., pp. 668–69.
58. Ibid., p. 667.
59. There are many apocryphal *utaibon* with the name of founder of the Fukuō line, Fukuō Moritada (Itō Masayoshi, *Fukuōryū kodenshoshū*, p. 521).

60. Sasaki, *Su'utai yoyo no ato*, p. 667. Ogawa never succeeded in creating his own school of *su'utai* in spite of his discovery of a secret treatise.

61. Ibid.

62. *Kyō habutae oridome*, p. 296.

63. The Fukuō school's monthly recitals continued until the Hōreki era (1751–61). The Kanze school held its monthly recitals at the same temple, on the eleventh day of the month. Takemura Sadakatsu's son Koreyuki (n.d.), who had switched from the Fukuō to the Kanze school, founded the Kanze school's monthly *su'utai* recital in 1716 to commemorate the passing of Kanze Shigenori, thirteenth head of the Kanze. The Katayama family, who became the Kyoto representatives of the Kanze in the eighteenth century, later took over this monthly *su'utai* meeting (Sasaki, *Su'utai yoyo no ato*, pp. 679–80).

64. Ibid., p. 674.

65. Ibid., p. 677.

66. Nonomura, *Nō no kokon*, p. 130.

67. Gondō, "Kansai nō no ie," p. 26.

68. Chisei continued the activities of the Fukuō school in Kyoto for thirty years after her husband's death. At her death, the Fukuō turned their mansion over to the Katayama, marking the symbolic passing of the mantle to the Kanze school, who dominated *su'utai* in Kyoto thereafter.

69. Nishiyama, *Edo Culture*, p. 195.

70. Larson, *Rise of Professionalism*, p. 48.

71. Nonomura, *Nō no kokon*, p. 220. For example, the Kyoto Kanze families maintained a variation of the strong song (*tsuyogin*) style called *nidan sage* found only in performances of Okina today (Fujita Takanori, pers. comm.).

72. Itō Marekoto, "Kansai nōgaku kindaishi," p. 22.

73. For an expanded discussion of Kanze Sakon's achievements, see Rath, "Remembering Zeami," pp. 199–202.

74. Itō Marekoto, "Kansai nōgaku kindaishi," pp. 23–24.

75. Kanze Sakon, *Kanzeryū hyakubanshū*, p. i.

76. Kanze Sakon, *Nōgaku zuisho*, p. 67.

77. Fujinami, *Utai rokujūnen*, p. 138.

78. Numa, *Nōgaku meijin no omokage*, p. 66.

79. Kanze Sakon, *Nōgaku zuisho*, p. 82. Numa So'u (*Nōgaku meijin no omokage*, p. 91) noted that this speech was made before a performance in Kyoto in 1938.

80. The Fukuō line also ended in the Meiji era with the death of the fourteenth-generation head, but one of its chief disciples, the Nakamura family, later revived the school and the family name.

Chapter 7

1. George, "Ritual Drama," p. 156.
2. Eric Hobsbawm (Hobsbawm and Ranger, *Invention of Tradition*, p. 1) includes ritual as part of a larger process of the "invention of traditions."
3. Shinmura, *Kōjien*, p. 1105.
4. Nose, *Nōgaku genryūko*, p. 1222.
5. Ibid., pp. 1219–24.
6. Omote and Amano, *Nō no rekishi*, p. 90.
7. Omote Akira (*Kitaryū no seiritsu to tenkai*, p. 181), in tracing the career of Kita Shichidayū, declared that his creation of the Kita school was monumental considering the fact that noh became a "ritual performing art" in the Edo period.
8. Groemer, "Noh at the Crossroads."
9. Keene, *Nō and Bunraku*, p. 39.
10. Ooms, "Neo-Confucianism and the Formation of Early Tokugawa Ideology," p. 33.
11. Nakamura Yasuo, *Noh, the Classical Theater*, pp. 129–30.
12. *Nippo jisho* is the Japanese name of *Vocabulario da Lingoa de Iapan com a declaraçâo em Portuguese*. which was published in Nagasaki in 1603–4; see Doi et al., *Nippo jisho*; Tanigawa, *Wakun no shiori*; Ishikawa, *Zoho gagen shūran*; and Murata, *Rigen shūran*.
13. Ikenouchi, *Nōgaku seisuiki*, 1: 5–7.
14. Rosenau, *Postmodernism and the Social Sciences*, p. xi.
15. Bell, *Ritual Theory, Ritual Practice*, p. 14.
16. Schechner, *Future of Ritual*, p. 228.
17. Ikenouchi, *Nōgaku seisuiki*, 2: 4–5.
18. Kume, "Nōgaku no kako to shōrai," pp. 1–2.
19. Akabori, "Shikigaku to shite no yōkyoku."
20. Cited in Ikenouchi, *Nōgaku seisuiki*, 2: 90–91.
21. Mehl, *History and the State in Nineteenth-Century Japan*, pp. 5–45.
22. Cited in Ikenouchi, *Nōgaku seisuiki*, 2: 95.
23. Ibid., 2: 182.
24. Ibid., 2: 72.
25. Fujitani, *Splendid Monarchy*, p. 163.
26. Akabori, "Shikigaku to shite no yōkyoku."
27. Kume, "Ōshū sensō yori etaru nōgaku no kyōkun."
28. Ōkuma, "Kokugeki to shite no nōgaku," pp. 5–6.
29. Fujitani, *Splendid Monarchy*, p. 227.
30. Kume, "Chōtei rappu buke shikigaku," pp. 27–30.
31. Ikenouchi, *Nōgaku seisuiki*, 2: 74.

32. Toki, "Kokuminsei to nōgaku to," pp. 3–10.

33. Robertson, "Mon Japan."

34. Kanze Sakon, *Nōgaku zuisho*, p. 190.

35. Ienaga, *Sarugakunō no shisōteki kosatsu*, pp. 3–64.

36. Yoshida Tōgo, *Nōgaku koten Zeami jūrokubushū*.

37. Matsumoto, *Nō kara kabuki e*, pp. 142–51.

38. Yokomichi and Kobayashi, *Nō, kyōgen*, p. 8.

39. Gluck, "The Invention of Edo," p. 273.

40. For more on Kanze Hisao's work in the postwar era, see Rath, "Remembering Zeami," pp. 202–5.

41. Kanze Sakon (*Nōgaku zuisho*, p. 121) termed Okina a *shikiten*. Other performers use the terms *gishiki* and *matsuri*, all of which are close synonyms for the word "ritual."

42. Moreover, any collection of noh plays that includes Okina prints the text before other plays; see, e.g., Kanze Sakon, *Kanzeryū hyakubanshū*, p. 2.

43. Some performers maintain austerities only for the morning of the performance; others have abandoned the practice entirely (Nishino and Hata, *Nō, kyōgen jiten*, pp. 11–12).

44. Kanze Sakon, *Nōgaku zuisho*, p. 125.

45. Morita Mitsuharu, *Nōgaku oboe no shochō*, p. 20.

46. Shigeyama, "Kyōgen hachijūnen," p. 121.

47. Nomura, *Nomura Manzō chosakushū*, p. 168.

48. Bethe, "Okina," p. 97; Teele, "Recollections and Thoughts on Nō," p. 77.

49. Salz, "Roles of Passage," pp. 123–24.

50. Amano, *Okina sarugaku kenkyū*, p. 32.

51. Morita Mitsuharu, *Nōgaku oboe no shochō*, p. 19. Komparu Kunio (*Noh Theater*, p. 4) stated that sake was used instead of water. For a photograph of the altar used for a Kanze school performance of Okina, see Honda, *Okina sono hoka*, p. 194.

52. Morita Mitsuharu, *Nōgaku oboe no shochō*, pp. 19–20.

53. Komparu Kunio, *Noh Theater*, p. 4.

54. In the Konparu, Kongō, and Kita schools of the *shimogakari* tradition, the role of Senzai is played by a kyōgen actor, who also carries the box that contains the masks for Okina and Sanbasō. In the Kanze and Hōshō versions of the *kamigakari* tradition, the person responsible for the mask box is a kyōgen actor, but the role of Senzai is acted by a *shite* actor.

55. Bethe, "Okina," p. 96.

56. The tortoise is said to live 10,000 years and the crane for 1,000. This passage is from a late Heian-era popular ballad (*imayō*). The Kanze

school's rendering of the "god-song" dates from the eighteenth century when Kanze Motoakira changed the verse *dōdō tarari* to *tōtō tarari* (see Chapter 6). The Konparu, Kongō, and Kita schools still sing the former version.

57. Kanze Sakon, *Kamiuta*, p. 2.

58. Omote Akira (*Nōgakushi shinko*, pp. 344–60) disputed all these propositions but offered no other theories about the word's meanings.

59. "Languages change because they express meaning, are functional and constantly used. Meaningless sounds do not change; they can only be remembered or forgotten" (Staal, "Meaninglessness of Ritual," p. 489).

60. Amano, *Okina sarugaku kenkyū*, p. 102. The mask used for the role of Chichinojō resembles an old man and is similar to the mask worn by Okina.

61. The Buddhist heaven of Tōriten (in Sanskrit, Trayastrimsa) is the second of the six heavens of bliss.

62. Amano, *Okina sarugaku kenkyū*, p. 39.

63. The theory that Shakyamuni's father created Okina is found in the early sixteenth-century *Zenpō zōdan*, the notes of a student of Konparu Zenpō; see Konparu Zenpō, *Zenpō zōdan*, p. 506.

64. *Hachijō kadensho*, pp. 516–19. Henry Pernet (*Ritual Masks*, p. 79) notes a similar polyvalency in masked performances in diverse cultural contexts. He criticizes scholars who give static interpretations of these performances and argues that they instead represent events and cosmic moments in shared lore.

65. Komatsu, *Kamigami no seishinshi*, p. 155.

66. Nakamura Itaru, *Muromachi nōgaku ronko*, p. 505.

67. Kinoshita Keiken, *Nōgaku unnōshū*, 1: 1–5. Kinoshita's text purported to contain the most important teachings of the noh profession, including descriptions of dance patterns (*katazuke*) and secrets (*narai*) conveyed only to select disciples. The author's subsequent banishment from the Kanze school for publishing this work speaks to the authority of his claims.

68. Yoshida Tōgo, "Okina shikisanban no koten ni tsuite."

69. For a discussion of the reconfiguration of Buddhism in this era, see Ketelaar, *Of Heretics and Martyrs in Meiji Japan*; on the relations between the government and Shinto in this period, see Hardacre, *Shintō and the State*, pp. 21–40.

70. According to Kongō Ukyō, Okina stood for Ninigi, Senzai for Amenokoyane no mikoto, and Sanbasō for Sarudahiko no mikoto (De Poorter, "Nō Which Is No Nō," p. 29).

71. Ōwada, *Nō utai hiketsu*, pp. 1, 5.

72. Komparu Kunio, *Noh Theater*, p. 3.

73. For a short discussion of the distinction between shamanistic possession and living deities, see Werblowski, "Some Reflections on Two-Way Traffic," p. 284.

74. Toida, *Nō*, pp. 35–36.

75. Nogami, *Nō*, p. 211.

76. Mircea Eliade, *Le chamanisme et les techniques archaiques de l'extase*; cited in Pernet, *Ritual Masks*, p. 119.

77. Yokomichi, *Nōgeki shōyō*, pp. 23–24.

78. In *Kyakuraika* (p. 248), Zeami wrote that the "dance of Okina is the basis for noh dance." Kanze Motoyoshi, *Sarugaku dangi*, p. 260.

79. Kanze Hisao, *Kokoro yori, kokoro tsutaeru hana*, p. 170.

80. Bethe, "Okina," p. 95.

81. E.g., Morita Mitsuharu, *Nōgaku oboe no shochō*, p. 13; and Komparu Kunio, *Noh Theater*, p. 3.

82. Kanze Hisao, *Kokoro yori, kokoro tsutaeru hana*, pp. 171–72.

83. Kita Roppeita ("Roppeita geidan," p. 11) acknowledged that there were many variations in the way to perform Okina, but he condemned such variations as contrary to the spirit of piety required to perform the dance. For similar reasons, he stated that "deity noh" such as *Takasago* should be performed without alteration.

84. Teele, "Recollections and Thoughts on Nō," p. 77.

Conclusion

EPIGRAPH: Foucault, *Archaeology of Knowledge*, p. 21

1. Baudrillard, *Simulacra and Simulation*, pp. 6–7.

2. Kongō, *Nō to nōmen*, p. 67.

3. Konparu Nobutaka, *Ugokanu yue ni nō to iu*, pp. 22, 126.

4. Hōshō, "Nōmen no hanashi," p. 110.

5. Kanze Sakon, *Nōgaku zuisho*, pp. 11–22.

6. Kanze Hisao, *Kanze Hisao chosakushū*, 2: 259, 285.

7. Suzuki, *Nō no omote*, p. 3.

8. Konparu Nobutaka, *Ugokanu yue ni nō to iu*, pp. 25–29.

9. Kongō, *Nō to nōmen*, p. 107.

10. A selection of Ukyō's personal writings on noh were published after his death; see Miyake, *Nōgaku geiwa*. In the same text (p. 202), the noh scholar Matsumoto Kamematsu discussed Ukyō's wish to destroy the Kongō family's secret writings. Matsumoto noted that a catalog of the lost texts was compiled before they were destroyed, but this record was lost during an air raid in World War II.

11. Konparu Nobutaka, *Ugokanu yue ni nō to iu*, pp. 22, 126.

12. Halbwachs, *On Collective Memory*, p. 73.
13. Larson, *Rise of Professionalism*, p. 40.

Appendix

1. In addition to their affiliation with their school, all professional noh performers are members of the Nōgaku kyōkai, and a select few are also invited to join the more exclusive Nihon nōgakukai. Both organizations help to regulate the noh profession.

2. In 1953 actors of the Izumi and Ōkura schools of kyōgen collaborated in a well-received production of the play *Buaku*. *Buaku* and the play *Shūron* are among the works that have been staged collaboratively since then, but such performances are rare (Koyama, "Staging Kyōgen," pp. 58–59).

Works Cited

Unless otherwise indicated, the place of publication for Japanese-language works is Tokyo.

Akabori Matajirō. "Shikigaku to shite no yōkyoku." *Yōkyokukai*, Mar. 1920, pp. 40–41.

Amano Fumio. *Nō ni tsukareta kenryokusha*. Kodansha, 1997.

———. *Okina sarugaku kenkyū*. Osaka: Izumi shoin, 1995.

———. "Okina sarugaku no seiritsu." *Bungaku* 7, no. 51 (1983): 166–78.

Amino Yoshihiko. *Igyō no ōken*. Heibonsha, 1992.

Anderson, Jennifer. *An Introduction to the Japanese Tea Ritual*. Albany: State University of New York, 1991.

Arai Tsuneyasu. *Kōkotsu to warai no geijutsu*. Shindokushosha, 1993.

———. *Nō no kenkyū: Kosarugaku no okina to nō no densho*. Shindoku-shosha, 1966.

Araki, James T. *The Ballad-Drama of Medieval Japan*. Rutland, Vt.: Tuttle, 1978.

Aston, W. G. *Nihongi: Chronicles of Japan from the Earliest Times to AD 697*. Rutland, Vt.: Tuttle, 1993.

Barthes, Roland. *Mythologies*. Trans. Annette Lavers. New York: Hill & Wang, 1972.

Baudrillard, Jean. *Seduction*. Trans. Brian Singer. New York: St. Martin's Press, 1990.

———*Simulacra and Simulation*. Trans. Sheila Faria Glaser. Ann Arbor: University of Michigan Press, 1994.

Bell, Catherine. *Ritual Theory, Ritual Practice*. Oxford: Oxford University Press, 1992.

Ben'yō utai. In *Nō*, vol. 3 of *Nihon shōmin bunka shiryō shūsei*, ed. Geinō-shi kenkyūkai, pp. 687–700. San'ichi shobō, 1973.

Berger, John. *Ways of Seeing*. London: British Broadcasting Corporation and Penguin Books, 1985.

Berry, Mary Elizabeth. *The Culture of Civil War in Kyoto.* Berkeley: University of California Press, 1994.

Bethe, Monica. "Okina: An Interview with Takabayashi Kōji, Actor of the Kita School." *Mime Journal,* 1984, pp. 93–103.

Bodiford, William. "Dharma Transimission in Sōtō Zen." *Monumenta Nipponica* 46, no. 4 (1991): 423–51.

———. *Sōtō Zen in Medieval Japan.* Honolulu: Kuroda Institute and University of Hawaii Press, 1993.

Bolitho, Harold. "The Han." In *Early Modern Japan,* vol. 4 of *The Cambridge History of Japan,* ed. John Hall, pp. 183–234. Cambridge, Eng.: Cambridge University Press, 1990.

Borges, Jorge Luis. *Ficiones.* Ed. Anthony Kerrigan. New York: Grove Press, 1962.

Brown, Steven. *Theatricalities of Power: The Cultural Politics of Noh.* Stanford: Stanford University Press, 2001.

Chamberlain, Basil Hall. *Kojiki: Records of Ancient Matters.* Rutland, Vt.: Tuttle, 1981.

Chibbett, David. *The History of Japanese Printing and Book Illustration.* Tokyo: Kodansha, 1977.

Clanchy, M. T. *From Memory to Written Record: England, 1066–1307.* 2nd ed. Malden, Mass.: Blackwell, 1993.

Cleary, Thomas, trans. *Transmission of Light [Denkoroku]: Zen in the Art of Enlightenment by Zen Master Keizan.* San Francisco: North Point Press, 1990.

Cohn, Jeremy. *The Friars and the Jews: The Evolution of Medieval Anti-Judaism.* Ithaca, N.Y.: Cornell University Press, 1982.

Daijōin jisha zōjiki. Ed. Tsuji Kinojō. Kadokawa shoten, 1964.

De Poorter, Erika. "Nō Which Is No Nō: The Ritual Play Okina" *Maske und Kothurn* 23 (1989): 21–30.

———. *Zeami's Talks on Sarugaku: An Annotated Translation of the "Sarugaku Dangi" with an Introduction on Zeami Motokiyo.* Amsterdam: J. C. Gieben, 1986.

Doi Tadao et al., eds. *Nippo jisho.* Iwanami shoten, 1980.

Dōmoto Masaki. *Chūsei geinōjin no shisō: Zeami atosaki.* Kadokawa shoten, 1992.

———. *Nō, kyōgen no gei.* Tōkyō shoseki, 1983.

Dumoulin, Heinrich. *Zen Buddhism: A History,* vol. 2, *Japan.* Trans. James Hesig and Paul Knitter. London: Macmillan, 1990.

Dykstra, Yoshiko. "Miraculous Tales of the Hasedera Kannon." In *Religions of Japan in Practice,* ed. George Tanabe, pp. 117–23. Princeton: Princeton University Press, 1999.

Eisenstein, Elizabeth. *The Printing Revolution in Early Modern Europe.* New York: Cambridge University Press, 1998.

Elison, George. *Deus Destroyed: The Image of Christianity in Early Modern Japan.* Cambridge, Mass.: Harvard University Council for East Asian Studies, 1988.

Farris, William Wayne. *Sacred Texts and Buried Treasures: Issues in the Historical Archaeology of Ancient Japan.* Honolulu: University of Hawaii Press, 1998.

Faure, Bernard. *The Rhetoric of Immediacy.* Princeton: Princeton University Press, 1991.

———. *Visions of Power: Imagining Medieval Japanese Buddhism.* Trans. Phyllis Brooks. Princeton: Princeton University Press, 1996.

Fischer-Schreiber, Ingrid, et al. eds. *The Shambhala Dictionary of Buddhism and Zen.* Boston: Shambhala, 1991.

Foucault, Michel. *The Archaeology of Knowledge and the Discourse of Language.* Trans. A. M. Sheridan Smith. New York: Pantheon, 1972.

———. "What Is an Author?" In *Rethinking Popular Culture: Contemporary Perspectives in Cultural Studies*, ed. Chandra Mukerji and Michael Schudson, pp. 446–64. Berkeley: University of California Press, 1991.

Fujinami Shisetsu. *Utai rokujūnen.* Hinoki shoten, 1981.

Fujita Takanori. *Nō no korosu.* Hitsuji shobō, 2000.

Fujitani, Takashi. *Splendid Monarchy: Power and Pageantry in Modern Japan.* Berkeley: University of California Press, 1996.

Fujiwara-Skrobak, Makiko. "Social Consciousness and Madness in Zeami's Life and Work: Or the Ritualistic-Shamanistic-Divine Aspects of Sarugaku for an Ideal Society." Ph.D. diss., University of California, Los Angeles, 1996.

Furukawa, Hisashi, "The Noh." In *Japanese Music and Drama in the Meiji Era*, vol. 3 of *Japanese Culture in the Meiji Era*, trans. and ed. Edward Seidensticker and Donald Keene, pp. 73–112. Obunsha, 1966.

Futaki Ken'ichi. "Hideyoshi seiken no girei keisei." In *Toyotomi Hideyoshi no subete*, ed. Kuwata Tadachika, pp. 143–73. Shinjinbutsu ōraisha, 1981.

Geinōshi kenkyūkai, ed. *Dengaku, sarugaku.* Vol. 2 of *Nihon shōmin bunka shiryō shūsei.* San'ichi shobō, 1974.

———. *Nihon geinōshi*, vols. 3, 4, and 5. Hōsei daigaku, 1986.

George, David, "Ritual Drama: Between Mysticism and Magic." *Asian Theatre Journal* 4, no. 2 (1987): 127–65.

Gluck, Carol. "The Invention of Edo." In *Mirror of Modernity: Invented Traditions of Modern Japan*, ed. Stephen Vlastos, pp. 262–84. University of California, 1998.

Gondō Yoshikazu. "Kansai nō no ie." *Kamigata geinō* 95 (1987): 25–29.

Goody, Jack. *The Logic of Writing and the Organization of Society.* Cambridge, Eng.: Cambridge University Press, 1986.

Goshima Kunimasa. "Buke sarugaku to Muromachi dono ni okeru kōgyō." *Geinōshi kenkyū* 85 (1984): 29–44.

Gotō Hajime. *Chūsei kamen no rekishiteki, minzokugakuteki kenkyū.* Taga shuppan, 1987.

———. *Nihon no kamen.* Mokujisha, 1989.

Grapard, Alan. "The Shinto of Yoshida Kanetomo." *Monumenta Nipponica* 47, no. 1 (1992): 27–58.

Groemer, Gerald. "Noh at the Crossroads: Commoner Performance During the Edo Period." *Asian Theatre Journal* 15, no. 1 (1998): 117–41.

Hachijō kadensho, in *Kodai, chūsei geijutsuron,* ed. Hayashiya Tatsusaburō et al., pp. 511–665. Nihon shisō taikei, vol. 23. Iwanami Shoten, 1995.

Halbwachs, Maurice. *On Collective Memory.* Trans. and ed. Lewis Coser. Chicago: University of Chicago Press, 1992.

Hall, John, "Rule by Status in Tokugawa Japan." *Journal of Japanese Studies* 1 (1974): 39–49.

Hane, Mikiso. *Peasants, Rebels and Outcasts: The Underside of Modern Japan.* New York: Pantheon Books, 1982.

———. *Premodern Japan: A Historical Survey.* Boulder, Colo.: Westview Press, 1991.

Hardacre, Helen. *Shintō and the State, 1868–1988.* Princeton: Princeton University Press, 1989.

Hare, Thomas Blenman. *Zeami's Style: The Noh Plays of Zeami Motokiyo.* Stanford: Stanford University Press, 1986.

Hata Yoshiaki. "Kadō ni okeru densho no seiritsu: sono seikaku o chūshin ni." *Geinōshi kenkyū* 16 (1967): 26–34.

Hayashiya Tatsusaburō. "Chadō zenshū no seiritsu: iemoto seido e no michizukuri." *Geinōshi kenkyū* 1 (1963): 1–11.

Hirose Mizuhiro. *Nō to Konparu.* Kyoto: Hatsune shobō, 1969.

Hobsbawm, Eric, and Terrence Ranger, eds. *The Invention of Tradition.* Cambridge, Eng.: Cambridge University Press, 1983.

Hoff, Frank. "The 'Evocation' and 'Blessing' of Okina: A Performance Version of Ritual Shamanism." *Alcheringa Ethnopoetics,* n.s. 3, no. 1 (1977): 48–60.

Honda Yasuji. *Okina sono hoka: nō oyobi kyōgenko no futatsu.* Meizendō shoten, 1958.

Horiguchi Yasuō. *Sarugakunō no kenkyū.* Ōfūsha, 1988.

Hōshō Kurō. "Nōmen no hanashi." *Yōkyoku kōza* 1, no. 11 (1926): 105–12.

Hosokawa Ryōichi. *Chūsei no mibunsei to hinin.* Nihon editāsukūru shuppanbu, 1994.

Ienaga Saburō. *Sarugakunō no shisōshiteki kosatsu.* Hōsei daigaku, 1980.

Ikenouchi Nobuyoshi. *Nōgaku seisuiki*. 2 vols. Sōgensha, 1992.

Ise Sadayori. *Nenjū jōreiki*. Ed. Hanawa Hokinoichi. In *Gunsho ruijū*, vol. 22, pp. 274–92. Zoku gunsho ruijū kanseikai, 1959–60.

———. *Sōgō ōzōshi*. Ed. Hanawa Hokinoichi. In *Gunsho ruijū*, vol. 22, pp. 573–626. Zoku gunsho ruijū kanseikai, 1959–60.

———. *Tadasugawara kanjin sarugaku nikki*. In *Gunsho ruijū*, vol. 19, pp. 717–23. Zoku gunsho ruijū kanseikai, 1959–60.

Ishiguro Kichijirō. *Chūsei engeki no shosō*. Ōfusha, 1983.

Ishikawa Masamochi. *Zoho gagen shūran*. Ed. Nakajima Hirotari. Koeki tosho, 1903–4.

Itō Marekoto. "Kansai nōgaku kindaishi." *Kamigata geinō* 95 (1987): 19–24.

Itō Masayoshi, ed. *Fukuōryū kodenshoshū*. Osaka: Izumi shoin, 1993.

———. *Konparu Zenchiku no kenkyū*. Kyoto: Akao shōbundō, 1970.

Kanmon gyoki. Ed. Hanawa Hokinokichi and Ōta Toshirō. 2 vols. *Zoku gunsho ruijū*, bui, no. 2. Zoku Gunsho ruijū kanseikai, 1991.

Kanzawa Teikan. *Okinagusa*. 6 vols. Nihon zuihitsu zenshū, vols. 19–24. Yoshikawa Kōbunkan, 1978.

Kanze Hisao. *Kanze Hisao chosakushū*. 4 vols. Heibonsha, 1981.

———. *Kokoro yori, kokoro tsutaeru hana*. Hokumizu U bukkusu, 1994.

Kanze Motonobu. *Yoza yakusha mokuroku*. Ed. Tanaka Makoto. Wan'ya shoten, 1975.

Kanze Motoyoshi. *Sarugaku dangi*. In *Zeami, Zenchiku*, ed. Omote Akira and Katō Shūichi, pp. 259–314. Nihon shisō taikei, vol. 24. Iwanami shoten, 1995.

Kanze Sakon, ed. *Kamiuta*. Hinoki shoten, 1994.

———. *Kanzeryū hyakubanshū*. Hinoki shoten, 1995.

———. *Nōgaku zuisō*. Kawade shobō, 1939.

Katagiri Noboru. "Edo jidai shoki shirōto nō yakushakō: 'Yakusha mokuroku' o chūshin ni." *Nōgaku kenkyū* 3 (1977): 73–116.

———. "Sarugaku 'Hieza' kō." 3 pts. *Nōgaku kenkyū* 6 (1980): 153–82; 7 (1981); 75–102; and 9 (1983): 87–118.

Kawashima Masao. *Chūsei Kyōto bunka no shūroku*. Kyoto: Shibunkaku, 1992.

———. "Shōmonji." In *Chūsei no minshū to geinō*, ed. Kyoto burakushi kenkyūjo, pp. 90–95. Kyoto: Aunsha, 1991.

Keene, Donald. "The Iemoto System (Nō and Kyōgen)." *Fenway Court 1992* (1993): 30–36.

———. *Nō and Bunraku: Two Forms of Japanese Theatre*. New York: Columbia University Press, 1990.

Ketelaar, James Edward. *Of Heretics and Martyrs in Meiji Japan: Buddhism and Its Persecution*. Princeton: Princeton University Press, 1990.

Kim, Yung-hee. *Songs to Make the Dust Dance: The "Ryōjin hishō" of Twelfth-Century Japan.* Berkeley: University of California Press, 1994.

Kinoshita Keiken. *Nōgaku unnōshū.* N.p.: 1890.

Kita Roppeita. "Roppeita geidan." In *Nō, kyōgen, bunraku,* vol. 3, *Nihon no geidan,* pp. 7–72. Kyūgei shuppan, 1978.

Kitagawa Tadahiko. *Zeami.* Chūō kōronsha, 1972.

Klein, Susan Blakeley. "Allegories of Desire: Kamakura Commentaries on the Noh," Ph.D. diss., Cornell University, 1994.

Kobayashi Eiichi. "Kinsei Honganji no nōgaku: utaizome, gosechi no hayashi o megutte." *Geinōshi kenkyū* 119 (1992): 1–24.

Kobayashi Kenji. "Edo bunka no naka no nō." *Kokubungaku* 9 (1956): 84–89.

Kobayashi Shizuo. *Yōkyoku sakusha no kenkyū.* Nōgaku shorin, 1942.

Kokin wakashū. Ed. Kojima Noriyuki and Arai Eizō. Shin Nihon koten bungaku taikei, vol. 5. Iwanami shoten, 1989.

Komatsu Kazuhiko. *Kamigami no seishinshi.* Hokuto shuppan, 1985.

Komoriya Chieko. "Honganji no nōgaku." *Geinōshi kenkyū* 15 (1966): 1–13.

Komparu Kunio. *The Noh Theater: Principles and Perspectives.* New York: Weatherhill, 1983.

Kongō Iwao. *Nō to nōmen.* Hirofumidō shobō, 1940.

Konparu Nobutaka. *Ugokanu yue ni nō to iu.* Kodansha, 1980.

Konparu Yasuteru. *Konparu Yasuteru denshoshū,* ed. Omote Akira and Oda Yukiko. Wan'ya shoten, 1978.

Konparu Zenchiku. *Enman'iza hekisho.* In *Konparu kodensho shūsei,* ed. Omote Akira and Itō Masayoshi, pp. 312–14. Wan'ya shoten, 1969.

———. *Enman'i keizu.* In *Konparu kodensho shūsei,* ed. Omote Akira and Itō Masayoshi, pp. 308–9. Wan'ya Shoten, 1969.

———. *Go'on jittei.* In *Konparu kodensho shūsei,* ed. Omote Akira and Itō Masayoshi, pp. 143–48. Wan'ya shoten, 1969.

———. *Go'on sangyokushū.* In *Zeami, Zenchiku,* ed. Omote Akira and Katō Shūichi, pp. 334–74. Nihon shisō taikei, vol. 24. Iwanami shoten, 1995.

———. *Meishukushū.* In *Konparu kodensho shūsei,* ed. Omote Akira and Itō Masayoshi, pp. 279–307. Wan'ya Shoten, 1969.

———. *Rokurin ichiro hichū (bunshōbon).* In *Konparu kodensho shūsei,* ed. Omote Akira and Itō Masayoshi, pp. 249–62. Wan'ya shoten, 1969.

Konparu Zenpō. *Go'on no shidai.* In *Konparu kodensho shūsei,* ed. Omote Akira and Itō Masayoshi, pp. 405–19. Wan'ya shoten, 1969.

———. *Zenpō zōdan.* In *Kodai, chūsei geijutsuron,* ed. Hayashiya Tatsusaburō et al., pp. 479–510. Nihon shisō taikei, vol. 23. Iwanami shoten, 1995.

Kornicki, Peter. *The Book in Japan: A Cultural History from the Beginning to the Nineteenth Century.* Boston: Brill, 1998.

Kotaka Kyo, ed. *Geinōshi nenpyō, Ōei 8—Genroku 8.* Meicho shuppan, 1992.

Koyama Hiroshi. "Staging *Kyōgen.*" *Acta Asiatica* 73 (1997): 39–60.

Koyama Hiroshi, Taguchi Kazuo, and Hashimoto Asao. *Kyōgen no sekai.* Iwanami kōza nō, kyōgen, vol. 5. Iwanami shoten, 1993.

Kume Kunitake. "Chōtei rappu buke shikigaku." *Nōgaku* 11, no. 8 (1913): 27–30.

———. "Nōgaku no kako to shōrai." *Nōgaku* 9, no. 7 (1911): 1–7.

———. "Ōshū sensō yori etaru nōgaku no kyōkun." *Nōgaku* 12, no. 12 (1914): 77–83.

Kuroda, Toshio. "Historical Consciousness and Honjaku Philosophy in the Medieval Period on Mount Hiei." Trans. Alan Grapard. In *The Lotus Sutra in Japanese Culture,* ed. George Tanabe and Jane Tanabe, pp. 143–58. Honolulu: University of Hawaii Press, 1989.

Kurokawa Doyu. *Yoshu fushi, Hinami kiji.* Ed. Yuasa Kichirō. Kyoto: Kyōto sōsho kankōkai, 1916.

Kyōgenki. Ed. Sakamoto Tetsuzō. Yūmeidō shoten, 1930.

Kyōgen shūsei. Ed. Nonomura Kaizō and Andō Tsunejirō. Shun'yōdō, 1931.

Kyō habutae oridome. Ed. Shisen Kyōto sōsho kankōkai. Shinshū Kyōto sōsho, vol. 6. Kyoto: Kōsaisha, 1968.

Kyōhō rokunen kakiage. In *Nō,* ed. Geinōshi kenkyūkai, pp. 211–56. Nihon shōmin bunka shiryō shūsei, vol. 3. San'ichi shobō, 1973.

Kyōto burakushi kenkyūjo, ed. *Shiryō kodai chūsei. Kyōto no burakushi,* vol. 3. Kyōto: Aunsha, 1984.

Larson, Magali. *The Rise of Professionalism: A Sociological Analysis.* Berkeley: University of California Press, 1977.

Law, Jane Marie. *Puppets of Nostalgia: The Birth, Death, and Revival of the Japanese Awaji Ningyō Tradition.* Princeton: Princeton University Press, 1997.

Lebra, Takie Sugiyama. *Above the Clouds: Status Culture of the Modern Japanese Nobility.* Berkeley: University of California Press, 1993.

Majima En'an (Shūsen'o). *Bushōgoma.* Ed. Omote Akira. Wan'ya shoten, 1958.

———. *Jikkanshōkei densho.* Ed. Omote Akira. Wan'ya shoten, 1992.

Mansai Jugō nikki. Ed. Hanawa Hokinoichi and Ōta Toshirō. 2 vols. Zoku gunsho ruijū, bui, no. 1. Zoku Gunsho ruijū kanseikai, 1988–89.

Marra, Michele. *Representations of Power: The Literary Politics of Medieval Japan.* Honolulu: University of Hawaii Press, 1993.

Mass, Jeffrey. *The Development of Kamakura Rule, 1180–1250: A History with Documents.* Stanford: Stanford University Press, 1979.

Matsumoto Kamematsu. *Nō kara kabuki e.* Yōkyoku hakkōsho, 1941.

McLuhan, Marshall. *The Gutenberg Galaxy: The Making of Typographic Man.* Toronto: University of Toronto Press, 1962.

———. *Understanding Media: The Extensions of Man.* Cambridge, Mass.: MIT Press, 1997.

Mehl, Margaret. *History and the State in Nineteenth-Century Japan.* New York: St. Martin's Press, 1998.

Miles, Clement A. *Christmas in Ritual and Tradition, Christian and Pagan.* London: T. Fisher Unwin, 1913.

Miyake Noboru, ed. *Nōgaku geiwa.* Hinoki shoten, 1976.

Moore, Ian Robert. *Formation of a Persecuting Society.* London: Basil Blackwell, 1987.

Morisue Yoshiaki. "Nō no hogosha." In *Nōgaku zensho,* ed. Nogami Toyoichirō, vol. 2, pp. 339–404. Sōgensha, 1942.

Morita Mitsuharu. *Nōgaku oboe no shochō.* Nōgaku shorin, 1992.

Morita Yoshinori. *Chūsei no senmin to zatsugei no kenkyū.* Yūzankaku, 1994.

Moriya Katsuhisa, "Urban Networks and Information Networks." In *Tokugawa Japan: The Social and Economic Antecedents of Modern Japan,* ed. Chie Nakane and Shinzaburō Ōishi; trans. and ed. Conrad Totman, pp. 97–123. University of Tokyo Press, 1990.

Moriya Takeshi. *Kinsei geinō bunkashi no kenkyū.* Tankōsha, 1992.

———. "Yūgei and Chōnin Society in the Edo Period." *Acta Asiatica* 33 (1977): 32–54.

Murai Yasuhiko. *Hana to cha no sekai.* San'ichi shobō, 1990.

Murata Ryōa. *Rigen shūran.* 3 vols. Koten kōkyūjo insatsubu, 1899–1900.

Murayama Shūichi. *Nihon onmyōdō shiwa.* Asahi Culture Books, 1987.

Nagao Akio. "Gobandate no seiritsu: omo to shite ennō kiroku kara." *Geinōshi kenkyū* 13 (1966): 13–24.

Nakamori Hiroshi. "Ōmi to nō, kyōgen." In *Nō, kyōgen no furusato to Ōmi: kamen ga tsutaeru chūsei no minshū bunka,* ed. Ōtsushi Rekishi Hakubutsukan, pp. 10–11. Ōtsu: Ōtsushi rekishi hakubutsukan, 1997.

Nakamori Shōzō. *Nō ga ima, oshietekureru koto.* Mainichi shinbunsha, 1990.

Nakamura Itaru. *Muromachi nōgaku ronko.* Wan'ya shoten, 1994.

Nakamura Yasuo. *Kamen to shinkō.* Shinchō sensho, 1993.

———. *Noh, the Classical Theater.* Trans. Don Kenny. New York: Walker/Weatherhill, 1971.

———. "Nō no koteika to iemoto seido: Kanze Motoakira o chūshin to shite." *Geinōshi kenkyū* 16 (1967): 8–25.

————. *Zeami densho yōgo sakuin.* Kasama shoin, 1985.

Nearman, Mark. "Behind the Mask of Nō." *Mime Journal,* 1984, pp. 20–64.

Nippon gakujutsu shinkōkai. *The Noh Drama: Ten Plays from the Japanese.* Selected by and trans. Special Noh Committee, Japanese Classics Translation Committee, Nippon gakujutsu shinkōkai. Rutland, Vt.: Tuttle, 1955.

Nishida Tomomi. *'Chi' no shisō: Edo jidai no shiseikan.* Kenseisha, 1995.

Nishikawa, Kyōtarō. *Bugaku Masks.* Trans. Monica Bethe. Tokyo: Kodansha, 1978.

Nishino Haruo. "Kyōhō zengo no shinsaku kyoku: kinsei yōkyoku-shikō." *Nōgaku kenkyū* 7 (1981): 103–36.

Nishino Haruo and Hata Hisashi, eds. *Nō, kyōgen jiten.* Heibonsha, 1987.

Nishiyama, Matsunosuke. *Edo Culture: Daily Life and Diversions in Urban Japan, 1600–1868.* Trans. Gerald Groemmer. Honolulu: University of Hawaii Press, 1997.

————. *Iemoto no kenkyū.* Yoshikawa kōbunkan, 1982.

————. *Iemotosei no tenkai.* Yoshikawa kōbunkan, 1982.

Nogami Toyoichirō. *Nō: kenkyū to hakken.* Iwanami shoten, 1948.

————. *Nōmen ronko.* Koyama shoten, 1944.

Nomura Manzō. *Nomura Manzō chosakushū.* Ed. Furukawa Hisashi and Kobayashi Seiki. Gogatsu shobō, 1982.

Nō no kinmō zui, ed. Omote Akira. Wan'ya shoten, 1980.

Nonomura Kaizō. *Nōgaku kokonki.* Shun'yodo, 1931.

————. *Nō no kokon.* Mokujisha, 1967.

Nose Asaji. *Nōgaku genryūkō.* Iwanami shoten, 1938.

Numa So'u. *Nōgaku meijin no omokage.* Hinoki shoten, 1953.

Ohnuki-Tierney, Emiko. *The Monkey as Mirror: Symbolic Transformations in Japanese History and Ritual.* Princeton: Princeton University Press, 1987.

Ōishi, Shinzaburō. "The Bakuhan System." In *Tokugawa Japan: The Social and Economic Antecedents of Modern Japan,* ed. Chie Nakane and Shinzaburō Ōishi; trans. and ed. Conrad Totman, pp. 11–36. University of Tokyo Press, 1990.

Ōkuma Shigenobu. "Kokugeki to shite no nōgaku." *Nōgaku* 7, no. 6 (1909): 4–6.

Omote Akira. *Kitaryū no seiritsu to tenkai.* Heibonsha, 1994.

————. *Nōgakushi shinko,* vols. 1 and 2. Iwanami shoten, 1979, 1986.

————. "Zeami to Zenchiku no densho." In *Zeami, Zenchiku,* ed. Omote Akira and Katō Shūichi, pp. 542–82. Nihon shisō taikei, vol. 24. Iwanami shoten, 1995.

Omote Akira and Amano Fumio, eds. *Nō no rekishi.* Iwanami kōza nō, kyōgen, vol. 1. Iwanami shoten, 1987.

Omote Akira and Itō Masayoshi. *Konparu kodensho shūsei.* Wan'ya shoten, 1969.

Omote Akira and Katō Shūichi. *Zeami, Zenchiku.* Nihon shisō taikei, vol. 24. Iwanami shoten, 1995.

Omote Akira and Takemoto Mikio, eds. *Nōgaku no densho to geiron.* Iwanami kōza nō, kyōgen, vol. 2. Iwanami shoten, 1988.

O'Neill, P. G. *Early Nō Drama: Its Background, Character and Development, 1300–1450.* London: Lund Humphries, 1958.

Ong, Walter J. *Orality and Literacy: The Technologizing of the Word.* Routledge, 1982.

Ooms, Herman, "Neo-Confucianism and the Formation of Early Tokugawa Ideology: Contours of a Problem." In *Confucianism and Tokugawa Culture,* ed. Peter Nosco, pp. 27–61. Princeton: Princeton University Press, 1984.

———. *Tokugawa Ideology: Early Constructs, 1570–1680.* Princeton: Princeton University Press, 1985.

Orikuchi Shinobu. *Nihon geinōshi nōto.* Chūō kōronsha, 1957.

Ortolani, Benito. *The Japanese Theatre: From Shamanistic Ritual to Contemporary Pluralism.* Rev. ed. Princeton: Princeton University Press, 1990.

Ōtani Tokuzō, ed. *Yōkyoku nihyaku gojū banshū sakuin.* Kyoto: Akao shōbundō, 1978.

Ōtsushi rekishi hakubutsukan, ed. *Nō, kyōgen no furusato to Ōmi: kamen ni tsutaeru chūsei no minshū bunka.* Ōtsu: Ōtsushi rekishi hakubutsukan, 1997.

Ōwada Tateki. *Nō utai hiketsu.* Gen'yōsha, 1935.

Oyudono no ue no nikki. Ed. Hanawa Hokinokichi. Zoku gunsho ruijū, bui, no. 3. Taiyōsha, 1943.

Oze Hoan. *Taikōki.* Ed. Hinotani Teruhiko and Emoto Hiroshi. Shin nihon koten bungaku taikei, vol. 60. Iwanami shoten: 1996.

Pernet, Henry. *Ritual Masks: Deceptions and Revelations.* Trans. Laura Grillo. Columbia: University of South Carolina Press, 1992.

Picken, Stuart D. B. *Essentials of Shinto: An Analytical Guide to Principal Teachings.* Westport, Conn.: Greenwood Press, 1994.

Pinnington, Noel, "Crossed Paths: Zeami's Transmission to Zenchiku." *Monumenta Nipponica* 52, no. 2 (1997): 201–34.

Plutschow, Herbert. *Japan's Name Culture: The Significance of Names in a Religious, Political and Social Context.* Folkestone, Eng.: Japan Library, 1995.

Rabinow, Paul. "Representations Are Social Facts: Modernity and Post-Modernity in Anthropology." In *Writing Culture: The Poetics and Politics of Ethnography*, ed. James Clifford and George E. Marcus, pp. 234–66. Berkeley: University of California Press, 1986.

Rath, Eric. "Challenging the Old Men: A Brief History of Women in Noh Theater." *Women & Performance: A Journal of Feminist Theory*, special issue: *Performing Japanese Women*, ed. Steven T. Brown and Sara Jansen, 12, no. 1 (issue no. 23) (2001): 97–111.

———. "From Representation to Apotheosis: Nō's Modern Myth of Okina." *Asian Theatre Journal* 17, no. 2 (2000): 253–68.

———. "Legends, Secrets, and Authority: *Hachijō kadensho* and Early Modern Noh." *Monumenta Nipponica* 54, no. 2 (1999): 169–94.

———. "Remembering Zeami: The Kanze School and Its Patriarch." *Asian Theatre Journal* 20, no. 2 (2003): 191–208.

Rimer, J. Thomas, and Masakazu Yamazaki, trans. *On the Art of the Nō Drama: The Major Treatises of Zeami*. Princeton: Princeton University Press, 1984.

Robertson, Jennifer. "Mon Japon: The Revue Theater as a Technology of Japanese Imperialism." *American Ethnologist* 22, no. 4 (1995): 1–27.

Rodrigues, João. *This Island of Japon: João Rodrigues' Account of 16th-Century Japan*. Trans. and ed. Michael Cooper. Kodansha, 1973.

Rosenau, Pauline Marie. *Postmodernism and the Social Sciences: Insights, Inroads and Intrusions*. Princeton: Princeton University Press, 1992.

Ruppert, Brian D. *Jewel in the Ashes: Buddha Relics and Power in Early Medieval Japan*. Cambridge, Mass.: Harvard University Asia Center, 2000.

Sagara Tōru. *Zeami no uchū*. Perikansha, 1990.

Sakamoto Setchō. "Nōgaku no genjō." *Yōkyoku kōza* 1, no. 9 (1926): 33–122.

Salz, Jonah. "Roles of Passage: Coming of Age as a Japanese Kyogen Actor." Ph.D. diss., New York University, 1997.

Sanari Kentarō, ed. *Yōkyoku taikan*. Meiji shoin, 1931.

Sarugaku dengi. In *Nō*, ed. Geinōshi kenkyūkai, pp. 257–90. Nihon shōmin bunka shiryō shūsei, vol. 3. San'ichi Shobō, 1973.

Sarugaku kikigaki, Ed. Zoku Gunsho ruijū kanseikai. In *Zoku gunsho ruijū*, vol. 19, pp. 242–58. Taiyōsha, 1943.

Sasaki Haruyuki. *Su'utai yoyo no ato*. In *Nō*, ed. Geinōshi kenkyūkai, pp. 657–84. Nihon shōmin bunka shiryō shūsei, vol. 3. San'ichi shobō, 1973.

Saunders, E. Dale. *Mudrā: A Study of Symbolic Gestures in Japanese Buddhist Sculpture*. Princeton: Princeton University Press, 1960.

Schechner, Richard. *The Future of Ritual: Writings on Culture and Performance*. London: Routledge, 1993.

Senga Kiyoko. "Toraya Ryūha to Toraya Yahe'e." *Geinōshi kenkyū* 119 (1992): 64–80.

Shigeyama Sensaku. "Kyōgen hachijūnen." In *Nō, kyōgen, bunraku*, pp. 85–196. *Nihon no geidan*, vol. 3. Kyūgei shuppan, 1978.

Shimazu Mazue et al. *Mitsuike kyūzō nōmen*. Gakken, 1992.

Shimotsuma Shōshin. *Shimotsuma Shōshin shū*, vol. 1, ed. Nishino Haruo. Wan'ya shoten, 1973.

———. *Shōshin kikigaki*. In *Shimotsuma Shōshin shū*, vol. 2, ed. Furukawa Hisashi, pp. 67–104. Wan'ya shoten, 1974.

———. *Sōdensho*. In *Shimotsuma Shōshin shū*, vol 3, ed. Katagiri Noboru, pp. 7–44. Wan'ya shoten, 1976.

Shinmura Izuru, ed. *Kōjien*. 4th ed. Iwanami shoten, 1993.

Shively, Donald. "Sumptuary Legislation and Status in Early Tokugawa Japan." *Harvard Journal of Asiatic Studies* 25 (1964): 123–64.

Staal, Frits. "The Meaninglessness of Ritual." In *Readings in Ritual Studies*, ed. Ronald Grimes, pp. 483–94. Englewood Cliffs, N.J.: Prentice Hall, 1996.

Stock, Brian. *The Implications of Literacy: Written Language and Models of Interpretation in the Eleventh and Twelfth Centuries*. Princeton: Princeton University Press, 1983.

Street, Brian. *Literacy in Theory and Practice*. Cambridge, Eng.: Cambridge University Press, 1984.

Suzuki Keiun. *Nō no omote*. Wan'ya shoten, 1960.

Takabayashi Ginji. *Geidō dokubon: Hokuryū shōshi*. Kyoto: published privately, 1961.

Tanahashi, Kazuaki, ed. *Moon in a Dewdrop: Writings of Zen Master Dōgen*. San Francisco: North Point Press, 1985.

Tanikawa Kotosuga. *Wakun no shiori*. 3 vols. Kōten kōkyūjo, 1908.

Teele, Rebecca, "Recollections and Thoughts on Nō: An Interview with Kongō Iwao, Head of the Kongō School of Nō." *Mime Journal*, 1984, pp. 74–92.

Teikin ōrai. Ed. Ishikawa Matsutarō. Heibonsha, 1973.

Tenshō kyōgenbon zen'yaku. Ed. Kanai Kiyomitsu. Fūkan shobō, 1998.

Thornhill, Arthur. *Six Circles, One Dewdrop: The Religio-Aesthetic World of Komparu Zenchiku*. Princeton: Princeton University Press, 1993.

Toida Michizō. *Nō: kami to kōjiki no geijutsu*. Serika shobō, 1985.

Toki Kō. "Kokuminsei to nōgaku to." *Nōgaku* 14, no. 1 (1916): 2–17.

Tokuda Rinchū Tōzaemon. *Rinchū kenmonshū*. Ed. Sakamoto Setchō. Wan'ya shoten, 1967.

Tokugawa jikki. Ed. Kuroita Katsumi. Shintei zōho kokushi taikei. Yoshikawa kōbunkan, 1976.

Tonomura, Hitomi. *Community and Commerce in Late Medieval Japan: The Corporate Villages of Tokuchin-ho*. Stanford: Stanford University Press, 1992.

————. "Forging the Past: Medieval Counterfeit Documents." *Monumenta Nipponica* 40, no. 1 (1985): 69–96.

Totman, Conrad. *Early Modern Japan*. Berkeley: University of California Press, 1993.

Ueda, Makoto. *Literary and Art Theories in Japan*. Ann Arbor: University of Michigan, Center for Japanese Studies, 1967.

Varley, Paul. "Chanoyu: From the Genroku Epoch to Modern Times." In *Tea in Japan: Essays on the History of Chanoyu*, ed. Paul Varley and Kumakura Isao. Honolulu: University of Hawaii Press, 1989: 161–94.

Wakita Haruko. "Chūsei hisabetsumin no seikatsu to shakai." In *Buraku no rekishi to kaihō undō, zenkindaihen*, ed. Buraku mondai kenkyūjo, pp. 67–182. Kyoto: Buraku mondai kenkyūjo, 1991.

Wakita Osamu. *Genroku no shakai*. Hanawa shobō, 1980.

Watanabe Shōgo. *Geinōshi bunkashi jiten chūsei hen*. Meichō shuppan, 1991.

Werblowsky, R. J. Zwi. "Some Reflections on the Two-Way Traffic or Incarnation/Avatāra and Apotheosis." *Journal of Japanese Religious Studies* 14, no. 4 (1987): 279–85.

Yamaguchi Shōji. *Nō ongaku no kenkyū: chihō to chūō*. Ongaku no tomosha, 1987.

Yamaji Kōzō. "Matsubayashi." In *Chūsei no minshū to geinō*, ed. Kyōto burakushi kenkyūjo, pp. 77–83. Kyoto: Aunsha, 1991.

————. *Okina no za: Geinōmintachi no chūsei*. Heibonsha, 1990.

————. "Senzumanzai." In *Chūsei no minshū to geinō*, ed. Kyōto burakushi kenkyūjo, pp. 42–47. Kyoto: Aunsha, 1991.

Yamamoto Naotomo. "Onmyōji." In *Chūsei no minshū to geinō*, ed. Kyōto burakushi kenkyūjo, pp. 121–27. Kyoto: Aunsha, 1991.

Yokomichi Mario. *Nōgeki shōyō*. Chikuma shobō, 1984.

Yokomichi Mario and Kobayashi Seiki. *Nō, kyōgen*. Iwanami shoten, 1996.

Yokomichi Mario and Koyama Hiroshi, eds. *Nōgaku zusetsu. Iwanami kōza nō, kyōgen*, vol. 8. Iwanami shoten, 1988.

Yonekura Toshiaki. *Waranbegusa kyōgen mukashi gatarisho kenkyū*. Kazama shobō, 1973.

Yoshida, Teigo, "The Stranger as God: The Place of the Outsider in Japanese Folk Religion." *Ethnology* 20, no. 2 (1981): 87–99.

Yoshida Tōgo, ed. *Nōgaku koten Zeami jūrokubushū*. Nōgakukai, 1909.

———. "Okina shikisanban no koten ni tsuite." *Nōgaku* 4, no. 1 (1906): 15–28.

Yoshikawa Kanehira. "Matsubayashi ni tsuite." In *Minzoku geinō*, ed. Nishitsunoi Masahiro, vol. 2, pp. 81–85. Ongaku no tomosha, 1990.

Zeami Motokiyo. *Fūshikaden*. In *Zeami, Zenchiku*, ed. Omote Akira and Katō Shūichi, pp. 13–65. Nihon shisō taikei, vol. 24. Iwanami shoten, 1995.

———. *Go'on*. In *Zeami, Zenchiku*, ed. Omote Akira and Katō Shūichi, pp. 206–32. Nihon shisō taikei, vol. 24. Iwanami shoten, 1995.

———. *Go'ongyokujōjō*. In *Zeami, Zenchiku*, ed. Omote Akira and Katō Shūichi, pp. 197–204. Nihon shisō taikei, vol. 24. Iwanami shoten, 1995.

———. *Kakyō*. In *Zeami, Zenchiku*, ed. Omote Akira and Katō Shūichi, pp. 83–109. Nihon shisō taikei, vol. 24. Iwanami shoten, 1995.

———. *Kyakuraika*. In *Zeami, Zenchiku*, ed. Omote Akira and Katō Shūichi, pp. 245–48. Nihon shisō taikei, vol. 24. Iwanami shoten, 1995.

———. *Shikadō*. In *Zeami, Zenchiku*, ed. Omote Akira and Katō Shūichi, pp. 111–19. Nihon shisō taikei, vol. 24. Iwanami shoten, 1995.

———. *Shūgyoku tokka*. In *Zeami, Zenchiku*, ed. Omote Akira and Katō Shūichi, pp. 183–96. Nihon shisō taikei, vol. 24. Iwanami shoten, 1995.

Index

Harvard East Asian Monographs
(* out-of-print)

Harvard East Asian Monographs

Harvard East Asian Monographs

Harvard East Asian Monographs

Harvard East Asian Monographs

Harvard East Asian Monographs